SharePoint 2010 Web Parts in Actio

D0901459

SharePoint 2010
Web Parts in Action

WICTOR WILÉN

MANNING

Greenwich
(74° w. long.)

For online information and ordering of this and other Manning books, please visit
www.manning.com. The publisher offers discounts on this book when ordered in quantity.
For more information, please contact

Special Sales Department
Manning Publications Co.
180 Broad Street, Suite 1323
Stamford, CT 06901
Email: orders@manning.com

Manning Publications Co.   Development editor: Susan Harkins
180 Broad Street, Suite 1323   Copyeditor: Liz Welch
Stamford, CT 06901   Typesetter: Gordan Salinovic
                                   Cover designer: Marija Tudor

ISBN 9781935182771
Printed in the United States of America
2 3 4 5 6 7 8 9 10 – MAL – 16 15 14 13 12 11

To my amazing wife and our two beautiful daughters

brief contents

contents

preface

I really love working with SharePoint! I've been doing it full-time for the last half decade, including lots of late nights and weekends. One area that I've found particularly interesting is Web Parts. I like the nature of a Web Part since it can act as a stand-alone application inside the powerful SharePoint platform—or it can interact both with SharePoint *and* other Web Parts. A couple of years ago I owned a company that built its own portal software (which integrated with SharePoint, but that's another story), and that product was based on a similar concept. When we started building our solutions on SharePoint, Web Parts was the way to go since we were used to the approach. One day I came up with an idea for a book about Web Parts. Yes, nearly all SharePoint platform books cover Web Parts, but not as deeply as I wanted to. I felt that there were much more to say about them. This book is the result.

As I was working on the outline, SharePoint 2010 was unleashed from Redmond, and I thought that this must be it—perfect timing. After signing a contract with Manning I thought, this can't be too hard, just start writing. I couldn't have been more wrong! Writing a book isn't easy, especially if English isn't your native language, and writing about a product that isn't yet production-ready doesn't make it any easier. But, you do learn a lot in the process, and that is why I decided, in the end, to continue. Nearly every day over the last eight months of writing this book, I learned something new about SharePoint, or about writing, and that's my reward.

Now it's your turn to learn something new. I hope you enjoy reading this book as much as I enjoyed writing it.

acknowledgments

This is the section I always read in a book, and one I've always wanted to write. From reading others' acknowledgments, I knew that writing a book is never a solo mission; there are many people involved in many ways. And it was no different for my book.

I'd like to start with thanking my family—Cecilia, Wilma, and Alicia. Before I embarked on this book project, I made sure that I had a great support system at home. My family helped and encouraged me in every way possible, even though they don't share my passion for SharePoint. (Not yet!) You are my everything.

This book wouldn't exist without the community that has evolved around Share-Point. All the amazing people who write books, blogs, and freely share information have helped bring SharePoint, and my knowledge of it, to where we are today. Being a part of this community, as well as being awarded MVP for SharePoint while writing this book, makes me very proud.

Next, I would like to thank the Manning crew, especially Michael Stephens who believed in the idea for this book and helped turn it into reality. Also, my agent Neil Salkind deserves a thank you for stitching the deal together. But the most important person during the writing process was Susan Harkins, my development editor at Manning. From day one she supported and coached me every step of the way. She has been an amazing teacher. Thank you, Susan!

Writing a book on a specialized topic takes a lot of research and review and I had great technical reviewers and experts who gave me inspiration, ideas, and suggestions along the way. Sincere thanks to the following reviewers who read the manuscript at different stages during its development—your input made this a better book: Jonas Bandi,

Amos Bannister, Margriet Bruggeman, Nikander Bruggeman, Berndt Hamboeck, Kunal Mittal, Niclas Goude, and Christina Wheeler. And special thanks to Waldek Mastykarz, Anders Rask, and Tobias Zimmergren for sharing their exceptional expertise with me, and to Tobias again, for a final technical proofread of the manuscript during production.

about this book

This book focuses on Web Part development in SharePoint 2010 using Visual Studio 2010. It takes you on a journey from learning what a Web Part is and how you can use Web Parts, to building your own Web Parts in different and advanced ways. When you have read it, you should be a fairly skilled SharePoint Web Part developer, ready to take on challenging projects.

How this book is organized

This book covers Web Part development from basic to advanced scenarios and is divided into three parts. Each chapter can stand on its own and you can use it as a reference when looking at a particular scenario.

The first part, consisting of chapters 1 and 2, is about Web Parts in general—to get you started. These two chapters explain the parts of a Web Part, how a Web Part fits into SharePoint, and how to use Web Parts in the SharePoint user interface, as well as in SharePoint Designer.

Part 2 is where the *action* begins. It consists of 11 chapters that start you off building basic Web Parts using Visual Studio 2010. You will learn how to build configurable and personalizable Web Parts and how to package and deploy them in a maintainable way. Once you have learned the basics, discussion of advanced topics in subsequent chapters, such as building contextual-aware and Silverlight Web Parts, will show you how to take your Web Parts one step further. One of these (chapter 8) is dedicated to troubleshooting; you will learn how to debug Web Parts and how to make troubleshooting easier—or avoid it entirely. New techniques introduced in SharePoint 2010, such as the Client Object Model, the Sandbox, and PowerShell are also covered. Part 2 ends with a chapter that focuses on design patterns and the latest guidelines released by Microsoft.

The third and final part (chapters 14 and 15) covers end-to-end scenarios where you learn how to connect Web Parts so that they interact with each other. In chapter 15 you learn how to deploy solutions of pre-configured site pages with connected Web Parts.

Finally, an appendix lists the most commonly used out-of-the-box Web Parts. For each Web Part, the corresponding class, feature, and its connection end-points are documented.

Who should read this book

SharePoint 2010 Web Parts in Action is a book for SharePoint developers. Web Parts is one of the core concepts of SharePoint and a requirement when you are building enterprise portal solutions. The book assumes that you have basic knowledge of SharePoint and development in ASP.NET using C#. Even if you're already a skilled SharePoint developer you will find details that you haven't seen before or even thought possible.

How to use this book

If you are new to SharePoint 2010 development you should read this book in order, from chapter 1 to the end. The first chapters will give you a good start and a smooth introduction to SharePoint Web Part development and Visual Studio. Experienced SharePoint developers should start with chapter 4. Even though this chapter may contain information that you already know, or think you know, it points out some commonly made mistakes. From there, the chapters will drill deeper and deeper into Web Part development. And you can always refer back to specific chapters when looking for a specific solution.

Code conventions and downloads

This book contains a lot of code listings and snippets. All compilable code is written using C# but since this is a SharePoint book you will also see XML snippets. All code is written using a `fixed font like this`, and if you are reading on an eReader or in PDF format, you will see that the code is color coded. Some code listings and snippets contain annotations to highlight important topics.

You can download the source code for many of the samples in this book from the publisher's website at www.manning.com/SharePoint2010WebPartsinAction.com.

Software requirements

To take full advantage of this book you need to have a copy of SharePoint 2010 Foundation and Visual Studio 2010 (not the Express version). Preferably, you should have access to a virtual environment. Chapter 3 has detailed information about software requirements.

Author Online

The purchase of *SharePoint 2010 Web Parts in Action* includes access to a private forum run by Manning Publications where you can make comments about the book, ask technical questions, and receive help from the author and other users. To access and subscribe to the forum, point your browser to www.manning.com/ SharePoint2010WebPartsinAction, and click the Author Online link. This page provides information on how to get on the forum once you are registered, what kind of help is available, and the rules of conduct in the forum.

Manning's commitment to our readers is to provide a venue where a meaningful dialogue between individual readers and between readers and the author can take place. It's not a commitment to any specific amount of participation on the part of the author, whose contribution to the book's forum remains voluntary (and unpaid). We suggest you try asking the author some challenging questions, lest his interest stray!

The Author Online forum and the archives of previous discussions will be accessible from the publisher's website as long as the book is in print.

About the author

Wictor Wilén is a SharePoint Architect at Connecta AB with more than 12 years of experience in the web content management and portal industry. He has worked for consulting companies, founded and sold his own software company, and experienced the beginnings of SharePoint back in 2001. He is an active SharePoint community participant, writer, tutor, and frequent speaker at local and international conferences. In 2010 Wictor was awarded the SharePoint Server MVP title by Microsoft for his community contributions. He can be found online at http://www.wictorwilen.se/. Wictor is based in Stockholm, Sweden.

about the cover illustration

The figure on the cover of *SharePoiont 2010 Web Parts in Action* is called "The Gentle-man." The illustration is taken from a French travel book, *Encyclopédie des Voyages* by J. G. St. Saveur, published almost 200 years ago. Travel for pleasure was a relatively new phenomenon at the time and travel guides such as this one were popular, introducing both the tourist as well as the armchair traveler to the inhabitants of other regions of the world, as well as to the regional costumes and uniforms of French soldiers, civil servants, tradesmen, merchants, and peasants.

The diversity of the drawings in the *Encyclopédie des Voyages* speaks vividly of the uniqueness and individuality of the world's towns and provinces just 200 years ago. Isolated from each other, people spoke different dialects and languages. In the streets or in the countryside, it was easy to identify where they lived and what their trade or station in life was just by what they were wearing.

Dress codes have changed since then and the diversity by region, so rich at the time, has faded away. It's now often hard to tell the inhabitant of one continent from another. Perhaps, trying to view it optimistically, we've traded a cultural and visual diversity for a more varied personal life. Or a more varied and interesting intellectual and technical life.

We at Manning celebrate the inventiveness, the initiative, and the fun of the com-puter business with book covers based on the rich diversity of regional life of two cen-turies ago brought back to life by the pictures from this travel guide.

about Web Parts

Before we start our journey into SharePoint 2010 Web Parts, let's take a look at the history of SharePoint and how Web Parts came to be.

Microsoft announced the concept of Web Parts in the middle of 2000, which was before SharePoint existed as a product. It seems like ages ago. The aim of Web Parts was the same then as it is now. At the time, Web Parts was a part of the since long-forgotten Digital Dashboard, an ASP, XML, and VBScript-based portal framework. "In Web Parts, we are providing the building blocks for next-generation digital dashboard solutions…," wrote Bob Muglia in June 2000, later President of Microsoft's Server and Tools Business.

When SharePoint Portal Server 2001, called Tahoe, was released, it was based on the Digital Dashboard and used Web Parts to create the portal. This was the first real step towards the SharePoint of today. SharePoint at the time was not based on Microsoft SQL Server but rather on the Microsoft Exchange Web Storage System (WSS) and its focus was on document management rather than portals.

In 2003, Windows SharePoint Services 2.0 and SharePoint Portal Server 2003 were released, based on the relatively new Microsoft .NET Framework, first released in 2002. Web Parts was introduced as a class in the SharePoint API and you had to compile your code into assemblies instead of simply writing a VBScript object. That's how Web Parts started and with SharePoint 2003 you could build scalable, customizable, and personalizable web portals.

Microsoft .NET Framework 2.0 was released in 2005 and by then Microsoft had enhanced and incorporated the Web Part concept into the ASP.NET framework. The

Web Part Manager was introduced to manage the Web Parts, which previously had been managed exclusively through zones. This new Web Part infrastructure allowed anyone to create their own Web Part-based site, using their own providers for storing customizations. For further reading on the internals of the ASP.NET 2.0 Web Part infrastructure, I recommend Manning's *ASP.NET Web Parts in Action* by Darren Neimke, published in 2006.

SharePoint 2007, Windows SharePoint Services 3.0, and Microsoft Office SharePoint Server 2007, was a huge release. SharePoint had finally become a major player in the portal market. It was based on ASP.NET 2.0 and therefore based on the ASP.NET built-in Web Part infrastructure. For backwards compatibility reasons the Web Part class introduced in SharePoint 2003 was kept, and you could use both versions for your Web Parts, both with different abilities.

The development tools for SharePoint and Web Parts, compared to other .NET-based projects, were inferior in the beginning and had to rely on the community for improvements. The lack of a visual editor for Web Parts made the Web Part development threshold high. The community around SharePoint has been extremely interesting, professional, and entertaining since the release of SharePoint 2007. The community understood early on the lack of proper development tools and a number of excellent tools were born, such as WSPBuilder by Carsten Keutmann (http://wspbuilder .codeplex.com) and STSDev by Ted Pattison et al. (http://stsdev.codeplex.com).

Today, we have SharePoint 2010. It's based on Microsoft .NET Framework 3.5 Service Pack 1, which is essentially Microsoft .NET Framework 2.0 with a set of extensions. So the baseline is still the same as in SharePoint 2007: we can still use both versions of the Web Part, but a new one has been introduced for the Visual Web Part, which is based on the ASP.NET 2.0 Web Part. SharePoint 2010, together with Visual Studio 2010 will affect the lives of developers: we can now, just as easily as for any other .NET project, design, build, and debug solutions. This is where we are now.

Fun Facts

SharePoint 2010 is version number 14 while SharePoint 2007 has version number 12. There is no clear answer why Microsoft skipped version 13, but one of the "tales" making the rounds says that number 13 was skipped due to superstition, just as many hotels don't have a floor numbered 13. SharePoint 2003 did have a version 11, which was chosen to align the version number with Microsoft Office's versioning.

With SharePoint 2010 Microsoft has dropped the name Office from the server product. Microsoft Office SharePoint Server 2007 became Microsoft SharePoint Server 2010. The main reason was to avoid confusion between the SharePoint Server product with the Office client suite; many users believed that you needed to have the Office client to work with SharePoint. The integration works best using the Microsoft Office suite compared to other suites.

SharePoint 2010 also comes in a hosted version, called SharePoint Online, which means that you don't have to invest in hardware for your own SharePoint installation.

You "rent" a slot in the ready-to-go SharePoint 2010 installations and pay per user, month, and usage, which means that you only have to pay for what you use. Previous versions of SharePoint Online were very limited in custom application development but the new SharePoint Online 2010 allows for third-party applications to run in the hosted environment. The market for Web Parts is an innovative one and there are several successful companies that thrive on making Web Parts.

SharePoint 2010 offers a lot of opportunities for you as a developer to make custom solutions for yourself and your clients. Many of those solutions will contain Web Parts, so let's get started!

> **NOTE** SharePoint 2010 comes in many flavors, from SharePoint Foundation 2010 (formerly called Windows SharePoint Services) to SharePoint Server 2010 (Microsoft Office SharePoint Server), and the feature set differs in both versions. For clarity, I'll use SharePoint 2010 throughout this book and, when applicable, note if a specific task or feature is not available in one of the versions. I'll use the term SharePoint when talking about SharePoint in general, with no specific version or SKU (Stock Keeping Unit) in mind.

Part 1

Introducing
SharePoint 2010 Web Parts

P art 1 introduces you to the world of SharePoint 2010 Web Parts. You'll learn what Web Parts are and how you can use them to build solutions using only the web browser and SharePoint Designer 2010. The first chapter explores the Web Part infrastructure and pages in SharePoint. Chapter 2 shows you how to use out-of-the-box Web Parts to build Web Part–based applications. All this is in preparation for part 2, where we'll dive into the development of SharePoint 2010 Web Parts.

Introducing
SharePoint 2010 Web Parts

1

This chapter covers

- Defining a Web Part
- Using Web Parts
- Knowing the difference between ASP.NET and SharePoint Web Parts

Web Parts are an essential part of Microsoft SharePoint 2010 and one of the first technologies that a new SharePoint developer starts using. You can describe a Web Part as a self-contained application that's used in a SharePoint site. SharePoint comes with a wide range of out-of-the-box Web Parts and you can download more from Microsoft.com. You can even buy additional Web Parts from third-party vendors or download the source code for some Web Parts from open-source sites such as CodePlex.

Users, developers, IT professionals, and administrators have embraced the SharePoint platform. SharePoint is one of Microsoft's most important products; it's their fastest-growing server product. SharePoint is making an impact on all types of organizations, from small businesses to large Fortune 500 companies.

A product like SharePoint is always a challenge to implement. It's a broad platform, and it's sometimes difficult to determine what parts to use. Developers have had mixed feelings about SharePoint throughout the years. From the beginning, there was a lack of extensibility and, when that extensibility came, there was a lack of accompanying documentation. Each new version of SharePoint has introduced new challenges for developers, ranging from the developer toolset to the software features. Until recently, skilled SharePoint developers have been rare, probably due to these obstacles, which made the threshold to become a great SharePoint developer quite high. Thanks to excited developers and the strong online community, together with an engaged product team from Microsoft, these obstacles have been addressed with the release of SharePoint 2010. And, this book is a guide to Web Parts development on this new platform.

Microsoft SharePoint is a platform for creating portals and websites where the end user can—without programming skills—create and build websites and solutions using a standard web browser. Using lists, users can store data in SharePoint and/or integrate with external line-of-business systems. Lists can be predefined, such as Contacts, Calendars, or Announcements, or users can create their own. Figure 1.1 shows how a SharePoint site might look using several Web Parts.

Web Parts are a fundamental component of SharePoint and have been since the beginning of the SharePoint era. Web Parts can be small or standalone applications that you deploy into your SharePoint installation. With Web Parts, you can extend the functionality of your SharePoint investment and create new applications or even integrate with your existing applications to create a gateway from your SharePoint portal. Most of Microsoft's products, such as Microsoft Dynamics AX and SQL Server Reporting Services, also integrate with SharePoint using Web Parts.

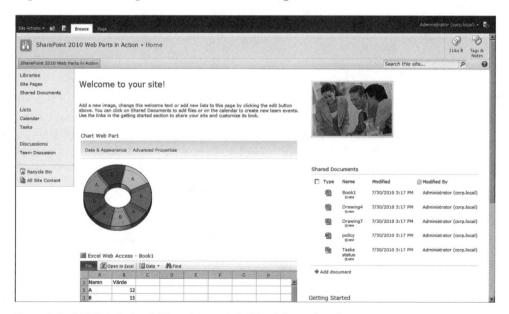

Figure 1.1   Add Web Parts of different types to build a rich user interface.

Building solutions and applications using Microsoft SharePoint 2010 allows you to keep your focus on the business logic, meet the customer's requirements, and implement the cool features. You don't have to worry about implementing security or authentication, building a framework for creating sites and pages, or creating a solution for deploying and distributing your features onto several servers in a controlled manner. The monitoring of your servers, software, and solutions is a task that's important for large-scale scenarios, and you get this ability with SharePoint.

Web Parts won't always be the best way to extend SharePoint. For instance, you'll usually create lists, content types, and site definitions in SharePoint projects. In addition, Web Parts aren't always the best tool for long-running calculations or jobs. In such cases, you might consider timer jobs, which you'll read about later in this book. You might even consider a custom service application. As a SharePoint developer, you must be able to handle many skills and methods, and Web Part development is just one of those skills. To be a good SharePoint developer, you need to know when to use a Web Part—and when not to. That includes knowing when to use an out-of-the-box Web Part, customize a Web Part, or go in an entirely different direction. By discerning the best solution, you'll save you and your customer a lot of time and money. In this chapter, I'll introduce you to the world of Web Parts.

1.1   What is a Web Part?

Before we dig down deep into developing Web Parts for SharePoint 2010, you should know what a Web Part is. As the name implies, it means *parts of a web*. Web Parts are the building blocks for building web pages in SharePoint. Web Parts are essentially ASP.NET web controls that inherit the web control base class in ASP.NET but have special abilities compared with ordinary ASP.NET web controls. These special abilities focus on giving the end user or administrator, and not the developer, the possibility to customize, move, and edit the control. Normally, ASP.NET controls are configured and programmed on the server side with no or limited options for the end user to modify its properties. Web Parts, on the other hand, are building blocks that the end user can choose from to build their own web page. For example, the user may decide that a particular Web Part should show the contents of a document library with a specific set of columns, that another Web Part should display a graph generated from a data source, and so on. The most used Web Part in SharePoint is the one that shows a view of a SharePoint list, such as a task list, a calendar, or a document library.

All Web Parts have a common set of properties, including the title, size, chrome layout, and other appearance settings. They also share a common set of methods. That way, they're initialized and rendered so that the web page that contains the Web Part doesn't have to know exactly which Web Part it's going to show—just that it's a Web Part.

In a Web 2.0 standard fashion, the Web Part infrastructure also handles personalization of Web Parts and Web Part pages, which means that every end user of the Web Part can have their own configured web page that looks different from the same page for other users.

An important part of the Web Part infrastructure is the ability to *connect* Web Parts. Connected Web Parts can send or retrieve information from one Web Part to another. This concept allows developers to create advanced web pages and dashboards that users can connect to via the web interface. SharePoint provides a special kind of Web Parts called *filter Web Parts*. They have one purpose: to deliver a filter to other Web Parts so that their content can be filtered. For example, suppose you have a product catalog Web Part. You can set up a filter Web Part that filters the product catalog when users choose a product category in the filter Web Part.

All these factors together are what makes Web Parts so interesting and useful when creating custom applications or solutions for SharePoint. You as a developer can create configurable applications that users can adapt to their method of work. The user might also combine the Web Parts by connecting them together and, from that, create their own applications or mashups.

> **NOTE**   A web page or web application built using different external sources or open APIs is often referred to as a *mashup*. You might consider everything in SharePoint, including Web Parts, Business Connectivity Services (BCS), and InfoPath, as external sources for mashups.

The concept of Web Parts isn't unique to SharePoint. All major vendors and platforms have their version of Web Parts that are more or less evolved. In the Java world you might know them as *portlets*, Google uses *gadgets* for their iGoogle site, and so on. Web Parts can also be used to connect portals from different vendors and platforms using, for instance, the Web Services for Remote Portlets (WSRP) standard, which allows you to publish content from one portal to another, or the recently ratified Content Management Interoperability Specification (CMIS) standard.

If you're an ASP.NET developer, you might be familiar with Web Parts, because that infrastructure exists in the ASP.NET 2 Framework. SharePoint is built on top of ASP.NET and has extended the Web Part infrastructure and introduced a number of new and improved features. Using Web Parts instead of building custom ASP.NET applications allows you to take advantage of the SharePoint feature set, including infrastructure, user management, deployment, and scalability. This enables you to focus on the business goals of the application instead of building a new infrastructure.

Web Parts are essentially ASP.NET `WebControl` objects or, to be more exact, ASP.NET `Panel` objects. Therefore, from a developer perspective, the first thing you need to learn is ASP.NET programming in the language of your choice: C#, Visual Basic, or even F#. SharePoint 2010 is built on the .NET Framework version 3.5 and ASP.NET 2, so anything in those frameworks can be used when developing Web Parts for SharePoint 2010. This book assumes that you're familiar with ASP.NET 2 development and we'll highlight only those areas where you have to be extra careful. One of the most important and, very often, underestimated concepts is the ASP.NET page and control life cycle. In the later chapters, you'll see examples of why this concept is so important.

> **NOTE**   All code samples throughout the book will use C#. You can download these samples from www.manning.com/wilen or www.sharepointwebpartsinaction.com.

1.2 Why use Web Parts?

Web Parts are just one but important component of the huge SharePoint product—without Web Parts, you couldn't enjoy the platform's flexibility. It's the Web Parts that make SharePoint as well as other Web Part–based portals interesting for both editors and end users. As mentioned earlier, building a new web page or site can be done without programming skills. Editors create their pages and choose Web Parts from a gallery. Then, they customize a Web Part and save the page—and, all of this is done from the browser. The Web Parts that users can choose are determined by the administrator (and the permissions on the Web Parts). A Web Part's configuration options are defined by the developer who created the Web Part.

One of the reasons Web Parts are easy to use when creating custom applications for SharePoint is that they can be self-contained or grouped together. The business logic and the user interface are based on the .NET and ASP.NET development, which lets you get started right away, if you're familiar with .NET development.

Because Web Parts share a lot of common features and they're managed in the same way, it's easy for the end user to get started with a new Web-Part–based application. If users are familiar with SharePoint, they know how to find, add, and edit a page's Web Part. This makes the adaptation of new features or applications in your SharePoint environment faster and easier.

You can deploy a Web Part to the site collections of the SharePoint environment that you want your Web Part to be able to run in, and you can even control who can use the Web Parts through the built-in permissions in SharePoint.

SharePoint 2010 comes with a number of Web Parts that you can use—which ones are available depends on which version of SharePoint you've installed. Appendix A, "Out-of-the-box Web Parts," contains references to the most used Web Parts and their corresponding edition. Web Parts come in a couple of different types. The basic Web Part shows user tasks, the contents of a list, or a graph. Then, you have Web Parts that need customization, such as the Content Editor Web Part or Forms Web Part. For more advanced use, there are the new XSLT List View Web Part or the Data Form Web Part; both need to be configured using SharePoint Designer, and you can use them to create more advanced applications than you can using just the web browser.

Also available are complete suites or standalone Web Parts that can be downloaded for free or purchased. In many cases, getting one of these off-the-shelf products can solve your problem for a much lower price compared with the cost of developing a Web Part. You can custom-design applications, perhaps, in combination with these standard products and build Web Parts that do exactly what you want.

When do you need to create your own Web Parts? The Data Form Web Part is an excellent tool and should be used whenever possible. It's great for connecting to an external data source or web service and, then, all you have to do is customize the view of the data. SharePoint 2010 also introduces a new way to connect to external data using External Lists in SharePoint. External Lists, in combination with the out-of-the-box Web Parts, can be used to create an interface for your custom database in SharePoint using just configuration techniques.

> **NOTE** BCS is the evolution of the SharePoint 2007 Business Data Catalog (BDC), which allows you to connect to external data sources such as databases or web services. Data sources can be visualized in an External List, which looks and acts like a standard SharePoint list for the user but the data still resides in the connected system. SharePoint Designer 2010 is the tool to use when creating external entities and mapping them to external data sources. In SharePoint 2007, BDC was an Enterprise feature but, in SharePoint 2010, a part of the BCS is available in the SharePoint 2010 Foundation edition.

Custom Web Part development takes all of these approaches one step further: you have full control of what's going to be shown and you can create an interface that lets your user interact with the Web Part in a more advanced and sophisticated way than with the standard Web Parts. Using agile development methods, you can even involve the users early in the development process and iterate until you have a satisfied customer. The developer has the power to make the Web Part configurable for the end user. Compare that to the Data Form Web Part, where the administrator configures the Web Part and, then, all the user can do is watch and use the result. Most configuration of the Data Form Web Part has to be done using the SharePoint Designer application—which normal users don't have access to—or requires skills in eXtensible Stylesheet Language for Transformations (XSLT)—which typical users generally don't understand.

> **NOTE** Agile development has become popular in recent years. It's a set of methodologies focusing on some simple principles, which include an iterative approach and early and continuous delivery. Some of the most popular agile methods are Scrum, test-driven development (TDD), and continuous integration.

As a Web Part developer, you have full control of the user interface. This is especially important when you're creating Web Parts for publishing sites, where you might need to control the exact output of the Web Part or if you're using a dynamic Ajax-based interface and you need to run client-side scripts.

Building custom Web Parts gives you access to the complete object model of SharePoint and can be used to modify or show content that the user normally wouldn't have seen using elevated privileges. For example, you might store data in a SharePoint list that's protected by permissions so that users aren't allowed to see the list. You can then create a Web Part that uses the System Account context, reads data from the list, presents that data to the user, or lets the user update the data.

SharePoint 2010 has been updated to support mobile devices better than its successor—and it's not just about the way it displays lists and libraries. SharePoint now has support for converting your Web Part pages into mobile views, and you can convert the Web Parts to mobile Web Parts using special mobile adapters. If you compare that to a no-code solution built using custom JavaScript, which relies on a powerful browser and perhaps isn't adapted to a smaller screen, you'll find that building Web Parts and mobile adapters will improve your user experience significantly.

Another interesting aspect of Web Part development is when you have an out-of-the-box Web Part or third-party product that you'd like to enhance. As long as the Web Part isn't sealed, you can subclass it to enhance your version and override its default logic. This is a common task, and I've seen and used several subclassed versions of the Content Query and the Search Web Parts (which are not sealed in Share-Point 2010).

Web Parts can be powerful, which isn't always a good thing. Because you can run whatever .NET code you like in your Web Part, there's a risk that malicious or badly written code may cause damage to your applications and data. SharePoint has several mechanisms that help you control those scenarios through policies applied during deployment. With the new *sandboxed* solutions, you can even allow Web Parts from less trusted sources to run in your SharePoint environment in a special protected process. The sandboxing feature in SharePoint 2010 will be discussed in more detail further in this book.

1.3 Introducing the Web Part infrastructure

Before we go further, let's explore some basic facts about site pages and Web Parts in SharePoint. If you've been working with SharePoint or ASP.NET, this might be old news to you but, nevertheless, it's always good to refresh your memory. This section examines the various components in the Web Part infrastructure that you'll encounter when building a page. In addition, you'll get your first look at a simple Web Part. You'll learn the different components and their responsibilities. Familiarize yourself with the technical terms because I'll use them throughout the book.

1.3.1 Web Part page

A Web Part page, which most often is the type of page you use to host Web Parts, is an ASP.NET page that inherits from or uses a specific SharePoint page class, the WebPart-Page. This class, in turn, is inherited from the standard ASP.NET Page class. The responsibilities of a Web Part page are:

- Connecting to the SharePoint context.
- Performing user authorization.
- Hosting the Web Part Manager.
- Hosting the Web Part zones.
- Hosting the special zones for Web Part properties and the Web Part Gallery.

To use Web Parts on a web page, that page needs to be equipped with one Web Part Manager and, optionally, Web Part zones. The Web Part Manager in SharePoint is defined in the master page, which makes it available to all pages using that master page. Figure 1.2 shows how the building blocks of a Web Part page are organized. Web Parts can live inside or outside a *zone*. When a Web Part is outside a zone and managed by the page, that Web Part is called a *static Web Part* and can't be customized by the end user using the web user interface. If a Web Part exists in a zone that's managed by the

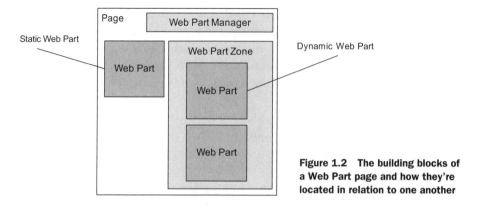

Figure 1.2   The building blocks of a Web Part page and how they're located in relation to one another

Web Part Manager, it can be customized and the customization can be persisted so that it's retained; it's then called a *dynamic Web Part*. The Web Part zones can also allow the user to add, remove, or move Web Parts that the user either can upload or find in the Web Part Gallery.

The Web Part Manager and Web Part zone objects are defined in the ASP.NET object model, but SharePoint uses its own implementation of these objects. .NET Framework has a provider model that allows developers to create their own backends for Web Part storage, and the SharePoint product team has created providers for SharePoint and enhanced them for SharePoint use. The customization and personalization of Web Parts are stored in the SharePoint content databases using the SharePoint implementation of the provider model.

1.3.2   *Web Part Manager*

The Web Part Manager control is responsible for handling the various Web Parts on a page. It deserializes and serializes Web Parts and their customizations from the content database, correctly places them in Web Part zones, and, optionally, connects them. During the Web Part page life cycle, a Web Part Manager fires and forwards all of the events on the different Web Parts. A Web Part Manager is responsible for:

- Persisting properties and customizations of Web Parts.
- Managing the Web Part connections.
- Managing the Web Parts in Web Part zones.
- Wiring up the events to the Web Parts.
- Managing standard and mobile views.

There can be only one Web Part Manager on a page. In SharePoint, a Web Part Manager is defined in the master page. Removing it from the master page or adding it directly to a page can make the page fail.

1.3.3   *Web Part zones*

A Web Part zone acts together with the Web Part Manager to render Web Parts onto the page. It's responsible for creating the chrome—any borders or styles around the

Web Part—as well as for rendering the necessary scripts to make the Web Parts able to react to drag-and-drop actions. A Web Part zone contains a set of properties that defines the layout of the zone. The responsibilities of a zone are:

- Defining the areas where Web Parts can be added.
- Defining the appearance (header, footer, frames, and so on) and the behavior of the zone.
- Specifying whether the Web Parts within a zone can be customized and/or personalized.
- Rendering the Web Parts in a zone.

Web Part zones and the wiki content controls have undergone a major overhaul since the 2007 version. In SharePoint 2010, the wiki content areas and the rich HTML fields for Publishing pages can be used as Web Part zones. Yes, you've heard that right! In a wiki (see figure 1.3) or a Publishing page, you can add your Web Parts into the wiki content or rich text between the paragraphs or even in the middle of a word.

NOTE Internally, SharePoint uses a hidden Web Part zone, with the id wpz, to manage the Web Parts in the wiki content. This Web Part zone is necessary so SharePoint can store its configuration. Each Web Part is marked in the wiki content using hidden DIV elements that reference the unique identifier of each Web Part (in the hidden zone).

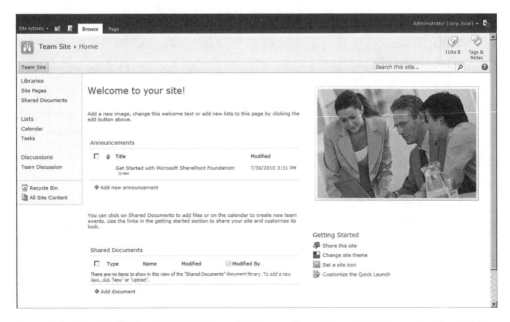

Figure 1.3   The default SharePoint 2010 Team Web is based on wiki pages. Wiki pages in SharePoint allow you to add Web Parts directly into the wiki content.

1.3.4   *Web Part elements*

The Web Part itself consists of several parts, as shown in figure 1.4. It has a content area, which you as a developer are focusing on. The content area is where a Web Part renders the content and the controls. The title of a Web Part can be configured through a property, but its layout is controlled primarily by the zone.

A Web Part has an Options menu, normally in the upper-right corner, and this menu contains actions called *verbs*. We'll discuss verbs in detail in chapter 4 but, for now, just know that a verb is defined as an action that belongs to the Web Part type. The action that's executed is controlled by the developer in the Web Part object. The Options menu also contains some other standard Web Part verbs, such as Minimize, Close, Delete, and Edit. The actions that appear reflect the user's permissions on the page and the Web Part's configuration.

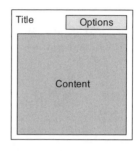

Figure 1.4   **A Web Part consists of a content area surrounded by the chrome. All Web Parts also have a title and a menu containing a set of verbs. You can configure the title and the menu so they don't display.**

1.3.5   *Web Part Gallery*

Each site collection in SharePoint has a set of galleries (sometimes called catalogs) containing the various artifacts that are used to build the sites in the site collection. One of these galleries is the Web Part Gallery. This gallery contains all the Web Parts that are available for the editors in that site collection. When creating a Web Part page, users can choose a Web Part from this gallery and add it to the page. Administrators can add new Web Parts to the gallery via web interface.

Each Web Part in the gallery has a set of metadata attached to it, such as a group for grouping Web Parts, as well as default values for the Web Part properties and permissions. The Web Part Gallery will be discussed in greater detail in chapter 2.

1.4   *Types of Web Parts*

One of the first questions Web Part developers ask themselves is why there are two implementations of the `WebPart` class: one ASP.NET version and one SharePoint version. These implementations have similarities as well as differences. The reason behind the two implementations is that, when SharePoint Portal Server 2003 and Windows SharePoint Services 2.0 were introduced, they were based on Microsoft .NET Framework 1.0 and ASP.NET 1.0, neither of which had the Web Part infrastructure. The Web Part infrastructure was introduced later in ASP.NET 2.0. In late 2006, when Microsoft Office SharePoint Server 2007 and Windows SharePoint Services 3.0 came out, they were built on top of ASP.NET 2.0 and implemented in such a way that they accepted both the old SharePoint Web Part implementation (to be backward compatible) and the ASP.NET Web Part implementation. What happened was that Microsoft rewrote the SharePoint 2003 Web Part implementation and made it inherit from the ASP.NET 2.0 Web Part, which made it compatible with SharePoint 2007.

How does this affect the situation for developers? Numerous discussions have taken place about the pros and cons of the different versions; one camp believes that you should use the old SharePoint-based Web Part due to its specific abilities, and another camp claims that the ASP.NET 2 Web Part is better because it's newer and Microsoft recommends it. In the next few sections, I'll explain when you should and should not use each version. The choice of implementation is really up to you—you have to evaluate the pros and cons of respective implementations. My recommendation, which also is Microsoft's recommendation, is that you should always start out with an ASP.NET 2 Web Part and only use a SharePoint Web Part if you need that implementation's specific features. Both versions are equally supported by SharePoint 2010, but this book will primarily focus on the ASP.NET 2 implementation. (When the SharePoint implementation is used, I'll point that out.) I'll highlight the differences and the advantages and disadvantages of the two versions and, finally, take a look at what has changed since the previous versions of SharePoint.

1.4.1   *ASP.NET 2 Web Parts*

The ASP.NET 2 Web Part was introduced when Microsoft released .NET Framework 2, together with a framework that allowed you to create your own providers for storing Web Part information, such as customization and zone information. This framework was used for building SharePoint 2007, and it's almost the same in SharePoint 2010.

ASP.NET Web Parts are defined in the `System.Web.UI.WebControls.WebParts` namespace in the `System.Web` assembly and are a part of ASP.NET. This means that if you write a Web Part using this implementation, you can start building it for a non-SharePoint environment; an example is a custom portal built with ASP.NET. Once you start adding references to the SharePoint assemblies and namespaces, you've lost this benefit and you are stuck with having your Web Part in SharePoint. Later in this book, we'll discuss various design patterns to use when building Web Parts, and you'll learn how to work around these issues.

ASP.NET Web Parts are the implementation that Microsoft recommends you use when building Web Parts for SharePoint. They're said to be the future of Web Parts. Nothing has really happened to Web Parts in the .NET Framework since the release of 2, and .NET Framework 4, which was released in early 2010, doesn't show any changes in the Web Part implementation.

SharePoint 2010 and Visual Studio 2010 features a new Web Part project type called Visual Web Parts (which we'll discuss further in chapter 3), and those Web Parts are based on the ASP.NET Web Part. Essentially, a Visual Web Part is a standard Web Part class that loads a user control (ASCX file), and this control can be edited using the Visual Studio 2010 visual designer. This will make your Web Part development experience more pleasant, and you'll save a lot of time because you don't have to manually create the controls and events and add them to the control tree.

What about .NET Framework 4?

Although .NET Framework 4 has been released, SharePoint 2010 is still built with .NET Framework 3.5 (Service Pack 1). The reason behind this is that the SharePoint team thought that it was too risky to work with the new framework, because .NET 4 still was in beta.

The .NET Framework 4 contains side-by-side execution of different .NET versions, which leads me to believe that we'll soon be able to run .NET 4 code in SharePoint. When you're installing Visual Studio 2010, which you'll do on your development machines, .NET 4 is a prerequisite.

When it comes to sandboxing (which means that the code is executed in a controlled and isolated environment), the only supported Web Part implementation is the ASP.NET Web Part. This is due to the sandboxing restrictions that don't allow you to dynamically load a user control or use the SharePoint Web Part implementation.

Here are the main benefits of using ASP.NET Web Parts:

- They're Microsoft's recommended choice for Web Part implementation.
- They're the future of Web Parts.
- They form the base of Visual Web Parts.
- They can be used to create non-SharePoint-hosted Web Parts.
- They support sandboxed deployment, unless standard Visual Web Parts are used.

NOTE   The freely downloadable Visual Studio 2010 SharePoint Power Tools contain a Visual Web Part that can be used in sandboxed solutions.

1.4.2 *SharePoint Web Parts*

SharePoint Web Parts remain in the SharePoint API due to large investments in these Web Parts since the time of SharePoint 2003 and because SharePoint Web Parts have some interesting features that ASP.NET Web Parts don't.

The Web Part implementation from SharePoint is defined in the `Microsoft.SharePoint.WebPartPages` namespace and exists in the `Microsoft.SharePoint` assembly. Once you derive your own Web Part from this class, your Web Part is tied to SharePoint and you can't reuse it in other ASP.NET-based solutions. The SharePoint Web Part inherits from the ASP.NET Web Part, so everything that you can do with an ASP.NET Web Part you can also do with a SharePoint Web Part.

The main reason for using this Web Part implementation is that it has some exclusive features when working with Web Part connections, features that the ASP.NET Web Part doesn't provide. The SharePoint Web Part can be connected to other Web Parts that either reside on other pages within the site or that don't exist in any zone (in other words, static Web Parts). The ASP.NET Web Part only accepts connections between Web Parts placed in zones and on the same page. The SharePoint Web Part can also handle client-side connections using the Web Part Page Services Component

(WPSC). This is no longer such a big deal because the new SharePoint 2010 Client Object Model, in combination with JavaScript, can be used to create a similar experience. Another reason for using the SharePoint Web Part is that it has a built-in feature for caching content.

Using this implementation might expose you to a risk, if you're looking for a long-lived product. You can't be sure that this implementation will be supported in upcoming versions of SharePoint.

The main benefits of using the SharePoint-based Web Parts are that:

- You can use cross-page connections.
- You can connect to static and dynamic Web Parts.
- These Web Parts offer built-in caching.
- You can take advantage of client-side connections using the Web Part Page Services Component.
- You might need SharePoint-based Web Parts for backward compatibility.

The single most important reason why developers choose the SharePoint Web Part implementation is that it can use connections between Web Parts that don't exist in Web Part zones or even on other pages. One example is when you have a dashboard page with a couple of zones and you've added a filter Web Part on your page but not in a zone, so that each page of this kind will always have that filter and the user can't remove it. Using the new Client Object Model (described in chapter 10) and JavaScript, you can reproduce a similar behavior if you need it by using the ASP.NET Web Part implementation.

Caching is important for high-scalability solutions, and the SharePoint Web Part has a built-in caching mechanism. If you need caching in your Web Part, then the SharePoint implementation might be a good candidate to start with. But the ASP.NET 2 Framework also has built-in support for caching in several ways. Using this ASP.NET caching mechanism, you can easily create your own caching and still be able to use the ASP.NET Web Part implementation. I strongly recommend that you implement caching yourself using the ASP.NET Web Part, and I'll show you how in chapter 9.

1.4.3 Changes in the Web Part infrastructure for SharePoint 2010

The Web Parts in SharePoint 2010 are derived from both implementations, but most of the new Web Parts derive from the ASP.NET 2 Web Part. This might be an indication of what Microsoft is trying to achieve for future versions of SharePoint. Even though, for the most part, ASP.NET Web Parts are used and SharePoint Web Parts are there for backward compatibility, there have been minor internal changes to the SharePoint Web Part implementation.

The SharePoint `WebPart` class hasn't changed much and doesn't offer developers any new features. Some internal changes have been made to the implementation related to the new SharePoint 2010 user interface, such as Ribbon integration.

The `WebPartZone`, `SPWebPartManager`, and other related classes have had some updates related to the Wiki Web Part zones. The updated `SPWebPartManager` also provides support for the mobile view of Web Part pages as well as mobile Web Parts. These changes are mostly internal to the assembly but, in later chapters, when we focus on these components, you'll see how you can use some of these enhancements.

One of the most notable changes is that the customization of a Web Part is *versioned* just as the Publishing Web Part page is versioned, which was not the case in earlier versions of SharePoint. This is an important improvement and it's crucial for you to be aware of it. If you roll back a page to a previous version, any changes to your Web Part customization will also be rolled back. The upside is that versioning makes it easier for you to experiment with customizations of a Web Part—if you'd like to go back to the original or working state, you just roll back the page.

To improve security and to prevent injection of malicious code, the Web Part infrastructure includes cross-site scripting (XSS) protection. We'll discuss this protection mechanism further in chapter 7.

1.5   Hello World example

You've just read about the basics of Web Parts and their infrastructure. Because this is a book for developers, what would be better than looking at a Web Part using the classic Hello World sample in a Hello World Web Part? This simple Web Part will write the text "Hello World" in the Web Part content area. The result for the end user should look sim-

Figure 1.5   A Hello World Web Part, showing the default Web Part options menu in the right corner

ilar to figure 1.5. The text is written in the content area and the title is automatically generated by Visual Studio. The Web Part options menu shown in the figure is the default menu of any Web Part.

The Hello World example in the following listing is quite basic if you're familiar with ASP.NET development. Using Visual Studio 2010, you first have to create a SharePoint project and then add a Web Part item to that project with the name `HelloWorldWebPart`.

Listing 1.1   Hello World Web Part

```
public class HelloWorldWebPart :
    System.Web.UI.WebControls.WebParts.WebPart {

    public override void CreateChildControls() {
        Label label = new Label();
        label.Text = "Hello World!";
        this.Controls.Add(label);
        base.CreateChildControls();
    }
}
```

The Web Part is defined in the HelloWorldWebPart.cs file. The class derives from the ASP.NET Web Part class, which exists in the `System.Web.UI.WebControls.WebParts` namespace and `System.Web` assembly. To add the `Label` control, you override the `CreateChildControls` method, and in the overridden method, a new `Label` control is created and added to the control tree. The `Text` property of the `Label` control gets the value of `"Hello World"`. Using Visual Studio 2010, you press F5 to build and deploy the Web Part into SharePoint 2010. The Web Part will be added to the Web Part Gallery during the deployment, and all you have to do is edit a page, locate the Web Part in the gallery, and add it to the page. This F5 deployment will be shown in greater detail in chapter 3.

As you can see from the sample code, the title and options aren't specified. The Web Part's title inherits from the base class and is, by default, the name of the class. Every Web Part has a set of default verbs that are added to the Options menu.

Later, I'll walk you through the steps involved in the creation and deployment of Web Parts using Visual Studio 2010, and I'll do the same with the Web Part Manager, zones, and connections. In SharePoint, along with the compiled assembly for the Web Part that you deploy to SharePoint, there are a few more files, and we'll cover them all as well. But, first, let's continue our look at the Web Part infrastructure.

1.6 SharePoint 2010 pages

We've gone through all the basics of the Web Part infrastructure in SharePoint 2010. Now, it's time to take a look at the pages where you use your Web Parts. To understand where you can use the Web Parts you're developing and where you have to use other approaches, you must have a good grasp of the concept of pages in SharePoint.

As previously stated, a page that has a Web Part Manager and, optionally, a zone can be used to host Web Parts, and this is almost the whole truth. SharePoint has two basic page types, application and site pages, and each serves its own purpose. These page types are based on a single ASP.NET master page that allows SharePoint to have a consistent interface framework.

First, we'll share some SharePoint basic knowledge. Pages exist in SharePoint sites. A SharePoint *site* represents a set of lists, libraries, groups, features, subsites, and so forth. These sites are grouped into *site collections*. Every site collection has a top-level site, which may have one or more subsites.

> **NOTE** The SharePoint API doesn't use the *site collection* and *site* naming conventions but, instead, uses *site* and *web*, where the `SPSite` object represents a site collection and `SPWeb` represents a site.

Sites in SharePoint 2010 have a special library called *site pages* (/SitePages/), which normally contains the web pages of a site, similar to the *Pages* library that the Publishing sites use to store the pages. The Site Pages library is new to SharePoint 2010. In SharePoint 2007, you either had to create a library on your own or resort to the more commonly used scenario: put your pages directly into the site. The advantage of a Site Pages library is that you can turn on versioning and/or workflows on all your site pages.

1.6.1   *Application pages*

First, we'll review application pages. Application pages are most often used as configuration pages for features or applications. Application pages can't host Web Part zones and therefore aren't dynamic Web Parts. You can use static Web Parts (those living outside a zone) though. A good practice is to use web or user controls instead of Web Parts when building application pages. These pages can't be controlled or edited by end users and should only be used for custom applications. They behave very much like a standard ASPX page. When you deploy or update application pages, you do so directly to the ASPX file in the file system. This is important; in a SharePoint farm, each server has a copy of these files and any changes and additions must be replicated to all servers (preferably using SharePoint Solution Packages, which is also the recommended way of doing this, as you'll see later in this book). Application pages are also known as *layout pages* because they exist in the Internet Information Services (IIS) _layouts virtual directory. The files are stored in the TEMPLATES\LAYOUTS subfolder of the SharePoint root (see the accompanying note) and virtualized as the _layouts subfolder of each SharePoint site.

> **NOTE** The SharePoint root is the folder where SharePoint stores its file on the server. It was previously and unofficially called the 12-hive, from version 12 in SharePoint 2007. It is located in c:\Program Files\Common Files\Microsoft Shared\Web Server Extensions\14\. Rather than writing the whole path I'll use {SharePoint Root} throughout this book.

1.6.2   *Site Pages*

Site pages are the pages in SharePoint that are created while a site is provisioned by the user or by different triggers. Typical site pages are the default or home pages created in a site, the AllItems.aspx list view page and the EditForm.aspx form page used to edit list items. These pages can be customized or modified by the end user using the browser, SharePoint Designer, or using other tools or techniques. There are a few different types of site pages; this book will focus on the Web Part and wiki pages. For publishing sites, there's a special type of page called the Publishing page that inherits from the Web Part page and is specifically designed to have a flexible layout. You can also create your own types of site pages by inheriting from or customizing any of the existing types.

WEB PART PAGES

A Web Part page is the simplest kind of site page. It's based on the master page, just like all other pages in SharePoint, and is equipped with a set of Web Part zones. The Web Part page is used for all form and view pages for lists and libraries. These pages are limited to changes in the Web Part zone, and in SharePoint 2010 the use of Wiki pages should be considered when creating pages.

WIKI PAGES

In SharePoint 2010, the default page becomes a wiki page, which has several benefits (compared with previous versions, where the default page type was a Web Part page).

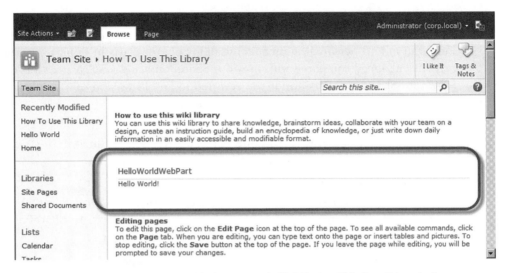

Figure 1.6   Wiki pages in SharePoint 2010 can contain Web Parts within the wiki content.

First, all text and content editing is easier and more user friendly with the WYSIWYG interface. Second, the wiki content areas have been hugely improved and now act as Web Part zones. In SharePoint 2007, the wiki content area was just a place where you could have content such as text, links, and images, with very limited editing possibilities. SharePoint 2010 wiki content areas can contain text, links, images, and Web Parts, and you have far better editing tools. The page editor can add and remove Web Parts in the wiki content and drag the Web Parts around and place them in appropriate positions, as shown in figure 1.6.

The wiki pages, inheriting from the `WikiEditPage` class, always contain a hidden Web Part zone that is used for storing the Web Parts that exist in the wiki content areas. In other words, the wiki content areas aren't Web Part zones. The wiki content contains special tags where Web Parts are placed. When SharePoint finds one of these tags, it locates the Web Part in the hidden zone and renders it into a buffer. Finally, this buffer is flushed out to the page.

> **NOTE**   *Wiki* is a Hawaiian word that means fast. A wiki typically is a website that allows for easy creation, editing, and linking between wiki pages using a specific syntax or editor. SharePoint 2010 uses a WYSIWYG editor and, using the `[[` and `]]` symbols, links to pages are created. If no page exists at the link, the editor will be asked to create a page once they click on the link.

PUBLISHING PAGES

Publishing pages are most often used in enterprise portals or public-facing websites. A Publishing page is a Web Part page that uses specific field controls to render the publishing content. A Publishing page inherits from `PublishingLayoutPage`, which inherits from the `WebPartPage` class. In many cases, Publishing pages also contain Web Part zones that the page editor can use to add extra information or functionality to the pages. Because SharePoint 2010 now can handle the versioning of a Web Part's customization and personalization state, usability of Web Parts in Publishing pages and sites is enhanced compared with previous SharePoint releases. This was a problem in previous SharePoint versions: if you reverted to an old version of a Publishing page, the configuration of the Web Part didn't change.

CUSTOM SITE PAGES

Site pages are normally based on one of two classes, both defined in the `Microsoft.SharePoint.WebPartPages` namespace:

- *WebPartPage*—A site page containing Web Part zones.
- *WikiEditPage*—A new type of site page introduced in SharePoint 2010, which contains the new Wiki field, which can host Web Parts. In SharePoint 2010, these pages are sometimes simply called Page (see figure 1.7).

By default, these site pages can't contain inline server-side code, such as custom logic and events. Assume that you create a new site page in a document library and want to add a submit button that runs some code when clicked. You can't do this using inline code without changing the security settings of your SharePoint web application. You can lower the security, but I don't recommend it because that exposes your web application to malicious code. Instead, you have two basic options that work equally well but have different purposes:

- *Create a Web Part*—This Web Part will display the button and handle the click event for you.
- *Subclass the site page*—Your new class will have the code that handles the click event and the site page ASPX code will define the button.

Using a Web Part for your custom code is the preferred way because you can reuse the logic much more easily. If you add the Web Part as a static Web Part (outside a zone), you can control on which pages the Web Part is available. The easiest way to achieve

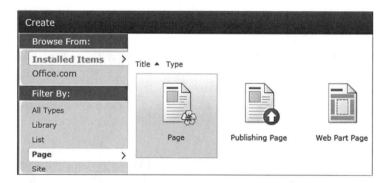

Figure 1.7   You can use the new Silverlight-based Create dialog box to search for and add new items to your site. Notice the option to download new items and templates from Office.com. If you don't have Silverlight installed, you'll see an HTML-based interface instead.

this is using SharePoint Designer, but that will customize the page (read more about customization below). If you add a Web Part to the page using the web interface to a zone, the editors of that page can move, customize, or even delete the Web Part, but you'll allow the page to stay in its original state (if it wasn't already customized).

Allowing inline server-side code in a Site page

To allow inline code in your site page, you have to edit the web.config file of the web application to lower the security. Do so by adding a new `PageParserPath` element to the `PageParserPaths` element like this:

```
<PageParserPath
    VirtualPath="/Library/*"
    CompilationMode="Always"
    AllowServerSideScript="true"
    IncludeSubFolders="true" />
```

Where `VirtualPath` is the path to the document library or site where you put your site page.

Once you do this, anyone can upload their own code to be executed in the virtual path, so be advised. Enabling inline server-side code isn't a good practice and you should use this approach only for testing and development purposes.

PAGE CUSTOMIZATION

The site pages are stored, just like the Web Part customizations, in the content database of your SharePoint instance. Compared with the application pages, you don't have to care about replicating changes between the SharePoint servers because the file resides in the database.

This is true in most cases. SharePoint has a mechanism called *page customization*, previously referred to as *ghosting*. This technique allows you to store the template of the site page on the disk ("ghost") and the database keeps a reference to the file on the disk instead. When you customize the page ("unghost"), data is added to the content database and the reference points to the database instead of the file system. The page customization makes SharePoint perform better because it doesn't have to keep a copy in the database for all provisioned pages—only the ones that the user explicitly customized. For example, the editform.aspx file for a contacts list uses the version stored on the disk for all contacts lists in the farm (unless the page is customized) and saves you a lot of database space and performance. Any updates to a file in the file system will immediately be visible for all noncustomized contacts list edit forms (for example, when you need to make some changes or when you apply a SharePoint service pack). You shouldn't modify a site page residing in the file system of the SharePoint frontend web servers because it's difficult to determine if and where this file has been customized and it will likely be difficult to get support if it breaks. Another disadvantage of editing files directly in the file system is that they might be overwritten when you update or upgrade SharePoint.

1.6.3   *Master pages*

A master page is the foundation of any page in SharePoint ASP.NET sites. A master page defines the basic layout, structure, and functionality of pages and contains placeholders where the pages can host their content. Each time a page is requested by a user, the page is created by replacing the placeholders in the master page with the content from the page, which merges the master page with the requested page.

SharePoint 2010 mainly uses one master page, called v4.master, compared with the previous SharePoint version, which had a separate master page for application pages. You can edit master pages or provide your own, but that's a completely different topic. The default master page is located in the SharePoint root under the TEMPLATE\GLOBAL folder.

> **NOTE**   SharePoint 2010 contains a completely new master page to support the new user interface and web browser compatibility. If you've invested heavily in the SharePoint 2007 UI and want to upgrade your site, it's good to know that the old master pages are still provided with the SharePoint 2010 upgrade and you can at any time select the interface you want to use: the old one or the brand-new one. Note that, once you switch from the 2007 interface to version 2010, you can't go back.

As a Web Part developer, be aware of a couple of things when working with master pages. The default master page delivered with SharePoint 2010 contains the important Web Part Manager object (`SPWebPartManager`), so there's no need to define your own in your site or application pages. It's defined close to the body tag of the page and has an id of m.

You can't add Web Part zones to the master page—only to the pages utilizing the master page, but you can add Web Parts directly to a master page. These Web Parts will be available on all pages using the master page and they'll be static, because they don't exist in a zone. This also means that the Web Parts can't be customized using the user interface, for instance, when editing a page. You have to use SharePoint Designer 2010 to customize the Web Parts.

1.7   *Summary*

This chapter was a brief introduction to the world of Web Parts in SharePoint, and you should now have the basic knowledge to begin building your own Web Parts. SharePoint is a platform that can be used to develop and deploy your custom applications. We walked through the basics of Web Parts in SharePoint 2010, and we introduced the building blocks of pages. Here's a summary of what you've learned so far:

- Web Parts are one of the building blocks in SharePoint.
- Web Parts can act alone or together with other Web Parts.
- The Web Part infrastructure is defined in ASP.NET 2.
- Web Parts are managed through a Web Part Manager object.
- Web Parts exist inside or outside of Web Part zones.
- Pages in SharePoint host the Web Part zones.

For a SharePoint Web Part developer, two tools are especially important: Visual Studio 2010 and SharePoint Designer 2010. The first is used for designing and building Web Parts and the latter for configuring Web Parts, pages, and sites. The rest of this book will cover most of the situations you'll be facing when building Web Parts, and you should have these tools close at hand.

Remember that you don't always have to develop your own Web Parts; there are plenty of configurable Web Parts that you can use to create your solutions. But, there are many situations when you need to develop your own custom Web Part to provide a unique functionality that your customer is requesting or to have full control of your application. Developing Web Parts isn't just about writing a piece of code that's injected into a SharePoint environment; you need to know how SharePoint uses the Web Parts and how you leverage SharePoint's features. We'll continue to explore Web Parts in SharePoint and how to make your Web Parts utilize the platform in the best possible way.

Using and configuring
Web Parts in SharePoint 2010

2

This chapter covers

- Features in the SharePoint 2010 interface
- The Web Part Gallery
- Out-of-the-box Web Parts in SharePoint 2010
- SharePoint Designer 2010

A key factor in becoming a great developer is a good understanding of how end users work with the tools that SharePoint 2010 provides. As a developer, you may often be asked to build a solution or a Web Part that accomplishes a specific task. Taking advantage of the out-of-the-box features can get you up to speed faster. Sometimes, you may even end up with a solution that requires no programming and no new code.

As you learned in the first chapter, the best SharePoint developers know how to leverage the platform and use the tools that SharePoint supplies. You'll most likely build better Web Parts if you know how your end users will use your Web Parts and how they'll create their own applications using them. In this chapter, we'll explore a few of those possibilities.

Once you know what users can accomplish using only the web interface and SharePoint Designer, you should use the same techniques. You can use the built-in Web Parts to create mockups and demos to show a concept application or to validate your solution with your customer even before you start programming. The out-of-the-box Web Parts can also be a part of your final solution, in combination with your custom Web Parts and pages.

2.1 The SharePoint 2010 user interface

The first thing you'll notice in SharePoint 2010—if you've worked with SharePoint before—is the new user interface. Menus have been drastically changed and moved around and the interface has a more modern design, but it won't be long before you find your way around and feel at home. SharePoint hides a lot of functionality to avoid cluttering the interface; for example, the Web Part options menu in the upper-right corner of the Web Part is visible only when you select it or hover over the Web Part with your mouse.

SharePoint has several new and improved features such as the Ribbon (you'll recognize it from Microsoft Office 2007) and Ajax dialog boxes and notifications. These components, which you'll learn about in the next section, make SharePoint efficient to work with. They also give you, the developer, a whole new way to interact with the users of your Web Parts.

> **TIP** If you're upgrading or have upgraded your SharePoint 2010 site from SharePoint 2007, you'll notice that the new version retains the SharePoint 2007 interface. This is because of the enhanced SharePoint upgrade procedure that uses the backward-compatible master pages. You can switch over to the new 2010 interface at any time, temporarily or permanently, using the Visual Upgrade option found under Site Settings.

2.1.1 The new SharePoint user interface and the Ribbon

Microsoft Office 2007 introduced a revolutionary and innovative interface, including the now well-known Ribbon interface. The Ribbon is the new combined menu and toolbar and is based on the user's current context; for example, if the user is editing a table, the table editing commands appear. This context-aware interface has now made it into SharePoint 2010 (see figure 2.1) and is one of the most significant UI changes for end users.

Figure 2.1 **SharePoint 2010 includes the Ribbon toolbar, introduced in Office 2007. The Ribbon is context aware, which means it changes its contents depending on what the user is doing.**

The Ribbon consists of a number of tabs that are divided into sections containing controls. These tabs are context aware and appear when needed. For example, when you're editing a page, the Editing Tools tab containing the Format Text and Insert tabs appears, as you can see in figure 2.1. The tabs and sections are dynamically loaded without any postbacks and screen refreshes, which makes the interface easy and fast to use. Even a Web Part, such as the SharePoint Server Media Web Part, can have its own Ribbon controls.

The Ribbon experience is extensible in that you can add and remove tabs, sections, groups, and controls to make a superior end user experience. Chapter 10 will introduce you to the Ribbon objects and show you how to create Ribbon- and context-aware Web Parts.

SharePoint has borrowed other features from the Microsoft Office UI, such as Live Previews and Galleries. Live Previews facilitate the editing process and allow you to preview your design changes without saving the information.

2.1.2 *Other interface improvements*

The Ribbon is not the only interface improvement in SharePoint 2010. There are several features that you as a developer can take advantage of and plug into. SharePoint is using Ajax-based dialog boxes and notifications as well as other JavaScript-based features that you can extend.

To avoid postbacks and make the web interface faster and more intuitive, SharePoint uses the new Ajax-based Dialog Framework, a JavaScript-based framework for creating modal dialogs. When you click to edit an item in a list, instead of going to a new page, which you did in SharePoint 2007, you're now presented with an in-browser overlay pop-up window.

Another dynamic interface feature is the status bar, which is located under the Ribbon. This bar is used to provide status messages to the user and optionally gives the user the opportunity to take some action without stopping work. The status bar can be used to alert users about configuration errors or that certain actions need to be taken. For example, the status bar is used when you have a save conflict on a Web Part page. In Central Administration (Central Administration is the SharePoint administration website), the status bar notifies administrators when the Health Analyzer has detected issues (see figure 2.2).

Notification messages are the small messages that appear below the Ribbon on the right side when, for instance, a page is loading or saving. The difference between the status bar and notification messages is that the status bar is used for more persistent user information whereas notification messages are used for transient information. Chapter 10 will show you how to utilize these new features in your Web Parts.

You can use all these features to create just the user experience that you want, and I'll show you how it's done in this book.

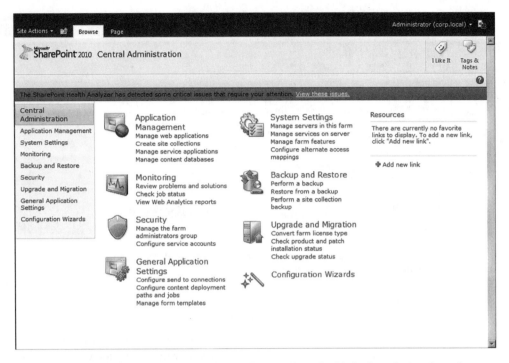

Figure 2.2　The Central Administration in SharePoint contains a Health Analyzer that analyzes the current state of the farm. If any critical errors are found, the Health Analyzer uses the status bar to notify administrators.

2.2　*The Web Part Gallery*

You choose Web Parts from the Web Part Gallery, which you'll find in the Ribbon menu when editing a page. The gallery is a site collection-based library that contains information and metadata about the Web Parts that are available to end users in that specific site collection. The gallery is used to publish the Web Parts that you build or install so that your users can select the Web Parts they want. Using the gallery or directly importing Web Parts is the only way for users to add Web Parts to a page.

Each site collection has its own gallery; you can access a gallery by choosing Site Settings and, under the Galleries section, clicking on Web Parts. SharePoint displays a list of all the available Web Parts in the gallery (see figure 2.3).

Not only does the Web Part Gallery host the Web Parts but it also contains metadata about how Web Parts are organized in groups as well as permissions for Web Parts. As a developer, you can deploy your default Web Part configuration into the gallery, and the site collection administrator can, at any time, change the configuration of any Web Part in the gallery. In this section, I'll walk you through the gallery so that you'll know where your Web Parts are deployed and how they can be used and configured after deployment.

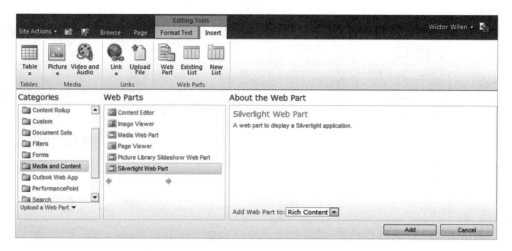

Figure 2.3   The Web Part Gallery contains all installed Web Parts for the current site collection and is used to locate and add Web Parts to pages.

2.2.1   *What is the Web Part Gallery?*

The Web Part Gallery is a special catalog created by SharePoint to host the site collection's Web Parts. When users are building Web Part pages using either the browser or SharePoint Designer, they pick the Web Parts they need by selecting them from the gallery. The gallery doesn't contain the compiled Web Part assembly; it's simply a list of Web Part items with metadata columns and a file attachment that contains a Web Parts control description file. This file contains the default value used by any created instance of the Web Part as well as the reference to the assembly and Web Part class. All Web Parts can also have a group value, which is used for organizing and grouping the Web Parts.

The Web Part Gallery contains a set of preconfigured templates for Web Parts that editors can choose from. When you're adding a Web Part to a page, the Web Part properties are copied from the control description file to the page. If you later go back and edit the Web Part in the gallery, this change won't affect Web Parts that have already been added. Chapter 3 will show you what the Web Parts control description file looks like and how it works. When I talk about Web Parts in the Web Part Gallery, I'm referring to the definition and configuration of a Web Part. That's also what end users are referring to when they talk about Web Parts. When a developer talks about a Web Part, they're most often talking about the Web Part class existing in an assembly.

When working with pages programmatically, you don't have to use only the Web Parts listed in the gallery—you can use any Web Part that you create through code. This topic will be discussed further in chapter 15 when we explore building pages and dashboards.

If you're adding Web Parts to a page, you also have access to a special group called *Lists and Libraries.* This category contains the XSLT List View Web Parts (see section 2.3.1) configured for all available lists and libraries in the site and shows a view of the selected list.

2.2.2   Uploading or adding new Web Parts to the gallery

To add new Web Parts to the gallery using the web interface, you can choose from two basic methods:

- Upload a Web Parts control description file (.webpart).
- Populate the gallery with Web Parts discovered in registered assemblies.

The first approach, uploading a Web Parts control description file, is also used behind the scenes when you install a SharePoint solution package containing Web Parts. You simply click the Upload Document button in the gallery and, when the file is uploaded, you're prompted to configure the Web Part with a title, description, and so forth, before you save the item.

In the second method, which involves discovery of Web Parts in registered assemblies, you click the New Document button in the gallery. SharePoint iterates all assemblies registered as safe in the web.config file and then searches for any classes inheriting from the `System.Web.UI.WebControls.WebParts.WebPart` class and displays a list of them. When you select one or more of the Web Parts in the list and click Populate Gallery, SharePoint creates the Web Parts control description files for you automatically and adds the Web Parts to the gallery. Using the populate method has a drawback: the Web Part won't get any default property values, which may result in unexpected behavior. Only use this approach when you have to or when you need to modify and upload a default control description file.

2.2.3   Editing Web Parts in the gallery

If you want to edit the metadata and information of a Web Part in the gallery, you first have to go to the Web Part Gallery, which you'll find in the Site Settings of the site collection. Note that, if you're in a subsite, you have to navigate to the root site and choose Site Settings. The Web Part Gallery is located under the Galleries section; just click the link to view the gallery.

The gallery is just like any SharePoint list and can be sorted and filtered. This is great if you have a lot of Web Parts, especially when you're using SharePoint Server 2010 and have a number of features activated. When you click on one of the Web Parts listed in the gallery, you'll see the Web Part Preview page, which shows you the Web Part in preview mode. To edit the Web Part metadata, select the Web Part, click the Documents tab in the Ribbon, and click Edit Properties (or you can click the edit icon that appears directly to the right of the Web Part name). A dialog box appears (as shown in figure 2.4), where you can edit the properties of the Web Part. These aren't the Web Part properties that are stored in the Web Parts control description file discussed in chapter 5; you're editing metadata about the Web Part configuration in this site collection. The dialog box lets you change the title, description, grouping, and other properties for the Web Part. Save the information by clicking the Save button in the Ribbon.

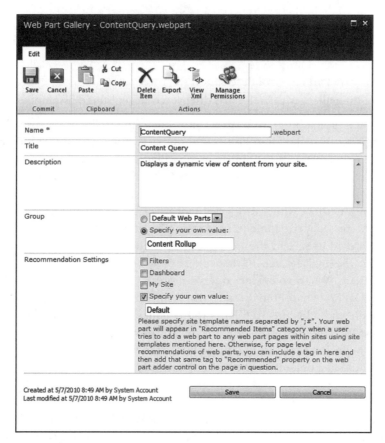

Figure 2.4   You can configure, group, export, and manage the permissions for the Web Parts in the Web Part Gallery catalog, accessed from the Site Settings page.

NOTE   A SharePoint feature is a set of functionalities packaged together to simplifies deployment and installation. A feature is targeted to a scope, such as a site or the entire farm, and can be activated to enable the functionalities defined in the feature and deactivated to remove them.

2.2.4   Grouping the Web Parts

Web Parts are grouped in the gallery, which helps end users find the relevant Web Part more easily. The groups are defined by the metadata on the Web Part in the gallery and can be changed by users who have appropriate permissions. Custom-developed and imported Web Parts appear in the *Custom* group unless otherwise specified. In chapter 3, you'll learn how to define these groups in your custom solution.

    If you want to change groups or add groups to a Web Part in the gallery, you have to edit the Web Part metadata. You can specify a new group name or use the default ones to group your Web Parts.

2.2.5   Permissions on Web Parts in the gallery

Not all users can add Web Parts to the gallery, but, by default, all users with permissions to edit a page can use all the Web Parts in the gallery. Only users with the Design or Full

Control permission level are allowed to add or edit Web Parts in the gallery. More specifically, you need the Manage Lists list permission to be able to edit the gallery.

Normally, there's no need to prohibit users from using all the Web Parts available in the gallery. Instead, you build Web Parts in such a way that they display a friendly error message if they're used or viewed by someone who shouldn't have access. For example, if you create a Web Part that reads information from a restricted content source and displays that data, you should make sure in your Web Part that *only* the intended users can see that information.

Sometimes, it's necessary to hide Web Parts from the editors so they don't use them. You can do this by modifying properties on the Web Part and then selecting Manage Permissions. The permissions are, by default, inherited from the gallery, which is, by default, inherited from the site. So you first have to break the permission inheritance and then set the permissions that you want the Web Part to have. This only prevents the editors from using the Web Part when creating a new page and it doesn't hide any Web Parts currently used on pages or prohibit users from seeing Web Parts.

2.3 Out-of-the-box Web Parts

SharePoint 2010 comes with a number of out-of-the-box Web Parts that are available for end users to use when they're creating pages and dashboards. The Web Parts that are included reflect which version of SharePoint is installed, which site template is used, and which features are enabled on the site collections. Not all Web Parts are available through the gallery. Some, like the Data Form and the XSLT List View Web Parts, need to be added and configured using SharePoint Designer. Some you have to add manually to the gallery.

The following sections cover the most important out-of-the-box Web Parts in SharePoint. I've separated them into the free version SharePoint Foundation 2010 and the license-based version SharePoint Server 2010 so that you can see the differences. For a full list of Web Parts and more details, see appendix A.

SharePoint edition details

The official SharePoint web site contains a detailed edition comparison diagram where you can see what features each edition contains. Compare the features of the SharePoint Foundation, SharePoint Server Standard and Enterprise at http://sharepoint.microsoft.com/en-us/buy/pages/editions-comparison.aspx.

2.3.1 SharePoint Foundation 2010

SharePoint Foundation 2010, which is the entry-level edition of SharePoint 2010, contains a set of Web Parts. They're either generic, for information display, or focused on building simple collaboration sites. Table 2.1 lists the Web Parts that you can find in the gallery in a SharePoint Foundation site.

Table 2.1   The Web Parts of SharePoint Foundation

Web Part name	Description	Group
HTML Form Web Part	Connects simple form controls to other Web Parts.	Forms
Picture Library Slide-show Web Part	Creates a slideshow of pictures from a picture gallery.	Content Rollup
XML Viewer	Imports an XML source and transforms it using an XSLT document. For example, it can be used to import an RSS feed, which is then transformed using a custom XSLT into displayable content.	Content Rollup
Relevant Documents	Displays relevant documents for the current user.	Documents
Content Editor	Used to add formatted text, tables, and images to a page. Can be used to add JavaScript functions to the page.	Media and Content
Image Viewer	Shows an image.	Media and Content
Page Viewer	Allows you to frame in another or external page in the page. This Web Part can be used to add framed custom external applications to a site.	Media and Content
Silverlight Web Part	Adds a custom Silverlight application to the page.	Media and Content
Site Users	Shows the current users and groups of a site.	People
User Tasks	Displays the current tasks for the user from the site where the Web Part is placed.	People

The generic Web Parts, such as Content Editor, HTML Form, and XML Viewer, can be used to create basic applications. For instance, you can use Content Editor to execute JavaScript code or insert custom HTML into a page. Using HTML Form, you can create an input form that creates a filter for other Web Parts.

The Silverlight Web Part—new in SharePoint 2010—allows you to add a Silverlight application to your site by either uploading a Silverlight XAP file to a document library or linking to an external XAP file. Using this Web Part and the Client Object Model (discussed in detail in chapter 11), you can create rich and advanced applications without even touching the server. Silverlight is a convenient way to extend your SharePoint site in situations when you aren't allowed to add server-side code and can't use sandboxed solutions.

Some of the out-of-the-box Web Parts aren't accessible from the Web Part Gallery and are often overlooked by developers. These include the Data Form Web Part (known as the Data View Web Part in SharePoint 2003) and the new XSLT List View Web Part, as shown in table 2.2. They can only be added to SharePoint programmatically or by using tools such as SharePoint Designer 2010. The configuration options of these Web Parts are advanced and that's one of the reasons they can't be created through the web interface. On many occasions you can use these Web Parts rather than developing a custom Web Part.

Table 2.2   SharePoint Foundation Web Parts not available in the web interface

Web Part name	Description
Data Form (DFWP/DVWP)	The Data Form Web Part can be used to create views from external sources such as Web Services and SQL Server databases. It's still called the Data View Web Part internally.
XSLT List View (XLV)	This is a new Web Part in SharePoint 2010 and replaces the List View Web Part. It's based on XSLT instead of Collaborative Application Markup Language (CAML).

The XSLT List View Web Part, new in SharePoint 2010, is superseding the old CAML-based List View Web Part. Instead of using CAML formatting to generate the output of the Web Part, the XSLT List View Web Part uses Extensible Stylesheet Language Transformation (XSLT). XSLT is a more standardized approach, and you'll find it easier to learn XSLT than CAML. I recommend that you get up to speed on XSLT; not only is it used in this Web Part, but it's also leveraged in other Web Parts, such as some of the Search Web Parts. The XSLT List View Web Part also has better performance and supports in-browser editing compared to its predecessor.

> **NOTE**   The Collaborative Application Markup Language (CAML) is an XML-based language that's used by SharePoint. It's mainly used to query the information in SharePoint but also provides support for defining data and rendering. Support for rendering in previous versions of SharePoint was provided in the List View Web Part, which has been replaced by the new XSLT List View Web Part.

The Data Form and XSLT List View Web Parts support rich customization with SharePoint Designer 2010, with support for extensible, shareable view styles and conditional formatting.

> **TIP**   To learn more about the Data Form Web Part and how to work with the out-of-the-box Web Parts without any code there is a great set of series and blog posts at the End User SharePoint section at www.nothingbutsharepoint.com.

2.3.2   *SharePoint Server 2010*

When using a SharePoint 2010 Server edition, you get a whole lot of Web Parts in the different features. SharePoint Server is essentially SharePoint Foundation with a set of features and services applied to it, which means that all the Web Parts listed in tables 2.1 and 2.2 also are available in SharePoint Server.

SharePoint Server comes in two major editions: Standard and Enterprise. The Enterprise edition has a number of features and Web Parts that aren't available in the Standard edition. This section doesn't separate the Standard and Enterprise Web Parts, but appendix A lists all Web Parts available in SharePoint Foundation, Standard, and Enterprise and indicates the edition in which they're accessible.

When you create a site, you won't see all these Web Parts in the site collection's Web Part Gallery by default. They'll appear only when features are turned on or installed. For example, you won't have access to the PerformancePoint Web Parts until the PerformancePoint feature is activated.

I've grouped the Web Parts using the same default groups in which the Web Parts appear in the gallery. First is the most used: Content Rollup.

CONTENT ROLLUP WEB PARTS

Content Rollup Web Parts are used to collect and merge content and information from lists and sites and create views. Table 2.3 lists the rollup Web Parts that are available in SharePoint Server.

The most interesting and the most used in this group is the Content Query Web Part (CQWP). It can, for instance, be used to show items of specific content types from all subsites and present them to end users. To use the CQWP, you have to activate the SharePoint publishing infrastructure feature on your site collection. The CQWP has had numerous improvements since the 2007 version; here are a couple most important ones:

- In-browser support to pass additional fields to the XSLT transformation
- Dynamic filters based on Page fields and query string parameters

If your solution calls for rolling up content, this is the Web Part you should start with.

Table 2.3   Content Rollup Web Parts in SharePoint Server 2010

Web Part name	Description
RSS Viewer	Shows an RSS feed.
Web Analytics	Displays configurable popular contents for the site or site collection.
Content Query (CQWP)	Dynamically rolls up content and information and creates a view for end users.

FILTER WEB PARTS

Filter Web Parts are used in combination with other Web Parts. SharePoint Server contains a set of great Web Parts, as shown in table 2.4. Filter Web Parts are used to filter the contents of other Web Parts using Web Part connections.

> ### Web Part Connections
>
> Web Part connections let you connect one Web Part to another to send data or information from one provider Web Part to a consumer Web Part. In chapter 14, I'll show you all the details you need to build custom connectable Web Parts. In section 2.4.3, you'll learn how to use Web Part connections.

Chapter 14 provides more information about connecting Web Parts and will give you more details on how these filter Web Parts work. In chapter 15, you're going to build dashboards and use some filter Web Parts.

Table 2.4   Filter Web Parts available in SharePoint Server 2010

Web Part name	Description
Text Filter	Filters a Web Part using a value entered by the user.
Current User Filter	Sends a user id to a Web Part.
Date Filter	Filters a Web Part with a selected date.
Filter Actions	Synchronizes two or more filter Web Parts.
SQL Server Analysis Server Filter	Filters a Web Part with values from a SQL Server Analysis Server cube.
Page Field Filter	Filters a Web Part based on metadata of the Web Part page.
Query String (URL) Filter	Filters a web part using query string parameters.
SharePoint List Filter	Filters a Web Part using a list of values.
Choice Filter	Filters a Web Part using a list of values entered by the page author.

MEDIA WEB PARTS

The publishing feature of SharePoint Server contains a media Web Part that can display audio and video using a Silverlight player. This Web Part takes advantage of the new SharePoint 2010 features such as the Ribbon for configuration and Silverlight integration. Unfortunately, the Web Part is *sealed*, which means that you can't modify or add features to it.

NAVIGATION WEB PARTS

The navigation Web Parts (see table 2.5) are used to enhance websites with improved features such as sitemaps and tag clouds (a visual representation of tags, often weighted) and the ability to display sites in the site directory.

Table 2.5   Navigational Web Parts for use with SharePoint Server 2010

Web Part name	Description
Sites in Category	Displays sites from a specific category in the site directory.
Categories	Displays the categories from the site directory.
Site Aggregator	Displays documents and tasks from selected sites.
Tag Cloud	Displays a tag cloud of tagged subjects.
Summary Links	Displays a list of grouped and styled links.
Table of Contents	Displays the sitemap of your site.

PEOPLE WEB PARTS

The People Web Parts (see table 2.6) are focused on users and their social activities. For example, you can add the Note Board Web Part to pages for users to create and share notes about that specific page.

Table 2.6   People Web Parts

Web Part name	Description
Contact Details	Displays contact details for a specified user.
Organization Browser	Silverlight-based Web Part for browsing the organization.
Note Board	Allows the user to make a note of the current page.

SEARCH WEB PARTS

SharePoint Server 2010 comes with a highly customizable search engine. The search and results pages are built using a set of Web Parts. In many projects, the search pages are customized with either the out-of-the-box Web Parts or custom-built ones. On many occasions, you may need to tweak the out-of-the-box Web Parts but you can't achieve what you want by modifying the properties; in such cases, you can subclass these Web Parts. Fortunately, the newly added Web Parts aren't sealed (most were in SharePoint 2007), so they can be subclassed and you can create your own inherited Web Parts from them. Table 2.7 shows the most important Search Web Parts and indicates whether they're sealed.

Table 2.7   Search Web Parts of SharePoint Server 2010

Web Part name	Description	Sealed
Advanced Search Box	Parameterized options for search	Yes
Federated Results	Shows the search results from a federated (external—non-SharePoint) location	No
People Refinement Panel	Used to refine people search results	No
People Search Box	A search box used to search for people	No
People Search Core Results	Displays the people search results	Yes
Refinement Panel	Refinements for search results	No
Related Queries	Displays queries related to the current	No
Search Best Bets	Displays the best bets of the search results	Yes
Search Box	Displays the search box to search for information	Yes
Search Core Results	Displays the results of a search or search actions	No
Top Answer	Displays the top federated results from a federated location	No
Visual Best Bets	Displays visual best bets	No

The Search Web Parts don't use Web Part connections to provide and consume information from one another. Instead, they use a special object on the page called `SharedQueryManager`, from which all Search Web Parts locate and retrieve information. The best way to learn how these Web Parts work is to go to a Search Center in your SharePoint site and edit the search and results page and see how the various Web Parts interact with one another.

MY INFORMATION WEB PARTS

SharePoint Server comes with My Information Web Parts, which can be integrated with Outlook Web Access (OWA), the web version of Microsoft Exchange Server. These Web Parts, listed in table 2.8, are normally used on the profile pages.

Web Part name	Description
My Mail Folder	Displays a mail folder from OWA.
My Calendar	Displays your calendar from OWA.
My Contacts	Displays your contacts from OWA.
My Inbox	Displays your inbox from OWA.
My Tasks	Displays your tasks from OWA.

Table 2.8 My Information Web Parts for integration with Outlook Web Access

BUSINESS DATA WEB PARTS

The Business Data Web Parts are used to leverage information from Business Connectivity Services (BCS). Even though BCS is a part of SharePoint Foundation 2010, these Web Parts are only available in SharePoint Server 2010. Table 2.9 lists the available Web Parts in this category.

Table 2.9 Business Data Web Parts in SharePoint Server 2010

Web Part name	Description
Business Data Actions	Lists available actions for a specified external content type.
Business Data Connectivity Filter	A filter Web Part that provides the consumer with a set of values from the Business Connectivity Services.
Business Data Item	Displays a specific item from an external content type.
Business Data Item Builder	Creates a BCS item using query string parameters and provides this item to other Web Parts.
Business Data List	Displays a list of items from an external content type.
Business Data Related List	Lists related items from one or more parent items.
Indicator	Displays a single status indicator.
KPI List	Displays a list of status indicators.

PERFORMANCEPOINT WEB PARTS

PerformancePoint Services are a new feature of SharePoint Server with business intelligence features. If you've configured PerformancePoint Services 2010 in your SharePoint Server farm and you've activated the PerformancePoint Feature, you'll get a handful of specialized Web Parts for that service application.

OFFICE CLIENT APPLICATIONS WEB PARTS

The Office Client Web Parts, listed in table 2.10, are part of the Enterprise edition of SharePoint Server and are used to display Office files. They include Excel Services, which can display a workbook as a web page and InfoPath Form, which can be used to display InfoPath-based forms as Web Parts that can be connected with other Web Parts.

Table 2.10   The Office Web Application Client Web Parts

Web Part name	Description
Excel Web Access	Shows an Excel Workbook as a web page.
InfoPath Form	Displays an InfoPath browser-enabled form.
Visio Web Access	Shows a Visio Web Drawing (.vwd file).
WSRP Viewer	Shows portlets from websites using Web Services for Remote Portlets (WSRP) 1.1. WSRP is an OASIS-approved standard for communications with remote portlets.

2.4   Working with Web Parts and pages

Web Parts, whether custom or default, are self-contained applications. You can create them so that end users can configure them, or you can provide no configuration options at all. Web Parts can be added to pages and may be connected with other Web Parts to create new applications or mashups.

Users with appropriate permissions can create and edit Web Part pages in Share-Point to create their own solutions. They're provided with a set of out-of-the-box Web Parts as well as those custom Web Parts that are installed in the site collection's Web Part Gallery. Using only a web browser, users can add Web Parts and connect them using the user-friendly SharePoint 2010 interface.

The following sections will show you how to create a page, add a Web Part, and filter it using a Web Part. We'll build a new page that contains a view of a library and use a connected HTML Form Web Part to filter the list.

2.4.1   Creating a page using the web interface

The task of creating a page has been improved in SharePoint 2010. In earlier versions, only publishing sites had the benefit of a decent user interface that was adapted for creating and editing pages. Nearly all SharePoint sites are now created with a Site Pages library to contain site pages.

To create a new page, all you have to do is either add a new page in the library the traditional way—by adding a new item to the library—or select Site Actions > New Page. These two methods differ slightly; the former will make you fill in the standard New Item form and then return to the library. The latter shows you a simple interface where you just enter the name of the page and, once the page is created, you enter Edit mode. The option to create a page isn't available on all sites; it depends on which definition or template the page is based on.

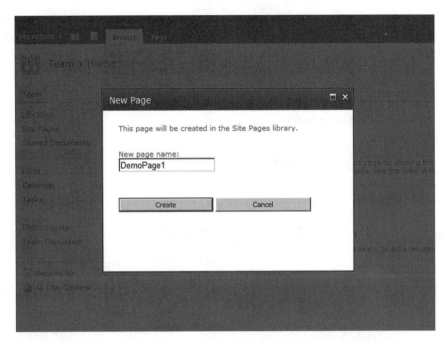

Figure 2.5   The New Page dialog box used to create new pages uses the new Dialog Framework. It improves usability by reducing the number of page loads and makes the interface user friendlier and faster.

To create the page, choose Site Actions > Create Page and enter the page name. Then you simply click Create. Figure 2.5 shows adding a new page called DemoPage1.aspx. You don't need to specify the .aspx file extension—it's automatically added to the file.

> **NOTE**   To be able to add or edit a page, you must have the permission level of *Contributor* on the list or the page itself. By default, Contributor has the Add, Edit, and Delete permissions on list items.

Now you have a page to which you can add Web Parts and content. Because you created it using the Site Actions menu, you should be in Edit mode. Next, I'll walk you through the steps to add Web Parts using this mode. (If you later want to edit the page, click the Edit button on the Quick Access toolbar or the Edit button on the Page tab of the Ribbon.)

2.4.2   Adding Web Parts using the web interface

When you're in Edit mode, the Ribbon will adapt its contents accordingly and you'll see two new tabs, Format Text and Insert, under the Editing Tools tab group. To insert a new Web Part, select the Insert tab and position your cursor in a Web Part zone or wiki content area. The Insert tab contains a group called Web Parts, and within that group, you have a Web Part button, as you can see in figure 2.6.

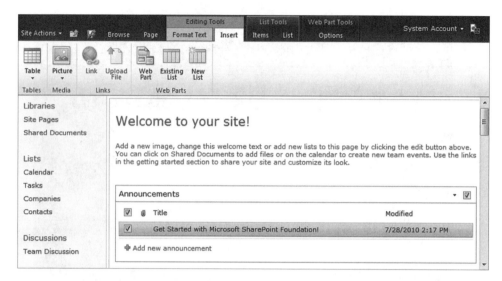

Figure 2.6   The Ribbon adapts to your current context. If you're editing a Web Part page, the tools for editing content and adding new Web Parts appears. And if you select a Web Part when editing the page, the Web Part tools and, optionally, Web Part–specific tabs appear.

To insert a Web Part, click the Web Part button, which opens the Web Part Gallery. Our first Web Part on this page is List View, which shows the Site Pages library. The List View Web Parts are automatically created for all lists and libraries in the site using the XSLT List View Web Part. They're located in the Lists and Libraries category in the gallery. Select the Site Pages Web Part and then click the Add button in the lower right of the gallery. If you placed your cursor in the wrong Web Part zone, you can use the Add Web Part To dropdown menu to change the target zone of your Web Part.

When you select a Web Part in the gallery, a preview of the Web Part appears to the right, along with the name and the description. You can modify the name and the description in the gallery. The preview of the Web Part is created by the developers of the Web Part. In chapter 5, I'll show you how to create a good preview of the Web Part, designed to help your users and spare you and your administrators support time.

Once you add the Web Part, the web page will be updated automatically. Note that this is done asynchronously in SharePoint 2010 compared with SharePoint 2007, which reloaded the whole page. You should now see the Site Pages library on your pages showing all the pages within it.

The Web Part will have all its default values set and you can now edit those properties. To begin, select the Web Part and click the Web Part menu, located in the upper-right corner of the Web Part, and choose Edit Web Part. The Web Part menu is only visible if you've selected the Web Part by clicking it once or if you hover over the Web Part with your mouse. The Web Part tool pane appears to the right. If your page is in Edit mode, you can also access the tool pane by clicking the Web Part Properties button on the Ribbon.

The tool pane consists of two types of Editor Parts, controls that are used for editing properties of a Web Part. Some of the Editor Parts in the pane are automatically created for every Web Part and you the developer can add new ones. (You'll learn more about Editor Parts in chapter 5.) Figure 2.7 shows editing properties for a list that uses the XSLT List View Web Part.

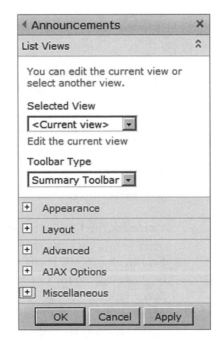

The following Editor Parts are automatically added to your Web Part:

- *Appearance*—Controls the visual style of the Web Part.
- *Layout*—Controls how the Web Part appears in the Web Part zone.
- *Advanced*—Contains advanced options.

To change the properties, just modify the values in the Editor Part controls and click OK. At that point, the editor pane closes. If you click Apply instead, the changes will be saved but the tool pane will still be available for you to make more changes.

Once the Web Part is added to the zone and

Figure 2.7   You edit the properties of a Web Part in the editor pane, which consists of Editor Parts. Each Web Part type has its own setup of Editor Parts.

you're done editing properties, you can save the page. Do so by clicking the Save button on the Quick Access toolbar or by clicking Save on the Page tab on the Ribbon.

2.4.3   Filtering a Web Part using Web Part connections

The ability to connect Web Parts is a powerful feature and can be done using the web interface. A common use is filtering a Web Part based on information in another. Web Parts connections can be used to build mashups that combine information from one or more sources. When you're connecting Web Parts, SharePoint is sending information from one Web Part, called the *provider*, to another Web Part, called the *consumer.*

In our earlier example, you added the SitePages Web Part to a page. If you'd like to filter this library depending on some input from your users, you could add an HTML Form Web Part and let that Web Part send values to the SitePages Web Part. The HTML Form Web Part consists of an editable Web Form that provides an input box and a button by default.

To connect the default HTML Form Web Part to the SitePages Web Part, you use the Web Part options menu and select Edit Web Part, just as you do when editing its properties. The options menu will then display a Connections option. Choose Connections > Provide Form Values To > Site Pages and a dialog box will appear, as shown in figure 2.8. You use this dialog box to configure the connection. First, on the Choose Connection tab, select the connection type—in this case, Get Filter Values From—and

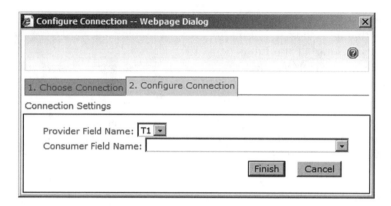

Figure 2.8   **Use the Configure Connection dialog box when connecting Web Parts to send values from one Web Part to another.**

then click the Configure button to continue to the next tab. On the Configure Connection tab, click the Provider Field Name dropdown list and select the name of the field in the HTML Form Web Part (the default is T1). Then, choose the consumer field name from the Consumer Field Name dropdown list; for this sample, specify the Name field. Then, click Finish to complete the connection configuration and save the page to store the changes.

To test your connection, enter the name of any page in the Site Pages library, such as Home.aspx, and then click OK in the HTML Form Web Part. The screen should refresh and you should now only see one page in the SitePages Web Part.

2.5   *Customizing and personalizing pages*

Our example using the out-of-the-box Web Part that you just connected illustrates just one way to create an application using Web Parts. In many cases you configure the Web Parts for your users using the Web Part's properties, and sometimes you allow users to configure the Web Parts themselves. Web Parts and Web Part pages have two major views: Shared and Personal. These views are also often referred to as *customized* or *personalized* views. The Shared view is the default view of a page and its Web Parts, managed by the page editor. All users will see the Shared view until they decide to make changes to the page. To do so, they'll create a Personal View of the page, in a process known as *personalization.*

It's important to understand the differences between the Shared and Personal views and the implications:

- The Personal view can only be seen by the user.
- The Personal view is the default view if it exists.
- Changes to Web Part properties in the Shared view won't override the Personal view properties.
- Not all properties can be changed in the Personal view.

Before you make any changes to a Web Part page, make sure that you are in the correct view by checking the Users menu in the upper-right corner. If it displays the option Show Personal View, then you're in the Shared view; if it says Show Shared

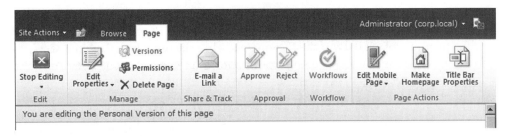

Figure 2.9 The status bar displays when the current page is edited in Personal view and this version of the page is only available to the current user.

View, you're in the Personal view; and if neither option appears, that also means you're in the Shared view. When you're in Edit mode and Personal view, the status bar will show that you're editing the personal version of the page, as shown in figure 2.9.

Chapter 5 describes how you as a developer can adapt your Web Part to take advantage of Shared and Personal views. For example, you can prohibit a user from changing a specific property on a Web Part in the Personal view. This section presents an overview of Shared and Personal views. We'll also explore the difference between closing and deleting Web Parts. Finally, we'll take a look at the Maintenance view, which can be used to look at all the available Web Parts without rendering them. You'll find this view handy if you have a Web Part that fails and prevents the page from rendering.

2.5.1 Shared view

Shared is the default view of a Web Part page. The Shared view uses the default values or those specified by the page editor. Any changes to the page and its Web Parts will be seen by all users who haven't personalized the page.

When a new Web Part is added to the Shared page, it also appears in all the Personal views, which may cause the Personal views to look different. When Shared Web Parts are deleted, they're also deleted from the Personal views together with all personalization.

2.5.2 Personal view

The Personal view is created once a user who isn't a page editor (and thus cannot change the Shared view) wants to change anything on the Web Part page. In the personalization process, SharePoint combines the Shared view with all the personal changes into the Personal view.

A user can add, edit, or close Web Parts from the Personal view without these changes being reflected in the Shared view. The user can't delete Web Parts that are created in the Shared view but can delete those that are added in the Personal view. Normally, properties such as Appearance and Layout can be changed, such as the height and width of a Web Part or how many items should be listed in a specific Web Part. Users can move Web Parts to different zones and customize the page. Web Parts in Wiki Content zones can't be moved or closed in the Personal view.

If a page is personalized, SharePoint uses the Personal view by default. If you want to make changes to the Shared view, select User > Show Shared View. Use the same menu to switch back to the Personal view by selecting Show Personal View.

If you're a wiki page editor and want to create a Personal view of the page, you have to add `PageView=Personal` to the URL of the page, as in

```
http://intranet/SitePages.aspx?PageView=Personal
```

Likewise, this parameter can be used to show the Shared view, by appending `PageView=Shared` to the URL. In standard Web Part pages, choose Users > Personalize This Page to create a Personal version of the page.

2.5.3   *Closing and deleting Web Parts*

One very important thing to keep in mind is that there's a big difference between closing and deleting Web Parts. Deleting a Web Part does exactly what it says; it removes the Web Part from the page, including all customization and personalization. Closing a Web Part, on the other hand, only makes the Web Part invisible—the Web Part is still loaded when the page is rendered but it doesn't do anything. If the user wants to remove a Web Part from a personalized page and the Web Part is added to the Shared view, the user only has the option to close the Web Part because it can't be deleted from the Personal view. Having a lot of closed Web Parts can cause performance implications for your site both in terms of speed and storage. In chapter 4, I'll show you why it can slow down your page, and, in chapter 5, you'll learn how to prohibit the users from closing Web Parts.

All closed Web Parts are accessible through a special group in the Web Part Gallery for the page called Closed Web Parts. This is a virtual group and only appears in the gallery when there are closed Web Parts. It doesn't correspond to any group in the site collection's Web Part Gallery; it exists only for the actual page. To restore a closed Web Part, select the Web Part from the Closed Web Parts group and add it back to any zone on the page.

2.5.4   *Maintenance view*

If you're editing a page and you want to ensure that any changes you make are reflected for all users, you can remove all Personal views for that page by appending `Contents=1` to the page URL—for example:

```
http://intranet/SitePages/Home.aspx?Contents=1
```

This will redirect you to the /_layouts/spcontnt.aspx page, called the Web Part Maintenance page (see figure 2.10). This page will display all Web Parts that are used on the page without loading and rendering them. It will show Web Parts that you won't see in the normal views—for instance, if they're closed, hidden, or in any way failing. This application page can be used to reset, close, or delete Web Parts.

If you have a Web Part that fails and crashes the whole page you're using, perhaps due to bad error handling in your code or someone else's, enter the Maintenance

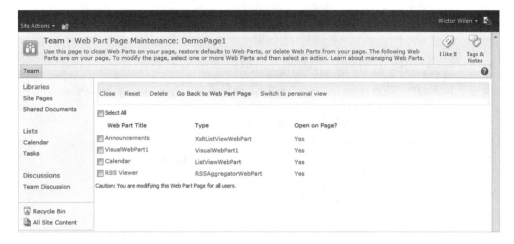

Figure 2.10   The Maintenance View of a page can be used to close, reset, and delete Web Parts from the Shared or Personal Views when, for instance, a Web Part fails to load and makes the whole page inaccessible.

mode of the page and delete the failing Web Part(s). Simply check all the Web Parts that you'd like to remove and click the Delete link. If you select to close a Web Part instead, it's not removed and you can restore it as described in the previous section.

You can reset Web Parts if you've reconfigured a Web Part in the Shared view and you'd like to remove all personal settings. This approach will reset the selected Web Parts in all Personal views to the current Shared view configuration.

Using the SharePoint web interface to customize Web Parts and build simple mashups is just one method. Sometimes using the free tool called SharePoint Designer 2010 is the better choice.

2.6   *SharePoint Designer 2010*

During recent years, no-code or assembly-free solutions have become quite popular. *No-code solutions* is the term used when you mean that you don't put any compiled code on the server. Instead, you use clever workarounds with the Data Form Web Part, JavaScript, jQuery, calculated columns, or other techniques. A user who has the knowledge of these techniques can accomplish a great deal. But this approach also has its drawbacks when it comes to users who don't master the techniques and mess up the functionality.

One of the items that should be in every SharePoint developer toolbox is SharePoint Designer 2010. This tool is a non-code-oriented application for customizing and editing your SharePoint sites. SharePoint Designer 2010 can be used to create reusable applications and features, something previous versions didn't allow. You can create solutions using SharePoint Designer and configure and export them as solution packages. You can then import these packages into Visual Studio 2010 and prepare them for deployment. For example, if you create a Web Part page or a dashboard or customize a site in SharePoint Designer, you can reuse the page, dashboard, or site by packaging it as a deployable and maintainable solution in Visual Studio.

> **SharePoint Designer fun fact**
>
> Before SharePoint Designer, Microsoft had an application called Microsoft FrontPage that you could use to edit and create web pages. FrontPage acted as an editing client to SharePoint 2003, using extensions to IIS called FrontPage Server Extensions.
>
> FrontPage received criticism for creating invalid HTML markup and for changing the HTML without telling you. When Microsoft released SharePoint Designer 2007, it discontinued the FrontPage product.

SharePoint Designer 2010 is a free and downloadable application that can be used to customize and control SharePoint 2010. Using SharePoint Designer, you can create new items such as sites, lists, and content types. You can also edit and configure these items as well as change the layout of pages and edit the master pages. SharePoint Designer can do everything that you do using the web interface and more. For example, using SharePoint Designer, you can create external content types and connect to the external data; you can't do this using the web interface.

You have to use SharePoint Designer 2010 if you're going to use the Data Form Web Part or customize list views using the XSLT List View Web Part. These two Web Parts are powerful and require a far more advanced user interface than the one available in SharePoint.

SharePoint Designer 2010 can only be used for editing SharePoint 2010 sites, and SharePoint Designer 2007 can't be used with SharePoint 2010. If you need to work with SharePoint 2007, you have to use SharePoint Designer 2007.

NOTE   You can download SharePoint Designer 2010 from http://sharepoint. microsoft.com/. If you do not have SharePoint Designer installed when choosing to open it using the Site Actions menu, you will be redirected to the download page of SharePoint Designer.

By now, you should be familiar with the web interface and how users and administrator can work with Web Parts. The following sections will explore similar scenarios but using SharePoint Designer 2010. We're also going to look at how to export and import a Web Part.

2.6.1   *Adding Web Parts to a page*

Just as you can use the web interface to add Web Parts to a page, you can use Share-Point Designer to do the same. The benefits of using SharePoint Designer instead of the web interface are:

- You can use the Data Form Web Part.
- You can use the XSLT Designer for the XSLT List View Web Parts.
- For other Web Parts, you can access more properties and customization options compared to the web interface.

When working with pages in SharePoint Designer, you can switch between Edit mode and Advanced Edit mode. Edit mode allows you to add and edit Web Parts and content in the zones, just as you'd do in the web interface. But, if you switch to Advanced Edit mode, you can edit the code outside of the zones. This mode allows you to add and configure static Web Parts (those not confined in a zone) or add ASP.NET controls.

2.6.2 Adding a Web Part using SharePoint Designer 2010

To add a Web Part to a page using SharePoint Designer, you have to open the site with the application. This can be done using one of two methods:

- Open SharePoint Designer 2010 and open the site by entering the address of your site.
- Use the Site Actions menu in SharePoint 2010 and choose Edit Site in SharePoint Designer.

Once you have your site opened, navigate to the library using the left-hand navigation in SharePoint Designer. Wiki Page libraries, which the Site Pages library is based on, are listed at the top level. If you're using another type of library to host your pages, you have to click List and Libraries and browse to your library. When you select one of the libraries, you'll see a list of all the pages and items in that library. To edit a page, right-click it and select Open from the context menu. If you, instead, click on a page, you'll see the item's Overview page in SharePoint Designer. On the Overview page, you can access the Edit page view by clicking Edit in the Customization dialog box.

When you're in the page's Edit mode, notice that the Ribbon has changed its context and you now have an Insert tab with a Web Parts group (see figure 2.11). To add a Web Part, place your cursor in one of the zones (or anywhere on the page if you've switched to Advanced Edit mode). Then, click the Web Part button and select one of the Web Parts from the dropdown list that appears. The Web Part will be added and selected where you positioned your cursor.

Figure 2.11 When you edit a page in SharePoint Designer, the Ribbon adapts to the editing context and makes the Insert tab visible. The Insert tab gives you access to the Web Part button, which is used to insert new Web Parts.

2.6.3 Configuring Web Parts using SharePoint Designer 2010

Web Parts can be configured using SharePoint Designer 2010. If you select a Web Part in SharePoint Designer or if you add a new one to a page, the Ribbon will display the Web Part Tools tab. This tab allows you to edit some of the common properties of a Web Part, such as chrome, size, and connections. If you need to edit the properties of the Web Part, you have to click the Properties button in the Web Part group on the

Format tab or right-click the Web Part and select Properties. The resulting dialog box is just a web page that reads the Editor Parts of the Web Part and shows exactly the same interface as you have in the web interface.

If you have properties that aren't accessible using the web browser or advanced properties that have no default web interface, such as arrays and complex types, you can use SharePoint Designer to set those properties. For example, if you have a property of your Web Part that's an array of strings, this property won't get a default property editing interface. Using SharePoint Designer, you can still change these complex properties by selecting the Web Part and then choosing View > Task Panes > Tag Properties in the Ribbon. This will display a task pane in SharePoint Designer that lets you edit all properties publicly exposed by the underlying .NET Web Part class. If you'd like to provide an interface for editing complex Web Parts in the web interface, you need to create your own custom Editor Part; read more about them in chapter 5.

2.6.4   Adding pages

SharePoint Designer lets you add new pages to libraries using the Navigation pane to the left and selecting a library. Once you select a library, the Pages tab will appear. On this tab click the Web Part Page button and select a page design to add a new page. Note that SharePoint creates a Web Part page (not a Wiki page, even if it's a Wiki Page library). You can then customize this page using the SharePoint Designer editing tools.

2.6.5   Editing pages and adding zones

When editing, you can add any ASP.NET control or custom control, including new Web Part zones, to a page. Most controls are available from the Toolbox in SharePoint Designer 2010, but not Web Part zones. To add a new Web Part zone, you have to enter code in the Code view of the page editor. Select to edit the page in Advanced Edit mode and then manually write the Web Part zone tags, as shown in listing 2.1. You access Advanced Edit mode by right-clicking on the page and selecting Edit File In Advanced Mode or by clicking the Advanced Mode button on the Edit tab.

Listing 2.1   Adding a Web Part zone to a page

```
<WebPartPages:WebPartZone
    runat="server"
    ID="MyZone"
    Title="My Zone">
    <ZoneTemplate></ZoneTemplate>
</WebPartPages:WebPartZone>
```

This Web Part Zone will have an ID called MyZone and a Title of My Zone. The Zone-Template is empty so there are no Web Parts in it. You will learn more about how to add zones to pages in the final chapter (15) of this book.

When you're editing pages in Advanced Edit mode using SharePoint Designer 2010 and you save the page, the page will be customized and will no longer be based on the site definition. SharePoint Designer 2010 will warn you when you're trying to customize a page. All customized pages will have a blue icon in front of them so that you can identify them. If you need to revert back to the original definition of the page, you can right-click or use the Ribbon button Reset To Site Definition to restore the original definition. If you reset a customized page, you'll lose all your customized settings.

2.6.6 *Import and export of solutions using SharePoint Designer*

One of the most powerful features in SharePoint Designer 2010 is the ability to import and export information and solutions. If you're creating and configuring Web Parts using SharePoint Designer, you can export the configuration to a file, which you can then later add to the Web Part Gallery in the same site collection or on a totally different farm, and use it as long as the Web Part assembly is installed. SharePoint Designer also allows you to directly publish a configured Web Part to the local Web Part Gallery so that you can reuse the configuration within that site collection. Publishing the Web Part configurations to the gallery is a good way to reuse configured Web Parts such as the Content Query and XSLT List View Web Parts.

You'll use the Ribbon to export Web Parts from SharePoint Designer. When you've selected a Web Part, the Format tab appears. This tab contains the group Save Web Part, which displays two buttons. The first button, To Site Gallery, saves the selected Web Part configuration to the local Web Part Gallery. The second button, To File, allows you to save the Web Parts control description file on your local drive. Note that for XSLT List View Web Parts the export buttons are located on the Web Part tab instead of the Format tab.

You also have the ability to save a site or a list as templates for reuse, and you can export pages edited in SharePoint Designer so that you can include them in a Visual Studio 2010 SharePoint solution.

> **NOTE** SharePoint Designer 2010 is *not* a tool that you should equip all users with, because it has a lot of powers. If you make changes to, for instance, the master page and it fails, your whole site will fail. To secure your SharePoint environment, you can lock down SharePoint Designer using settings in the sites or the Central Administration tool.

2.7 *Exporting and importing Web Parts*

When working with SharePoint, you most often have several environments, such as development, test, staging, and production, to secure and validate your implementation. You start with building and configuring your Web Parts in the development environment before it moves to the test environment and so on. If you have a Web Part with a lot of configuration options and would like to move it into another environment, you might find it hard to reconfigure the Web Part in the new site. Managing the Web Part configurations is especially important in application life cycle management scenarios when you're scripting your environments and configurations.

In this section, you'll learn how to export and import a configured Web Part and how to prohibit users from exporting a Web Part. You'll find this information valuable as you start developing your Web Parts, and it will save you some time if you export the Web Parts instead of manually typing everything.

2.7.1 Exporting a Web Part

A Web Part can be exported to a Web Parts control description file (using the .webpart extension), which contains information about which Web Part is exported and the current state of all the Web Part's properties. The file is an XML file and can be viewed using Notepad or any XML editor. You'll learn more about the .webpart file in chapter 3.

You can export a Web Part from the web interface by editing the page and then using the Options menu of the Web Part that you'd like to export. Then choose the Export verb. You will be prompted to save the file locally to your machine and the file should have the .webpart file extension. This file contains XML that describes which Web Part class and assembly to use and the default values of the Web Part properties. Once you've saved this file, you can use any text-editing tool, such as Notepad or Visual Studio 2010, to change the values of the properties.

2.7.2 Importing a Web Part

If you have a Web Parts control description file (a .webpart file) that you either created yourself or received from someone else, you can upload this definition to the Web Part Gallery. Note that, in order to get the Web Part to work, you need to have the corresponding Web Part assembly installed in your environment; otherwise, the Web Part will fail with an error message.

To add a Web Part to the gallery using a .webpart file, open the Web Part Gallery and upload the file using the options on the Library Tools > Documents tab. Once the file is uploaded, you can specify metadata on the Web Part such as the title, description, and group, just as you'd do on any item that's added or uploaded into SharePoint.

You can add a preconfigured Web Part to a page without uploading it to the Web Part Gallery. Use the Ribbon to add a new Web Part and, when the Web Part Gallery shows up in the interface, click Upload A Web Part under the Categories list. This Web Part will appear in the category Imported Web Parts and can then be added to the page. The uploaded Web Part configuration is only temporarily available in the gallery to the user editing the specific page and won't be available once you exit Edit mode.

.webpart or .dwp file definitions?

In SharePoint 2003, the Web Parts control description files had the extension of .dwp, but, in SharePoint 2007, it changed to .webpart. Both files contain XML to define the Web Part but the XML schema differs. The .dwp files contains version 2 of the schema (SharePoint version 2), and the .webpart uses version 3 of the schema (SharePoint 2007 was version 3).

If you export a Web Part based on the old SharePoint Web Part implementation, you'll get a .dwp file with version 2 of the schema instead of a .webpart file.

2.7.3 *Prohibiting the export of a Web Part*

You'll find yourself in situations when you don't want your users to be able to export your Web Parts; you might store confidential data in properties or there might be other reasons. The Web Part defines a property called Export Mode that defines how a Web Part can be exported. It can have one of the following values:

- Do Not Allow
- Non-sensitive Data Only
- Export All Data

You can access this property by editing the Web Part's properties and changing the Export Mode property's value under the Advanced category.

- More details on sensitive data and Export mode are discussed in chapter 5.

2.8 Summary

This chapter summarized the features in the web interface and in SharePoint Designer 2010. What you've seen so far are mostly end-user tasks, and this is essential knowledge for you as a developer. If you understand how end users work with SharePoint, you'll likely design and build Web Parts that will be more usable.

At this point, you should be acquainted with the various parts of the SharePoint 2010 interface and the features that we'll address later in the book. If you're new to SharePoint 2010, then give yourself some extra time to become accustomed to the new interface. You should also explore the possibilities of the new SharePoint Designer 2010, which is a whole new experience compared with the previous SharePoint Designer version, 2007. You can accomplish a lot with this application and the out-of-the-box Web Parts, especially the new XSLT List View Web Part, and you should have these at hand in your toolbox.

By now you're probably anxious to see some code—and that's where we're heading next.

Part 2

Developing SharePoint 2010 Web Parts

Part 2 covers 11 full chapters of Web Part development topics. In part 1, you learned what Web Parts are, how you can use them, and how you can configure applications with them. But, you'll eventually end up with a scenario requiring you to build your own custom Web Part—and that's why you're reading this book.

We'll start from the ground up by introducing you to Visual Studio 2010 and the SharePoint Development Tools. You'll learn how to build Web Parts using best practices to avoid falling into traps, in many cases, using standard ASP.NET techniques. So if you've been building ASP.NET applications and controls, you'll find quite a lot of common tasks and I'll show you the differences.

The longest chapter of this book, chapter 5, will walk you through the various ways that you can make your Web Parts customizable. Next, in chapter 6 you'll learn how to localize your Web Parts and use resources such as JavaScripts and images. An essential part of SharePoint development is how you package and deploy your solutions, and, in chapter 7, I'll show you just that.

Sooner or later you'll get to the point that your Web Part and solution misbehave, and then it's time to troubleshoot those problems. Chapter 8 is all about troubleshooting and how to avoid running into these situations. Once your Web Part is up and running, you may need to fine-tune it for performance. Chapters 10 and 11 focus on the new features introduced in SharePoint 2010, such as integration with the Ribbon menu and other dynamic features of the SharePoint web interface.

Silverlight is a key component of the Microsoft web technologies, and you'll learn how Silverlight can be used in combination with Web Parts. Chapter 12 gives you insight into how to turn your Web Parts into mobile-friendly components so that your users can access on any devices the functionality that you build. Chapter 13 discusses design patterns; you'll see how to build robust and testable Web Parts using proven patterns and techniques.

I hope you have a great time reading through this part of the book and enjoy the code samples. You can download most of the code samples from the book's website at http://www.manning.com/wilen and use them as a reference for your own projects.

Building Web Parts
with Visual Studio 2010

This chapter covers

- Using Visual Studio 2010
- Taking advantage of SharePoint Developer Tools
- Building Visual Web Parts
- Building traditional Web Parts

You should now have a fairly good understanding of what Web Parts are and how end users will work with them. It's time to start building some of your own. Previous versions of SharePoint lacked the tools and applications to create a good development experience, which made it hard to be productive. You had to use tools provided by the community, create your own, or do a lot of manual editing of XML-based manifests and configuration files. The new SharePoint Developer Tools that ship with Visual Studio 2010 solve these problems and allow you to focus on the fun part: development.

Developing Web Parts for SharePoint 2010 isn't just about wiring up components in a control that you can then use to build pages or applications in SharePoint as you might do when working in ASP.NET applications. Solutions built for SharePoint need a few extra steps before they can be invoked in the host environment. This chapter shows you how to build, package, and deploy SharePoint Web Part solutions using the new development tools for SharePoint 2010 in Visual Studio 2010. These tools allow you to focus on programming tasks rather than packaging the solution.

We'll begin by reviewing the requirements for the development environment. Then, I'll walk you through two ways of building Web Parts; Visual Web Parts and traditional Web Parts. During these walkthroughs, we'll look into the various files and artifacts that your SharePoint Web Part solution consists of in Visual Studio and explore the features of the development tools. We'll also discuss the extensibility of Visual Studio and the development tools. The last section of this chapter will explain how to upgrade solutions built for earlier SharePoint versions to SharePoint 2010.

3.1   *Requirements for your development environment*

Before we start with the programming tasks, you need to prepare your development workstation. Earlier versions of SharePoint required that you work directly on a Windows Server machine with SharePoint installed. This was because it wasn't possible to install SharePoint on a Windows client operating system (OS) in a supported way. You could build and package your solutions on a client workstation and then later manually add the solution to the server for testing. But, this procedure was unsupported, took a lot of time, and didn't allow you to debug your solution. And it's something I really can't recommend.

SharePoint 2010 has support for installation on a 64-bit Windows 7 or 64-bit Windows Vista Service Pack 1 machine so that you can develop, build, test, and debug directly on your normal client OS. This strategy is good for some scenarios, such as showing demos, testing, and small development tasks. But I recommend that you invest in hardware that allows you to run virtual machines (VMs) in which you have your SharePoint 2010 installation, Visual Studio 2010, and other tools. VMs allow you to create an environment that looks similar to your production environment, and you can more easily create new machines when necessary. VMs also let you take snapshots of your environment, which allows you to roll back the server when you mess up your machine instead of having to reinstall your client OS. You need 64 bit–capable hardware with enough RAM to host your VMs. The recommended minimum amount of RAM is 4 GB for a development machine. Even though it might work pretty well, I recommend that you use 8 GB on your client. This allows you to have a local client installation of SharePoint Foundation and enough memory to spin up a VM. It's the speed of the disks that matters (along with the amount of RAM). Hosting VMs on external USB drives isn't recommended. If you can convince your boss to invest in one or more solid-state disks, you can achieve great performance on a laptop.

Your development workstation or VM should have at least SharePoint Foundation 2010 or SharePoint Server 2010 installed along with Visual Studio 2010 and SharePoint Designer 2010. SharePoint Designer isn't a necessity when developing for SharePoint but, as you've seen in previous chapters, it can add great value for rapid application development. To get started quickly without setting up an environment of your own, download the evaluation image from Microsoft at www.microsoft.com/ downloads/ and search for "2010 Information Worker Demonstration and Evaluation Virtual Machine."

3.2   *Developing for SharePoint 2010 in Visual Studio 2010*

Visual Studio 2010 is the primary development environment that you'll use to build your Web Parts and other SharePoint 2010 projects. You can use other environments or tools, but the SharePoint Developer Tools for Visual Studio 2010 will save you a lot of time and allow you to be more productive than before. The Developer Tools are a new addition to the Visual Studio suite, even though there were extensions for Visual Studio 2005 and 2008 that you could download. The new SharePoint Developer Tools are targeted for SharePoint 2010 development only.

> **NOTE**   There were extensions for SharePoint 2007 (Microsoft Office Share-Point Services [MOSS] 2007 and Windows SharePoint Services [WSS] 3) called Visual Studio Extensions for Windows SharePoint Services (VSeWSS) that could be downloaded to Visual Studio 2005 and, then, 2008. These extensions were criticized and never exited the Community Technology Preview (CTP) stage. For SharePoint 2007 development, the community moved faster than Microsoft and created great tools that offered more flexibility than VSeWSS. The two most popular community contributions were STSDev (http:// stsdev.codeplex.com) and WSPBuilder (http://wspbuilder.codeplex.com).

The SharePoint Developer Tools in Visual Studio allow you to edit and configure your SharePoint solutions using visual designers instead of working with the XML files directly. You can just hit F5 to run and debug your project, just like any other solutions built with Visual Studio. In the following sections, we'll walk through the initial Share-Point 2010 development experience with Visual Studio 2010 and look at the various types of projects that you can create.

Visual Studio 2010 comes in many flavors, ranging from the free edition, called Visual Studio 2010 Express, to the top-notch edition, called Visual Studio 2010 Ultimate (which contains everything you need from design, development, testing, and life cycle management). All editions (except for the free Express edition) have the Share-Point Developer Tools.

You need to run Visual Studio 2010 as administrator if you have the User Account Control enabled on your server or workstation—deployment and debugging need full access to the processes and the files in SharePoint root.

To create a project in Visual Studio, always start with a project template. The Share-Point Developer Tools install a set of templates for SharePoint projects, and we're going to use some of them throughout this book.

The SharePoint Extensions for Visual Studio 2010 come with a set of project templates for SharePoint 2010 development. They range from an empty project to specialized projects like Web Parts, lists, and workflows. To create a SharePoint project, you need to start a new project in Visual Studio by selecting File > New > Project. The New Project dialog box will display all the available project templates.

The first time you open this dialog box, select the target framework for your project. The default framework in Visual Studio is version 4.0, but SharePoint 2010 is based on Microsoft .NET 3.5 Service Pack 1, so select version 3.5 as your target framework. Visual Studio will change your project so that .NET Framework 3.5 is used even if you select version 4 when you create SharePoint projects. You change the target framework using the dropdown list in the New Project dialog box. After selecting the framework, look at the SharePoint templates in the template category selector on the left, as shown in figure 3.1. Select Visual C# > SharePoint > 2010 to view the available templates for SharePoint 2010 development. Depending on your Visual Studio edition and the extensions you've installed, the templates will vary. Because SharePoint is based on Microsoft .NET, you can use the language of your choice, such as Visual Basic, F#, or C++. If you prefer to use Visual Basic, select Visual Basic > SharePoint > 2010 to display those templates, which are exactly the same as for C#. This book will use C# in all code and samples. The reason for choosing C# is that it's currently the most popular .NET programming language and you'll find most samples and demos on the Internet and that sites such as CodePlex use it.

In the New Project dialog box, specify the name of your project, the solution, and the location in the file system. A Visual Studio 2010 solution is a collection of projects; you can add more projects later. Don't confuse the Visual Studio solution with a SharePoint 2010 solution: each project based on the SharePoint templates will result

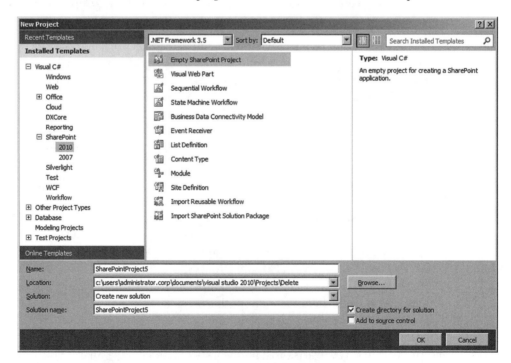

Figure 3.1   **The New Project dialog box in Visual Studio 2010 shows the available SharePoint 2010 templates and includes a brief description of the selected template.**

in one SharePoint solution package. You can't create a SharePoint project using the Visual Studio 2010 SharePoint Developer Tools on a machine that doesn't have Share-Point 2010 installed.

The default templates in Visual Studio 2010 for SharePoint 2010 development are listed in table 3.1. When working with Web Parts, you'll mainly use the Empty Share-Point project and the new Visual Web Part template—which is the one you'll use when building the first Web Part in this book.

Table 3.1 All out-of-the-box SharePoint 2010 templates in Visual Studio 2010

Template Name	Description
Blank Site Definition	Creates a site definition.
Business Data Connectivity Model	Creates a model for the Business Connectivity Services.
Content Type	Creates a content type.
Empty SharePoint Project	Creates an empty SharePoint 2010 solution in which you can add items and Features.
Event Receiver	Creates an event receiver.
Import Reusable Workflow	Imports workflows from SharePoint Designer 2010.
Import SharePoint Solution Package	Imports WSP files that have been exported from SharePoint 2010.
List Definition	Creates a list definition.
Module	Creates a module.
Sequential Workflow	Creates a sequential workflow.
Site Definition	Creates a site definition project.
State Machine Workflow	Creates a state machine workflow.
Visual Web Part	Creates a project with a Visual Web Part item.

As you can see, you have a lot of different options and project templates to select from. Choose the appropriate one to get an easy start; you can easily add project items later to add more functionality. You can even create your own templates or download new ones using the Visual Studio Extension Manager.

3.3   *Building your first Visual Web Part*

Previous developer tools for SharePoint lacked a good visual designer environment. Visual Studio 2010 contains a new project item called *Visual Web Part*. To illustrate how a Visual Web Part works (and how the SharePoint Developer extensions in Visual Studio 2010 work), I'll guide you through your first Visual Web Part project. We'll create a Visual Web Part project with a Visual Web Part that takes text input and displays it in the Web Part when you click a button. The following sections will show you how to create and build the project and then eventually deploy the solution and use the Web

Part by adding it to a page. When you're creating a project for SharePoint, Visual Studio will guide you through the setup using a wizard. During this first Web Part project, we'll explore the other files that are created within your SharePoint project.

3.3.1 *The Visual Web Part template*

When creating a solution in Visual Studio, you always start with a project template. The first template that we're going to use is the *Visual Web Part* template. Visual Web Parts employ a user control to build the user interface. The user control is loaded by the Web Part class during runtime and rendered. Using a user control enables you to use a visual designer in Visual Studio to design and build your Web Part. This allows for more rapid development and increased productivity. If you're an ASP.NET developer, you'll be familiar with the Visual Studio interface and this method of building Web Parts.

The disadvantage of using Visual Web Parts is that these Web Parts are dependent on files that live in the SharePoint Root in the file system. These files are loaded and compiled dynamically during runtime, which isn't allowed in Sandboxed mode. (You'll learn more about Sandboxed mode in chapter 7.) The Visual Web Parts also require that you write some plumbing code when writing custom Web Part properties (see chapter 5) because you have two classes that need to be updated: the Web Part class and the control template class.

NOTE   The Microsoft SharePoint Tools team has released a set of extensions for Visual Studio 2010 that's available for download using the Extension Manager in Visual Studio. In the extension manager, search for "SharePoint Power Tools" to find the extension. These tools contain a sandbox-compatible Visual Web Part.

First, you need to create a new SharePoint 2010 project using the Visual Web Part template in Visual Studio, as described earlier. Make sure that you're using Microsoft .NET 3.5 as your target framework.

> ### Naming projects in Visual Studio
> You should carefully name your projects when working with SharePoint. Do this for other projects as well. With a good naming convention, it's easier to locate the source of any failures during troubleshooting. A good convention is to use your company name and the name of the project.
>
> Throughout this book I'll use the following standard: `WebPartsInAction.ChNN.<Project name>`, where `NN` is replaced by the chapter number and `<Project name>` with the actual project we're creating.

Our first project is going to be called `WebPartsInAction.Ch3.VisualWebPart`. Note that, when you enter a project name in the Name field, your Visual Studio solution will be assigned the same name automatically. If you plan to create several projects within your solution or if you prefer to have another name for the solution, you can change the solution's name by entering a separate name for it in the Solution Name field. Another benefit of using a naming convention is that the default namespace in your project will use the name of the project. When you've selected the template and specified a project name, click OK; the SharePoint Customization wizard appears.

3.3.2 The SharePoint Customization wizard

The SharePoint Customization wizard will appear for all SharePoint 2010 templates in Visual Studio 2010 and have different configuration steps depending on the chosen template. The first step in the wizard asks you which site you'd like to use for debugging and what trust level you'd like to have for the solution, as shown in figure 3.2. The site URL you enter must be a local site; this is also the site that's going to be started when you debug your solution and the site in which your solution will be deployed.

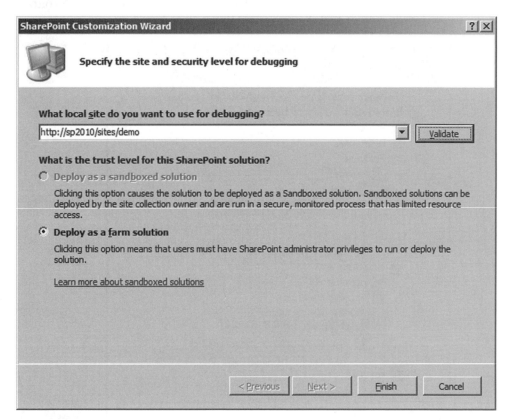

Figure 3.2 The SharePoint Customization wizard when creating a Visual Web Part; note that the Deploy as a sandboxed solution option is disabled.

You have two trust levels to choose from:

- *Sandboxed solution*—The solution will run in a secure, protected, and monitored process; chapter 7 will show you more details.
- *Farm solution*—The solution will run as a fully trusted component (in the global assembly cache) in the farm.

Because this is a Visual Web Part project, you don't have an option to select the trust level; it has to be a Farm solution, also known as a full-trust solution. To end the wizard, click Finish, and Visual Studio will create the solution, project, and project items for you.

3.3.3   Explore the SharePoint Project Items

Once you finish the wizard, you're taken to the Visual Studio environment and your project is created. When creating a Visual Web Part, Visual Studio automatically creates a Package, a Feature, and a Visual Web Part for you. You can browse these items using the Solution Explorer in Visual Studio; click View > Solution Explorer if you don't see the Solution Explorer in your environment. Figure 3.3 shows the Solution Explorer after we've created a Visual Web Part and, as you can see, it contains several SharePoint project items, nodes, and source code files.

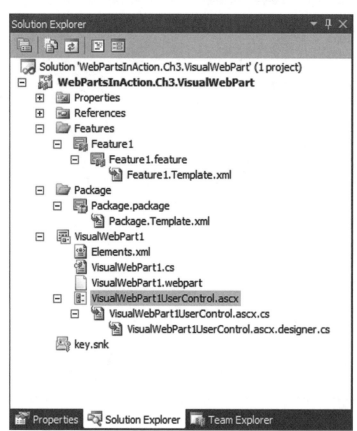

Figure 3.3
The Solution Explorer in Visual Studio 2010 allows you to navigate the files in your project.

NOTE The items in a Visual Studio 2010 SharePoint project are also called SharePoint project items (SPIs). For example, a Visual Web Part is a SPI, even though it contains several files.

THE PACKAGE PROJECT ITEM

The *Package*, found under the Package root node in your project, describes the SharePoint files, assemblies, and Features included in the solution package. At some point, Visual Studio will create a Windows SharePoint Package (WSP) file of your Package, based on what's defined in the Package editor. The resulting file is a cabinet (CAB) file with all the files you need for your solution. Chapter 7 will tell you more about the WSP file. You'll also use the Package editor when you need to include references to other assemblies, as you'll see in later chapters.

The package project item consists of an XML file called the package manifest, and you edit it using a designer or manually by writing XML code. When editing the package project item manually, you work with a special file called package.template.xml, which is, during the packaging process, merged with the actual package manifest.

THE FEATURE PROJECT ITEM

Visual Web Part projects always include a Feature, found under the Feature node in the project. A *Feature* is a set of components, definitions, and actions that are deployed onto a specified scope. Each Package can contain several Features. Visual Studio has a designer that you can use to edit the Feature in the same way you do with the Package. You can also edit the underlying XML manually by using a template file, as you do with Packages. The designer can be used to add items to or remove them from your Feature. When we build the next Web Part, we'll take a closer look at the Feature designer.

THE VISUAL WEB PART PROJECT ITEM

The Visual Web Part project item, located in the project root, consists of no more than six files. First you have the user control, which is the file ending with .ascx. This is the control that the Web Part will load and display, and it contains all controls and events. The user control also makes this Web Part editable by the Visual Studio control designer, which allows you to visually design the control. The user control also has two code-behind files: one that you'll use for your custom code-behind code and one that's used by the Visual Studio designer to define the controls, properties, and events that you edit using the designer. The Visual Web Part has another code file—VisualWebPart1.cs, as you can see in figure 3.3; this is where the Web Part class is defined and this Web Part class loads the user control.

NOTE Partial class definitions were introduced in C# 2. Using the `partial` keyword on classes allows the class to be split over several files. Visual Studio uses partial classes to separate the code generated by the designers and the code that the developer edits. For instance, the user control in the Visual Web Part is split into two files: one for you to add logic to and one appended with designer.cs, which is used by the Control designer.

The Feature needs to know how to add the Web Part to SharePoint. You specify this information in the elements.xml file, called the elements manifest, which you see in the following code snippet. This file contains instructions to SharePoint to add the Web Part to the gallery as well as its name and group. The elements manifest also references the Web Part controls description file (.webpart), which contains the reference to the Web Part class and assembly as well as its default property values. This is the file that's added to the Web Part Gallery.

```xml
<?xml version="1.0" encoding="utf-8"?>
<Elements xmlns="http://schemas.microsoft.com/sharepoint/" >
  <Module
    Name="VisualWebPart1"
    List="113"
    Url="_catalogs/wp">
    <File
        Path="VisualWebPart1\VisualWebPart1.webpart"
        Url="WebPartsInAction.Ch3.VisualWebPart_VisualWebPart1.webpart"
        Type="GhostableInLibrary" >
      <Property
        Name="Group"
        Value="Custom" />
    </File>
  </Module>
</Elements>
```

The elements manifest file has a `Module` element that specifies the destination of the items. The `File` element identifies the source of the Web Parts control description file to upload using the `Path` attribute and specifies the destination using the `Url` attribute. If you change the name of your Web Parts control description file, you need to manually update the `Path` property to reflect your change.

To specify properties for the file in the Web Part Gallery, you use the `Property` element. It's important to specify into which categories the file will be placed in the Web Part Gallery; you do this by editing the `Group` property. By default, Visual Studio 2010 adds files to the Custom category. You should change this setting to something related to your solution. Here, we're changing the value from `Custom` to `My Web Parts`:

```xml
<Property Name="Group" Value="My Web Parts" />
```

The Web Parts control description file that SharePoint creates for you looks like the following listing.

Listing 3.1 The default Web Part control description file for a Visual Web Part
---

```xml
<?xml version="1.0" encoding="utf-8"?>
<webParts>
  <webPart xmlns="http://schemas.microsoft.com/WebPart/v3">
    <metaData>
      <type name="WebPartsInAction.Ch3.VisualWebPart.VisualWebPart1.
      VisualWebPart1,$SharePoint.Project.AssemblyFullName$" />
      <importErrorMessage>$Resources:core,ImportErrorMessage;
      </importErrorMessage>
```

Declares class and assembly ❶

```
    </metaData>
    <data>
      <properties>
        <property name="Title" type="string">VisualWebPart1</property>
        <property name="Description" type="string">
        My Visual WebPart
        </property>
      </properties>
    </data>
  </webPart>
</webParts>
```

Sets property
default values ❷

The default Web Part control description file contains two interesting parts. One is the `type` element ❶, which has a `name` attribute. The `name` attribute specifies the Web Part's class, including the namespace, followed by a special Visual Studio 2010 parameter that's replaced with the full assembly name during the packaging process. If you change the name or namespace of your Web Part, you must manually change it here.

The second part of the Web Parts control description file is the `properties` element, in which you set the default values of the Web Part's properties. By default, Visual Studio adds the `Title` and `Description` properties ❷. Change the values of these property elements so that they look like this:

```
<property name="Title" type="string">My Visual WebPart</property>
<property name="Description" type="string">
  Visual Web Parts rock!
</property>
```

When this Web Part is deployed to the Web Part Gallery, it'll have the title and description as specified here. The title in the Web Part header will also use the `Title` property as the default value.

> **TIP** In chapter 2, you learned how to export a Web Part. You can save some XML typing if you deploy your Web Part and configure it using the web interface. Using the *export* verb, you can download a .webpart file from which you just copy and paste the properties instead of manually typing them into the file. Make sure that you don't overwrite the `metaData` tag or the Visual Studio token used for the full assembly name. You'll learn more about the contents of this file in chapter 5.

3.3.4 *Adding functionality to your Visual Web Part*

The Visual Web Part you just created contains no controls or content by default, but you can add them by double-clicking on the Visual Web Part item in the Solution Explorer (or expand the item and click on the user control file). Visual Studio will open the User Control designer in Source mode. You can switch between Design and Source mode using the buttons in the lower-left corner of the user control file. You can also use Split mode, which allows you to edit the source and directly see the preview in the designer, or vice versa.

To add controls to the user control, you have two options. You can use the Toolbox, found under View > Toolbox, to drag and drop controls to your user control. The drag-and-drop approach works for both the Design and the Source modes. The second option is to write the control code in the Source editor. If you've worked with Visual Studio before, you'll be familiar with this way of working.

ADDING CONTROLS TO THE VISUAL WEB PART

In this first sample, you're going to add three controls: a `TextBox`, a `Label`, and a `Button` control. These are standard ASP.NET controls, and you'll find them in the Standard group in the Toolbox. Drag and drop the controls into your user control. Then, add a `<br/>` tag after each control so that it looks a bit nicer. If you switch to Design mode, you'll immediately see a preview of how your Web Part will look. Note that the preview won't take themes or SharePoint CSS into consideration, but you'll get a fair view of how you've organized your controls.

Note that you should use the closed line break tag `<br/>` instead of `<br>`. This closed tag must be used to comply with the XHTML standard that's used in the SharePoint 2010 interface.

ADDING EVENTS TO THE VISUAL WEB PART

Our Web Part will take the value from the `TextBox` when the user clicks the button and will write that value into the label, so we need to add an event to the button control. To add the click event, switch to Design mode and double-click on the button. Visual Studio will then automatically create a new method in the code-behind of the user control and wire that method to the control by adding an attribute to the control tag in the user control source. Once this is done, Visual Studio will open the code-behind file and place your cursor at the new method. Add the code to the new method that takes the value from the `TextBox` and wires it into the label. The following snippet shows what the click event method should look like after you add the code. The method takes the `Text` property from the `TextBox` and assigns it to the `Text` property of the label:

```
protected void Button1_Click(object sender, EventArgs e) {
    Label1.Text = TextBox1.Text;
}
```

The next snippet shows the markup source of the user control after you add the event to the button. The control, import, and register directives are omitted before the first line and the `Label` control has been manually modified so that it has an empty string as the default value for its `Text` property. You can see the automatically added `onclick` event, which is hooked to the newly created method in your code-behind:

```
<asp:TextBox ID="TextBox1" runat="server"></asp:TextBox>
<br/>
<asp:Label ID="Label1" runat="server" Text=""></asp:Label>
<br/>
<asp:Button ID="Button1" runat="server" Text="Click me!"            Attribute added
    onclick="Button1_Click"/>                                        automatically
```

EXAMINING THE WEB PART CLASS

Before you build and deploy your Visual Web Part, let's see how the Web Part invokes the user control. The Visual Web Part project item consists of a Web Part class file that contains the implementation of the class that inherits from the `System.Web.UI.WebControls.WebParts.WebPart` class.

The first thing to notice is a constant definition that points out the location of the user control file that's used. This location points to the TEMPLATE\CONTROLTEMPLATES folder in the SharePoint Root folder; that's where the user control file is placed during deployment.

```
private const string _ascxPath =
    @"~/_CONTROLTEMPLATES/VisualWebPart1/
    VisualWebPart1/VisualWebPart1UserControl.ascx";
```

The `CreateChildControls` method is automatically created for you by Visual Studio. This method will load the user control using the constant and add the control to the control tree of the Web Part class.

```
protected override void CreateChildControls() {
    Control control = Page.LoadControl(_ascxPath);
    Controls.Add(control);
}
```

If you look at the class definition, you'll notice that the Web Part inherits from the ASP.NET Web Part class. You can change which class the Web Part inherits from if you're using another base class or would like to use the SharePoint Web Part implementation.

3.3.5 *Build and deploy the Visual Web Part*

The SharePoint Developer Tools for Visual Studio 2010 use the same approach as any other Visual Studio project, so you can just press F5 to run and debug your project. But, before you do that, I'll guide you through the details of what happens when you press F5 or select Debug > Start Debugging.

First, Visual Studio compiles your project, which means that Visual Studio uses the correct language compiler and builds a .NET assembly file (a DLL file) of your source code. During the compilation, any warnings and errors will be reported in the Visual Studio Output and Error List windows. In this example, the Web Part class and user control code-behind files are compiled. Any errors in the user control markup source (the .ascx file) won't be detected; this file will be compiled during runtime. For example, if you add the button click event manually and incorrectly spell your event method in the user control source, the compiler won't detect the mistake.

After the compilation phase, Visual Studio needs to package the solution into a format that SharePoint understands: a Windows SharePoint Package (WSP). This file contains all the necessary files to deploy your solution into SharePoint and includes the compiled assembly, your Feature definitions, .webpart files, user controls, and other resources. You can manually invoke packaging by selecting Build > Package in Visual Studio.

The SharePoint Developer Tools contain a set of deployment configurations that are invoked after the compilation and packaging processes when you press F5 to debug your solution. To open the properties for your project, do one of the following:

- Double-click the Properties item in your project.
- Right-click the project name and select Properties.
- Click the Properties button.

As shown in figure 3.4, SharePoint projects have a special tab for configuring the deployment configuration. Visual Studio 2010 comes with two configurations out of the box:

- *Default*—Retracts the old solution, adds the new one, and activates the Features.
- *No Activation*—Retracts the old solution and adds the new one without activating the Features.

You can choose which deployment configuration to use in your project and even *create* your own. Each configuration contains a number of deployment steps; you can watch the steps by selecting a configuration and clicking View. Each configuration has two sets of steps: one for deployment and for retraction. You might want to change from the Default configuration to the No Activation configuration if you'd like to manually activate the Feature, perhaps when you need to debug or test just that activation situation. At the bottom of the SharePoint Configuration tab is a check box called

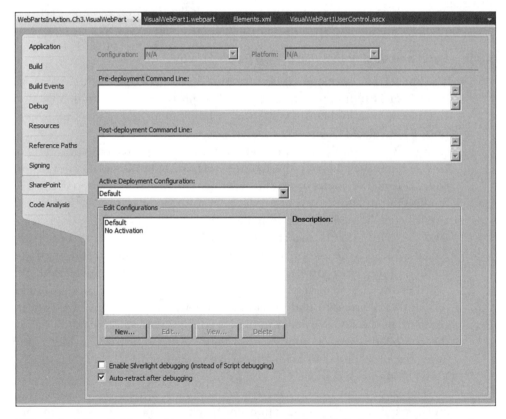

Figure 3.4   A SharePoint project has a special properties tab for selecting and editing deployment configurations.

Auto-retract After Debugging. This check box is selected by default, which means Visual Studio will always retract your solution when you're done with debugging. I find it convenient to deselect this check box to avoid retracting the package when going in and out of the debugging mode.

Depending on your solution and your needs, you can easily create your own deployment configuration by clicking the New button and then selecting the steps you want to use for deployment and retraction. You can also specify a command-line action to invoke before and after deployment. If you have specific needs, you can create custom deployment steps with a Visual Studio extension; see section 3.8 for more information.

You can manually deploy a project or solution by selecting Build > Deploy Solution and retract it by selecting Build > Retract. It's during the deployment step that Visual Studio will use the URL you specified while creating the project in the SharePoint Customization wizard. That URL will be the target of your deployment. Once you've deployed your solution without any errors and warnings, you can go to the site and test it.

During the deployment, Visual Studio also checks for any conflicts of Features and files. Conflicts may occur, for example, when you're building Web Parts and you give the Web Parts in different projects the same name. In a conflict, Visual Studio will detect that a .webpart file with that name exists in the gallery and will remove the previous one. As a general rule, try to name your Web Parts control description files appropriately so you don't encounter conflicts. Visual Studio automatically resolves conflicts with Web Parts in the gallery by removing the old .webpart file and adding the new one, but for other conflicts, such as list instances, Visual Studio will instead ask you for your input on how to resolve the conflict.

To perform all these steps with just one keystroke, press F5. Visual Studio 2010 will then do all these steps for you and, after the deployment, start Internet Explorer and browse to the site to which you deployed the solution. Finally, Visual Studio attaches the debugger to the ASP.NET worker process and Internet Explorer so that you can debug your solution.

3.3.6   *Take your Web Part for a test drive*

To run your Web Part for the first time, just press F5. It will take a few seconds for Visual Studio 2010 to perform the build and deploy the Web Part. Once it's ready, you'll find yourself on the SharePoint site that you configured in the wizard. If this is the first time you've used Visual Studio to debug the application, you'll see a dialog box that asks if you want to enable debugging on the website. Click Yes to configure the web.config file so that you can debug your project. Visual Studio will automatically launch Internet Explorer with the welcome page of the site specified in the SharePoint configuration wizard. Choose Site Actions > New Page to create a new page where you'll host your deployed Web Part or use an existing page. The page will open in Edit mode.

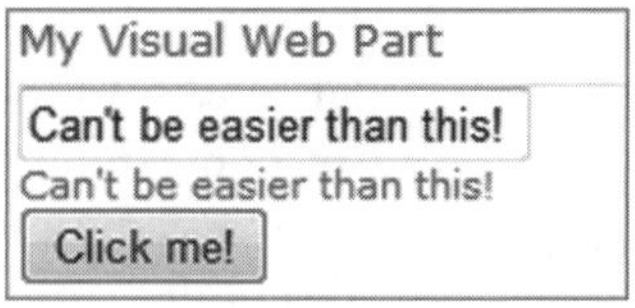

To add your Web Part to the page, position the cursor in the wiki content area and then use the Ribbon to open the Web Part Gallery. Select the My Web Parts category that you defined in the elements manifest. In that category, you'll find the Web Part called VisualWebPart1. Select it, click Add, and then save the page. Now, test the Web Part by making an entry in the text box, as shown in figure 3.5, and clicking the button.

> My Visual Web Part
>
> | Can't be easier than this! |
>
> Can't be easier than this!
>
> [Click me!]

Figure 3.5   The first Visual Web Part project that prints the value of the text box in a label when the button is clicked

If you go back to Visual Studio 2010 without closing Internet Explorer, you can navigate to the code-behind file for your user control and set a breakpoint in the `Button1_Click` method where you assign the value to the label. Do so by clicking in the gray area in the left of the Source Code editor or by pressing F9. Then, return to Internet Explorer and once again click the button. Visual Studio will interrupt the execution of the program when it hits the breakpoint, and you can debug your solution just as you would any other .NET-based application. Visual Studio automatically attaches to the IIS Worker Process, w3wp.exe, for debugging the compiled code and to Internet Explorer for script debugging when you press F5.

If you want to run your solution without any attached debugger, you can press Ctrl-F5 or choose Debug > Start Without Debugging. Visual Studio will then perform all building and packaging and finally start Internet Explorer but without attaching the debugger.

SharePoint 2010 needs a lot of resources, such as RAM and CPU. If you don't have a powerful machine, the deployment and debugger attachment process can take a while. You have a couple of options to speed up this process. First, you can run your solution without attaching the debugger by pressing Ctrl-F5. A second option is to manually start Internet Explorer and use the Deploy Solution command to test your solution. If you need to debug your session after using one of these methods, you can always attach the Visual Studio debugger to the IIS Worker Process manually.

3.4   *Traditional Web Part projects*

The traditional way of building Web Parts didn't involve any visual designers, so we had to build our Web Parts and control trees manually. The Visual Web Part has drastically changed the way we develop Web Parts and has helped us to be more productive. But, the Visual Web Part has some disadvantages that can't be overlooked. For example, Visual Web Parts can't be run in Sandboxed mode (which isn't a huge issue thanks to the downloadable SharePoint Power Tools mentioned earlier), and they require some extra plumbing when you're working with Web Part properties. The Visual Web Parts also have a slightly larger memory footprint than a traditionally built Web Part, which can be important in large scenarios and highly scalable solutions. Also, whenever you need to subclass another Web Part, you have to use traditional Web Parts.

Traditional Web Parts are built in nearly the same way as Visual Web Parts except that you need to programmatically add all controls and you don't have the visual aids. I'll walk you through building the same Web Part you built as a Visual Web Part to illustrate the differences in developing with the visual aids and without. This technique can also be used in combination with the Visual Web Part or even when you combine several user controls into a single Web Part.

3.4.1 Create an empty SharePoint project

There are no out-of-the-box templates for creating Web Part projects, but Web Parts can be added to any SharePoint project in Visual Studio. For a simple Web Part project, you should start with the *Empty SharePoint Project* template. This template contains no items or Features when created. When you've selected the template, give it the name `WebPartsInAction.Ch3.WebPart1` and click OK to create the project. The SharePoint Customization wizard will start, just as with the Visual Web Part. The big difference here is that you can select which trust level you'd like to use for your SharePoint solution—the Visual Web Part only offered the option of creating fully trusted solutions. With the empty Web Part project, you can also choose to deploy your solution to the protected and monitored SharePoint sandbox process.

This time you're going to deploy your solution to the sandbox. Begin by selecting Deploy As Sandboxed Solution, enter the name of the site to use for debugging, and click Finish. The Sandboxed Solution option in the SharePoint Customization wizard is set as the default option. This is an indication on how Microsoft wants us to develop SharePoint solutions and I agree that, whenever it's possible, the sandbox should be used. When building solutions for Office 365 and SharePoint Online, Sandboxed Web Parts is the only to go. You'll learn more about this as we move along in this book.

3.4.2 Adding the Web Part to the project

As I mentioned, when your empty SharePoint project is created, it doesn't contain any Features or items, just a Package. To add a Web Part, click Project > Add New Item and browse to the SharePoint > 2010 template folder. There, you need to select the Web Part project item and give it a name. Always try to add items using a meaningful name instead of the suggested name so you don't have to go through your files and classes renaming things. Name this Web Part item `MyWebPart`. Renaming an item can be quite painful because it can involve modifying several files and references.

When you've added the Web Part item to the project, Visual Studio will add the Web Part class, the Web Parts control description file (.webpart), and a Feature elements manifest file (elements.xml). These files are grouped together in the Solution Explorer. Visual Studio also adds a new Feature to your project, which references the project item that includes the elements.xml and the .webpart file that's connected to the Web Part, as you can see in figure 3.6.

At any time, you can add more Web Parts or other items to the project as long as you don't violate the restrictions Visual Studio enforces when you use a sandbox-targeted project, which will be discussed in chapter 7. For instance, you can't add a Visual Web Part to this current project.

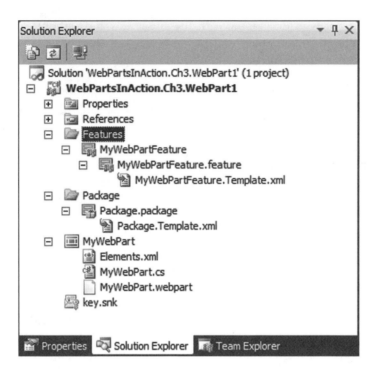

Figure 3.6   **The Solution Explorer in Visual Studio shows you all the files and Features of your Web Part project. The Web Part files are grouped together into a SharePoint project item.**

Rename the Feature to `MyWebPartFeature` by right-clicking the Feature, selecting Rename, and typing a name. If you want, double-click on the Feature you just renamed and the Feature designer will open in Visual Studio, as shown in figure 3.7.

Figure 3.7   **Use the Feature designer in Visual Studio to edit your Features. You can change the title, description, and scope as well as configure which items should be part of the Feature.**

You can use the designer to give the Feature a title and description that will be shown to web interface users. The Feature designer also contains functionality for changing the scope of your Feature. A Web Part project must always have the scope set to Site, which means that it's deployed to a site collection because the Web Part Gallery exists at the site collection level. Using the Feature designer, you can also add SharePoint items to or remove them from the Feature. You'd do this, for example, if you have multiple Features in your solution and you'd like to have different Web Parts in the different solutions. For now, though, let's leave our Feature as is. When you've changed the title and description, save and close the Feature designer.

3.4.3 Adding controls to the Web Part

The Web Part class file is automatically opened in Source Code view when you add the Web Part item to the project. Because this project item doesn't support any visual editing, you only have this view of the Web Part. The class file looks similar to the corresponding Visual Web Part class except for the code that loads the user control.

NOTE For the code samples in this book, I've stripped out most namespace declarations and all `using` statements.

You have to add controls to your Web Part manually, using the `CreateChildControls` method (except in certain scenarios that we'll cover in later chapters). The following listing shows what our code looks like after we've added a text box, a label, and a button.

Listing 3.2 Adding controls to the `CreateChildControls` method

```
protected TextBox textBox;                              ❶ Defines controls
protected Label label;
protected Button button;

protected override void CreateChildControls() {
    textBox = new TextBox();
    label = new Label();                                ❷ Instantiates controls
    button = new Button();

    button.Text = "Click me!";

    this.Controls.Add(textBox);
    this.Controls.Add(new LiteralControl("<br/>"));
    this.Controls.Add(label);                           ❸ Adds controls
    this.Controls.Add(new LiteralControl("<br/>"));        to control tree
    this.Controls.Add(button);

    base.CreateChildControls();
}
```

First, you define the text box, label, and button controls as protected local variables ❶. These controls are created in the `CreateChildControls` method ❷, and then you add them to the Web Part controls collection in the order that you want your controls to appear ❸.

Use the `LiteralControl` control to add the `<br/>` tags that you used in the Visual Web Part to write each control on a new line. This control is great for creating HTML markup that doesn't need any connected control. For example, if you need to write HTML content in the Web Part, you can use the `LiteralControl` and build a string with HTML instead of using several ASP.NET controls. The more controls you use, the more processing is needed. In addition, the view state of the page may grow larger.

3.4.4 *Adding the button-click event manually*

Because you can't take advantage of the designer and automatically hook up the control events, you have to manually add the click event to the button. The event is wired up to the button control after the control is created in `CreateChildControls`. Using IntelliSense in Visual Studio helps you write the code. When you type += after the `Button.Click` event and press the Tab key, Visual Studio writes the code for you. If you press Tab a second time, it also creates the event handler method skeleton for you. The source code row you wrote should look like this:

```
button.Click += new EventHandler(button_Click);
```

And the automatically created event handler looks like this:

```
void button_Click(object sender, EventArgs e) {
    throw new NotImplementedException();
}
```

Replace the exception with the assignment of the text box text to the label just as we did in the Visual Web Part example. To complete your Web Part, your event handler code should look like this:

```
void button_Click(object sender, EventArgs e) {
    label.Text = textBox.Text;
}
```

As in the Visual Web Part example, you can change which base class the Web Part will use here but, because this sample is deployed to the sandbox, you can't use a base class that inherits from the SharePoint implementation. Doing so will result in a run-time error when you add the Web Part to a page, even though the compilation will work fine.

3.4.5 *Testing and debugging your Web Part*

To run your Web Part, press F5 (just like you did with the Visual Web Part), and Share-Point 2010 will open if the compilation succeeds. Any compilation or packaging errors will be reported and stop the debugging process.

Once Internet Explorer has opened the SharePoint site, create a new page using the Site Actions menu. Or, you can edit the page you used earlier by clicking the Edit Page icon, inserting the Web Part on the page, and verifying that it's working.

Because you just created a sandboxed solution, this Web Part is running in the isolated sandbox process. Visual Studio deployed it to a special gallery in the site collection called the Solution Gallery. Click Site Actions > Site Settings and then click Solutions under the Galleries header to access the Solutions Gallery. This gallery holds the WSP files that can be used within the site collection, and they're all running in the sandbox. Verify that your newly created solution is there. Visual Studio attaches the debugger to Internet Explorer and to the SPUCWorkerProcess.exe process (instead of the IIS Worker Process) that's the host for the sandbox.

> **NOTE** In chapter 7, you'll learn more about sandboxed solutions and the Solution Gallery.

3.5   *Upgrading SharePoint 2007 projects*

You've just seen how to build Web Parts in two different ways. But, what if you've already worked with SharePoint 2007 and created solutions for it using Visual Studio or other tools? Then you can, in most cases, use these solutions as-is in SharePoint 2010. Share-Point 2010 is mostly backward compatible so, just like any other project, you should be sure to test your solutions thoroughly before deploying them into production. If you need to update or edit the projects, you should move the solutions to a SharePoint project in Visual Studio 2010. If you need to upgrade your solutions, there are several methods you can use.

3.5.1   *Upgrading from Visual Studio Extension for WSS 1.3*

For SharePoint 2007, Microsoft has a VSeWSS extension for Visual Studio 2008. Projects created with this tool aren't directly compatible with the new developer tools in Visual Studio 2010. But, the SharePoint Developer Tools for Visual Studio 2010 contain a migration tool for this specific situation. This tool shows up as a new SharePoint project template called Import VSeWSS Project and lets you import the old project file. Because the structure of the new tools for SharePoint 2010 differs a lot from VSeWSS, you should thoroughly test your new project. The tool is provided by Microsoft but has no official support.

> **NOTE** The VSeWSS Import Tool for Visual Studio 2010 can be downloaded from http://code.msdn.microsoft.com/VSeWSSImport. The tool is distributed as source code and needs to be compiled before usage.

3.5.2   *Upgrading from other project types*

If you have previously used tools like STSDev or WSPBuilder, then there are no tools for importing these solutions to a SharePoint Project in Visual Studio 2010. I suggest that you start a new project and then manually add each item from the old project to the new one. This will ensure that your solution will work with Visual Studio 2010. Another approach might be the Import SharePoint Solution Package project, which allows you to import a WSP file into a new Visual Studio project. This approach doesn't import the source code from the assemblies, but it might give you a faster way to start migrating larger solutions.

   If you're trying to upgrade your project so that you can use it to upgrade an already existing solution in SharePoint, you have to carefully export the solution manifest and, most importantly, the solution id. You must manually add and edit the manifest in the Visual Studio 2010 SharePoint project. You have to choose this approach to upgrade your solution if you have a SharePoint 2010 installation that's upgraded from SharePoint 2007.

3.6   *SharePoint Project settings in Visual Studio*

When you created the two previous Web Parts, you used the SharePoint Customization wizard and it asked you for a specific URL and a deployment type (Sandbox or Farm solution). What do you do if you switch servers or discover that the SharePoint sandbox is too limited for your use? These settings are handled and stored by the Visual Studio project and can be changed at any time. You can access and change the settings by selecting the project in the Solution Explorer and then pressing F4 to open the Properties pane, as shown in figure 3.8. Don't confuse this with the project properties that you open when you double-click the Properties item or right-click on the Project and select Properties in the Solution Explorer.

Using this toolbox window, you can change the URL of the site collection you're using for debugging purposes by modifying the Site URL property. You can change the deployment type from fully trusted to sandboxed solutions by modifying the Sandboxed Solution property, which you set to True if it will be deployed to the sandbox.

Startup Item is a special property that, in an empty SharePoint project, has the value of (None) by default. But, as soon as you add the Web Part item to the project, you're able to change this property to the name of your Web Part or any other SharePoint

Figure 3.8   The Project Properties window shows the debugging URL and whether the project is a sandboxed solution. You can also use this window to specify which of the SharePoint project items you'd like to use when debugging the project.

items in the project. Selecting a Web Part project item here makes the browser start at the default URL. But, when you choose a List instance item, for example, the debugging session will start at the URL of the List instance.

3.7 *SharePoint Server Explorer in Visual Studio*

In this chapter, we've looked at several improvements for SharePoint developers, and there are still some more that can make the development experience even better. The Server Explorer in Visual Studio 2010 lets you connect to a local SharePoint site if the SharePoint Developer Tools are installed. Open the Server Explorer by selecting View > Server Explorer. Using this window, you can add new SharePoint sites so that you can browse the details of the site and its subsites and perform actions on the various items. To add a new SharePoint site to the Server Explorer, right-click on SharePoint Connections and select Add Connection (see figure 3.9).

Figure 3.9 shows the Server Explorer with the Sites node expanded. You can use the Server Explorer to get information about the various items in a SharePoint site, for example, to determine the id of a field or a content type. If you have a site or a list selected, you can right-click the node and choose View In Browser to open your web browser and view the item. By default, the Server Explorer provides just read-only

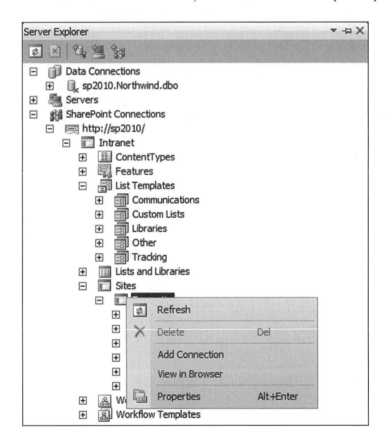

Figure 3.9 Use the Server Explorer in Visual Studio 2010 to explore your SharePoint site collection and see the contents within it.

property views of the items, but the extensibility options of Visual Studio 2010 allow you or third parties to customize the nodes, insert new nodes, and add functionality.

3.8   *Extensibility in Visual Studio 2010*

Visual Studio 2010 has been designed so that it can be extended in various ways to improve your productivity and interactivity. You might encounter situations when you need to customize the SharePoint development tools with new project templates or project items or create extensions for the deployment process.

The set of project templates and project item templates in Visual Studio can be customized to fit your needs. Perhaps you've created a base class from which to derive your Web Part projects and you've customized the elements manifest and Web Parts control definition files. You can create an extension to the SharePoint Developer Tools using Visual Studio with your customizations and share it with your colleagues. You can also extend the Server Explorer with new functionality or information.

The extensions that you create are built using a special project template called the VSIX project in Visual Studio. The result is a VSIX file that you can install on any machine with Visual Studio 2010. You can also upload your extensions to the Visual Studio online gallery to share your creative ideas with the community. When you're creating a project in Visual Studio, select Online Templates in the New Project dialog box and search for available extensions and templates. Enable, disable, or uninstall your extensions using the Tools > Extension Manager in Visual Studio.

> **NOTE**   The Community Kit for SharePoint—Development Tools Edition is a Visual Studio 2010 extension that's available for download (http://cksdev.codeplex.com or www.communitykitforsharepoint.org). These extensions contain numerous improvements to the SharePoint Developer Tools, and I highly recommend that you install and use these extensions. For example, with these extensions, you can browse the Web Part Gallery and copy Web Part configurations.

3.9   *Summary*

This concludes our walkthrough of your first Visual Web Part and traditional Web Part using Visual Studio 2010. This chapter explored the two ways of creating Web Parts and introduced the SharePoint Developer Tools in Visual Studio 2010. You learned the build, package, and deploy routines used when working with SharePoint, both to a fully trusted location and into a sandbox. In the next chapter, we'll continue to build Web Parts and take a deeper look on how to build the user interface.

Building
the user interface
4

This chapter covers

- Understanding the flow of events in Web Parts
- Working with the view state
- Validating user input
- Creating custom controls
- Using SharePoint controls

When you build the user interface (UI) for your Web Part, you should consider more than just how it looks. You need to factor in how the user will interact with your Web Part. Some Web Parts require no interaction and just show lists or display information. But, often Web Parts resemble applications that allow users to interact with the underlying business logic. In this chapter, you'll learn how to create the UI and appearance of your Web Parts using the underlying techniques in the ASP.NET and SharePoint platforms.

The UI is built using controls. A control can be a text label, a button, or something more complex, such as a data grid. Controls can also be combined to create composite controls. These controls can be ASP.NET, SharePoint, or custom controls.

Some controls produce the HTML that's used by the browser, and some only act on the server side. This chapter will start by exploring the ASP.NET basics and showing how you can utilize the ASP.NET controls and features in your Web Part. Remember that Web Parts are defined in ASP.NET and aren't specific to SharePoint.

Once you know how to use the various controls to build an interface that your users can interact with, we'll focus on achieving the desired visual appearance for your Web Parts. We'll look at the default SharePoint style sheets and themes and see how you can use them in your Web Parts. The look and feel is not all about the colors and fonts of the interface. SharePoint has come a long way in terms of usability and accessibility. Finally, we'll show you how to add *verbs* to your Web Part. Verbs are specific actions that can be invoked on Web Parts.

4.1   ASP.NET and Web Parts

First, let's look at Web Parts on the ASP.NET side. The Web Part infrastructure and SharePoint are built on Microsoft .NET Framework 3.5. Web Parts are essentially ASP.NET controls that have been extended with functionality—for example, with features that allow the users to customize the controls. But, when you're working with Web Parts, you're working with ASP.NET, so you can use all features of the ASP.NET and .NET Frameworks.

Because ASP.NET is the foundation of Web Parts, we'll review the basics of how controls are created and used in ASP.NET. During the ASP.NET page life cycle, all controls and Web Parts go through a number of steps, and each step invokes a method or event on each control and subcontrol. The order of these events is one of the key features that all ASP.NET and SharePoint developers need to be aware of. Failing to understand the concept of events and their order can make developing Web Parts difficult and often results in poor design decisions. Each event has its specific purpose and should be used accordingly.

ASP.NET contains features such as validators for validating input (which is a great way to improve the usability of your Web Part). Using validators in Web Parts requires you to do some extra configuring that isn't often needed in ASP.NET projects. Another feature of ASP.NET that's of interest is the view state, which maintains the state of a control between postbacks. Normally, you don't need to worry about view state because ASP.NET does the work for you, but some scenarios require you to handle view state manually.

Because Web Parts can be used and added to pages by users, you can't as a developer predict exactly how your Web Parts are going to be used. To prevent your Web Part from interfering with other Web Parts or multiple instances of itself, you have to take certain precautions when building them.

4.1.1   Adding controls to the Web Part

The interface of a Web Part consists of one or more controls. These controls render HTML, JavaScript, or style sheets to the web browser. You can use any ASP.NET controls in your Web Part or you can create your own. All controls on a page, including the Web Parts, are organized into a hierarchy called a *control tree*. Thus, each control has a parent and a collection of child controls. Unless you create a custom rendering of your Web Part, the controls will be rendered in the order in which they exist in the tree.

When building Web Parts, you start by adding new child controls to the Web Part. The controls should always be added in the `CreateChildControls` method as a first option, which is the first method that you should override in your Web Part implementation. This method is used by all ASP.NET controls and isn't specific to Web Parts. `CreateChildControls` is specifically intended for creating the subcontrol tree of a control. There are situations when you can't add the controls in that method, such as when the child controls depend on other Web Parts or information isn't available at this point in the event flow. But try to add as many controls as possible in the `Create-ChildControls` method.

Another common method used to add child controls, `OnPreRender`, is called before the Web Part is rendered and immediately before the view state of the Web Part is saved. The disadvantage of adding controls in the `OnPreRender` method is that any events attached to the controls in the control tree won't fire. This is because all postback events are fired before the `OnPreRender` method is called. You won't have problems adding controls or modifying the properties of a control in this method if it just has to do with the appearance.

4.1.2 The event flow for a Web Part

Taking advantage of the event flow is a key to building great Web Parts and will save you a lot of troubleshooting. The event flow is quite similar to the event flow of an ASP.NET web control but has additional events that the Web Part infrastructure requires. As an exercise, you could create a simple Web Part and override all events and then use a debugger to step through all the events.

The event flow differs slightly when you load a page or if you, for example, click a button that invokes a postback. This differentiation is one of the major issues developers stumble over when starting to build Web Parts or ASP.NET controls in general.

NORMAL PAGE LOAD EVENT FLOW

Figure 4.1 shows the event flow for a Web Part when a page loads. First, the constructor is called; you can use this constructor to initialize any default values of your Web Part. After the object is constructed, the Web Part Manager sets the properties of the Web Part using the persisted values from the SharePoint content databases using .NET reflection techniques. Only properties with persisted values are set. Then, the `OnInit` method is called to initialize your Web Part and properties. The `TrackViewState` is called to indicate that the tracking of the view state starts before the `OnLoad` method is called. The `OnLoad` method can be used to perform actions on the Web Part regardless of its state.

Then it's time for the `CreateChildControls` method that's building the UI and control tree. This method is followed by `OnPreRender`, which is used to perform the

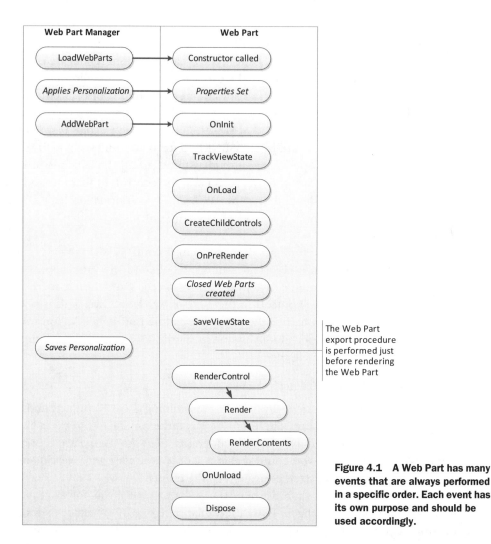

Web Part Manager	Web Part
LoadWebParts →	Constructor called
Applies Personalization →	*Properties Set*
AddWebPart →	OnInit
	TrackViewState
	OnLoad
	CreateChildControls
	OnPreRender
	Closed Web Parts created
	SaveViewState
Saves Personalization	
	RenderControl
	Render
	RenderContents
	OnUnload
	Dispose

The Web Part export procedure is performed just before rendering the Web Part

Figure 4.1   A Web Part has many events that are always performed in a specific order. Each event has its own purpose and should be used accordingly.

final adjustments before the Web Part is rendered. The SaveViewState method allows you to hook into the view state of the object and customize the view state if you want. The view state is only loaded on postbacks (which you'll see later when we go through the postback event flow). Later in this chapter, I'm going to show you how to use the view state. Notice that, before the SaveViewState method is invoked on all Web Parts, the Web Part Manager will create all Web Parts on the page that are closed and invoke their constructor. This means that, even though the Web Part is closed, its constructor will be called. Avoid placing calculations or other resource-consuming operations in the constructor of the Web Part because they can be performance killers.

RenderControl calls the appropriate render methods and must never be overridden. This method ensures that the control is rendered through control adapters (which you'll learn about in chapter 12). RenderControl calls the Render method, which draws the chrome of the Web Part and then calls the RenderContents method. You shouldn't override the Render method either because that method verifies that the Web Part connections are valid and, if they aren't, the method renders an error message. If you need to overwrite any of the render methods, you should override Render-Contents to start with. There are scenarios when you need to override the Render method—for instance, if you have to inject code or handle errors late in the event flow.

Returning to the event flow, the next event is the OnUnload method, which you can use to do any cleanup. Finally, the Dispose method is invoked.

Note that all these event methods are for the ASP.NET-based Web Part. If you create a Web Part based on the SharePoint implementation, the event flow is the same except for the rendering methods.

All events are executed in sequence for all Web Parts and controls in the order in which they're added to the zones. For example, all OnLoad methods are executed on all Web Parts before any calls to CreateChildControls.

When you're exporting a Web Part, the export file is generated just before the Web Part is rendered and after the personalization state is saved by the Web Part Manager. The Web Part Manager retrieves all properties of the Web Part and creates the XML file, which is returned to the client.

POSTBACK EVENT FLOW

The event flow is different when you're doing a postback, such as a response to a button click. A postback is a technique used by ASP.NET pages to post back data to themselves and to retain all control values. Figure 4.2 shows the event flow for a postback. The events following the TrackViewState until the SaveViewState are different compared with a normal page load. First, the Load-ViewState method is called if the Web Part has any saved view states. Following that is the CreateChildControls method before the OnLoad method (the opposite order

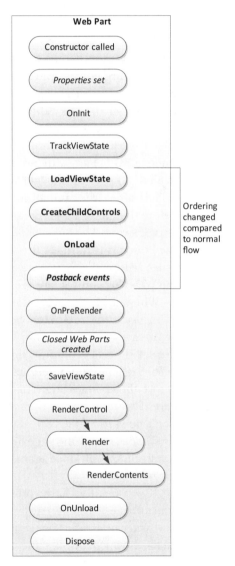

Figure 4.2 The event flow of a Web Part during a postback is slightly different from the flow during a normal load. Most significant is that the OnLoad event is executed after the CreateChildControls event.

compared with a nonpostback load). After the OnLoad event, all of the postback events on the controls are performed. If you need to update the controls or the control tree in response to a postback event such as a button click, you can do so in the OnPreRender method.

If you delete a Web Part from a page, then all events up to TrackViewState will be called, followed by an OnDeleting event and an OnUnload event. There are no events for when a Web Part is minimized or closed. These states can be checked using the Web Part property ChromeState and the method IsClosed, respectively.

EVENT FLOW WHEN EDITING PROPERTIES

When you're editing and saving Web Parts, you'll encounter some new events in the event flow. The properties are edited in the tool pane, which consists of Editor Parts (see chapter 5). The Editor Parts read the properties from the Web Part and, if the properties are changed and saved, the Editor Part writes the properties back to the Web Part. Figure 4.3 shows the event flow when a Web Part with an Editor Part is loaded. The OnEditModeChanged event is called after the initialization and just before the Editor Part is created in Create-EditorParts. The SyncChanges method of the Editor Part retrieves the values of properties before the view state is loaded and the Web Part controls are created.

When saving the properties after editing them using the tool pane, you invoke the ApplyChanges method after OnLoad, as figure 4.4 shows. A common mistake is using OnLoad to build your interface, which occurs before the changes are applied to the Web Part. The result? Your updated properties won't be used by the controls immediately. You have to reload the page or, if you clicked Apply, click Apply once again to actually use the new values.

If you need to have your controls and control tree available earlier in the event flow, you can use the EnsureChildControls method, which invokes the CreateChild-Controls event. Don't manually call Creat-eChildControls. This method ensures that any control adapters applied to the control are used. It also sets the ChildControlsCreated property of the control to true to avoid

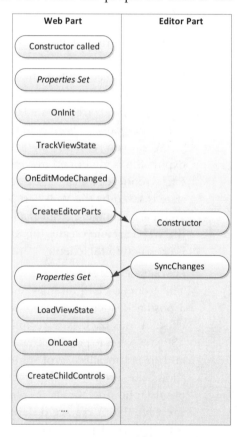

Figure 4.3 A Web Part that loads an Editor Part adds a few new events to the normal event flow. The Web Part instantiates the Editor Part and the Editor Part eventually reads the properties from the Web Part.

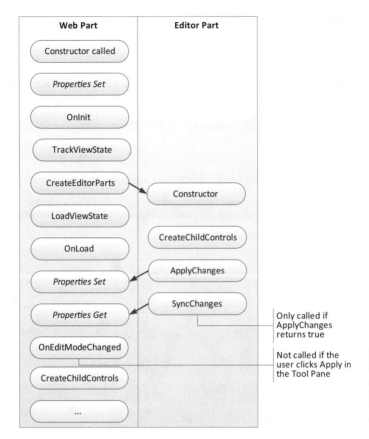

Figure 4.4 When the changes made in an Editor Part are
applied to the Web Part, the
properties are pushed back
to the Web Part after the
`OnLoad` event.

the multiple calling of the `CreateChildControls` method. As a best practice, you should always set this property in your own implementations of the `CreateChildControls` method:

```
protected override void CreateChildControls() {
    // create controls
    this.ChildControlsCreated = true;
}
```

Setting this property to `false` may be necessary when you have to rebuild your control tree in response to an event. Calling `EnsureChildControls` after setting it to `false` will ensure that the `CreateChildControls` method is invoked.

4.1.3 Working with view state

The *view state* is a standard ASP.NET feature that allows controls to maintain their state between page reloads. You can use the view state in Web Parts just as you do with any other ASP.NET controls. Using view state is handy if you build your control tree dynamically and need to persist values between postbacks. The view state is nothing unique to SharePoint, and manually controlling the view state isn't often necessary. There are some Web Part situations where you need to use it, such as when you're working with Web Part connections (discussed in chapter 14). For now, let's start with the basics of manually managing the view state.

> **TIP** You can disable view state for specific controls by setting the `EnableViewState` property of the control to `false`.

To demonstrate how you can solve persisting the state of dynamically added controls, look at listing 4.1, which contains a simple Web Part with a button and a counter variable. The counter is incremented on every click and shown in the Web Part. This sample will also illustrate when to use the `OnPreRender` method to add controls.

Listing 4.1   A Web Part with view state

```
public class ViewStateWebPart : WebPart {
    public ViewStateWebPart() {
    }
    int counter = 0;                                     ❶ Initializes counter

    protected override void CreateChildControls() {
        Button button = new Button() {
            Text = "Click me!"                           ❷ Creates button
        };
        button.Click += (s, e) => {
            counter++;                                   ❸ Creates anonymous click delegate
        };
        this.Controls.Add(button);
        base.CreateChildControls();
    }

    protected override void OnPreRender(EventArgs e) {
        this.Controls.Add(
            new LiteralControl("Count = "                ❹ Prints counter value
                + counter.ToString()));
    }
}
```

`counter` is a local variable ❶ and initialized to 0 every time the class is loaded. In the `CreateChildControls` method, you add a button ❷ that increments ❸ the value of `counter`. If you added a control that printed the value in the `CreateChildControls`, you wouldn't see the changed value. The postback event is fired after the `CreateChildControls` event, as seen in figure 4.2. To see the changed variable value, you can take advantage of the `OnPreRender` method and add a `LiteralControl` with the counter value ❹. If you test this Web Part, you'll see that `counter` is incremented but only once, to the value of 1. This is because the variable is initialized to 0 every time the class is created.

A common method for solving problems like this is to have a hidden control that contains the value instead of a private variable. The hidden control will automatically save its view state. The downside is that you're adding an unnecessary control to the control tree. A better solution is to use the view state to resolve this problem and persist the value of the counter between postbacks. By overriding SaveViewState in the Web Part, as shown here, the counter value will be saved to the view state after the button click event:

```
protected override object SaveViewState() {
    return counter;
}
```

The SaveViewState method returns the current state of the Web Part—in this case, the value of counter. The counter value will then be retrieved after the postback by the overridden LoadViewState method, implemented as follows, before the Create-ChildControls:

```
protected override void LoadViewState(object savedState) {
    if (savedState != null) {
        counter = (int)savedState;
    }
}
```

To retrieve the view state for the Web Part, the LoadViewState method converts the saved state to an integer and assigns it to counter. This ensures that counter correctly increments each time you click the button.

Note that, if you create a custom view state, saving and loading will override any default view state of other controls in the Web Part. To combine your own view state with the default view state, you could create an array that contains the default view state and your custom values, as shown in the following listing.

Listing 4.2 SaveViewState **and** LoadViewState **preserves the default view state**

```
protected override object SaveViewState() {
    object state = new object[2];
    object[0] = counter;
    object[1] = base.SaveViewState();
    return state;
}
protected override void LoadViewState(object savedState) {
    if (savedState != null) {
        object[] state = (object[]) savedState;
        counter = (int)state[0];
        base.LoadViewState(state[1]);
    }
}
```

The SaveViewState method creates an object array that stores the custom value and the default view state. The method then returns this array. The view state is loaded by LoadViewState, which casts the savedState argument into an object array. The first value of the array is cast to your custom variable, and the second value in the array is used as an argument to the base implementation of LoadViewState.

4.1.4 Using validators

Validators are a part of the ASP.NET Framework. They're special controls that validate the input of other controls. The validation is performed both on the server side and

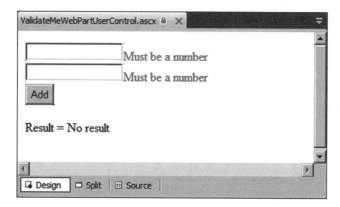

Figure 4.5 The Designer view in Visual Studio shows a Visual Web Part with two validated text boxes, a button, and a result label.

on the client side for the out-of-the-box validators. You should take advantage of these controls. The problem with validators in Web Parts is that the Web Parts can be added multiple times to a page and together with other Web Parts that use validators. This can result in validation collisions if you don't set it up correctly.

To resolve this problem, use the `ValidationGroup` property of the controls and validators. Figure 4.5 shows you a Visual Web Part that has two text boxes, a button, and a label, as well as a validator for each text box.

The validators validate that the text boxes contain only a number using regular expression validators like this:

```
<asp:RegularExpressionValidator
    ID="RegularExpressionValidator1"
    runat="server"
    ControlToValidate="TextBox1"
    ErrorMessage="Must be a number"
    ValidationExpression="\d+">
</asp:RegularExpressionValidator>
```

If you add two or more of these validator Web Parts to a page and enter invalid values in one of them and, in one of the other Web Parts, click the button, the Web Part with invalid values will invalidate the click because it can't validate. This is because the validation is done on all controls with validators on the current page when you click the button, not only in the Web Part you're clicking on. To solve the problem, you need to use the validation groups. You can't use a declarative approach and enter a name of the validation group because this name will be the same for all your Web Parts. Instead, you need to set the validation group name programmatically to get a unique value.

This is a Visual Web Part, and we need to set the validation group in the user control code-behind. The code is added into an overridden `OnPreRender` method, as in the following listing.

Listing 4.3 Adding dynamic validation groups to a Visual Web Part

```
protected override void OnPreRender(EventArgs e) {
    TextBox1.ValidationGroup = ClientID;
    TextBox2.ValidationGroup = ClientID;
    RegularExpressionValidator1.ValidationGroup = ClientID;
```

```
        RegularExpressionValidator2.ValidationGroup = ClientID;
        Button1.ValidationGroup = ClientID;
        base.OnPreRender(e);
}
```

The `ValidationGroup` property is set on all controls and validators to the `ClientID` of the Visual Web Part user control. This will guarantee that the validation group name is unique within the page. The `ClientID` property, which exists on all controls, is an identifier generated by the ASP.NET runtime, which is guaranteed to be unique for the page. In this case, the `ClientID` of the Web Part is used to ensure uniqueness for the validation group.

> **TIP**   A good practice is to disable all or some validators while in Edit mode for the Web Part or page to prevent the validators from blocking the editing operations. Using validation groups can also avoid blocking the editing operations.

4.1.5 *Custom controls and user controls*

Building the UI using a large amount of controls in the Web Part might not always be the best option. Instead, consider moving some of your controls to custom server controls or user controls. This arrangement will make your code easier to understand and follow. Creating custom user controls also makes the control reusable to other Web Parts or pages that you build. If you're creating a solution and targeting the sandbox, then you can't use user controls but, instead, have to rely on creating server controls. User controls are based on ASCX pages that are deployed into the {SharePoint Root} (which isn't allowed by the sandbox).

To show you how to create a user control, let's go back to our earlier validation example and create a user control consisting of a text box that only accepts integers. Start by creating a Visual Web Part project. Once you've set it up, select the project, right-click, and choose Add > New Item. In the resulting dialog box, select the SharePoint 2010 category in the left pane and add a user control. Give the control the name `RequiredNumberField`. Visual Studio will add a new SharePoint mapped folder called ControlTemplates, which corresponds to the {SharePoint Root} and TEMPLATE\CONTROLTEMPLATES folder. In this folder, Visual Studio also creates a subfolder with the name of your project and adds the user control to this subfolder. Your Solution Explorer should look like the one shown in figure 4.6.

Figure 4.6   The Visual Studio Solution Explorer can be used to add the SharePoint mapped folders in order to include the files that will be deployed to the SharePoint root.

NOTE Visual Studio 2010 uses the SharePoint mapped folders in your project to enable developers to add content to specific folders within the {SharePoint Root}. Items added to any of these mapped folders will be included in the resulting package and deployed to the farm and will be copied into the corresponding folder in the SharePoint root of all servers in the farm.

Open the user control you just added and add the code shown in the following listing. This code will add the text box and necessary control validators.

Listing 4.4   A `TextBox` control with two validator controls

```
<asp:TextBox ID="TextBox1" runat="server"
    Width="60px" ></asp:TextBox>
<asp:RegularExpressionValidator
    ID="RegularExpressionValidator1" runat="server"
    ErrorMessage="Only integers allowed"
    ControlToValidate="TextBox1"
    ValidationExpression="\d+"
    Display="Dynamic">
</asp:RegularExpressionValidator>
<asp:RequiredFieldValidator
    ID="RequiredFieldValidator1" runat="server"
    ErrorMessage="A value is required"
    ControlToValidate="TextBox1"
    Display="Dynamic">
</asp:RequiredFieldValidator>
```

❶ Declares TextBox to validate

❷ Defines validation regular expression

First, you add the text box ❶ and set a smaller width than the default. Then you add two validators: the first uses a regular expression ❷ to make sure it's one or more digits, and the second makes sure that the text box has a value. Both of the validators have the `Display` property set to `Dynamic`, which ensures the validator appears only when invalid.

After creating the control interface, you need to make some adjustments in the code-behind. You should specify which validator group to use so that you can get the value from the text box. The following listing shows the code you add to the user control.

Listing 4.5   The code-behind of the custom validated input control

```
protected override void OnInit(EventArgs e) {
    TextBox1.Style.Add("text-align", "right");
    base.OnInit(e);
}

public string ValidationGroup {
    get;
    set;
}

public int Value {
    get {
        return int.Parse(TextBox1.Text);
    }
    set {
```

❶ Right-aligns text

❷ Contains Validation group property

❸ Defines Control value

```
            TextBox1.Text = value.ToString();
        }
    }
    protected override void OnPreRender(EventArgs e) {
        RegularExpressionValidator1.ValidationGroup = this.ValidationGroup;
        RequiredFieldValidator1.ValidationGroup = this.ValidationGroup;
        TextBox1.ValidationGroup = this.ValidationGroup;
        base.OnPreRender(e);
    }
```

❹ Overrides prerendering logic

The `OnInit` method adds a style to the text box so that the content of the text box is right-aligned ❶. Then, two properties are added to the control. The first one ❷ is a string property that's used to set the validation group of this control, and the second one ❸ extracts the value of the text box as an integer. To properly set the validation group on the text box and validators, the `OnPreRender` method ❹ needs to be over-ridden. In this method, the validation group is set on each control. At this point, you've created a reusable user control that you can use to request an integer input from the user.

The next thing to do is to add this user control to the Visual Web Part. First, add a `Register` directive to the user control of the Visual Web Part like this:

```
<%@ Register
    src="~/_CONTROLTEMPLATES/WebPartsInAction.Ch4.CustomControls/
➥   RequiredNumberField.ascx" tagname="RequiredNumberField"
    tagprefix="rnf" %>
```

Now you can use the control in your code. Add two instances of the user control like this:

```
<rnf:RequiredNumberField ID="RequiredNumberField1" runat="server" />
<br/>
<rnf:RequiredNumberField ID="RequiredNumberField2" runat="server" />
<br/>
```

Then you need to add a button and a label to this Visual Web Part. When you've added the button, go to the Design mode of the control and double-click the button. The double-click will automatically generate the click event handler in the user control and its code-behind. The code for the label and the button will look like this:

```
<asp:Button ID="Button1" runat="server" Text="Add"
    onclick="Button1_Click" />
<br />
<asp:Label ID="Label1" runat="server" />
```

In the code-behind for the Visual Web Part control, edit the button click event handler so that it adds the values from the two custom user controls. You need to cast the `RequiredNumberField` objects into the correct class because Visual Studio has added these controls as `UserControl` objects:

```
Label1.Text = (((RequiredNumberField)RequiredNumberField1).Value
    + ((RequiredNumberField)RequiredNumberField2).Value).ToString();
```

Finally, add code to the `CreateChildControls` method so that the validation group is set on the custom controls and the button:

```
protected override void CreateChildControls() {
    base.CreateChildControls();
    ((RequiredNumberField)RequiredNumberField1).ValidationGroup =
        this.ClientID;
    ((RequiredNumberField)RequiredNumberField2).ValidationGroup =
        this.ClientID;
    Button1.ValidationGroup = this.ClientID;
}
```

Once you've done this, your calculator Web Part is done. Deploy it and test it. You'll see that the validation works even if you add several calculators to the same page. But, most importantly, you've seen that you can create composite custom controls and avoid cluttering your Web Part code with styling and logic for the subcontrols. I recommend that you use this efficient technique when you're creating controls or subcontrols that you plan to reuse.

This sample used a user control as base. Because standard user controls can't be used in sandboxed solutions, I suggest using web controls when you create reusable controls. This will keep you from limiting yourself to one type of deployment.

4.2   SharePoint controls

You've seen how you can add controls to your Web Parts and, so far in this book, you've added standard ASP.NET web controls. You can use these controls to display content to your users or allow them to interact with your Web Part. If you need custom functionality not found in the default controls, you can create your own controls, either by creating classes or using user controls. SharePoint also contains a set of web controls and user controls that you can use to create your custom Web Parts. These controls are specifically designed to interact with SharePoint features and the SharePoint interface.

This section will guide you through some of the controls that SharePoint allows you to use. Some controls are available from within the Toolbox in Visual Studio. I'll show you both the standard SharePoint controls available in Visual Studio and some other controls that I've found useful and that also have some documentation. Most of the controls in SharePoint are unfortunately not documented or not even supported for use in custom applications. Even though you can use the undocumented controls, I don't recommend you do because they can be changed between service releases of SharePoint.

> **TIP**   If you'd like to use the controls that SharePoint uses and can't find documentation in the SharePoint SDK or on the MSDN website, you'll find a lot of information on blogs using your favorite search engine. You can also always use the .NET Reflector tool (www.red-gate.com/products/reflector/) to analyze the source of the controls and find out how they work.

4.2.1   Default SharePoint controls in Visual Studio

Let's start our exploration of the SharePoint controls in Visual Studio. When you install Visual Studio with the SharePoint Developer Tools, you'll see a new tab in the Toolbox (figure 4.7) called SharePoint Controls. The controls in this tab come from the `Microsoft.SharePoint` assembly and are added to the tab because they have the `ToolboxData` attribute specified on the class declaration.

The Toolbox contains the SharePoint `DateTimeControl`, which allows you to select a date and a time. ASP.NET has no date and time control by default, just a calendar control. This `DateTimeControl` is configurable and is built so that it renders using the default SharePoint styling and theme.

> **TIP** You can also add your own controls to the Toolbox. You just have to add the `ToolboxItem` attribute or the `ToolboxData` attribute with appropriate parameters. After a successful build

Figure 4.7 The Toolbox in Visual Studio contains a few default SharePoint controls that you can use when building Web Parts.

of your project, the controls should appear in a new tab in the Toolbox when you're editing user controls or ASPX pages. Sometimes, you have to restart Visual Studio to make the controls appear. Also note that the default Web Part project items have the `ToolboxItem` attribute with the value `false` when created; this is to stop them from appearing in the Toolbox by default.

4.2.2 Standard SharePoint controls

SharePoint uses several custom controls specifically built for use with SharePoint. The controls are defined in the SharePoint assemblies and also exist in the TEMPLATE\ CONTROLTEMPLATES folder in the {SharePoint Root}. Several of these controls can be used in your Web Parts and solutions. Most of the controls that are available in the SharePoint assemblies don't have any documentation. Even though you can use them in your Web Parts, I recommend that you don't use them because Microsoft offers no support for these controls. Covering all these controls would be enough material for a book on its own. Instead, I'll show you some of the most useful controls in SharePoint that are documented.

THE SPGRIDVIEW CONTROL

There are many occasions when you need to present data or information in a grid. ASP.NET includes a `GridView` control that can be connected to a data source. The ASP.NET `GridView` control can be used in your Web Parts, just like any other ASP.NET control. But, if you use this control in a Web Part, you'll find that you need to customize it to achieve the SharePoint look.

SharePoint has its own grid view control called the `SPGridView`. It uses the built-in CSS styles of SharePoint, which means you have to do less interface customization than you would with the ASP.NET `GridView` control. The `SPGridView` inherits from the ASP.NET `GridView` control and can, therefore, be used as a normal grid view. The `SPGridView` has a set of features that's not available in the ASP.NET `GridView` control;

SPGridViewWebPart		
Title	**Priority**	**% Complete**
Install SharePoint 2010	(1) High	100 %
Install Visual Studio 2010	(2) Normal	75 %
Have Fun!	(1) High	67 %

Figure 4.8   The SharePoint `SPGridView` control can be used to create a data-bound grid that takes advantage of the SharePoint UI features.

these features include grouping, filtering, and the ability to add context menus to the rows. The disadvantage of the `SPGridView` is that it doesn't support autogeneration of columns, so you have to define all the fields in the grid.

To illustrate how this control works, let's look at a sample Visual Web Part that shows all items in a list. This sample will also use the SharePoint-specific data source control, `SPDataSource`, but you can use any data source control. The data is taken from a Tasks list in a SharePoint site and shows the Title, Priority, and % Complete columns (see figure 4.8).

Listing 4.6 shows the code that you add to a Visual Web Part user control. It contains a `SPGridView` control, which defines the fields in the grid, and an `SPDataSource` object that queries a list in SharePoint.

Listing 4.6   `SPGridView` control and `SPDataSource` object used in a Visual Web Part

```
<SharePoint:SPGridView
    runat="server"
    ID="gridview"                          Set this
    AutoGenerateColumns="false"            to false
    DataSourceID="datasource">
    <Columns>
        <SharePoint:SPBoundField
            DataField="Title"
            HeaderText="Title"
            SortExpression="Name"
            ShowHeader="true" />           ➊ Data binding
        <SharePoint:SPBoundField              controls
            DataField="Priority"
            HeaderText="Priority"
            SortExpression="Name" />
        <SharePoint:SPBoundField
            DataField="% Complete"
            HeaderText="% Complete" />
    </Columns>
    <EmptyDataTemplate>
        No tasks
    </EmptyDataTemplate>
</SharePoint:SPGridView>
<SharePoint:SPDataSource              ➋ Data source
    runat="server"                       control
```

```
    ID="datasource"
    DataSourceMode="List"
    SelectCommand="<Query></Query>">
    <SelectParameters>
        <asp:Parameter Name="WebUrl" DefaultValue="/" />
        <asp:Parameter Name="ListName" DefaultValue="Tasks" />
    </SelectParameters>
</SharePoint:SPDataSource>
```

**❸ Control that retrieves
data from list**

**❹ Query
command**

First, the `SPGridView` control is added to the page and connected to the data source
(defined later). This grid contains three columns that you bind to using the `SPBound-Field` controls ❶. The `SPBoundField` is a special SharePoint control, but you can use
any ASP.NET data binding fields. If no items are found in the data source, you print a
nice message for the user using the empty data template. The data source is defined
with the `SPDataSource` control ❷. This control reads data from a list ❸ using the
specified CAML query ❹ and parameters.

The `SPGridView` control is powerful and you can configure it to sort and group the
columns. Using the special data binding control `SPMenuField`, you can attach a menu
to the rows in the `SPGridView`. Find out more about the `SPGridView` and `SPDataSource`
at Microsoft's MSDN SharePoint Developer Center at http://msdn.microsoft.com/
en-us/library/microsoft.sharepoint.webcontrols.spgridview.aspx.

USING PICKER CONTROLS

SharePoint contains a set of picker controls you can use to select users, groups, Business Connectivity Services (BCS) entities, and more. These picker controls can save
you a lot of time and design effort. Figure 4.9 shows the People Picker control in
action when you configure permissions of a site. The user has the option of writing
the username and clicking the left icon to validate the user or clicking the address
book icon to browse for a user.

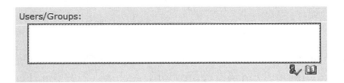

**Figure 4.9 The People
Picker control allows end
users to easily select and
browse users and groups.**

If you need to select a user or a group in your Web Part, you can use the People Picker
control. Let's see how to use this control in a Visual Web Part. This Web Part contains
a picker control that allows you to select a user. Once you do, you can click the Press
Me button to print the name of the selected user (see figure 4.10).

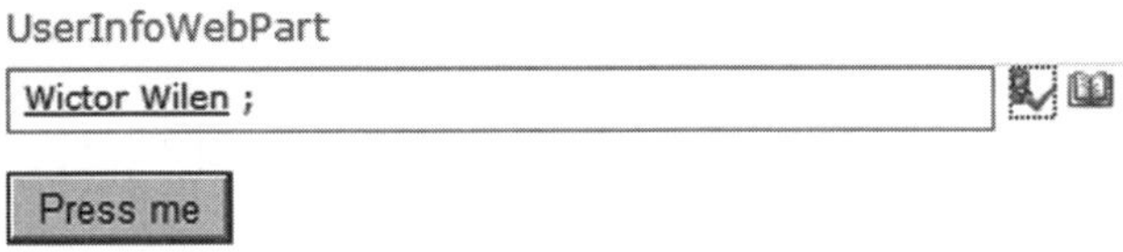

UserInfoWebPart

Wictor Wilen ;

Press me

**Figure 4.10 Use the People
Picker control in your custom
Web Parts to select users and/
or groups.**

The following code snippet shows the code required for this Web Part. You add the code to the user control of the Visual Web Part:

```
<SharePoint:CssRegistration runat="server" Name="Layouts.css" />
<SharePoint:PeopleEditor runat="server" ID="peopleEditor"
    MultiSelect="false"
    SelectionSet="User" />
<br />
<asp:Button ID="btn" runat="server" Text="Press me"
    onclick="btn_Click" />
<br />
<h1><asp:Label runat="server" ID="lbl" /></h1>
```

The first line registers the Layouts.css file. This CSS registration is necessary to achieve the default styling of the picker control. The picker control is added and configured, and then a button control and a label control are added. The button contains a click event in the code-behind that looks like the following code snippet; it adds the name of the selected user to the label:

```
lbl.Text = peopleEditor.Accounts[0].ToString();
```

OTHER USEFUL CONTROLS

We've looked at two useful controls and several more are available in the SharePoint API. Most of them contain very little documentation, and you have to experiment and test to find out how the controls work. Some controls aren't intended to be used by anyone other than Microsoft.

Here are some controls that you should consider using in your Web Parts:

- `CssRegistration`—Registers a CSS file with the page (see the previous code snippet)
- `GroupedDropDownList`—*A grouped cascaded dropdown list*
- `ScriptLink`—Adds JavaScript files to the page to avoid redundant registrations of script files
- `SPDatePickerControl`—A picker control for selecting dates

The `ScriptLink` control is of particular interest. It allows you to register JavaScript files in a page, thus avoiding redundant registrations, such as when you register it in multiple Web Parts on the same page. This control has a few other powerful features as well. For instance, it can handle debug versions of JavaScript files. Add one JavaScript file called MyScript.js and another called MyScript.debug.js into the Layouts folder and use the ScriptLink control to register the MyScript.js file. By default, the MyScript.js file will be used but, if you're debugging your SharePoint web application and the web.config is configured for debugging, the MyScript.debug.js file will be used instead.

```
<SharePoint:ScriptLink
    runat="server"
    Name="MyScript.js"
    Localizable="false"/>
```

This allows you to have one debug version of the JavaScript that might contain debugging code and a production version that might be optimized, obfuscated, or minified (see chapter 9). Notice that the `Localizable` attribute is set to `false`. If you set it to `true`, SharePoint expects the file to exist in the Layouts/*<LCID>* folder, where LCID is the current language identifier of the user. Having the `Localizable` attribute set to `true` and using multiple-language versions of the JavaScript files allows for localization of the JavaScript code. You'll learn more about localization in chapter 6.

To investigate these other controls, take a look at the application pages in the Layouts folder or the SharePoint user controls in the ControlTemplates folder. These files, in combination with the .NET Reflector tool, let you do some interesting investigations of the SharePoint APIs.

4.3 Look and feel of Web Parts

The visual appearance of the user interface is important, as I've stated before. Maintaining a consistent look between your Web Parts and SharePoint is one key to user adoption and will make your Web Parts look more professional.

Adapting your Web Part to the SharePoint user interface look isn't a hard task. There are several simple methods you can apply to make this happen. In the previous section, you learned how to use SharePoint controls to build user interaction. These controls use the styles defined in the SharePoint Cascading Style Sheets (CSS). If you use the ASP.NET controls to build the user interface, by default they're not styled. So I'll show you how to use the standard SharePoint CSS classes in your Web Parts and controls. Once in a while you'll find that those CSS classes aren't enough and you have to add custom CSS styling to your Web Parts. This can be done in several ways. We'll take a look at the various approaches and their pros and cons as well as how you can adapt your CSS files to the new SharePoint themes.

Another important part of styling is web browser adaptation and web compliancy. If you're developing Web Parts for a broad use, you must make sure that your Web Part works with all the major browsers that SharePoint supports. You should also make sure that your Web Parts can be used by people with disabilities. I'll show you this through some relevant examples. Finally, we'll examine a simple way to enhance your Web Parts with icons.

4.3.1 CSS in SharePoint

The SharePoint layout relies on CSS, and you as a developer should take advantage of these CSS classes and definitions. Using the out-of-the-box style sheets will make your solution look SharePoint native and adapt more to the interface. The CSS files are located under the {SharePoint Root} in the TEMPLATE\LAYOUTS\1033\STYLES. The 1033 represents the language code of the installation and may be different for you, or you might have several of these folders if you have multiple language packs installed. The major CSS definitions are contained in corev4.css, which is the main CSS file for the SharePoint 2010 user interface. There's also a file called core.css, which is used when SharePoint is running in the SharePoint 2007 user interface mode. You can store language-independent CSS files in the TEMPLATE\LAYOUTS\STYLES folder to avoid multiple copies of your CSS files.

Whenever you need to style something in your Web Part, I recommend that you take a look at this CSS file to find a class that you can use. A good technique is to use the Developer Tools available in Internet Explorer or the FireBug extension for Firefox. Using these tools, you can select a specific element in a Web Page and inspect the current style and classes of the element. Figure 4.11 shows how the Internet Explorer 8.0 Developer Tools can inspect an element on the page to find out what classes are used and where they're defined.

The default CSS file in SharePoint 2010, corev4.css, contains several CSS classes for Web Parts. These styles are named `ms-WP*` and they define the chrome and title of the Web Part. The body of a Web Part always has the class `ms-WPBody`, and the corev4.css contains definitions for standard HTML elements used beneath an element with that class. For example, all links, header tags, table cells, and table headers have definitions, which means that they normally require no styling.

> **NOTE**   You should never modify the default SharePoint CSS files because doing so isn't supported. Always add custom CSS definitions and files, which override the default styles.

Elements such as text boxes, dropdowns, and buttons don't have any default styling in the Web Part body, which means that you have to set a CSS class for those elements. For input elements, you should use the `ms-input` class, and buttons should use any of the `ms-ButtonHeightWidth`, `ms-NarrowButtonHeightWidth`, or `ms-ButtonHeightWidth2` classes. Figure 4.12 shows the difference between styled and nonstyled input elements in a Web Part.

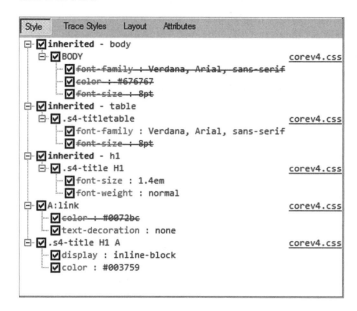

Figure 4.11   Use the Internet Explorer 8.0 Developer Tools when you need to inspect the HTML and CSS elements.

Style vs non-style

| No styles |
| Item 1 ▾ Text   Button |

| SharePoint styles |
| Item 1 ▾ Text   Button |

Figure 4.12 Applying the standard SharePoint CSS classes to input elements will help your Web Part adapt to the SharePoint interface. The top elements have no styles attached and the lower elements use the default SharePoint CSS classes.

4.3.2 Custom style sheets

You'll eventually find that you need to add custom styling to your Web Part that isn't available in any of the default CSS files. You have several approaches for adding this styling to the controls and Web Parts. To illustrate, let's take a look at an ASP.NET Panel, which results in a HTML div element for which we'll set a custom style. We'll set height, width, background color, border, and a change in the font in this Panel object. It should look like figure 4.13.

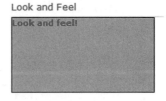

Figure 4.13 Web Parts can use custom style sheets to enhance the user experience.

APPLYING STYLES DIRECT TO THE CONTROLS

The easiest and fastest way is to add the styling directly to the control. You can do this by using the HTML style attribute or the specific properties of the control. When you're applying the styles directly to the control, the code looks like this:

```
<asp:Panel ID="panel"
    runat="server"
    BorderColor="Black"
    BorderWidth="1px"
    BackColor="Silver"
    Font-Bold="true"
    ForeColor="Red"
    Width="200px"
    Height="100px">
Look and feel!
</asp:Panel>
```

As you can see, it takes a lot of code to apply styling to this control using the control's inline properties. It's easy for the developers to read and change, but the resulting HTML in the browser is bad. This sample uses a Visual Web Part; if you'd do the same for a traditional Web Part, you'd need a lot more code. All these attributes on the Panel element automatically create a style attribute on the resulting HTML div element, as shown here:

```
<div id="ctl00_m_g_ced118c3_25b7_45ab_bd42_fb660837b12a_ctl00_panel"
    style="color:Red;background-color:Silver;
    border-color:Black;border-width:1px;border-style:solid;
```

```
        font-weight:bold;height:100px;width:200px;">
        Look and feel!
</div>
```

This `style` attribute consists of approximately 150 characters that are transferred to the client. If you have several of these Web Parts, that number is multiplied. This approach is ineffective and, for high-performance websites, can be a bottleneck.

CREATING CSS CLASSES

The second alternative is to create a CSS class of this style, add a `style` tag to the Web Part or Visual Web Part user control, and then set the `CssClass` property of the `Panel` control. The following listing shows this plan in action.

Listing 4.7   A Web Part with a custom CSS class

```
<style type="text/css">                              Adds style
    .looks {                       Defines      ❶ element
        border:1px solid black;    ❷ CSS class
        background-color:Silver;
        font-weight:bold;
        color:Red;
        width:200px;
        height:100px;
    }
</style>                                         ❸ Specifies CSS
<asp:Panel ID="panel" runat="server" CssClass="looks" >      class to use
Look and feel!
</asp:Panel>
```

An inline `style` element ❶ is defined; it contains the CSS selector class definition ❷. The same styling as in the previous snippet is used. The CSS class is then applied to the `Panel` object ❸ using the `CssClass` attribute.

Using this technique, you separate the design of the control from the interface logic, an approach that makes the code cleaner. The resulting number of characters doesn't decrease that much, unless you're reusing the CSS class several times within your Web Part. This approach is only recommended if you need to change the CSS selectors or class names during runtime. A common example is when the page editor can change the look and feel using properties on the Web Part.

USING CSS FILES

An even better way is to put this CSS class in its own CSS file and deploy that file with the solution. This approach reduces the amount of data transferred from the server by reducing the size of the page and allowing the web browser to cache the CSS file. To add a CSS file to your project, you add the Layouts folder to the project. Do so by right-clicking the project in the Solution Explorer and selecting Add > SharePoint "Layouts" Mapped folder. This will add the Layouts folder to the project, and its contents will be deployed to the Layouts folder in the SharePoint Root. Visual Studio will also, by default, create a subfolder with the name of your project (see figure 4.14). Add the CSS file to the project by right-clicking the subfolder of the Layouts folder and selecting Add > New

Item. In the New Item dialog box, select the Web template category and the Style Sheet template. Enter a name for your style sheet and click the Add button.

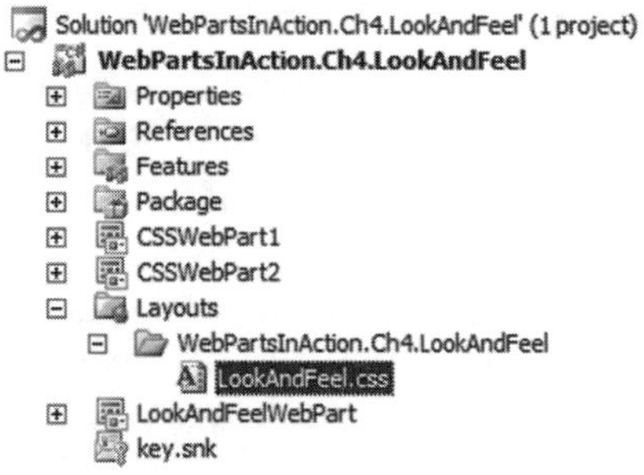

Deploying the CSS files or any files for that matter to the Layouts folder will only work for farm solutions. If you need to add a CSS file to a sandboxed solution, you must deploy the file into a library or folder in the site. We'll discuss this further in chapter 6.

In the style sheet file, add the CSS classes you need in your Web Part. For our sample, copy the CSS class from the previous sample and change the CSS selector name to `looks2` like this:

Figure 4.14 CSS files are added to the project using the Layouts folder. By default, Visual Studio adds a subfolder to the Layouts folder with the name of your project.

```
.looks2 {
    border:1px solid black;
    background-color:Silver;
    font-weight:bold;
    color:Red;
    width:200px;
    height:100px;
}
```

Then, remove the `style` tag in the Visual Web Part user controls so that it only contains the `Panel` control with the `CssClass` attribute. If you deploy this now, the Web Part wouldn't have any styling applied to it because you haven't yet told the Web Part or SharePoint to load this CSS file. Do so now by adding the `CssRegistration` control to the Web Part as follows:

```
<SharePoint:CssRegistration runat="server" ID="cssreg"
    Name="/_layouts/WebPartsInAction.Ch4.LookAndFeel/LookAndFeel.css" />
<asp:Panel ID="panel" runat="server" CssClass="looks2" >
Look and feel!
</asp:Panel>
```

In this snippet, you've added the `CssRegistration` control. The `Name` attribute references the CSS file. The `CssRegistration` control tells SharePoint that you need to have this CSS file for this page, and SharePoint will automatically create the appropriate HTML code to reference it. SharePoint also makes sure that even if you have multiple Web Parts, only one instance of the CSS file will be loaded. If there are no registrations for the CSS, it won't be loaded. You could add the CSS reference in the master page, but the CSS would be loaded even if you didn't need it.

All three methods produce three similarly looking Web Parts. The first way is a quick and dirty solution; the second slightly better with some usage scenarios; and the third one, with the CSS file, is the one I recommend that you use. It has a clear separation of the layout and the control logic and produces efficient code for the browsers.

4.3.3 SharePoint themes

SharePoint 2010 contains a completely new theming engine, which makes it easy to create new themes and produces more efficient CSS files. A *theme* defines a set of colors and fonts. If themes are enabled on your site, SharePoint sends dynamically created CSS files to the user. These CSS files are created from base CSS files and the selected theme. The base CSS files contain standard CSS syntax together with a set of tags that tells SharePoint how to replace colors and fonts with the values from the theme. The theme engine can even change the colors of images used in a style sheet.

> **TIP** You can create themes in SharePoint using Microsoft Office applications such as PowerPoint 2010. You export the theme from PowerPoint or any Office 2010 app as a .thmx file by selecting a design and then saving it to your local machine. The .thmx file is a zip file containing definitions for fonts, colors, and images. You can upload the .thmx file to the Themes Gallery of a site collection and then use it by modifying the site theme.

If you create styles, the Web Part may not fit into the target environment, depending on the theme used. In that case, you should create a style sheet that adapts to the current theme. Do so by creating a CSS file that contains the attributes that replace the colors, fonts, and images in your CSS file with the corresponding values of the theme.

To create this style sheet, you need to add a new CSS file to the SharePoint Layouts mapped folder. Begin by creating a folder under the Layouts folder called 1033. (The number 1033 corresponds to the English US locale and you can switch it for other locales.) Under the 1033 folder, create another folder called Styles and, under that folder, a new folder called Themable, as shown in figure 4.15. Then add a new CSS file to the 1033 folder and edit it so that it looks like the following listing.

Listing 4.8 A themable CSS

```
.looks3 {
/* [ReplaceColor(themeColor:"Dark1")] */     border:1px solid black;
/* [ReplaceColor(themeColor:"Light1")] */    background-color:Silver;
    font-weight:bold;
/* [ReplaceFont(themeFont:"MajorFont")] */   font-family:Verdana;
/* [ReplaceColor(themeColor:"Dark2")] */     color:Red;
    width:200px;
    height:100px;
}
```

In this listing, CSS comments are added to the style sheet, which includes attributes that the SharePoint theme parser uses. The attributes specify an action with parameters. ReplaceColor is used to replace the color specified in the CSS with a color value from the selected theme. In this sample, you use three different theme colors to replace the original ones. To use the theme fonts, you can use the ReplaceFont attribute. If you have images or sprites in your CSS, you can use the RecolorImage attribute to recolor the image and adapt it to the theme.

Figure 4.15   Adding CSS files that contain themed CSS selectors to the correct folder structure under the Layouts folder

The `CssRegistration` of the Web Part needs to be updated so that it understands that you've now created a themed CSS file. The following code snippet shows the Web Part with the new CSS class and with a correctly configured `CssRegistration` control:

```
<SharePoint:CssRegistration runat="server" ID="cssreg"
    EnableCssTheming="true"
    Name="themable/ThemedLookAndFeel.css" />
<asp:Panel ID="panel" runat="server" CssClass="looks3" >
Look and feel!
</asp:Panel>
```

The `CssRegistration` control has a new attribute called `EnableCssTheming`. This attribute tells SharePoint that you'd like to use themes for this CSS. In the `Name` attribute, you only need to specify the name of the CSS file prepended with `themable/`. If you don't have `themable/` before the CSS filename, an exception will be thrown when you render the Web Part.

Once you've deployed this Web Part, you can go in and change the theme of the site and see how the Web Part changes its interface. Figure 4.16 shows what the Web Part looks like when you've enabled one of the out-of-the-box themes.

If you need to make changes to the CSS file after you've deployed it and enabled a theme, you must reenable the theme to make the changes visible. This is because SharePoint dynamically generates the themed files only when the theme changes. You could do this using a feature receiver and use the Theme Engine API to apply the theme while activating the feature and reset it when deactivating. The Theme Engine API is found in the `ThmxTheme` class under the `Microsoft.Share-Point.Utilities` namespace in the `Microsoft.Share-Point` assembly.

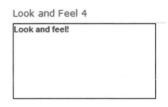

Figure 4.16   Web Parts with custom CSS styles can be configured so that they take advantage of the colors and fonts defined in the SharePoint theme.

4.3.4 *Web compliancy*

SharePoint 2010 has changed a lot in the web compliance area compared to earlier versions. SharePoint 2010 uses well-formed XHTML code out of the box. This allows for better browser compatibility and performance, and also makes it possible for SharePoint to be used by more web browser alternatives such as Firefox and Google Chrome. Previous SharePoint versions suffered from being optimized for Microsoft Internet Explorer and its interpretation of HTML and JavaScript. This made adapting SharePoint to other web browsers difficult; building public websites could be a nightmare.

To maintain this XHTML-compliant state of SharePoint, it's necessary that your Web Parts also conform to the XHTML standard. If you're only using standard ASP.NET controls, these controls will help you with this. But if you're building Visual Web Parts or using `LiteralControl` controls and adding your own HTML elements, you need to be sure to follow these simple rules:

- Elements must not be nested (`<a><b></a></b>` isn't valid whereas `<a><b></b></a>` is valid).
- Elements must be closed (`<br/>` is valid but not `<br>`).
- Element names must be in lowercase (`<br/>` is valid but not `<BR/>`).
- Attributes must be in lowercase (`onclick` is valid but not `onClick`).
- Attributes must always have a value (`selected="true"` is valid but not `selected`).
- Attribute values must be enclosed within quotation marks (`selected="true"` is valid but not `selected=true`).

Another thing to consider is to avoid using `<b>` for bold and `<i>` for italics and similar elements. These types of elements are discouraged in the XHTML standard; instead, you should move such formatting elements to the CSS definitions.

SharePoint 2010 is also, by default, Web Content Accessibility Guidelines (WCAG) 2.0 compliant. WCAG 2.0 is a set of recommendations intended to make web content accessible to people with disabilities such as visual impairment and movement disorders. The guidelines include recommendations that state you should be able to navigate using the keyboard and that all nontext content have a text alternative (such as titles on images). The full guideline can be found at www.w3.org/TR/WCAG20/. I highly recommend that you read through these guidelines and apply them to all your Web Parts.

The following listing is a sample that shows how you can enhance your Web Part and use some of the WCAG 2.0 guidelines.

Listing 4.9 Controls in a Web Part that's enhanced for accessibility

```
<asp:Label ID="label" runat="server"
    Text="Enter text here"
    AssociatedControlID="textBox"/>
<asp:TextBox ID="textBox" runat="server"
    ToolTip="Enter text here"/>
<asp:Button ID="button" runat="server"
    Text="Click me"
```

```
    ToolTip="Click here to submit"
    AccessKey="C"/>
<asp:RequiredFieldValidator ID="rfv"
    ControlToValidate="textBox"
    runat="server"
    ErrorMessage="You need to specify a value" />
```

The sample in this listing contains a text box and a button, both with descriptive tool-tips. The text box is preceded by a `Label` control containing descriptive text and an association (using the `AssociatedControlID`) to the text box. By providing this label and association, you ensure that this control conforms to WCAG 2.0 Guidelines 3.3.2 and 1.3.1. Guideline 2.1 says that all functionality should be accessible using the keyboard. The user can use the Tab key to navigate to the form controls and, in this case, also use the Alt+C keyboard shortcut because the `Button` control has the `AccessKey` attribute specified. By providing a validation control that verifies that the user has entered a value in the text box before submitting the information, using the required field validator the Web Part also conforms to Guideline 3.3.1, Error Identification.

4.3.5   *Web Part icons*

Before finishing this look-and-feel section, I want to show you how to make your Web Part more identifiable using an icon. Each Web Part can have two icons: one that identifies the Web Part in the Web Part Gallery and one that identifies the Web Part on a page. Using an icon is an easy trick to enhance your Web Part and, normally, requires no programming.

The Web Part definition contains two properties that specify the icons. The first property, `CatalogIconImageUrl`, specifies the URL to the file location of the icon image. The image must be a 16×16 pixel image of PNG, GIF, or JPEG format. This icon is used in the Web Part Gallery to identify the Web Part (see figure 4.17). I strongly recommend that you use this catalog icon. It will help your users find the Web Part and it gives a professional impression.

The second icon property, `TitleIconImageUrl`, can be used to show an icon in the Web Part's title bar to the left of the title. The icon should be the same size and type as the catalog icon. I don't think that you should always use this title icon. It can be helpful

Figure 4.17   Using catalog icons for the Web Parts enhances the Web Part Gallery experience and makes it easy for users to find the Web Parts.

in some situations but it can also affect the visual appearance of the Web Part and web page in a negative way if other Web Parts don't have icons.

You have the option of either specifying these icons in the Web Part control description file (.webpart) or by overriding the properties on your Web Part class. The easiest way is to modify the .webpart file.

To add the icons to your Web Part, first include the icon images in your Web Part project. Do so by adding the SharePoint Images mapped folder by right-clicking the project and then selecting Add > SharePoint "Images" Mapped Folder. Visual Studio will then add the folder to the project and create a subfolder with the name of your project. In that subfolder, you add the icon of your choice. Figure 4.18 shows what the Solution Explorer looks like after adding the icon.

After adding the icon or icons, you need to edit your Web Part control description file because you can have different icons for the catalog and the title. The file is located inside your Web Part project item. The following snippet shows what the properties section of the .webpart file looks like after adding the icon properties:

Figure 4.18   Add images to the project using the SharePoint Images mapped folder. Visual Studio creates a subfolder using the name of your project.

```
<properties>
    <property name="Title" type="string">WCAG 2.0 Web Part</property>
    <property name="TitleIconImageUrl" type="string">
        /_layouts/images/WebPartsInAction.Ch4.WCAG/Icon.png</property>
    <property name="CatalogIconImageUrl" type="string">
        /_layouts/images/WebPartsInAction.Ch4.WCAG/Icon.png</property>
</properties>
```

The properties have been added to the Web Part control description file and the `TitleIconImageUrl` points to the location of the title icon image. The `CatalogIconImageUrl` points to the location of the catalog icon image—in this case, the same one.

Using this technique, you can also edit already existing Web Parts and set custom icons for them. To prevent users from changing your icons and adding default icons to your Web Parts, you only need to override the two properties in your Web Part class. Edit the setter of the properties to do nothing and the getters to return a constant location to the icon image files.

4.4   Web Part verbs

In chapter 1, I briefly described the Web Part verbs. A Web Part verb is a Web Part–specific action that's accessible from the Web Part options menu. Typical default verbs are Minimize, Close, and Edit Web Part. A verb can be used to add actions to a Web Part so that it doesn't interfere with the default Web Part interface. For example, say you'd like to implement a print function of a graph Web Part. Instead of adding a button on the Web Part that says Print, you can add a verb that's available in the Web Part options menu. Clicking on this verb could, for instance, take the user to a page that shows the graph in a printer-friendly way.

When using verbs in a Web Part, you have to pay special attention to the event flow, especially if you're using server-side events for the verbs. The events don't execute where you'd expect them to execute, compared to normal server-side events: they're actually performed before the Web Part control tree is built. Once again, it's important to know the flow of events.

4.4.1 Adding verbs to a Web Part

Web Part verbs aren't often used in custom Web Parts probably because most developers aren't aware of them. So I'll show you a simple sample where you add two different verbs (see figure 4.19). The first will be a verb that executes code on the server side and changes the background color of a panel control. The second executes JavaScript code and shows a JavaScript alert box.

To add verbs to a Web Part, you have to override the Verbs property of the Web Part.

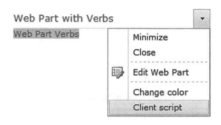

Figure 4.19   Verbs can be added to the Web Part options menu to include actions in the Web Part. The verbs can invoke client-side JavaScript or server-side events.

This property returns a WebPartVerbCollection, which is a collection of WebPartVerb objects. Each WebPartVerb object corresponds to one verb in the Web Part options menu. Listing 4.10 shows the complete Web Part source. The Web Part contains a Label control and we'll change its background color.

Listing 4.10   A Web Part that has two custom verbs

```
public class WebPartWithVerbs : WebPart {
    Label label;
    protected override void CreateChildControls()
        label = new Label();
        label.BackColor = Color.LightBlue;
        label.Text = "Web Part Verbs";
        this.Controls.Add(label);

    }
    public override WebPartVerbCollection Verbs {
        get {
            List<WebPartVerb> verbs = new List<WebPartVerb>();

            WebPartVerb verb1 = new WebPartVerb("Change_Color",
                (sender, args) => {
                    EnsureChildControls();
                    label.BackColor = label.BackColor == Color.LightBlue ?
                        Color.LightYellow : Color.LightBlue;
                });
            verb1.Text = "Change color";
            verb1.Description =
                "Click here to change the background color";
            verbs.Add(verb1);
```

❶ Creates server-side verb

❷ Sets option menu text

```
        WebPartVerb verb2 = new WebPartVerb("Client_Click",
            "alert('You clicked me')");
        verb2.Text = "Client script";
        verbs.Add(verb2);

        return new WebPartVerbCollection(verbs);
    }
  }
}
```

3 Creates JavaScript verb

The `Label` control is created in the `CreateChildControls` method. The verbs are added to the Web Part by overriding the `Verbs` property. First, a list that's used to hold the `WebPartVerb` objects is created. The first verb will be the one that executes server-side code. To create a verb, a `WebPartVerb` object is created and given an id **1**. As the second parameter to the constructor, the code uses a lambda expression for the event code that will switch the background color of the `Label` control. All verbs need a title, and that's set using the `Text` property **2** along with (optionally) a description. The Verb object is finally added to the local list of verbs. The second verb **3** is a client-side script verb. The script is passed as the second argument to the constructor. This second verb is also added to the list. To return a collection of all verbs, a `WebPartVerbCollection` object is created and returned; the list is passed to the constructor as an argument.

That's all you need to add a server-side and a client-side verb to a Web Part. If you deploy the Web Part and click on the Web Part options menu, you'll see the two verbs you created. If you click the Change Color verb, a postback will take place and the background color of the label will change. The script verb doesn't invoke a postback and just executes the JavaScript.

You can customize a verb even further. You can add an icon for each verb to describe the action a bit more, and you can enable or disable them and even hide them. Web Parts can also have a checked state. When the checked state of a Web Part is set to `true`, a check mark appears next to the verb title. You can take advantage of this if you have a Web Part with two display modes—one normal and one detailed—and your verb switches between those modes. Then, when the detailed mode is used, you set the checked state of the verb to `true`. Note that, if you need to persist the changes made via the verbs to the Web Part, you must add custom logic.

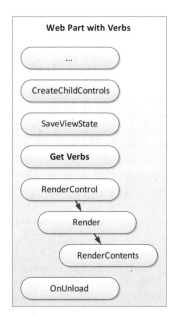

Figure 4.20   SharePoint retrieves the custom verbs after the `SaveViewState` method is called on the Web Part before rendering it.

4.4.2   *Event flow when using Web Part verbs*

If you're using server-side verbs, you need to be aware of the event flow of the Web Part and the verbs. The verbs are loaded after the `SaveViewState` method is called, as figure 4.20 shows.

WARNING The `Verbs` property is retrieved five times, so make sure that you don't perform any heavy operations here or at least implement some temporary caching. The reason that it's called five times is that SharePoint internally accesses the `Verbs` collection four times to check whether it has any verbs before it retrieves them.

When a server-side verb is invoked, the event flow is quite different from a normal postback (see figure 4.21). The `Verbs` property is retrieved after the `OnLoad` method and, after that, the verb events are invoked. This means that, if you're referencing any of the controls built in the `CreateChildControls` method, you have to use the `Ensure-ChildControls` method in your verb event handler. In listing 4.10, we did just that.

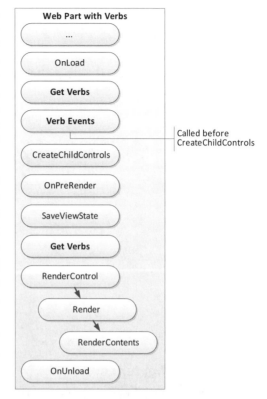

Figure 4.21 The server-side verb events are invoked before the `CreateChildControls` method. The verbs are retrieved two times in this flow: just before the verb events and then once again after the view state is saved.

4.5 Summary

This is one of the core chapters of this book and hopefully a chapter that you'll return to many times. I can't emphasize enough the importance of knowing the event flow of Web Parts and how important it is to build a user interface that adapts to the SharePoint look and feel. Microsoft put a lot of effort into making SharePoint 2010 comply with a lot of standards and to widen the range of browsers that are supported. One single Web Part can destroy all of this.

Visual Web Parts, which you learned about in chapter 3, will allow developers to start building Web Parts in a faster and easier way. This means that we'll see more and more development of Web Parts and with very different results. In the previous versions of SharePoint, it was harder to build Web Parts and that wasn't always bad. It was easier to place all the visual appearance styling in a CSS file than to write tons of code in the Web Part. Because you have direct access to the HTML markup using Visual Web Part, a lot of the UI design that could be replaced with CSS will be placed in the user controls. I don't want you to be one of those who build the Web Parts that others are going to show as bad practice.

In the next chapter, we'll take a look at how you can make your Web Parts customizable and personalizable. That's another chapter that contains essential knowledge for every Web Part developer.

Making
Web Parts customizable

5

This chapter covers

- Adding properties to Web Parts
- Learning the default Web Part properties
- Using custom Editor Parts
- Dealing with complex properties

One of the key features of Web Parts is that the user can customize them. The Web Part infrastructure was designed with this in mind; it provides several features to aid the developer. Web Parts and other controls in ASP.NET have properties that can be used to control the logic, appearance, and behavior. These properties are normally set in the code by the programmer, but Web Parts can be exposed and customized using the web interface.

This chapter shows how you as a developer can expose the properties to your end users so that they can customize or personalize them. You'll learn the default Web Part properties; you'll add your own properties and eventually create a custom interface for interacting with them. Properties can be simple types, such as strings or integers, which SharePoint supports. For advanced types and properties, there's no out-of-the-box support for editing, which means that you need to implement the logic yourself for those.

SharePoint Server 2010 also includes support for targeting Web Parts to groups and audiences. I'll show you how this works behind the scenes and explain how to implement a similar targeting behavior for SharePoint Foundation.

Apart from the actual user interface of the Web Part, the editing of the properties is where your Web Part meets the end user. It's therefore a necessity to have the end-user experience in mind when making your Web Parts customizable.

5.1 *Web Part properties*

A Web Part is based on an ASP.NET control and has properties that can be set by the developer. Compared to regular ASP.NET web controls, the Web Part has properties that are marked with special attributes that allow them to be editable in the web interface. Height and Width are good examples of such properties. You can set the default values of these properties and then the users can modify them using the web interface. The Web Part infrastructure and SharePoint contain the functionality to automatically create an interface for editing the Web Part properties and then save these values. This means that for simple properties you don't need to do anything other than mark the property as customizable.

To understand how Web Parts properties can be customizable, let's start by building a Web Part for which you'll create a few customizable properties. You'll see how to add various attributes to control the customization scope, categorization, and storage of the property values. These properties will use the Web Part infrastructure and the automatically generated web interface for editing them. To make the Web Parts user friendly, you should specify default values, and I'll show you a few options for doing just that. You'll also investigate the problems that might occur with Web Part properties when you're using Visual Web Parts or when you're using your Web Parts as static Web Parts.

To begin, let's use a custom Web Part that reads information from an RSS feed and presents it to the user. This RSS Web Part will initially have the following customizable properties:

- The RSS feed URL
- The number of items to show

Our RSS Web Part will be built in such a way that the properties can be customized using either the web interface or SharePoint Designer 2010. You'll use Web Parts based on the ASP.NET Web Part implementation for the sample of this chapter. But I'll also show you the differences in the Web Part properties when using the SharePoint implementation of Web Parts.

5.1.1 *Adding a property*

Adding a property to a Web Part involves a few simple steps. First, you define the actual property in the class by creating a public read and write property. Then, you have to decorate this property with Web Part–specific attributes so that the Web Part infrastructure can determine which properties will be available to the user.

To create the RSS Web Part, create a new project in Visual Studio using the Empty Project template and then add a Web Part item to that project. Give the Web Part the name of `RssWebPart`. You should select Farm Solution for this project, because later you'll use functionality not available in the sandbox. Once you've set up your project, navigate to and open the Web Part code file.

The first property you'll add is the URL to the RSS feed. This is a string property; call it `RssFeedUrl` and make it public. Your code should look like this when you're done:

```
public string RssFeedUrl {
    get;
    set;
}
```

Note that you're using the automatic getter and setter notation, introduced in C# 3.0, just to make the code look cleaner. If you deploy your Web Part after just adding this public property and then choose to customize the Web Part, you won't see the property in the Web Part tool pane. This is because you haven't yet told SharePoint that this is a customizable property. The property would still be available if you created the Web Part programmatically, or declaratively in an ASPX page. For example, you could use the following code snippet in an ASPX page in SharePoint using SharePoint Designer, which would instantiate the Web Part and set the value of the property:

```
<webparts:RssWebPart
    runat="server"
    id="rssWebPart"
    RssFeedUrl="http://feeds2.feedburner.com/WictorWilen"/>
```

To further customize this Web Part, add another property that tells the Web Part how many blog posts to show from the RSS feed. Use an `int` for the property and call it `ItemCount`:

```
public int ItemCount {
    get;
    set;
}
```

You'd like these properties to show up in the tool pane when editing the properties of the Web Part. Do this by adding two attributes to the two Web Part properties: `Web-Browsable` and `Personalizable`. For properties that have the `WebBrowsable` attribute, the Web Part framework in SharePoint will automatically generate a user interface and a valid input field, based on the type of the property. Because the first property is a string, SharePoint will generate a standard text input field. For the second property, another input field will be generated for inserting integers.

The `Personalizable` attribute tells the Web Part Manager that the value of this property is going to be stored in the SharePoint content database. SharePoint takes care of storing and retrieving these values. The parameter to the attribute, which you'll look at in section 5.1.7, tells SharePoint how to store this attribute and in which mode it can be edited. You'd like these properties to be available in Shared mode, so specify that in the parameter. The RSS feed URL property should look like this after you add the attributes:

```
[WebBrowsable]
[Personalizable(PersonalizationScope.Shared)]
public string RssFeedUrl {
    get;
    set;
}
```

You need to do the same for the `ItemCount` property. If you now build and deploy this Web Part, you'll be able to edit it. You can change and save the properties that appear under the Miscellaneous section in the tool pane, which uses the automatically generated web interface, as shown in figure 5.1.

You can now set the property values and click Apply to apply them and stay in Edit mode. If you click OK, the property pane will close and save your properties.

The `Personalizable` attribute can only be used on properties that match the following rules:

- They must be public.
- They must have both the set and get accessors.
- They can't have parameters.
- They can't be indexed.

Now open your site in SharePoint Designer and choose to edit the page in which you added the Web Part. Select the Web Part you just added and then, in the Ribbon, select View > Task Panes > Tag Properties. You'll see a new pane (called Tag Properties) listing all the Web Part properties. Scroll down to the Misc section and you'll see the custom properties, as shown in figure 5.2. SharePoint Designer will pick up all public properties and make them available for editing using the Tag Properties pane. You can also manually edit a property as an attribute to the Web Part tag in Source Code mode.

Figure 5.1 Custom Web Part properties with the `WebBrowsable` attribute applied will be visible in the Miscellaneous section of the tool pane. The tool pane interface for the properties has been automatically generated by SharePoint based on the type of the properties.

Figure 5.2 The Tag Properties panel in SharePoint Designer can be used to change the values of a Web Part or a control. This figure shows the custom properties of the custom RSS Web Part in the Misc category.

If you remove the `WebBrowsable` attribute from one of the properties and redeploy your solution, you'll see that it disappears from the tool pane in the web browser. The property will still be available from SharePoint Designer 2010. You can use this technique to hide certain properties from users who only access the Web Parts using the web interface. As a good practice, you should use the `WebBrowsable` attribute and set the parameter to `false` if you don't want to show it in the web interface:

```
[WebBrowsable(false)]
```

This will make your code easier to understand because it shows that you've made a choice not to show it in the web interface (and not that you just forgot to add the attribute!).

5.1.2 *Customizing the property*

You can see in figure 5.1 that the properties are displayed using the name of the property, which typically isn't user friendly. To fix this, there's another attribute you can use: `WebDisplayName` allows you to specify a friendly name to display in the web interface. To further enhance the user experience, add the `WebDescription` attribute, which lets you enter a brief description of the property. Figure 5.3 shows how your Web Part should look like after you add a custom display name.

Figure 5.3 The automatically generated tool pane of the RSS Web Part uses the attributes of the custom properties to generate the input fields and their descriptions.

The `WebDisplayName` and `WebDescription` attributes are added with the `WebBrowsable` and `Personalizable` attributes on your properties. The final code should look like the code in listing 5.1.

Listing 5.1 The two configurable Web Part properties for the RSS Web Part

```
[WebBrowsable]
[Personalizable(PersonalizationScope.Shared)]
[WebDisplayName("RSS feed Url")]
[WebDescription("Enter the Url to the RSS feed")]
public string RssFeedUrl {
    get;
    set;
}
[WebBrowsable]
[Personalizable(PersonalizationScope.Shared)]
[WebDisplayName("Items to show")]
[WebDescription("The number of RSS feed items to show")]
public int ItemCount {
    get;
    set;
}
```

To view the changes, click Build > Run to compile, deploy, and start the debugger. Once Internet Explorer has started, you can add the Web Part to a page, select it, and edit it if so desired. Your tool pane should look like figure 5.3. Hover your cursor over any of the input fields to see the description. SharePoint Designer will still display the actual property name. Note that if you don't specify the `WebDescription` attribute, the display name will be used as the description.

5.1.3 Custom categories

All properties that you make available for editing in the web interface are categorized under Miscellaneous by default. This category is the default used when you haven't specified any category for the property. To specify a category on the Web Part, you add another attribute to the Web Part called `SPWebCategoryName`. This attribute takes as a parameter a string that's the name of the category. To add `SPWebCategoryName`, you have to include the namespace `Microsoft.SharePoint.WebPartPages` in the source file by using the `using` statement. But when you compile your project, you'll get an error telling you that there's an ambiguous reference to the `WebPart` class. This is because the Share-Point Web Part implementation resides in that newly added namespace. To work around the issue, you should edit the `using` statement so it looks like this:

```
using SP = Microsoft.SharePoint.WebPartPages;
```

This creates an alias for that namespace and you can add the attribute to your properties as follows instead of writing out the full namespace:

```
[SP.SPWebCategoryName("Feed Properties")]
```

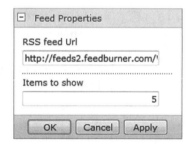

Deploy your solution and go back to the page where you added the Web Part and edit it. When the property pane is open, you can see that your properties are no longer in the Miscellaneous section but in the category called Feed Properties, as shown in figure 5.4. SharePoint Designer will still categorize these properties in the Misc section, as in figure 5.2.

You can also use the `Category` attribute defined in `System.ComponentModel`. This attribute is defined in the Microsoft .NET Framework and doesn't require any references to the SharePoint

Figure 5.4 Custom categories can be applied to properties using the `SPWebCategoryName` attribute.

assemblies. It's used by the property tool pane in SharePoint Designer and also works in the SharePoint web interface. The SharePoint category attribute has precedence over the .NET Framework attribute in the web browser. If you don't specify the .NET Framework `Category` attribute, the property will be shown in the Misc section in SharePoint Designer. Using both of these attributes at the same time allows you to have your property appear in different categories in the web interface and SharePoint Designer editor. Read more about attribute precedence in section 5.1.5.

> **NOTE** If you try to add custom properties to one of the default categories in SharePoint, your property will end up in the Miscellaneous section.

5.1.4 *Default values on properties*

At this point, you haven't added a body to the Web Part so that it displays the configured feed, so let's do that next. The content of the Web Part is generated in the `CreateChildControls` method, in which you add the code shown in listing 5.2. This code requires you to add a `using` statement to the `System.Linq` and `System.Xml.Linq` namespaces.

Listing 5.2 Building the interface of the RSS Web Part

```
protected override void CreateChildControls() {
    XElement feed = XElement.Load(this.RssFeedUrl);

    BulletedList bulletedList = new BulletedList();
    this.Controls.Add(bulletedList);
    bulletedList.DisplayMode = BulletedListDisplayMode.HyperLink;

    var items = feed.Descendants("item").Take(this.ItemCount);

    foreach (var item in items) {
        bulletedList.Items.Add(new ListItem() {
            Text = item.Descendants("title").First().Value,
            Value = item.Descendants("link").First().Value
        });
    }
    this.ChildControlsCreated = true;
}
```

The RSS feed is loaded using the `XElement.Load` method. The `BulletedList` control is used to show the feed items; its display mode is set to `HyperLink` so that the user can click each item in the list. Each feed item is then retrieved using LINQ to XML. Using the LINQ extension methods `Descendants` and `Take` the first `ItemCount` number of `item` elements are fetched from the feed. For each feed item, the method will create a new `ListItem` object. The method sets the object's `Text` property to the feed item's title and the `Value` property to its URL.

If you build and deploy this Web Part and add it to a page, you'll get an `Argument-NullException`. This is because `RssFeedUrl` is a `string` whose default value is `null`, and when the Web Part tries to load the feed, it uses the default value (`null`) of the string type. To fix this issue, you can define a different default value—by initializing it in the constructor, for example. But even if you add a new default value, you must take care of any exceptions in case the user makes an invalid entry.

The code in listing 5.2 has no error handling or default values, which will cause it to throw an exception. So let's continue adding code to the listing.

DEFAULT VALUES IN THE WEB PART DESCRIPTION FILE

The most common method of setting default values is to use the Web Parts control description file and set the default values using the `property` element. You do this in

Visual Studio by opening the .webpart file, located under the Web Part node in the Solution Explorer. To add a default value to a property, you add a new `property` element with a `name` attribute and a value. For the RSS Web Part, add two `property` elements to the file, like this:

```
<property name="RssFeedUrl">
http://feeds2.feedburner.com/WictorWilen/</property>
<property name="ItemCount">5</property>
```

If you deploy the solution and add the Web Part to a page, you'll see five blog posts from the specified feed. When you edit the Web Part, you can enter new values to override the default values. Any updates to the default values in the .webpart file won't be reflected in Web Parts that you've already added to the page—they're copied to the Web Part when you insert it to a page.

If you'd like to supply the user with two or more property configurations of your Web Part, you can add a new .webpart file to your solution. First, right-click the .webpart file in your Web Part item in the Solution Explorer and choose Copy. Then right-click the Web Part item and choose Paste. You have now cloned the .webpart file. Rename the new file to `RssWebPart2.xml`. When you copy the file or add a new .webpart file to the Web Part item, Visual Studio detects this and automatically updates the elements manifest for the item. If you open the elements.xml file, you should see that the `Module` element looks like this:

```
<Module Name="RssWebPart" List="113" Url="_catalogs/wp">
    <File Path="RssWebPart\RssWebPart.webpart"
          Url="RssWebPart.webpart"
          Type="GhostableInLibrary">
      <Property Name="Group" Value="Custom" />
    </File>
    <File Path="RssWebPart\RssWebPart2.webpart"
          Url="RssWebPart2.webpart"
          Type="GhostableInLibrary">
      <Property Name="Group" Value="Custom" />
    </File>
</Module>
```

Open the new .webpart file and change the values of the `RssFeedUrl` and `ItemCount` properties to `http://feeds2.feedburner.com/SharePointWebPartsInAction` and 5, respectively. You should also change the `Title` property so that you can easily see the difference between the two Web Parts. When you deploy this package to the Web Part Gallery, the site collection will be populated with two configurations of the same Web Part.

HARDCODED DEFAULT VALUES

Another approach for default values, which doesn't exclude the former one, is to initialize the properties in your Web Part class—for example, in the constructor. You should always have initial values of your properties that are configured so that you get no exceptions or other failures in your Web Part.

Default values are most important for reference typed properties, such as strings, which have no default values. Those properties are initialized as null and can cause null reference exceptions. Value typed properties such as integers and enumerations always have a default value. It's a good idea to set a default value for those as well so that the Web Part is configured even if it has no Web Parts control description file.

THE DEFAULTVALUE ATTRIBUTE

The `DefaultValue` attribute won't set any default values for your Web Part. This attribute is only used by visual designers or code generators to provide default values to member properties when inserting code (although it might be a good practice to use this attribute in case your Web Part is used in these scenarios). To set a default value on the `ItemCount` property, add this attribute line to the property:

```
[DefaultValue(10)]
```

HANDLING MISSING PROPERTY VALUES

There are situations when you can't have any default values or you'd like the user to configure the Web Part as soon as it's added to the page. A good convention is to inform users that the Web Part needs configuration before they use it. SharePoint has a JavaScript function that displays the Web Part's tool pane, which the user can open to edit the properties of the Web Part. You can add a link that invokes this JavaScript method to your Web Part interface if the Web Part isn't configured. In the `Create-ChildControls` method of your Web Part, add a check if the feed URL is null or an empty string. Then add the link with the JavaScript, as in listing 5.3. Insert this code *before* the code from listing 5.2 that you previously added.

Listing 5.3   Handling of missing or invalid values in a Web Part

```
if (String.IsNullOrEmpty(this.RssFeedUrl)) {
    HyperLink hl = new HyperLink();
    hl.NavigateUrl = String.Format(
        "javascript:ShowToolPane2Wrapper('Edit','129','{0}');",
        this.ID);
    hl.ID  = String.Format("MsoFrameworkToolpartDefmsg_{0}", this.ID);
    hl.Text = "Click here to configure the Web Part";
    this.Controls.Add(hl);
}
```

This snippet checks if the feed URL is null. If it is, the code creates a link control with a SharePoint built-in JavaScript function that opens the tool pane. The JavaScript needs the id of the Web Part to open the correct tool pane. Figure 5.5 shows how the Web Part will look if it has no default values using the technique just described.

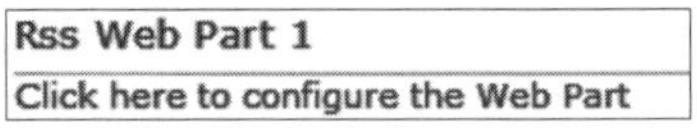

Rss Web Part 1
Click here to configure the Web Part

Figure 5.5   A nonnconfigured Web Part should show a user-friendly interface that helps the user configure it.

NOTE   The `ShowToolPane2Wrapper` JavaScript method is an internal and unsupported method in SharePoint that might be deprecated or changed in future versions.

5.1.5   Properties used in the Web Part class and defined in SharePoint

The SharePoint-based Web Part also uses attributes to customize how properties are used and their appearance. There's some dissimilarity, though, in which attributes are used. The attributes `WebDisplayName` and `WebDescription` were introduced in the ASP.NET 2 Framework and Web Parts based on the SharePoint implementation used the `FriendlyName` and `Description` attributes, respectively. The `FriendlyName` attribute is defined in the `Microsoft.SharePoint` assembly in the `Microsoft.SharePoint.WebPartPages` namespace. The `Description` attribute is, just like the previously discussed `Category` attribute, defined in the .NET Framework.

Web Parts based on the SharePoint implementation can also use a special attribute called `Resource` for localization. The attribute takes three parameters containing resource identifiers for the name, category, and description. SharePoint then uses the `LoadResource` method in the SharePoint Web Part implementation to load the localized value. This attribute can't be used on ASP.NET-based Web Parts.

SharePoint 2010 still supports all these variants for backward compatibility. You can even combine the different attributes, but then it's important to know which attribute SharePoint prioritizes first. Table 5.1 shows in which order SharePoint uses the attributes.

Table 5.1   The order in which SharePoint selects the attributes on Web Part properties when displayed in the web interface

Order of usage	Display name	Description	Category
1	WebDisplayName	WebDescription	SPWebCategoryName
2	Resources	Resources	Resources
3	FriendlyName	Description	Category

Note that only Web Parts derived from the SharePoint Web Part implementation can use the `Resources` attribute. Also, don't forget to use both the `SPWebCategoryName` and `Category` attributes to support categories in SharePoint Designer. As a best practice don't use the `Resources` attribute in your Web Parts because it might be deprecated in future versions.

5.1.6   Properties in Visual Web Parts

If you're building a Visual Web Part, you have to define the properties in the Web Part class, not the user control. SharePoint or SharePoint Designer won't pick up or store properties that are defined in any underlying control. You need to include extra plumbing when working with Visual Web Parts and Web Part properties to ensure that the properties are copied or referenced to the user control (if it needs the properties). The values of the properties exist in the Web Part before the `OnInit` method, as you saw in chapter 4, so you can use the property value in the `CreateChildControls` method.

For a Visual Web Part that should print the value of a Web Part property in the user control, you need to copy the value from the Web Part to the user control. One way to accomplish this, is to add a public property on the user control that exposes the `Text` property of a `Label` control as follows:

```
public string LabelText {
    get {
        return label1.Text;
    }
    set {
        label1.Text = value;
    }
}
```

This property is set in the `CreateChildControls` of the Web Part when the user control is created. The following code also casts the control loaded by `Page.LoadControl` into the type of the user control:

```
protected override void CreateChildControls() {
    VisualWebPart1UserControl control = Page.LoadControl(_ascxPath)
        as VisualWebPart1UserControl;
    control.LabelText = this.Text;
    Controls.Add(control);
}
```

As you can see, you need to do more coding if you want to use the values of Web Part properties in the Visual Web Part user control.

5.1.7   *Personalization*

SharePoint has the power to use personalized pages and Web Parts. Personalization support allows users to configure the content and Web Parts, resulting in a dynamic and interesting interface. Personalization isn't always a good thing, though; it demands maintenance and support and could possibly break Web Part applications. As a Web Part developer, you have the ability to control what parts can be customized and what parts can be personalized.

The `Personalizable` attribute controls whether a property can be edited by users and specifies whether its value needs to be stored (serialized into the content database). You used it in the previous sample to set the property to be editable by setting the personalization scope to Shared. When a property has the personalization scope set to Shared, it can only be changed by authors who are permitted to edit the page. You can also set the scope to User, which is the default mode. If the scope is set to User, then any user with personalization permissions can change the value of this property. User-scoped changes are only reflected on the page of the user who changed the property, not for any other user. When a user is editing a page or Web Part in Personal mode, only properties scoped to User can be changed. If a property has Shared scope, it can be edited in both Personal and Shared mode.

Web Parts based on the SharePoint implementation might have the `WebPartStorage` attribute instead of the `Personalizable` attribute. The `WebPartStorage` attribute is still valid for backward compatibility, but when you're upgrading or building a new Web Part, use the `Personalizable` attribute. The `Personalizable` attribute will take precedence over the `WebPartStorage` attribute once the Web Part has been modified by the user.

5.1.8 Storing URLs in Web Part properties

Storing a URL in a Web Part is as simple as creating a property with the `string` or `System.Uri` type. The Visual Studio Code Analysis tools suggest using the `Uri` type, because it's a part of the .NET design guidelines from Microsoft.

Storing URLs to SharePoint can be problematic if the Web Part is exported and then imported on another server. The address to the server might be different and that might potentially break your application. To resolve this issue, use the `ManagedLink` attribute. This attribute, which can be set on properties that have a Shared personalization scope, converts absolute addresses into server relative addresses, and vice versa. The attribute has two parameters:

- The `Fixup` parameter indicates whether the value of the property should be corrected by removing redundant `..` and `.` characters as well as canonicalizing the protocol and server address.
- The `ConvertServerLinksToRelative` specifies whether the links should be converted from server links to relative links. Both these properties are set to `true` by default. The following property would convert http://server/SitePages/Home.aspx to /SitePages/Home.aspx:

```
[WebBrowsable(true)]
[Personalizable(PersonalizationScope.Shared)]
[Microsoft.SharePoint.WebPartPages.ManagedLink]
public Uri ManagedFixup {
    get;
    set;
}
```

Even if an absolute URL is entered in the property, SharePoint will store and display the URL as a site-relative URL. If the `ConvertServerLinksToRelative` is set to `false`, the property will be stored as is but with a canonicalized server address. For instance, http://SERVER/default.aspx will be converted to http://server/default.aspx.

5.1.9 Static Web Parts

Static Web Parts—that is, Web Parts that don't exist in a Web Part zone—can't be customized or personalized. Their properties can be set programmatically but not in the user interface, and the values aren't stored in SharePoint.

Say you've built your Web Part so that it's in a nonconfigured state and provides the user with a link to open the tool pane for the Web Part. As shown in listing 5.3 earlier, the user will get an error when clicking the link for a static Web Part. The error is thrown because static Web Parts can't be edited in the web interface. To prevent this configuration link from being rendered and thus avoiding the error, you could use the IsStatic property of the Web Part, as in listing 5.4. This property returns true for all Web Parts that are static.

Listing 5.4   Handling of invalid configuration in a static Web Part

```
if (String.IsNullOrEmpty(this.RssFeedUrl)) {
    if (this.IsStatic) {
        Label label = new Label();
        label.Text = "Not configured";
        this.Controls.Add(label);
    }
    else {
        // Code from listing 5.3
    }
}
```

When you need controls outside of the zone, Web Parts aren't always the best solution. Instead, consider using standard web controls or other approaches such as delegate controls.

> **TIP**   You can learn more about delegate controls at the Microsoft MSDN site: http://msdn.microsoft.com/library/ms463169.aspx

5.1.10   *Web Part previews*

When you click on a Web Part in the Web Part Gallery, the Web Part preview page (/_layouts/WPPrevw.aspx) appears with a preview of the Web Part. This page renders the Web Part as a static Web Part using the default properties from the Web Part control description file.

The preview is generated by the WebPartPreview control that loads the Web Part as a static Web Part. To create a custom preview of your Web Part, use the following code in the CreateChildControls method:

```
if ( this.Parent is WebPartPreview ||
    base.DesignMode ) {
        this.Controls.Add(new Literal() {
            Text = "Preview mode"
        });
    }
```

This snippet checks whether the parent control is a WebPartPreview control or whether it's been generated in a designer such as SharePoint Designer or Visual Studio. If one of these conditions is true, the code builds the preview of the Web Part.

5.1.11   *Error handling in Web Part properties*

When working with Web Part properties, you'll need to have some kind of error handling for the properties. For instance, you might have a string property that should be a valid URL or a decimal number. It's a good practice to handle the validation of these properties directly in the property instead of in the user interface code. You have two options:

- Use Editor Parts (explained in section 5.3)
- Use the WebPartPageUserException

The WebPartPageUserException is a specific exception that's handled by the Web Part infrastructure and shows a friendly error message in the user interface instead of the default SharePoint error message. Let's say that you have a Web Part property that must contain a valid URL and that property is defined as a string. A correct way to implement this property is as follows:

```
private string m_url;
[WebBrowsable]
[Personalizable(PersonalizationScope.Shared)]
public string RssFeedUrl {
    get{
        return m_url;
    }
    set {
        if(!Uri.IsWellFormedUriString(value, UriKind.Absolute)) {
            throw new WebPartPageUserException("Not a well formed URL");
        }
        m_url = value;
    }
}
```

The setter method of this property uses the static method IsWellFormedUriString of the Uri class to verify that the URL is a valid absolute URI. If it's not, a WebPartPageUserException is thrown with an error message that informs the user of the error; otherwise, the value is accepted and stored in the private variable.

5.2   Common Web Part properties

All Web Parts are derived from the WebPart class defined in the System.Web.UI.WebControls.WebParts namespace and have a set of common properties. These properties are divided into three main groups:

- Appearance
- Layout
- Advanced

You can use these properties when you're developing your Web Parts. You can also override them if you need to make any changes. You're going to look at the three groups and focus on some of the important default properties. Each of these groups is handled by special SharePoint controls, which can't be modified.

5.2.1   Appearance properties

The Appearance group is focused on the general layout of the Web Part with properties such as Title, Width, and Height. Title is displayed in the header of the Web Part. Width and Height are by default set to adapt to the Web Part zones but can be set to fixed sizes.

This group also contains *chrome* configurations. The chrome is everything surrounding the Web Part, such as the title bar and border. You can specify the type and state of the chrome. Chrome State can be set to either Minimized or Normal and can be changed from the Web Part Options menu as well. Chrome Type specifies whether the border and/or title of the Web Part are shown. Table 5.2 lists all available properties in the Appearance group.

Table 5.2 Appearance Web Part properties

Property name	Description
Title	Specifies the title of the Web Part.
Height	Specifies the height of the Web Part. The default is Adjustable Height.
Width	Specifies the width of the Web Part. The default is Adjustable Width.
Chrome State	Specifies the initial state of the Web Part. Possible values are Normal and Minimized.
Chrome Type	Specifies the style of the chrome. Possible values are Default, None, Title and Border, Title Only and Border Only.

5.2.2 *Layout properties*

The Layout group contains configuration options related to how the Web Part is placed and how it acts within the Web Part zone. Using these properties, you can change the zone of the Web Part and its position within the zone. These configurations are seldom used because the rich web interface has support for dragging and dropping the Web Parts. Most of these properties are only valid for Shared mode.

One interesting feature in the Layout group is the ability to hide a Web Part. A hidden Web Part isn't displayed in the browser but can still execute actions and connect with other Web Parts. In comparison, a closed Web Part doesn't act at all on a page. All available properties in the Layout group are listed in table 5.3.

Table 5.3 Layout Web Part properties

Property name	Description
Hidden	Specifies whether the Web Part is visible. Can't be used in wiki content zones.
Direction	Specifies the direction of text in the Web Part.
Zone	Specifies in which zone the Web Part is located.
Zone index	Specifies the index of the Web Part in the zone. Can't be changed in wiki content zones.

5.2.3 *Advanced properties*

The Advanced group contains specific Web Part configuration options. You can use these properties to prohibit users from closing or hiding Web Parts and control what properties can be exported. This group is only available in Shared mode.

You can control which properties can be exported by the users, when using the Export command from the Web Parts menu. The Export Mode property in the Advanced group controls what's exported; this property has the following possible values:

- *Do Not Allow*—The Web Part can't be exported and the Export command is hidden in the user interface.
- *Export All Data*—All properties are exported.
- *Non-Sensitive Data Only*—Only nonsensitive properties are exported.

When you have properties that you don't want users to export, such as a password or other sensitive information, you can set the property to Sensitive. To do so, use the `Personalizable` attribute and set the `IsSensitive` parameter of the attribute to `true`. The default value is `false`. The following attribute will make the property a user-scoped property, and the second parameter sets the `IsSensitive` property of the attribute to `true`:

```
[Personalizable(PersonalizationScope.User, true)]
```

A property with a `Personalizable` attribute configured like this won't be exported if the `ExportMode` property of the Web Part is set to `NonSensitiveData`.

The export mode can be changed using the advanced properties, but if you want to prevent administrators or developers from changing this value, you can override the `ExportMode` property and hardcode the `NonSensitiveData` value. The following snippet shows how:

```
public override WebPartExportMode ExportMode {
    get {
        return WebPartExportMode.NonSensitiveData;
    }
    set {
    }
}
```

The advanced properties contain other configuration properties that you can set, as shown in table 5.4.

Table 5.4 Advanced Web Part properties

Property name	Description
Allow Minimize	Determines whether the Web Part can be minimized.
Allow Close	Allows users to close the Web Part. Set to `false` to prevent users from closing the Web Part.
Allow Hide	Indicates whether the Web Part can be hidden.
Allow Zone Change	Indicates whether the zone of the Web Part can be changed.
Allow Connect	Controls whether Web Part connections can be used for this Web Part.
Allow Editing in Personal View	Controls whether the user can change this Web Part in the personal view.

Table 5.4   Advanced Web Part properties *(continued)*

Property name	Description
Help URL	Specifies the URL for this Web Part's help page. The help link appears in the Web Parts menu when you enter it.
Help Mode	Determines how the browser opens the Help URL.
Catalog Icon Image URL	Specifies the icon shown in the Web Part Gallery.
Title Icon Image URL	Specifies the icon shown in the Web Part title.
Import Error Message	The error message that is displayed when an error occurs while importing this Web Part.

In SharePoint Server Standard or Enterprise edition, the advanced properties have an additional property called Target Audiences. Audience is a feature of SharePoint Server that allows you to have dynamic groups based on a set of rules. This property allows you to select an Audience for this Web Part; no other Audiences will see the Web Part. This property is added by a runtime filter in the Server edition of SharePoint. You can create your own runtime filter if you need a custom filter or if you'd like to add similar functionality to SharePoint Foundation. You'll learn how in section 5.5.

5.3   *Custom Editor Parts*

So far, you've covered how you can use a declarative programming approach to make your Web Parts customizable. Using simple property types and specific attributes, SharePoint takes care of creating a user interface for customizing the Web Parts. You now know how to create a property that can be edited by users and administrators. But if you'd like to have validation on your input fields or have dependencies between them, this approach doesn't work. To be able to add these functionalities to the properties, you have to create a custom Editor Part. You've already seen a few Editor Parts in the previous section:

- The tool pane consists of Editor Parts.
- The Layout property, `LayoutEditorPart`, is an Editor Part.
- The properties that you marked as `WebBrowsable` appear in another Editor Part, the `CustomPropertyToolPart`.

This section shows you how to create custom Editor Parts with validation and properties. You'll continue working with our RSS Web Part and add a custom Editor Part to it. To learn how to validate your input and create dependencies between the properties, you'll extend the functionality of the RSS Web Part.

> **TIP**   With the .NET Reflector tool, from Red Gate Software Ltd., you can inspect and browse the contents of any assembly. To understand how the built-in Editor Parts work, take a look at `CustomPropertyToolPart`, `LayoutEditorPart`, and other Editor Parts in the `Microsoft.SharePoint` assembly. You can download the Reflector tool for free at http://www.red-gate.com/products/reflector/.

5.3.1   Create a custom Editor Part

In our RSS Web Part, two properties are simple input values. They work as they should without validation, but the user could write anything in those text boxes. The feed URL should be validated so that it's a correct URL and the number of items to show should always be an integer equal to or larger than 1.

To create a custom Editor Part, the first thing you do is add a new class to your Web Part item. Right-click the Web Part item and select Add > Class. For this example, enter the name `RssWebPartEditorPart` as the name of the class.

To create the Editor Part, make sure that your class inherits from the base `Editor-Part` class, defined in the `System.Web.UI.WebControls.WebParts` namespace. To inherit from the `EditorPart`, you edit the class definition like this:

```
class RssWebPartEditorPart: EditorPart
```

The user interface of the Editor Part is built by creating the input fields in the `CreateChildControls` method, as shown in listing 5.5.

Listing 5.5   Creation of the controls in the Editor Part

```
protected TextBox m_feedUrl;
protected TextBox m_itemCount;

protected override void CreateChildControls() {
    m_feedUrl = new TextBox(){ID = "feedUrl"};
    m_itemCount = new TextBox() {ID = "itemCount"};

    this.Controls.Add( new Label() {
        Text = "Feed Url:<br/>",
        AssociatedControlID = m_feedUrl.ID
    });
    this.Controls.Add(m_feedUrl);

    this.Controls.Add( new Label() {
        Text = "<br/>Items to show:<br/>",
        AssociatedControlID = m_itemCount.ID
    });
    this.Controls.Add(m_itemCount);

    this.Title = "Feed Properties";

    base.CreateChildControls();
    this.ChildControlsCreated = true;
}
```

The input fields are defined as `protected` and created in `CreateChildControls`. The controls are then added to the child controls collection. The Title property is set to the title of the Editor Part; this is especially important if you have several Editor Parts. Notice how the `Label` controls are added and associated with the input form controls.

To read information from the Web Part that's being edited, the `EditorPart` has a method called `SyncChanges`. You have to override this method and read the property values from the Web Part and then set the values of the local Editor Part controls, as in listing 5.6.

Listing 5.6   The `SyncChanges` method

```
public override void SyncChanges() {
    EnsureChildControls();
    RssWebPart webPart = this.WebPartToEdit as RssWebPart;
    if (webPart != null) {
        m_feedUrl.Text= webPart.RssFeedUrl;
        m_itemCount.Text = webPart.ItemCount.ToString();
    }
}
```

The `SyncChanges` method retrieves the Web Part that it's associated with and then assigns the values from the Web Part to the local controls.

The property values are written back to the Web Part when you click OK or Apply in the tool pane. When saved, the `EditorPart` invokes a method called `ApplyChanges` that you need to implement so that it copies the values from the Editor Part to the Web Part. The Listing 5.7 shows you how this method is implemented.

Listing 5.7   The `ApplyChanges` method

```
public override bool ApplyChanges() {
    EnsureChildControls();
    RssWebPart webPart = this.WebPartToEdit as RssWebPart;
    if (webPart != null) {
        webPart.RssFeedUrl = m_feedUrl.Text;
        webPart.ItemCount = Int32.Parse(m_itemCount.Text);
    }
    return true;
}
```

Just as in the `SyncChanges` method, you have to retrieve the associated Web Part and then set the properties of the Web Part to the values of the local controls. Finally, you have to return `true` to indicate that the operation was successful. If the `ApplyChanges` method returns `false`, then the `SyncChanges` method won't be invoked, because you instruct SharePoint that an error has occurred.

This is all that's needed to create the custom Editor Part. The next step is to associate the Editor Part with the Web Part, instead of the automatically generated controls.

5.3.2   *Add the custom Editor Part to the Web Part*

The Editor Part you created is currently only a class defined in the solution and has no connection to the Web Part. To make the Web Part use this Editor Part instead of using the interface generated from the properties marked with the attributes discussed earlier, you need to make the Web Part implement the `IWebEditable` interface. Edit the class definition for your Web Part so that it looks like this:

```
public class RssWebPart : WebPart, IWebEditable
```

This interface exposes one property and one method and tells SharePoint and ASP.NET that this control exposes custom Editor Parts. The property is called

`WebBrowsableObject` and should return a reference to the Web Part or control that's going to be edited by the Editor Part controls. The method called `CreateEditorParts` returns a collection of `EditorPart` controls. A Web Part can have several Editor Parts, which can be useful if you want to group or organize your configuration for a better user experience.

> **TIP** To see how a class or interface is defined, you can use Visual Studio to show you the definition by selecting the class or interface. Then press the F12 key or right-click and select Go To Definition. If you do this on `IWebEditable` in your Web Part class definition, you'll see the definition of the property and method.

To implement the property and method, right-click on `IWebEditable` in your class definition and select Implement Interface > Implement Interface Explicitly. Visual Studio will then create the implementation of the interface at the end of your Web Part source code file.

Listing 5.8 shows how the `WebBrowsableObject` property returns the Web Part object. As you can see, the `CreateEditorParts` creates a collection of Editor Parts and returns the collection.

Listing 5.8 Implementation of the IWebEditable interface

```
EditorPartCollection IWebEditable.CreateEditorParts() {
    List<EditorPart> editors = new List<EditorPart>();
    RssWebPartEditorPart editorPart =
        new RssWebPartEditorPart();
    editorPart.ID = this.ID + "_editorPart";        ❶ ID must
    editors.Add(editorPart);                             be set
    return new EditorPartCollection(editors);
}

object IWebEditable.WebBrowsableObject {
    get {
        return this;
    }
}
```

In the `CreateEditorParts` method, you have to create a `List<EditorPart>` object to add your custom Editor Parts. You have to specify a unique identifier for each Editor Part ❶. A good convention is to use the id of the Web Part and append `_editorPart`. The `EditorPart` object is added to the list and finally returned from the method. The `WebBrowsableObject` is used by the Editor Part to get a reference to the Web Part that's being edited. This method needs to return the object itself.

The ASP.NET Web Part definition already exposes this interface. Instead of explicitly implementing this interface, you could just override the `CreateEditorParts` method. I'll show you the explicit method here so you'll see how the interface works.

Now your Editor Part is associated with the Web Part. Build and deploy the solution to SharePoint so that you can add the Web Part to a page. When the Web Part appears on the page, you can edit its properties. Your custom Editor Part will appear on the right and look like figure 5.6.

In figure 5.6, you can also see that the automatically generated interface is still available. To remove the properties from that category, you need to modify the `WebBrowsable` attribute so that it has the value set to `false` or remove the attribute from the property. Once that's done, you can once again deploy your project and test the Web Part.

5.3.3 *Validating properties*

You can further enhance your custom Editor Part with validation. Validation ensures that users enter a correct value to avoid error messages in the Web Parts. If you have a percentage input, you could validate the property so that its value is between 0 and 100. Not only does the validation avoid unnecessary error messages, it also improves the overall user experience.

You should use validation when it's applicable, but you shouldn't rely on it. The validation is only used when users are editing the Web Part

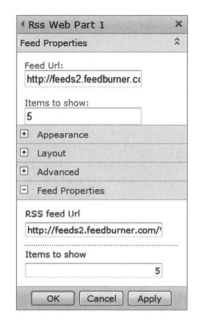

Figure 5.6   Adding an Editor Part to the Web Part allows the developer to control the logic in the tool pane. The properties may appear both in a custom Editor Part and in the default interface if the `WebBrowsable` **attribute is present on the property declaration.**

in the web interface using the custom Editor Part. If they're editing the Web Part in code or manually editing it with SharePoint Designer, the custom Editor Part and its validation won't be used. As usual, you always need good error handling in your Web Part. Chapter 8 explains how to implement good exception handling and error messages.

In the RSS Web Part, the RSS feed URL should be validated so that it's a valid URL. You accomplish this by adding a regular expression validation control. Add the control in the `CreateChildControls` method, directly after adding the feed URL text box:

```
RegularExpressionValidator regValidator = new RegularExpressionValidator {
    ControlToValidate = m_feedUrl.ID,
    ValidationExpression = @"([^:]+)://(([^:@]+)(:([^@]+))?@)?
        ([^:/?#]+)(:([d]+))?([^?#]+)?(\?([^#]+))?(#(.*))?",
    ErrorMessage = "Please provide a valid Url"
};
this.Controls.Add(regValidator);
```

Because you also created a text box for entering the number of items to fetch, you have to make sure that the user is entering an integer. For that validation, add a range validator:

```
RangeValidator rangeValidator = new RangeValidator {
    ControlToValidate = m_itemCount.ID,
    MinimumValue = "1",
    MaximumValue = "100",
    Type = ValidationDataType.Integer,
    ErrorMessage = "Enter a value between 1 and 100"
};
this.Controls.Add(rangeValidator);
```

Build and deploy the Web Part once again and try different settings for the feed URL and the number of items to verify that your validation and Web Part works. If you enter invalid values, you'll see the error message shown in figure 5.7.

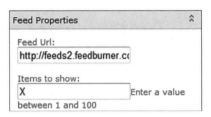

One problem with validators is that if you enter invalid data and try to click the Cancel button in the tool pane, nothing happens. The Cancel button invokes the validators and therefore can't perform its cancel action because

Figure 5.7   Validators can be used in custom Editor Parts to validate the user input.

they're invalid. You can work around this by turning off the validation of the Cancel button. Cast the Zone property of the Editor Part to a ToolPane object and then change the behavior of the Cancel button like this:

```
ToolPane pane = this.Zone as ToolPane;
if (pane != null) {
    pane.Cancel.CausesValidation = false;
}
```

This code snippet is added to the CreateChildControls method and casts the Zone property of the Editor Part to a ToolPane object. This ToolPane object corresponds to the tool pane and exposes the Cancel button so you can turn off its validation.

5.3.4   *Property dependencies*

If you're creating advanced Editor Parts, you might need to create one that adapts to the selections that the user is making. You can use standard ASP.NET postbacks to make the Editor Part react to the user's actions.

Suppose you want to add caching to the RSS Web Part. Wouldn't it be great to have the caching and cache time configurable? Just add two properties to the Web Part: one indicating if caching is on and another specifying the time to cache the data:

```
[Personalizable(PersonalizationScope.Shared)]
public bool CacheData {
    get;
    set;
}
[Personalizable(PersonalizationScope.Shared)]
public int CacheTime {
    get;
    set;
}
```

Because you're going to use these properties in your Editor Part, you only need to specify the `Personalizable` attribute so that the values are stored correctly. To be able to edit these values, add a `Check box` and another `TextBox` to your Editor Part:

```
protected Check box m_cache;
protected TextBox m_cacheTime;
```

Create these controls in the `CreateChildControls` method after the other controls. Listing 5.9 shows how the controls are created and added to the controls collection.

Listing 5.9   Event handlers and postbacks added to the Editor Part controls

```
this.Controls.Add(new Label(){
    Text = "<br/>Cache data:<br/>",
    AssociatedControlID = "cache"});
m_cache = new Check box() { ID="cache" };
m_cache.CheckedChanged += new EventHandler(m_cache_CheckedChanged);
m_cache.AutoPostBack = true;
this.Controls.Add(m_cache);

this.Controls.Add(new Label(){
    Text = "<br/>Cache time:<br/>",
    AssociatedControlID="cacheTime"});
m_cacheTime = new TextBox() { ID = "cacheTime" };
this.Controls.Add(m_cacheTime);
```

First create the check box and add an event handler when the checked status changes. To make the Editor Part reload immediately, set the `AutoPostBack` property of the check box to `true`, which will trigger the event handler. The event handler is a simple method that enables the cache time text box, if it's checked, and disables the text box otherwise:

```
void m_cache_CheckedChanged(object sender, EventArgs e) {
    m_cacheTime.Enabled = m_cache.Checked;
}
```

Now, when you change the checked status of the cache check box, the cache time text box will be disabled or enabled. Modify the `ApplyChanges` method so that you copy the values from the controls to the properties of the Web Part:

```
webPart.CacheData = m_cache.Checked;
webPart.CacheTime = int.Parse(m_cacheTime.Text);
```

In `SyncChanges`, copy the properties from the controls of the Editor Part to the Web Part. You also need to enable or disable the text box depending on the cache settings:

```
m_cache.Checked = webPart.CacheData;
m_cacheTime.Enabled = webPart.CacheData;
m_cacheTime.Text = webPart.CacheTime.ToString();
```

That's all you have to do to get a more dynamic Editor Part and to make it more intuitive for the end user. Now deploy the Web Part and test different settings (see figure 5.8). The actual caching isn't yet implemented—you'll take a closer look at caching in chapter 9.

Figure 5.8   Custom Editor Parts can be used when properties are dependent on other properties. The Cache Time text box shown here is disabled because the check box isn't selected.

5.3.5   *Visual appearance of the Editor Part interface*

So far, you've just added controls to the Editor Part without considering the visual appearance. This aspect is just as important as the functionality, and it makes the Web Part look more professional. The best practice is to use a layout that looks as much as possible like the out-of-the-box Editor Parts, such as the Editor Parts used for the common properties. For example, the automatically generated text boxes have a corresponding button that you can click to edit the text in a dialog box. These classes exist in the SharePoint internal API and aren't accessible for use in custom code.

> **NOTE**   The `Microsoft.SharePoint` assembly contains a class called `Builder-Button` that creates the button used to display a dialog box for entering text in an Editor Part. This class is marked as internal and can't be used by custom code. With the use of .NET Reflector, you can inspect that class and understand how it works to build a similar experience for your Editor Parts.

All styling of the Editor Parts have to be done manually. The best way to enhance your Editor Parts is to look at the out-of-the-box Web Parts and mimic their visuals. Most of the styling is done with a set of CSS classes. Table 5.5 contains some of the classes used to build the tool pane interface.

Table 5.5   CSS classes used when creating custom Editor Parts

CSS Class Names	Description
UserSectionTitle	Used on the titles of the categories.
UserGeneric	Used for the main DIV element or panel control surrounding all other controls.
UserSectionHead	Used on an inner panel control for headings.
UserSectionBody	Used on an inner panel control containing input controls.
UserControlGroup	Used inside a UserSectionBody panel when multiple controls are used.
UserInput	Used on text box input controls.
UserSelect	Used on drop-downs.
UserDottedLine	Used on panel controls to create a separator.

Apart from these classes, you should specify the width of text boxes as 176 pixels. For numeric input, set the `text-align` CSS attribute to `right` and the number of columns to 10. These values are the ones used internally by SharePoint when creating custom Editor Parts.

If you rearrange the Editor Part and apply the CSS classes in table 5.5, the Editor Part will look like figure 5.9. Compare that interface to the one in figure 5.8 and you'll see the improvements.

Figure 5.9
Building a professional-looking interface for custom Editor Parts enhances the user experience.

Creating this interface takes a lot of code. Listing 5.10 shows how the figure 5.9 interface is built.

Listing 5.10   Styling of the controls in the Editor Part

```
Panel genericPanel = new Panel() {            ⬅——❶ Header
    CssClass = "UserGeneric"
};
this.Controls.Add(genericPanel);
genericPanel.Controls.Add(
    new LiteralControl("RSS Web Part configuration<br/><br/>"));

Panel headPanel = new Panel() {               ⬅    First section
    CssClass = "UserSectionHead ms-bold"     ❷   header
};
headPanel.Controls.Add(new Label() {
    Text = "Feed Url",
    AssociatedControlID = m_feedUrl.ID
});
genericPanel.Controls.Add(headPanel);        ❸  First section
                                              ⬅   body
Panel bodyPanel = new Panel() {
    CssClass = "UserSectionBody"
};
genericPanel.Controls.Add(bodyPanel);        ❹  First control
Panel groupPanel = new Panel() {             ⬅   group
    CssClass = "UserControlGroup"
};
bodyPanel.Controls.Add(groupPanel);
m_feedUrl.CssClass = "UserInput";
m_feedUrl.Width = Unit.Pixel(176);
groupPanel.Controls.Add(m_feedUrl);
groupPanel.Controls.Add(new LiteralControl("<br/>"));
regValidator.Display = ValidatorDisplay.Dynamic;
groupPanel.Controls.Add(regValidator);       ❺  Second section
                                              ⬅   header
headPanel = new Panel() {
    CssClass = "UserSectionHead ms-bold"
};
headPanel.Controls.Add(new Label() {
    Text = "Items to show",
    AssociatedControlID = m_itemCount.ID
});
genericPanel.Controls.Add(headPanel);
bodyPanel = new Panel() {
    CssClass = "UserSectionBody"
};
genericPanel.Controls.Add(bodyPanel);
groupPanel = new Panel() {
    CssClass = "UserControlGroup"
};
bodyPanel.Controls.Add(groupPanel);
m_itemCount.CssClass = "UserInput";
m_itemCount.Style.Add("text-align", "right");
m_itemCount.Columns = 10;
groupPanel.Controls.Add(m_itemCount);
```

```
groupPanel.Controls.Add(new LiteralControl("<br/>"));
rangeValidator.Display = ValidatorDisplay.Dynamic;
groupPanel.Controls.Add(rangeValidator);

genericPanel.Controls.Add(new Panel() {          ⊲——❻ Separator
    CssClass = "UserDottedLine"
});
headPanel = new Panel() {
    CssClass = "UserSectionHead ms-bold"
};
headPanel.Controls.Add(new Label() {
    Text = "Caching",
    AssociatedControlID = "cache"
});
genericPanel.Controls.Add(headPanel);
bodyPanel = new Panel() {
    CssClass = "UserSectionBody"
};
genericPanel.Controls.Add(bodyPanel);
groupPanel = new Panel() {
    CssClass = "UserControlGroup"
};
bodyPanel.Controls.Add(groupPanel);
m_cache.Text = "Enable caching";
groupPanel.Controls.Add(m_cache);
groupPanel.Controls.Add(new Label() {
    Text = "<br/>Cache time:<br/>",
    AssociatedControlID = m_cacheTime.ID
});
m_cacheTime.CssClass = "UserInput";
m_cacheTime.Style.Add("text-align", "right");
m_cacheTime.Columns = 10;
groupPanel.Controls.Add(m_cacheTime);
```

The first control you need to create is UserGeneric ❶, which will be the control that you add to the Editor Part control tree. Next, add a LiteralControl with a description of the Editor Part to be followed by the input for the properties. Each group of properties has a head ❷ with a title and then a body ❸, ❺ and a group ❹. The group contains the input fields. The text boxes are configured to use a CSS class and a width. Just before the validator, a line break is inserted and the validator is changed to a dynamic validator so that it doesn't occupy space while not visible. This procedure is repeated for each property group. For the numeric input fields, you have to modify the text alignment and the number of columns. The two major groups of properties are separated by a dotted line ❻.

5.4   *Advanced properties*

Until now, you've looked at simple properties such as strings, Booleans, and numbers. What if you need to store something more complex, such as a coordinate or an array of items? The easiest way is to build a custom Editor Part for the property. This complex property could be converted into a complex representation or into several properties at the backend. The downside of this approach is that the developers working with this

Web Part in code or in SharePoint Designer will find it difficult to interpret its usage without proper documentation. It'll likely result in more errors and troubleshooting. A better approach is to leverage .NET features such as type converters. Doing so will allow you to use the out-of-the-box interfaces in SharePoint, Visual Studio, and SharePoint Designer to convert a complex object into a string representation.

This section shows you how to create a custom Web Part property for a coordinate property that can be edited in both the web interface and SharePoint Designer and then be stored and retrieved.

5.4.1   Define the property

In this example you'll create a new Empty SharePoint project called WebPartsInAction.Ch5.CoordinateWebPart, choose to use a farm solution, and add a new Web Part project item called CoordinateWebPart. Start with adding a new class to the project called Coordinate and define the coordinate class, as in listing 5.11.

Listing 5.11   The definition of the Coordinate class

```
[Serializable]
public class Coordinate {
    public float Latitude;
    public float Longitude;
    public override string ToString() {
        return this.Latitude.ToString(CultureInfo.CurrentCulture) +
            ":" +
            this.Longitude.ToString(CultureInfo.CurrentCulture);
    }
}
```

As you can see, this class has been marked as Serializable so that it can be serialized. It's a simple class with Latitude and Longitude fields and a ToString method that creates a visual representation of the class. Also, notice that you're using the CultureInfo.CurrentCulture (from the System.Globalization namespace) as a parameter to the ToString method to make sure that the float values are correctly displayed in all cultures.

In the Web Part, add a property as shown in listing 5.12 where CreateChildControls writes the value of the coordinate in a Label control.

Listing 5.12   The Coordinate Web Part definition

```
public CoordinateWebPart() {
    this.CurrentPosition = new Coordinate();
}

protected override void CreateChildControls() {
    this.Controls.Add( new Label() {
        Text = CurrentPosition.ToString()
    });
    base.CreateChildControls();
}

[WebBrowsable]
```

```
[Personalizable]
public Coordinate CurrentPosition {
    get;
    set;
}
```

In the constructor of the Web Part, initialize the local `Coordinate` variable to avoid any null reference exceptions. The `CreateChildControls` that's overridden adds a new `Label` control to the child controls collection that prints the value of the coordinate. The Web Part also contains a property called `CurrentPosition` that's personalizable.

5.4.2 Problems with complex types

At this point, deploy the Web Part into SharePoint and add it to a page. You'll see that it nicely prints the value of the `Coordinate` property. Then select it and notice that the property isn't available for editing. SharePoint doesn't understand how to create interfaces for properties of complex types.

If you open the page in SharePoint Designer, you'll see an error telling you that SharePoint can't convert a `Coordinate` object from its string representation. Switch to the code view and locate the Web Part tag, and notice that it has a `CurrentPosition` attribute with a correct value. The value of the attribute is generated from the `ToString` implementation of the `Coordinate` class. It should look like this:

```
<WpNs0:CoordinateWebPart
    runat="server"
    CurrentPosition="0:0"
    ...>
</WpNs0:CoordinateWebPart>
```

Using SharePoint Designer, change the value of the `CurrentPosition` attribute to `1:1` and save the page. Then open the page in the web browser. You'll see a similar error as before stating that SharePoint can't create the `Coordinate` object from its string representation. The .NET Framework doesn't know how to convert the string representation of the `Coordinate` class into a `Coordinate` object. Note that if you added the Web Part to a wiki page, you won't see the error. You have to go to the Web Part maintenance page (by adding `?contents=1` to the URL) to see that it fails.

You're facing two issues with a property like this:

- Creating a `Coordinate` object from its string representation
- Creating an interface for editing the property

The easiest way to work around these issues is to create two properties for `Coordinate`: a `Latitude` and a `Longitude` property. Doing so would solve both problems, but that's not the best approach. Instead, you can leverage some of the .NET Framework's features.

5.4.3 Create a type converter

The .NET Framework has classes and methods that allow you to convert types from one to another. The `ExpandableObjectConverter` class, defined in `System.Component-Model`, is a base class that converts an expandable object to another representation. In this scenario, you'll use this class to create an automatic conversion from the `Coordinate` class to a string representation, and vice versa.

To create the converter, start by adding a new class to the project; name it `CoordinateConverter`. It's common to name converters with the object name and append `Converter` to the class name. Add `using` statements so that you have access to the converter and globalization namespaces:

```
using System.ComponentModel;
using System.Globalization;
```

Then make the class inherit from `ExpandableObjectConverter` and implement it, as shown in listing 5.13.

Listing 5.13   The expandable `Converter` class for the `Coordinate` object

```
class CoordinateConverter : ExpandableObjectConverter {
    public override bool CanConvertTo(ITypeDescriptorContext context,
        System.Type destinationType) {

        if (destinationType == typeof(Coordinate))
            return true;
        return base.CanConvertTo(context, destinationType);
    }

    public override object ConvertTo(ITypeDescriptorContext context,
        CultureInfo culture, object value,
        System.Type destinationType) {

        if (destinationType == typeof(System.String) &&
            value is Coordinate) {
            Coordinate coord = (Coordinate)value;
            return coord.ToString();
        }
        return base.ConvertTo(context, culture, value, destinationType);
    }

    public override bool CanConvertFrom(ITypeDescriptorContext context,
        System.Type sourceType) {
        if (sourceType == typeof(string))
            return true;
        return base.CanConvertFrom(context, sourceType);
    }

    public override object ConvertFrom(ITypeDescriptorContext context,
            CultureInfo culture, object value) {
        if (value is string) {
            try {
                string s = (string)value;
                string[] arr = s.Split(':');
                Coordinate coord = new Coordinate();
                coord.Latitude = Single.Parse(arr[0],
                    CultureInfo.CurrentCulture);
                coord.Longitude = Single.Parse(arr[1],
                    CultureInfo.CurrentCulture);
                return coord;
```

1 Convert Coordinate to string

2 Convert to string from Coordinate

```
            }
        catch {
            throw new ArgumentException("Cannot convert '" +
                (string)value + "' to type a Coordinate");
        }
    }
    return base.ConvertFrom(context, culture, value);
}
}
```

In this Converter class, you need to implement four methods. The CanConvertTo method checks if this converter can convert to a Coordinate object. If this method returns true, then the .NET Framework needs the ConvertTo ❶ method to convert the object. This method returns the string representation of the Coordinate object if the destination type is a string and the value is a Coordinate. The third method, CanConvertFrom, is used to check if the converter can convert the object of the specified type to the type of the converter. This method returns true if the source type is a string. If it returns true, the conversion process needs the ConvertFrom ❷ method to perform the conversion. The method takes the supplied string value and splits it, and then creates a Coordinate object and sets the values. Finally, it returns the Coordinate object.

To let SharePoint and other applications using the Coordinate class know which converter to use, add the TypeConverter attribute to the Coordinate class. This attribute specifies the type of converter to use for the object at runtime. The class declaration of the Coordinate class should look like this:

```
[Serializable]
[TypeConverter(typeof(CoordinateConverter))]
public class Coordinate
```

When you're done, deploy your Web Part and return to the page where you added the Web Part. If you select the Web Part, you'll see that under the Miscellaneous section the property is available for editing. If you enter a new Coordinate and save the Web Part, the value is shown in the Web Part and stored.

If you choose to enter an invalid coordinate, you'll get the error message shown in figure 5.10.

When you've entered a valid coordinate, open the page in SharePoint Designer. Select the Web Part and choose View Tag Properties. Then scroll down to the Misc section and watch the CurrentPosition property. Just as in the web interface, you can edit the property and if you enter an invalid value you'll get an error message (see figure 5.11).

This property can be further enhanced by adding an Editor Part in which you have input fields for the Coordinate, Latitude, and Longitude, to avoid error

Figure 5.10   Complex properties implemented with .NET type converters are automatically validated in the Editor Parts.

Figure 5.11   SharePoint Designer doesn't allow invalid values for complex properties that have a custom type converter.

messages. The combination of the converter and an Editor Part makes the editing of your Web Part easy and understandable in both the web interface and using Share-Point Designer.

5.5   Runtime filters

In section 5.2, you looked at the standard Web Part properties and saw that the Share-Point Server has an extra property for targeting the Web Part to an audience. For instance, you might want to target one Web Part only to the Sales team and another one to the Support team. In this approach, the same page can be used for multiple audiences without cluttering the user interface with Web Parts that the current user doesn't need. It's a powerful feature that I miss in SharePoint Foundation because I often need to target Web Parts to specific groups or users. But the good news is that you can create your own runtime filter and create similar functionality yourself. This is something that's not very well known or documented, so I'm going to show you how to create this custom filter. You'll do this exercise as an end-to-end sample so that you can take the code and use it as is in your solutions.

The runtime filter in SharePoint is a specific class derived from the `IRuntimeFilter2` interface. This class is registered in the web.config file and is called for every Web Part when rendering a page. A specific method in the class tells SharePoint whether it should be shown to the user. In this section you'll create a custom runtime filter that can be used to target the Web Part using the site collection groups. This will give you the option to target Web Parts to specific groups even in SharePoint Foundation.

5.5.1   The AuthorizationFilter property

The `WebPart` class definition contains a string property called `AuthorizationFilter`. This property is used to store values of the runtime filter that applies to that specific Web Part. The `AuthorizationFilter` property isn't directly editable from the web interface; you can only edit it using a runtime filter. The value of the property depends on the implementation of the runtime filter. This property is passed, by the

WebPartManager object, to the runtime filter during page rendering to check whether the property has a valid value for the filter. You'll use the name of the groups separated by commas as a string representation of the filter.

5.5.2 Create a runtime filter

To create a filter, you must create a project that contains a class that derives from the IRuntimeFilter2. This project must be a farm solution because it has to be registered in the global assembly cache (GAC). The first thing you need to do is add a new class item to your project; call it SiteGroupsRuntimeFilter. Make the class public so that it's accessible from other assemblies.

This newly added class has to implement the IRuntimeFilter2 interface (from the Microsoft.SharePoint.WebPartPages namespace). It should look like this:

```
public class SiteGroupsRuntimeFilter: IRuntimeFilter2
```

To create the interface methods, you right-click on IRuntimeFilter2 and select Implement Interface > Implement Interface from the context menu. This will create the skeleton for the five methods that you need to implement. In this example, you're implementing the IRuntimeFilter2, which is the predecessor of the now deprecated IRuntimeFilter interface (used in SharePoint 2003).

THE ISFILTERACTIVE METHOD

The first method you'll implement is IsFilterActive, which must return a Boolean value indicating whether this filter should be active. Make this method return the value true all the time so that it's always visible:

```
public bool IsFilterActive() {
    return true;
}
```

You can use this method to conditionally use your filter on a specific site or site collection. The SharePoint Server Target Audiences implementation of the filter uses this method to enable the targeting only if the User Profile Service is enabled and online. For instance, you can make this method depend on a configurable setting so that administrators can turn the filter on or off.

THE INITIALIZESTRINGS METHOD

The InitializeStrings method returns an array of strings, of which you only need to specify one: the title of your runtime filter property. The reason that it returns an array of strings is that SharePoint 2003 used four different strings to create the user interface. The method also takes a parameter indicating the culture used so that the returned strings can be localized. Your implementation of the method should look like this:

```
public ArrayList InitializeStrings(CultureInfo cultureInfo) {
    return new ArrayList(new string[] { "Target Groups" });
}
```

Note that you need to add using statements to System.Collections and System.Globalization.

THE VALIDATEISINCLUDEDFILTER METHOD

To make sure that you're storing correct values in the Web Part's `AuthorizationFilter` property, the `ValidateIsIncludedFilter` is used. It takes a string as input and you add logic to validate that the string is correct and returns a correct string. The method is used after the user has inserted the values but before they're saved to Share-Point. Normally this method just returns the original value like this:

```
public string ValidateIsIncludedFilter(string persistedString) {
    return persistedString;
}
```

THE CHECKRUNTIMERENDER METHOD

The method used to check the `AuthorizationFilter` property is called `CheckRuntimeRender`. This method takes the value of the filter and contains your logic to determine if the Web Part will be shown. Listing 5.14 shows how it's implemented to check whether the user is a member of any of the groups in the filter.

Listing 5.14   The `CheckRuntimeRender` method

```
public bool CheckRuntimeRender(string IsIncludedFilter) {
    SPContext context = SPContext.Current;
    if (String.IsNullOrEmpty(IsIncludedFilter)) {
        return true;
    }

    string[] filterArray = IsIncludedFilter.Split(new char[] {','});
    foreach(SPGroup group in context.Site.RootWeb.SiteGroups) {
        if (filterArray.Contains(group.Name) &&
            group.ContainsCurrentUser) {
            return true;
        }
    }
    return false;
}
```

First this method checks if the filter is empty, and if there's no value, it returns `true`. Then it splits the incoming filter value on comma characters and iterates over the groups in the site collection. The method checks if the group exists in the filter and that the user belongs to that group. If that's the case, it returns `true`; otherwise, it returns `false`.

THE GETTOOLPANECONTROL METHOD

The last method that you need to implement is `GetToolPaneControl`. This method returns a web control that's serves as the user interface when editing the property. This method needs to instantiate a `WebControl` that has the `IToolPaneControl` implemented. In the next section you'll create a control called `SiteGroupsFilterControl` and the code for this method should look like this:

```
public IToolPaneControl GetToolPaneControl() {
    return new SiteGroupsFilterControl() { ID="SiteGroupsFilterControl" };
}
```

This method creates the control and assigns it an id. Note that you haven't yet created the `SiteGroupsFilterControl`, so Visual Studio will show you an error if you try to compile it.

5.5.3 Create the user filter control

The control that you need for the web interface is a class inherited from the `WebControl` class. and you create it by adding a new class item to the project. Name it `SiteGroups-FilterControl`. You could also add a new ASP.NET Server Control item instead, but you'll use the empty class to show all steps. First you have to make it inherit from the `Web-Control` class and implement the `IToolPaneControl` interface that's needed by the `GetToolPaneControl` method in the runtime filter. Add these using statements:

```
using System.Web.UI.WebControls;
using Microsoft.SharePoint;
using Microsoft.SharePoint.WebPartPages;
```

Then modify your class definition as follows:

```
public class SiteGroupsFilterControl: WebControl, IToolPaneControl
```

You have to implement the `IToolPaneControl` interface on this control. It only contains one simple property, called `Text`, that's used to get the value from the control. Implement it using an automatic property like this:

```
public string Text {
    get;
    set;
}
```

To avoid any null reference exception to this property, initialize the property to an empty string in the constructor. Create a constructor like the following and initialize the property:

```
public SiteGroupsFilterControl() {
    this.Text = String.Empty;
}
```

Create the user interface using any method that you normally use to work with web controls. In this sample you'll build the user interface using a list box that you create in the `CreateChildControls` method, as in listing 5.15.

> **Listing 5.15 The runtime filter control for selecting the target groups**

```
protected ListBox listBox;

protected override void CreateChildControls() {
    listBox = new ListBox();
    listBox.ID = "Groups";
    listBox.SelectionMode = ListSelectionMode.Multiple;

    SPContext context = SPContext.Current;

    var currentSelection = Text.Split(new char[] { ',' });
```

```
    foreach (SPGroup group in context.Site.RootWeb.SiteGroups) {
        listBox.Items.Add(
            new ListItem() {
            Text = group.Name,
            Selected = currentSelection.Any( g => g == group.Name )});
    }
    this.Controls.Add(listBox);
    base.CreateChildControls();
}
```

The `ListBox` is defined as a protected property of the class. In the `CreateChildControls` method, the `ListBox` is created and initialized. The current value of the filter is fetched from the `Text` property and split into an array. All groups of the site are iterated and added to the list box. Using the array of the current selection, you use a lambda method to check whether the item should be selected. Finally, you add the `ListBox` to the control collection.

To get this to work, you have to do one final thing: Push back the value to the `WebPartManager` via the `Text` property. Do this by modifying the web control so that it also implements the `IPostBackDataHandler` interface, which is defined in the `System.Web.UI` namespace. This handler catches the data from the postback and updates the current state of the control:

```
public class SiteGroupsFilterControl:
    WebControl,
    IToolPaneControl,
    IPostBackDataHandler
```

The `IPostBackDataHandler` interface has two methods; you need to use one. Using the `LoadPostData` method, you can intercept the postback values and update the `Text` property. The `RaisePostDataChangedEvent` is left empty, as in listing 5.16.

Listing 5.16 The `LoadPostData` method

```
public bool LoadPostData(string postDataKey,
    System.Collections.Specialized.NameValueCollection postCollection) {

    this.EnsureChildControls();

    var id = from key in postCollection.Keys.Cast<string>()
        where key.EndsWith("$" + listBox.ID)
        select key;

    if (id.First() != null) {
        this.Text = postCollection[id.First()];
        if (this.Text == null) {
            this.Text = String.Empty;
        }
    }
    return true;
}

public void RaisePostDataChangedEvent() {
}
```

The `LoadPostData` method makes sure that the child controls collection is created and then locates the postback id for the list box control. This is done using a LINQ query that finds the control ending with the id of the list box. The $ sign is used by ASP.NET to generate the unique postback names for the controls in the control tree. Each control is given the id of their parent control, which is appended with the $ sign and then the id of the actual control. The value of the list box that was posted back to the control is then set to the `Text` property.

To inform the ASP.NET runtime that you want to catch the postback data, you first have to register it. The registration is done in the overridden `OnPreRender` method. Override the `OnPreRender` method and add the following:

```
this.Page.RegisterRequiresPostBack(this);
```

This is all the logic necessary for your runtime filter. Next you need to register it in SharePoint.

5.5.4 Register the runtime filter

The registration of the runtime filter is done in the web.config file in the SharePoint section with the `RuntimeFilter` element. To finish this sample, so that you can take the complete code and put it to work, you'll create a *Feature receiver* for registering the runtime filter. The Feature receiver will add the necessary XML to web.config when the Feature is activated and remove it when deactivated.

First you need to add a Feature to your project. Name the Feature `SiteGroupsFil-ter` and then add a more descriptive title and description using the Feature designer. Set the scope to `WebApplication` because it will affect web.config and all sites using that specific web application. Once you've finished with the following steps and deployed this solution, using Central Administration you can turn this filter on and off for the different web applications.

Now, add the Feature receiver to the project by right-clicking on the Feature and selecting Add Event Receiver. This will add a new class to your project, under the Feature. You must override the `FeatureActivated` and `FeatureDeactivating` methods, as in listing 5.17.

> **Listing 5.17 The feature event receiver for the runtime filter**

```
public override void FeatureActivated(
    SPFeatureReceiverProperties properties) {

    SPWebApplication webApplication = properties.Feature.Parent as
                                SPWebApplication;
    if (webApplication != null) {
        addRemoveModification(webApplication, false);      ◁──┐ Add
    }                                                         ❶ modifications
}
public override void FeatureDeactivating(
    SPFeatureReceiverProperties properties) {
```

```
        SPWebApplication webApplication = properties.Feature.Parent as
                                SPWebApplication;
        if (webApplication != null) {
            addRemoveModification(webApplication, true);          ◁──┐  Remove
        }                                                          ❷  modifications
    }
}
private void addRemoveModification(
    SPWebApplication webApplication,
    bool remove) {

    string assembly = this.GetType().Assembly.FullName;
    string className = typeof(SiteGroupsRuntimeFilter).FullName;

    SPWebConfigModification modification =
        new SPWebConfigModification(
            "RuntimeFilter",
            "configuration/SharePoint");

    modification.Owner = this.GetType().FullName;
    modification.Type = SPWebConfigModification.
        SPWebConfigModificationType.EnsureChildNode;

    modification.Value = String.Format(
        "<RuntimeFilter Assembly='{0}' Class='{1}'/>",
        assembly, className);

    if (remove) {
        webApplication.WebConfigModifications.Remove(modification);
    }
    else {
        webApplication.WebConfigModifications.Add(modification);
    }

    webApplication.Farm.Services.GetValue<SPWebService>().
        ApplyWebConfigModifications();
    webApplication.Update();}
```

The Feature receiver by default contains a set of methods that are commented out when created by Visual Studio. Uncomment the FeatureActivated and FeatureDe-activating methods. The Feature receiver applies the web.config modification when the feature is activated ❶ and removes it when deactivated ❷. The modification takes place in the custom method. This method creates a web.config modification object for the RuntimeFilter element. The advantage of using the modification objects compared to editing the XML in web.config is that the modification objects will be replicated over all frontend servers in the farm. The element is defined using the full assembly and class names.

That was the complete walkthrough of creating a runtime filter. All that's left is to deploy and test it.

5.5.5 *Use the filter*

To deploy and test your runtime filter, you press F5 and wait for the operations to complete. Open a Web Part page and add a Web Part to it. Then open the properties of the

Web Part and in the tool pane go to the Advanced section. Your filter will show the groups in your site (see figure 5.12).

Using this simple Feature, runtime filter, and control, you have a working solution for targeting your Web Parts to groups in your site collection. You could further enhance this filter by adding a button to clear the current filter or add an Everyone group as a default.

Figure 5.12 The custom runtime filter can be used to target Web Parts to specific groups within the site collection.

5.5.6 Overriding the default Target Audiences filter

SharePoint Server comes with a standard runtime filter using audiences to filter the Web Parts. Each web application can have only one filter, so if you need a custom filter you have to replace the standard filter with your custom one.

To enhance the standard SharePoint Server filter, you can subclass the out-of-the-box filter. The web.config file in a SharePoint Server web application will look like this:

```
<RuntimeFilter
Assembly="Microsoft.Office.Server, Version=14.0.0.0,
        Culture=neutral, PublicKeyToken=71e9bce111e9429c"
Class="Microsoft.Office.Server.Audience.AudienceManager"
BuilderURL="audience_chooser.aspx" />
```

As you can see, this standard definition has an extra attribute called `BuilderURL`. This attribute was used in previous versions of SharePoint and is no longer needed.

5.6 Summary

This concludes the chapter on Web Part properties, one of the most important and interesting topics you'll encounter when creating reusable self-contained applications. You've seen how easy it is to add a property and tag it with a set of attributes to have SharePoint automatically generate an interface for editing the Web Part properties. Using these attributes, you can control how and when the properties are edited and stored. If you need to configure or control the editing of properties with, for example, validation, you can use custom Editor Parts. Editor Parts also allow you to create properties that are dependent on one another. A configurable Web Part with sufficient options will greatly increase the productivity of the users.

You also looked at complex properties that by default can't be edited with the web interface or SharePoint Designer. By leveraging some of the .NET Framework features, you can give SharePoint the ability to convert an object to and from a string representation so that it can be edited. Finally, You explored a sample where you created a filter that can target Web Parts to groups within SharePoint. Content targeting is important in modern applications and will make your applications more usable.

This was a long chapter filled with samples and code that you can use in your applications. Next up on the agenda is how you can enhance your Web Part and its properties with localization and resources and how you can store generic application configurations.

Web Part
resources and localization

This chapter covers
- Adding resources for your Web Parts
- Deployment methods for resources
- Localizing Web Parts

Web Parts are interface focused and are the building blocks of many successful SharePoint sites. A good user interface design is user friendly. I've discussed how you can add controls and logic to a Web Part; now you'll explore how you can add images, scripts, and style sheets to your solution. These attached items are *resources*. This chapter covers two types of resources:

- Linking and embedding resources such as images, scripts, and style sheets
- Localization resources containing culture-specific resources

Images and style sheets are important when building a good-looking interface. Use them to enhance the user experience and accessibility. There are several ways to add them to your solution, ranging from farm-deployed to assembly-embedded resources. Choosing a method depends on how you plan to use and access them, and I'll guide you through the various scenarios. The techniques in this chapter aren't applicable to just Web Parts—you can use them in user and delegate controls, pages, and other SharePoint projects and Features.

Localization of Web Parts is an important aspect when building reusable Web Parts. Localization means that you make the Web Part aware of which language the user is currently using in SharePoint and adapt your Web Part to that language, decimal numbers, and time format. The localization of a Web Part may be time consuming and often requires thorough testing, but if you're aiming for a global market this step is a necessity.

6.1   Linking and embedding resources

When building Web Parts, the most common resources you should include are images, style sheets, and script files. In chapter 4, you briefly looked at how to add a CSS file to take advantage of the SharePoint themes in a Web Part. In this chapter, you'll follow up that discussion and look at all your options for including style sheets and other resources in your Web Part.

Resources such as images and scripts can be included in a SharePoint solution in several ways. Let's review all your options:

- Deploying resources in the SharePoint root
- Deploying resources to the Web Part resource storage
- Embedding resources in the assemblies
- Deploying resources into the SharePoint sites

Each of these scenarios has its advantages and disadvantages. Your decision will depend on usage and how you plan to deploy the solution.

6.1.1   Using the SharePoint root folders

Each SharePoint site collection has a virtual directory called _layouts that's mapped to the {SharePoint Root}\TEMPLATE\Layouts folder. This folder looks the same for all site collections and web applications in the farm. The _layouts folder also contains a number of subfolders, one of which is the images folder. That folder is also a virtual directory, mapped to the {SharePoint Root}\TEMPLATE\Images folder. Any files deployed into these subfolders will be available for every site collection in the farm, even if the solution isn't installed on the web application or deployed to the site collection. Figure 6.1 shows how a SharePoint web application looks in the Internet Information Services (IIS) Management Console. You can see the _layouts folder and the images folder beneath it.

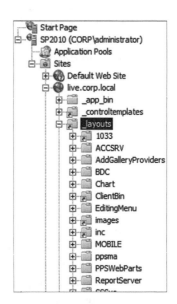

Figure 6.1   The _layouts folder and other folders are mapped to the physical paths in IIS as virtual directories.

> **NOTE**   The virtual directories in IIS are mapped to physical paths in the SharePoint root. Don't modify these paths or in any other way tamper with the settings in IIS.

Using these SharePoint mapped folders is an easy way to add resources to a Web Part project. Visual Studio provides great integration for adding the folders and including files in them. To add a SharePoint mapped folder, right-click the project and select

Add, or you can use the Project menu in the Visual Studio menu. You have three options to add the SharePoint mapped folders, as you can see in figure 6.2. You can directly add the Images and Layouts folders or select the third option that opens a dialog box in which you can select any of the folders in the SharePoint Root folder. The Images folder is used for images and the Layouts folder for other files such as scripts, style sheets, or Silverlight binaries.

Figure 6.2   Adding the SharePoint mapped folders

When you're adding the SharePoint mapped folders, Visual Studio will create a subfolder in the project with the name of your project. You have the option to add your files into that folder or the root folder, or you can create a new one. A good convention is to use the folder that Visual Studio creates for you. This folder name should be unique, and it keeps you from accidentally overwriting files with the same name from another solution.

To create a Web Part that displays an image located in the SharePoint root Layouts folder (see figure 6.3), you need to create a new Web Part project. In the SharePoint Customization wizard, select to deploy it as a farm solution. This is because the image will eventually be deployed into the SharePoint Images mapped folder, which is mapped to a physical path on the server's hard drive. This can only be achieved by using a farm solution because sandboxed solutions don't allow you to add files to the physical drive of the server.

Figure 6.3   Web Parts that use the /_layouts/ images folder to store images must be deployed as farm solutions because sandboxed solutions don't allow files to be written to the file system.

When the project is created, add the Images mapped folder and then add the image to the subfolder with the project name. Add the image file by right-clicking the project and selecting Add > New or Add > Existing Item. Then add a Visual Web Part in which you type the following code:

```
<h3>An image in the /_layouts/images folder</h3>
<img src="/_layouts/Images/WebPartsInAction.Ch6.ImagesAndScripts/
   Annotation.png" />
```

The src attribute of the img element points to the file image that you added to the project. As you can see, the path to the image is a server-relative URL. Because you're adding this image to the file system, it's available in all site collections so you don't have to care about any site-relative URL.

URL strings in SharePoint

SharePoint uses three forms of URL strings:

- An *absolute URL* is a URL that starts with the protocol and server address, like this: http://server/[sites/][web site]/.
- A *server-relative URL* starts from the top-level website, beginning with a forward slash, like this: /[sites/][web site]/.
- The third form is the *website-relative URL* (also called just site-relative), which doesn't start with a forward slash.

One of the advantages of having these resources residing in the file system and mapped through IIS virtual directories is that you can use IIS compression and caching techniques to improve the performance of your application. Another advantage is that you can share the resources between solutions. The disadvantage of using these shared-linked resources is that they're available from any site or site collection in the farm. This can be problematic if the resource contains sensitive data. Keep in mind that if you don't carefully name your folders and files they may collide with other solutions, which can lead to unwanted scenarios.

6.1.2 *Using class resources*

Another method of including resources in the solution involves using the special Web Part resource storage. This storage is another virtual directory mapped in IIS that's specifically made to host resources for Web Parts and separate them from other Web Parts. It works similar to storing the resources in the SharePoint mapped folders except that SharePoint makes sure that each assembly and class gets its own separate folder. The resources are stored in the _WPRESOURCES IIS virtual directory; under that directory SharePoint creates one folder for each assembly and version. Just as with the mapped folders,, these files reside in the file system. This method has the same advantages and disadvantages, except that file conflicts are more unlikely to occur because each assembly and version automatically gets a new folder tree.

To add an image as a class resource in a Web Part, you need to add the image to your Web Part project item. Right-click on the Web Part, click Add > Existing Item, and select the image to include. When the file is added to the project, you have to select the item and edit its properties. Edit properties by right-clicking the item and selecting Properties or by pressing the F4 key. The Properties window contains information about how the project item should be handled during compilation and packaging of the solution. Specifically, you must change Deployment Type to make this item a class resource. By default, the Deployment Type property of the added image has the value

_WPRESOURCES versus WPRESOURCES

There are two different WPRESOURCES directories: _WPRESOURCES and WPRE-SOURCES. _WPRESOURCES is used for solutions that are deployed as farm/full-trust solutions, and WPRESOURCES is used by solutions that are deployed to a web application (see chapter 7).

For farm solutions, the _WPRESOURCES directory is the same for all web applications across the farm, but WPRESOURCES exists on the web application level so those resources aren't shared across web applications.

NoDeployment, which means that this item won't be included in the solution or deployed. You must change the value of Deployment Type to ClassResource. When you do, Visual Studio will change the value of the Deployment Location property. The deployment location is the path in the _WPRESOURCES folder and consists of two parts. The first part, called the root, is the ClassResourcePath, which is the automatically generated path created from the assembly name and version. The second part, called the path, is a configurable folder that by default is set to the name of your project and the name of the project item. This will generate a very long path by default, and I recommend that you expand the Deployment Location property and change the value of the Path part to something shorter or just leave it empty. Figure 6.4 shows the Properties window with the default values for a class resource item.

Once the image item in the project is changed to a class resource, Visual Studio automatically adds it to the package of the solution. It adds the item as a `ClassResource`

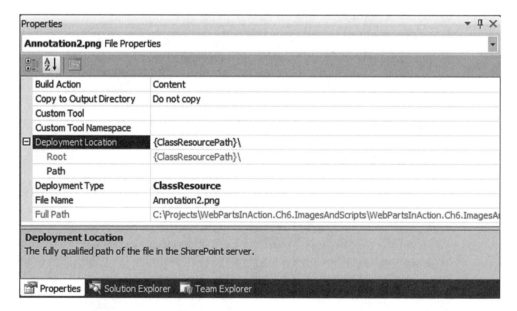

Figure 6.4 Using the Properties window of a project item in Visual Studio, you can configure how the item is going to be deployed and to which location.

element in the package manifest. To view the manifest, double-click on the package in the Solution Explorer and select the Manifest tab. The `ClassResource` element should look like this if you set the path in the Deployment Location property to Empty:

```
<ClassResources>
    <ClassResource Location="Annotation2.png" />
</ClassResources>
```

The root part of the Deployment Location property consists of the name of the assembly, the version, and the public key token. For example, it could look like this:

```
/_WPRESOURCES/WebPartsInAction.Ch6.ImagesAndScripts
⇒ /1.0.0.0__b96bfa3ca5f92c49
```

Using the server-relative path in code may be problematic, especially if you change the version of the assembly. So you don't have to hardcode this path, the SharePoint Web Part Manager provides a static method called `GetServerRelativeClassResourcePath` that automatically generates the path for you. To add an image as a class resource into a Visual Web Part, you must set the `ImageUrl` property in the code-behind to be able to use the method to get the class resource path like this:

```
<h3>An image using ClassResources</h3>
<asp:Image runat="server" id="WPImage" />
```

In the code behind the `ImageUrl` property set the `OnInit` method. It uses the static method of the `SPWebPartManager` object and appends the name of the image like this:

```
protected override void OnInit(EventArgs e) {
    WPImage.ImageUrl =
        SPWebPartManager.GetServerRelativeClassResourcePath(
            SPContext.Current.Web,
            typeof(WebPartWithImage))
        + "/Annotation2.png";
    base.OnInit(e);
}
```

`GetServerRelativeClassResourcePath` needs two parameters. First, it needs the current site, `SPWeb`, to get the relative path to the _WPRESOURCES folder. The second parameter is the type of the class—in this case, the Web Part—so that it can generate the folder names. You need to use the type of the Web Part because the Visual Web Part is dynamically compiled and therefore isn't a part of the Web Part assembly.

Worth considering when using class resources is that SharePoint configures IIS to set content expiration (caching) rules on the _WPRESOURCES folder but not on the WPRESOURCES folder. Chapter 9 will discuss this topic in more detail.

6.1.3   Embedded resources

The two previous methods add files to the file system and these files are accessible from any site collection on any web application in the farm. There are situations when you don't want the resources to reside in the file system or be accessible from anywhere except when called from your Web Part. Then you should use the standard ASP.NET technique to embed the resources within the assembly. This is done by embedding the files into the assembly file. These files are then retrieved from the assembly using the `WebResource.axd` handler. This assembly resource handler is called using a set of query string parameters that contain encrypted information about which assembly to retrieve the resource from and the name of the resource. The handler will then load the resource stream from the assembly and send it back to the client. You can't use this method for sandboxed Web Parts; the handler doesn't have access to the assembly existing in the sandbox, so it can't access and load the resources.

To add embedded resources to a project, you add the item or add an existing item to the project, just as with the class resource items. The Deployment Type property of the resource should be set to NoDeployment and the Build Action property to Embedded Resource so that the compiler knows that it should embed the item into the assembly. To make this embedded resource available for the ASP.NET asscmbly resource handler, you have to add a `WebResource` assembly attribute. You add the assembly attribute to the AssemblyInfo.cs file; find the AssemblyInfo.cs file by expanding the Properties node of the project in the Solution Explorer. The attribute should look like this:

```
[assembly: System.Web.UI.WebResource(
"WebPartsInAction.Ch6.ImagesAndScripts.WebPartWithImage.Annotation3.png",
"image/png")]
```

The first parameter in the attribute represents the resource name. By default, it has the name of the project along with the project item and the filename of the resource. In this case, `WebPartsInAction.Ch6.ImagesAndScripts` is the project name, `WebPartWithImage` is the name of the Web Part, and `Annotation3.png` is the filename. The second parameter is the content type of the resource. Because this image is a PNG, the content type is set to `image/png`.

The path to the image is a reference to the WebResource.axd with a set of encrypted parameters. This URL to the image must to be set in code and not in the user control. In a Visual Web Part, you add the Image control in the user control like this:

```
<h3>An image as embedded resource</h3>
<asp:Image runat="server" id="EmbedImage" />
```

The `ImageUrl` property of the Image control is set in the code-behind of the Visual Web Part user control using the `ClientScript` object of the current page. The `ClientScript` object has a method called `GetWebResourceUrl`, which takes two parameters. The first parameter is the type of the Web Part that's used to resolve the current assembly. The second parameter is the exact name of the resource that was used in the `WebResource` assembly attribute. The following code is added to the `OnInit` method to make the Web Part show the embedded resource:

```
EmbedImage.ImageUrl = Page.ClientScript.GetWebResourceUrl(
   this.Parent.GetType(),
   "WebPartsInAction.Ch6.ImagesAndScripts.WebPartWithImage.Annotation3.png"
);
```

Because this is a Visual Web Part, you need to use `this.Parent.GetType()` to be able to resolve the assembly. If the type was retrieved using `this.GetType()`, it would've only returned the assembly of the dynamically created user control. When you're using the `GetWebResourceUrl` method in a standard Web Part, you should use `this.GetType()`.

6.1.4 Resources in SharePoint libraries

None of the previous methods I discussed for including resources are available for use in sandboxed solutions, so how do you add images and other resources to those solutions? Because sandboxed solutions are deployed into a site collection and they live in and have access to only that site collection, you could add the resources to the site collection. You could add the resources to the Site Assets library, the Style Library, or a custom library. This approach also allows users to edit the resources. The best way is to create a custom folder, instead of a list or a library, in the site collection. This strategy prohibits users from tampering with the data, unless they have access to SharePoint Designer.

To create a Web Part that shows an image that you can deploy as a sandboxed solution, you start as you normally would with an empty SharePoint project in which you'll add a Web Part item. You add the resources to the solution in a new SharePoint project item of the type Module and assign it a unique name so that it won't collide with other solutions. The Module item contains two files: elements.xml and a sample file called sample.txt. Remove the sample file and add the image to the Module item. The elements.xml file should look like listing 6.1 when you've added the image.

> **Listing 6.1 Adding resources using modules in a SharePoint feature**

```
<Elements xmlns="http://schemas.microsoft.com/sharepoint/">
    <Module
        Name="Resources">
        <File
            Path="Resources\Tick.png"
            Url="Resources/Tick.png" />
    </Module>
</Elements>
```

The element manifest of the Module item includes a `Module` element whose `Name` attribute contains the name of the folder you want to create. For each resource that should be included, a `File` element is added. This element has a `Path` attribute that specifies the source of the file. The `Url` attribute specifies the destination of the resource. Ordinarily you don't have to add the `File` elements manually; Visual Studio will create a new `File` element each time you add a new item to the Module SharePoint item and remove the redundant elements when you remove a file.

In the Web Part, an image control is added that points to the image added by the module. Because the resources added to the solution are added to the site collection, you need to be sure to add the correct path to the resource. The Web Part class should look like listing 6.2.

> **Listing 6.2   Adding an image to a Web Part using the server-relative URL**

```
public class SandboxedWebPartWithImage : WebPart {
    protected override void CreateChildControls() {
        this.Controls.Add(
            new Image {
                ImageUrl = SPContext.Current.Site.ServerRelativeUrl +
                    "/Resources/Tick.png"
            });
    }
}
```

The Image control is created with an `ImageUrl` property that's a concatenation of the relative URL to the site collection and the path to the image. Using the site collection–relative URL ensures that the path to the image is correct on subsites.

The SharePoint API has a utility class called `SPUtility`, which contains numerous utility and helper methods. When creating site collection- or site-relative URLs, you can use the tilde syntax in combination with the `GetServerRelativeUrlFromPre-fixedUrl` method of the `SPUtility` class. The tilde syntax means that, instead of concatenating the URL as in listing 6.2, you can write the URL like this:

```
~sitecollection/Resources/Tick.png
```

This URL can then be processed by the `GetServerRelativeUrlFromPrefixedUrl` method, which creates the correct URL to be used by the client. This helper method can be used as shown next to translate the previous URL into a relative URL. The URL is stored in a string that you can use to set the image link property of the image control:

```
string url = SPUtility.GetServerRelativeUrlFromPrefixedUrl
    ("~sitecollection/Resources/Tick.png");
```

Unfortunately this helper method doesn't work in Sandboxed mode and you won't notice this fact until you test the Web Part. To make your solution work in Sandboxed mode, you have to build the URL manually by concatenating the strings.

6.1.5   *URL Expression Builder in SharePoint 2010 Server*

The publishing features in SharePoint 2010 Server edition have an Expression Builder class called `SPUrlExpressionBuilder`, defined in the `Microsoft.Share-Point.Publishing` assembly. This class is registered in the web.config (in the expressionBuilders section) with the `SPUrl` prefix. You can use this expression in ASPX pages or ASCX controls—for instance, in a Visual Web Part—to easily create server-relative or site-relative URLs like this:

```
<asp:Image
    runat="server"
    ID="img"
    ImageUrl="<%$SPUrl:~SiteCollection/Style Library/Images/image.png%>"/>
```

When the page containing this image is rendered, it'll make a server-relative URL from the expression in the `ImageUrl`. To create a website-relative URL, you use the `~Site` prefix instead of `~SiteCollection`.

6.2   Localization resources in Web Parts

You're living and working in a global world where you interact with people from all over the world. Not only is the language different from country to country, but you also treat dates and numbers differently. It would be great if everyone spoke the same language and used the same date and currency formatting—but that's not the reality.

SharePoint 2010 supports various cultures and languages. You can't expect everyone to be fluent in a single language. People feel more confident in using their native language when collaborating or having high-level discussions. If you develop solutions that might be used in organizations that use multiple languages, or if you're building solutions that will be sold on a global market, you need to make sure that the solution is culture aware and supports multiple languages. The procedure of translating the user interface is called *localization*.

> **Cultures in .NET**
>
> The term *culture* is used in .NET and defines a set of properties for a culture such as language, sublanguage, country, calendar, sorting conventions, date and time formats, and so forth. All cultures have a name that consists of a two-letter language code and a two-letter region code—for example, en-US for English and the United States.
>
> One specific culture is the "invariant culture," which is culture insensitive; it's associated with the English language but not with any country or region.

You install SharePoint using the English version and then apply language packs to support more languages. All sites are created with a default language, which means that all texts and labels will use that language. In previous versions of SharePoint, a site created in one language remained in that language and you couldn't switch to other languages. SharePoint 2010 lets you enable users to switch to the language of their choice, as long as the necessary language pack is applied.

Let's look at all the options you have when localizing your Web Part solutions and making them available for a global market. The user interface that you're building with the Web Part should be localized as well as the features, Web Part properties, and the editing interface. You have to make several choices, depending on what part of the solution you're localizing and if you're deploying a farm or a sandboxed solution.

6.2.1   Localization methods

There are several methods and techniques available to localize SharePoint items. I recommend that you use resource (.resx) files (a Microsoft .NET framework native feature). You could create your own mechanisms for localizing Web Parts, but using the resource files approach is the only one that will work. To make a solution fully localizable, the Web Part interface and optional Editor Parts need to be localized as well as the Web Parts control description files (.webpart) and the SharePoint Feature that installs it.

You can choose among several methods of including resource files into a Visual Studio solution and SharePoint project, but none of them covers all possible aspects. The resource files in a SharePoint solution package are deployed into different locations, and use of the resources depends on the location. Table 6.1 shows the various locations that you can use to deploy resource files.

Table 6.1 Resources can be included in a solution via numerous methods.

Location	Usage
{SharePoint Root}/ Resources	Resources in this location are accessible from all web applications and can be used by Web Parts, Features, and Web Parts control description files.
{Feature}/Resources	Resources in this location are only accessible and usable by the Feature.
{wwwroot}/ App_GlobalResources	Resources in this location are accessible from only that web application and can be used in Web Parts and user control files.
Satellite assemblies	The default resources are embedded into the assembly and the other cultures have separate culture-specific assemblies.

Deploying resource files into the {SharePoint Root}/Resources folder is a good approach to use when localizing your Web Parts. This technique covers all scenarios (except for the case when you're localizing the user control in Visual Web Parts). For Web Parts, the combination of using this folder and {wwwroot}/App_GlobalResources is the best alternative. Even though you could use the Feature's local resources, having more files to work with will probably cause you trouble. For sandboxed Web Parts the only options you have are Feature local resources and culture-specific assemblies. You can't deploy resource files as root or application global resources.

A resource file is an XML file with the extension of .resx and contains key/value pairs. There's one resource file for each culture, and there should be one resource file that's culture invariant as fallback. The filename of the resource file must be appended with the culture. For example, if the invariant culture resource file is named Resources.resx, then the English (US) resource file must be named Resources.en-US.resx and the Swedish resource file must be named Resources.se-SV.resx. A standard convention is to have the invariant resource file containing the same content as the English (US) resource file. You should also carefully name your resource files so they don't overwrite other resource files (or aren't overwritten).

Because resource files aren't tied to your assembly or code, you can easily localize other SharePoint solutions or have other, for instance a translation agency, localizing yours. To localize an existing solution, make a copy of the resource file, change the culture, and then edit the .resx file. It's smart to create a SharePoint solution package of the resource files so that you can install it as a language pack and deploy it to the farm.

Visual Studio provides an editor for resource files that simplifies editing. Just double-click on an .resx file in the Solution Explorer and the Resource editor will open, as shown in figure 6.5.

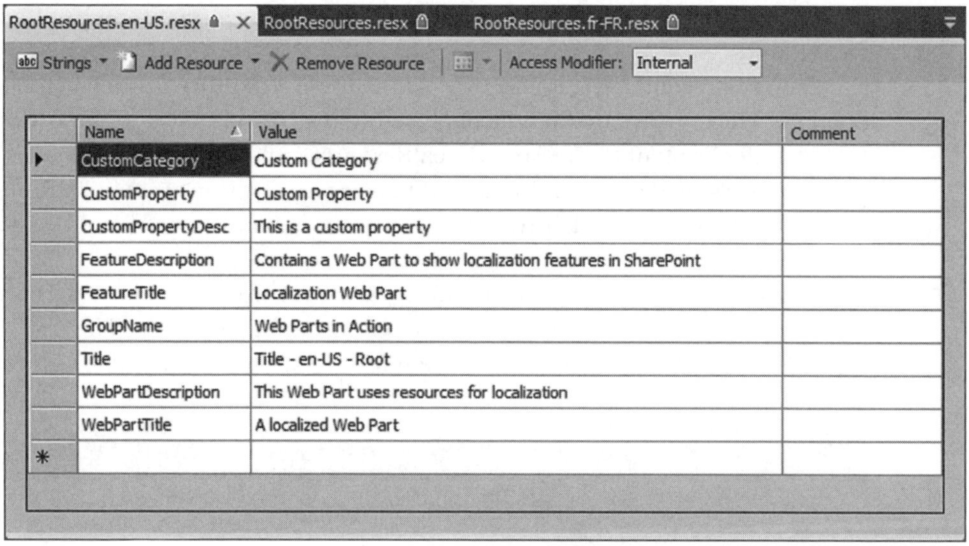

Name ▲	Value	Comment
CustomCategory	Custom Category	
CustomProperty	Custom Property	
CustomPropertyDesc	This is a custom property	
FeatureDescription	Contains a Web Part to show localization features in SharePoint	
FeatureTitle	Localization Web Part	
GroupName	Web Parts in Action	
Title	Title - en-US - Root	
WebPartDescription	This Web Part uses resources for localization	
WebPartTitle	A localized Web Part	
*		

RootResources.en-US.resx ✕   RootResources.resx   RootResources.fr-FR.resx

Strings ▼   Add Resource ▼   ✕ Remove Resource   ▪ ▼   Access Modifier: Internal

Figure 6.5   The Resource editor in Visual Studio allows you to add resource items and values.

The Resource editor allows you to edit the name and value of each resource item as well as add a comment. Using comments can be valuable when translating the resource files to other cultures to provide details about the context of the resource item.

6.2.2 *Localizing code*

The first thing you'll localize are the controls you're creating for the user interface. This step is probably the hardest part of localization because all strings or resources in the source code of the Web Part have to be replaced with calls to utility methods. Fortunately the SPUtility class has a method called GetLocalizedString that you can use to localize strings. To use this method in a Web Part, you have to deploy the resource files for localization to the {SharePoint Root}\Resources folder or the App_GlobalResources folder in the web application.

To localize a control in a Web Part, you have to add a resource file to the solution. Do so by adding a new item to the Web Part. Right-click the Web Part item in the Solution Explorer and select Add > New Item. In the Add New Item dialog box, select the SharePoint 2010 category and then select the Global Resource File item and click Add. Always assign unique names to the resource files so that they don't overwrite resources from other solutions. When you click Add, Visual Studio asks which culture to use for the resource file. The first resource file you add should have the Invariant Language culture. When Visual Studio adds the file to the solution, it'll create a file using the filename specified, and if any other culture than the invariant is selected, it'll append the culture to the filename automatically. For example, if you name your resource file MyAppGlobalResources and select the English (United States) culture, Visual Studio will name the file MyAppGlobalResources.en-US.resx. You should always add one invariant culture to serve as the fallback when no culture-specific resource file is found.

When the resource file is added to the solution, it will have a deployment type of RootFile, which means that it'll be deployed to the SharePoint Root Resources folder. To switch deployment to the App_GlobalResources folder in the web application, edit the properties of the file and change Deployment Type to AppGlobalResource. As long as you're working with a Web Part and not user controls or Visual Web Parts, you can deploy it as a Root File, as you'll learn in the next section.

Listing 6.3 shows how to add a localized `Label` control to a Web Part. This example localizes the `Text` property using the SharePoint utility methods. The text displayed depends on which culture is used in the interface and which installed resources exist in the solution.

Listing 6.3 Adding a localized `Label` control to a Web Part

```
protected override void CreateChildControls() {
    Label label = new Label();
    label.Text = SPUtility.GetLocalizedString(
        "$Resources:Title",
        "MyAppGlobalResources",
        (uint)CultureInfo.CurrentUICulture.LCID);
    this.Controls.Add(label);
}
```

The `SPUtility.GetLocalizedString` method is used to localize the `Text` property. The helper utility method takes a first argument, which represents the resource key. Resources are expressed using a resource expression, which has the following format:

`$Resources:``[file,]key`

`file` is an optional parameter and isn't used in this example. The file is instead used as the second argument to this method. Finally, the current locale identifier of the user interface is passed. You can easily turn this into your own helper method to make your code look cleaner by creating a new method that only takes the resource key as an input parameter.

> **TIP** You can also use the ASP.NET `HttpContext.GetGlobalResourceObject` method to retrieve resources from the App_GlobalResources folder.

6.2.3 *Localizing Visual Web Part user controls*

User controls in Visual Web Parts don't have access to resources other than those deployed into the App_GlobalResources folder. This means that if you're building Web Parts based on Visual Web Parts, you have to use two kinds of resources:

- Resources deployed to {SharePoint Root}/Resources (for Features and .webpart files)
- Resources deployed to {wwwroot}/App_GlobalResources (for Web Parts)

The Visual Web Part user controls can take advantage of the ASP.NET resource syntax, which means that you don't have to use the SPUtility class to localize. The ASP.NET resource handler is only aware of App_GlobalResources, so when using this syntax you can't use resources in Root Resources or Feature local resources. Listing 6.4 shows the same example as listing 6.3 but using a Visual Web Part.

Listing 6.4 Using the ASP.NET resource syntax in a user control

```
<asp:Label
    ID="label"
    runat="server"
    Text="<%$Resources:MyAppGlobalResources,Title %>" />
```

The Text property of the Label control uses inline scripts to localize the property. The same syntax you used for the SPUtility class is employed here, except that you must specify the name of the file. You can use the SPUtility class in the code-behind of the Visual Web Part if you prefer that syntax.

6.2.4 Localizing the Feature

The solution won't be completely localized until you localize the Feature that includes your Web Parts. Even though this Feature isn't seen by most end users, I recommend that you do this. For a Feature containing Web Parts, only the title and description of the Feature is of interest for localization.

To localize a feature, you can use Feature local resource files or resources in the {SharePoint Root}/Resources folder. Unless you have specific needs, I suggest that you place your resources in the Root Resources folder.

Restrict features to specific cultures

There's one situation when you need to use the local resources for a Feature: when you're restricting a Feature to a specific culture.

For example, say you don't want a Feature to install if the corresponding resources aren't available. You can then set the RequiresResources property of the Feature to true. Doing so will prohibit the Feature from showing up in the administration interface if no local resource files match the currently used culture.

To localize the Feature, start by adding a root resource file or by adding new resource items to existing root resource files. Then you have to set the Feature to use these resource files. Do so by opening the Feature in the Feature designer; then in the properties window, set Default Resource File to the name of your resource file. To access the properties window while in the Feature Designer, you can either press F4 or select View > Properties Window. You should only enter the name of the file without the extension and culture postfix. Then change the Title and Description settings to use the resource items using the resource expression syntax, as shown in figure 6.6. Because you've specified the default resource file you want to use, you don't have to supply the filename.

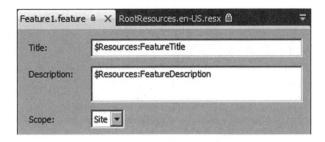

Figure 6.6 **The Feature can be localized using Feature local resource files.**

> **NOTE** If you don't specify a default resource file, the default will be core.resx, which resides in the {SharePoint Root}/Resource folder.

Not only the title and description can be localized in a Feature—you can also localize other parts, such as the elements manifest. The elements manifest of a Web Part normally contains the name of the group in the Web Part Gallery that the Web Part will be deployed to. This group name can be localized. The localized name of the group will be used when the Web Part feature is activated and the gallery is populated using the default language setting of the site, not the user's settings.

To localize the group name of the Web Part, add the name to either the Feature local resources or the root resources. The resource expression is added to the Value attribute of the Property element like this:

```
<Property Name="Group" Value="$Resources:RootResources,GroupName;" />
```

This sample uses a resource file called RootResources and a resource item called GroupName. You can also localize the name of the Web Part file in the gallery and other items in the element manifests.

6.2.5 *Localizing the Web Parts control description file*

The Web Parts control description file (.webpart) contains the default property values for a Web Part and should be localized. The procedure is the same here as when localizing Features, but you can only use resources stored in the {SharePoint Root}/ Resources folder. This also means that you can't localize the .webpart file for Sandboxed solutions. Figure 6.7 shows a Web Part that has been localized into French and has been installed in a site collection that has French as the default language.

Just as with the group name in the element manifest, the resource used for the properties is the default language of the top-level site of the site collection when deployed. Remember to always have a fallback invariant culture resource file or set the Requires Resources property of the feature to true to avoid invalid translations. It's especially important to localize the Title and Description property values, which appear in the Web Part Gallery.

To localize the property values in the Web Parts control description file, you add resources to a root resources file and then use resource expressions in the property elements. Listing 6.5 shows how a .webpart file can be localized.

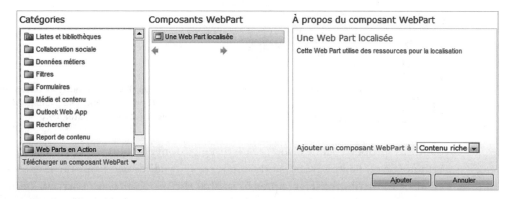

Figure 6.7 The Web Part Gallery uses the default language settings of the site for the groups and Web Parts added to the site collection.

Listing 6.5 Localizing a Web Parts control description file

```
<webParts>
  <webPart xmlns="http://schemas.microsoft.com/WebPart/v3">
    <metaData>
      <type name="WebPartsInAction.Ch6.Localization.WebPart,
                 $SharePoint.Project.AssemblyFullName$" />
      <importErrorMessage>
        $Resources:core,ImportErrorMessage;                    ❶ Localized import
      </importErrorMessage>                                        error message
    </metaData>
    <data>
      <properties>
        <property name="Title" type="string">        ❷ Localized Web
          $Resources:RootResources,WebPartTitle;           Part title
        </property>
        <property name="Description" type="string">    ❸ Localized Web
          $Resources:RootResources,WebPartDescription;     Part description
        </property>
      </properties>
    </data>
  </webPart>
</webParts>
```

The default .webpart file that's created contains the import error message ❶, which is already localized using the core resource file. The Title ❷ and Description ❸ are localized using the RootResources file deployed into {SharePoint Root}/Resources.

6.2.6 Localizing Web Part properties

You just saw how to localize property values, but you also have to localize property names. As you'll recall from chapter 5, you created custom properties and added attributes with the name, description, and category for each property. They're hardcoded values that can't be localized out of the box. To be able to localize these property names, you must extend the Web Part framework with custom attributes. Figure 6.8 shows a Web Part property that is localized.

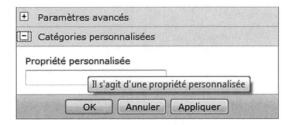

Figure 6.8   A correctly localized Web Part property contains a localized title, description, and category.

To localize property names, you create three custom attributes, one for each standard attribute: name, description, and category. They all derive from the corresponding default .NET attribute (see chapter 5) so that the properties are correctly handled by SharePoint and the Web Part infrastructure and that they behave like the default attributes. The three attributes that you'll create are:

- LocalizedWebDisplayNameAttribute—Localized version of WebDisplayName
- LocalizedWebDescriptionAttribute—Localized version of WebDescription
- LocalizedWebCategoryAttribute—Localized version of SPWebCategoryName

The implementation of these attributes will be similar—the only differences are the names of the attribute classes and the classes they derive from. You can find full implementations of these classes for you to use in your projects in the source code for the book. Listing 6.6 shows the implementation of the LocalizedWebDisplayNameAttribute.

Listing 6.6   Implementation of the localized Web Part property display name

```
[AttributeUsage(AttributeTargets.Property,
    AllowMultiple = false, Inherited = true)]          ◁──┐  Define
public class LocalizedWebDisplayNameAttribute          ❶  attribute
    : WebDisplayNameAttribute {        ◁── Create new
                                       ❷  display name attribute
    private bool m_isLocalized;

    public LocalizedWebDisplayNameAttribute() {        Use default core
    }                                                      resources
    public LocalizedWebDisplayNameAttribute(string displayName)
        : this(displayName, "core") {                  ◁──┘
    }

    public LocalizedWebDisplayNameAttribute(string displayName,  ◁──┐
        string resourceFile)
        : base(displayName) {                          Define
                                                   constructor ❸
        this.ResourceFile = resourceFile;
    }                                     Set, access resource
                                      ◁── file manually
    public string ResourceFile {
        get;
        set;
    }

    public override string DisplayName {
```

```
get {                                          ❹ Check for
    if (!m_isLocalized) {                          cached value
        this.DisplayNameValue =
            SPUtility.GetLocalizedString("$Resources:"    ❺ Translate
            + base.DisplayName,                              resource
            this.ResourceFile,
            (uint)CultureInfo.CurrentUICulture.LCID);

        m_isLocalized = true;
    }                                          ❻ Return
    return base.DisplayName;                       translation
}
    }
}
```

The localized display name is an attribute that can be used only on properties, and listing 6.6 allows it to be used just once on each property ❶. This attribute inherits from the WebDisplayNameAttribute ❷. The constructor ❸ takes the name of the resource item and the resource file to be used. Resource files can either be root resource files or stored in App_GlobalResources. The overridden DisplayName property is used to translate the resource item. First it checks if it has already been translated ❹, and if not, it uses the SPUtility.GetLocalizedString ❺ to translate the item. Finally, it returns the DisplayName ❻ of the base class, which has now been translated.

When you've created all three attributes, you can add them to the properties of the Web Parts. Listing 6.7 shows how a property can be localized using these three attributes.

Listing 6.7 Using the localized Web Part property attributes

```
[Personalizable]
[WebBrowsable(true)]
[LocalizedWebDisplayName("CustomProperty", "RootResources")]
[LocalizedWebDescription("CustomPropertyDesc", "RootResources")]
[LocalizedWebCategory("CustomCategory", "RootResources")]
public string CustomProperty {
    get;
    set;
}
```

Instead of using the standard attributes, the display name, description, and category attributes have been replaced with the localized versions of these attributes. SharePoint will still identify these attributes because they inherit from the standard classes that SharePoint searches for.

6.2.7 *Localizing using satellite assemblies*

A common method for localization is to use satellite assemblies containing the resources. Satellite assemblies are culture-specific assemblies that contain the resources of only one culture. These assemblies are registered together with the main assembly for the solution, and the resources are available through automatically generated classes. Using satellite assemblies isn't easy, and you must do some configuration.

Another downside is that you can only access the resources from within your Web Part code and you can't reuse the resources in manifests or .webpart files.

The easiest way to create satellite assemblies is to right-click the project and select Properties. In the Project Properties editor, select the Resources tab and choose to create a default resource file. The default resource file will be the invariant fallback resource file and its resources will be embedded in the main assembly. The resource file will be added to the project under the Properties node, as you can see in figure 6.9, and called Resources.resx. To add more cultures, just copy the default resources file and append the filename with the culture code.

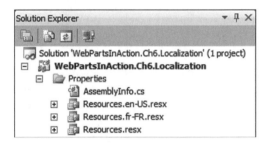

Each new resource file will result in a separate assembly. They'll all have the same name but they'll be located in separate subfolders in the build output folder. These built assemblies aren't included in the SharePoint solution package by default. Consequently, they

Figure 6.9 Embedded resources in the project will be compiled to culture-specific satellite assemblies.

aren't deployed to SharePoint. To include them in the WSP file, you have to open and edit the package. In the Package editor, switch to the Advanced tab, where you can add additional assemblies. To add one of the resource assemblies you've created, click the Add button and select Add Existing Assembly.

In the Edit Existing Assembly dialog box, set the Source Path field to one of the satellite assemblies. You can find them in your project folder under the bin\<configuration>\<culture>\ folder. All the satellite assemblies have the same name, so you have to edit the Location field of the assembly and prefix it with the culture, as shown in figure 6.10. For each assembly, repeat this procedure. Because you had to select the assemblies from one of the solution configuration folders (such as Release or Debug), you have to change the assembly references when switching between configurations.

> **TIP** You can avoid changing the references for the satellite assemblies by using a post-build script that copies the satellite assemblies into a custom folder. Then you reference the assemblies in this custom folder instead of the standard build output folders.

The resources can be used by any application that references the main assembly if you change the Access Modifier setting of the invariant resources to public (via the Project Properties window in the Resources tab). By default, the resources are available only for internal use. To use these resources in your code, you use the automatically generated resource classes:

```
Controls.Add(new Label {
    Text = Properties.Resources.Title
});
```

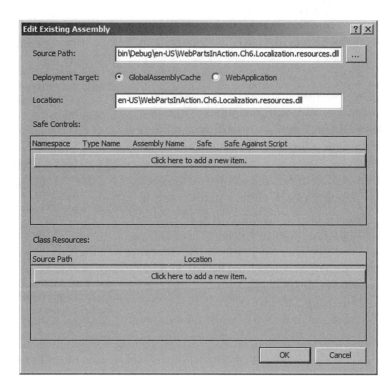

Figure 6.10
The Package designer lets you add existing assemblies, which you'll find necessary when deploying satellite assemblies.

I don't recommend that you make satellite assemblies your main approach to localizing your Web Parts—there are just too many issues, such as:

- Resources are only available from code.
- The Solution Package needs editing between release and debug builds. When you add the satellite assemblies to the package, they're tied to one output directory, which is different between release and debug builds.
- Compilation is necessary to build the satellite assemblies. RESX files can be edited without compilation

6.2.8 Localizing style sheets, scripts, and images

So far you've only looked at localizing text resources, but there are often situations when Web Parts need resources such as CSS files, JavaScript files, and images. These files might require localization—especially texts in JavaScript files or images containing text. Fortunately SharePoint has good support for this.

The {SharePoint Root}/Template/Layouts folder provides support for culture-specific folders. Most of the default JavaScript files of SharePoint reside in the culture-specific folders in the Layouts folder. When you add a new language pack for SharePoint, a new folder for the language pack is created in the Layouts folder. The name of the folder represents the locale identifier (LCID) instead of the short form of the culture name that's used with the resource files.

Each culture-specific folder within the Layouts folder has two subfolders by default: one used for images and one used for style sheets, as you can see in figure 6.11. Scripts and other files are stored in the folder.

In chapter 4 you saw how to make a style sheet Share-Point theme aware. You added the CSS files into the Layouts/1033/Styles folder. A similar procedure is used to localize other file types. Start with adding the Share-Point Layouts mapped folder. You can safely remove the default folder created with the name of your project. Create one new folder for each culture that's going to be supported using the LCID number. Scripts are added directly to the culture folder. To use localized scripts in your Web Parts, use the `ScriptLink` control. Do not hardcode or add the script manually. The `ScriptLink` control ensures that your JavaScript is included just once in the resulting page. With the `ScriptLink` control, you specify the name of the script and (optionally) if it's localized. In a user control, it can look like this:

Figure 6.11   The Layouts folder mapped to the _layouts virtual directory contains one culture-specific folder for each installed language.

```
<SharePoint:ScriptLink
    runat="server"
    Name="CustomScript.js"
    Localizable="true" />
```

This code makes sure that SharePoint loads the script file with the name Custom-Script.js. Because `Localizable` is set to `true` (which is the default value), it will create a reference to the file in the correct culture folder in the Layouts folder. If `Localizable` is set to `false`, it will look for the script file directly in the Layouts folder.

Style sheets use a similar control called `CssRegistration`. If you specify the name of the CSS file, it automatically assumes that the style sheet is in the Styles folder under the culture-specific folder. If the `EnableCssTheming` property is set to `true`, the file must be in the Styles/Themable folder:

```
<SharePoint:CssRegistration
    runat="server"
    Name="ThemedLookAndFeel.css"
    EnableCssTheming="true" />
```

If you need to reference culture specific images or other files in code, you can concatenate the path to the files by using the LCID value. In C#, you should use the current UI culture to get the LCID:

```
int lcid = CultureInfo.CurrentUICulture.LCID;
```

In JavaScript you can access the LCID using one of two methods. The first one is available as soon as the Document Object Model (DOM) has loaded:

```
var lcid =_spPageContextInfo.currentLanguage;
```

The other one requires that the SharePoint JavaScript files and the SP.* objects be loaded:

```
var lcid = SP.Res.lcid;
```

If you need to reference the images, scripts, or other files in the manifest files or files that can use resource expressions, you can use the core resource file to get the current LCID. The core resource files contain a resource item that always returns the current UI LCID, like this:

```
$Resources:core,Language;
```

Finally you always have the option to have values other than text in your resource files. You can use paths to files and scripts that are language dependent in the resource files.

6.2.9 *Other localization considerations*

You've learned how to localize text, images, scripts, and style sheets in SharePoint. To create applications that can be used by many different languages and cultures, you also need to make sure that you handle input data in the correct way. Another important thing is to thoroughly test your Web Part using different languages. The lengths of text may vary, which may affect your overall design.

One common mistake that I've seen in several products, including Microsoft's, is the simple case that the decimal separator is treated differently in different cultures. For example, the Swedish write decimals using a comma whereas a dot is used in the United States. Another common mistake is that dates are formatted differently. The Microsoft .NET Framework contains all the functions that you need to avoid these common mistakes.

In listing 6.8, you have a Web Part that takes a decimal value as input and then prints the value. Although this example is simple, it shows you how to avoid two basic mistakes: parsing the input incorrectly and printing it incorrectly.

Listing 6.8 Using correct parsing of culture-specific input

```
TextBox tb = new TextBox();
Button btn = new Button();
btn.Text = "Click me";
Label lbl = new Label();

this.Controls.Add(tb);
this.Controls.Add(btn);
this.Controls.Add(lbl);

btn.Click += new EventHandler((s, e) => {
    decimal d = Decimal.Parse(tb.Text, CultureInfo.CurrentUICulture);
    lbl.Text = d.ToString(CultureInfo.CurrentUICulture);
});
```

When a user clicks the button, the Web Part converts the value from the text box into a decimal variable. As an argument to the `Parse` method, the current UI culture is

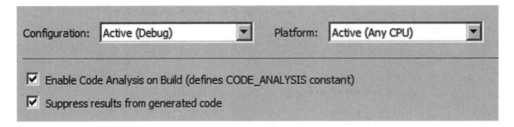

Figure 6.12   Using Visual Studio Code Analysis helps you avoid common mistakes such as forgotten culture-specific conversions.

passed, ensuring that the decimal parsing is done using the correct culture information. The value is printed using the Label control, and the decimal value is converted to a string using the ToString method with the current UI culture as an argument.

Visual Studio includes a feature called Code Analysis that helps you avoid these mistakes (I recommend that you always enable this feature). The code analysis can be run manually by selecting Build > Run Code Analysis. You can also enable this feature to run every time you compile your project by opening the Project Properties window, selecting the Code Analysis tab, and selecting the Enable Code Analysis On Build check box, as shown in figure 6.12.

6.3   *Summary*

Localization of the Web Part can be tricky and time consuming, but the work will be worth it in the end. I recommend that you consider localizing your Web Part project when you start a new project—it's always harder to implement localization when you're done with the project. Even if you choose not to localize the interface, at least enable Code Analysis in Visual Studio and follow the design rules.

Now that you can attach items and scripts to your Web Part solutions, you'll use this knowledge in upcoming chapters, especially when you're building advanced Web Parts that uses the scripting capabilities of a web browser. Adding images and styling to your Web Parts is an easy trick to enhance the overall user experience.

7

Packaging, deployment, and security

This chapter covers

- Working with solution packages
- Working with SharePoint Features
- Deploying solutions
- Activating and deactivating SharePoint Features
- Upgrading solutions and Web Parts

Using Visual Studio 2010 to develop your Web Parts makes it easy to create, package, and add your solutions to SharePoint. In previous versions of SharePoint and Visual Studio, this process wasn't automated, which forced developers to learn how to script SharePoint solution deployment. Even though the new toolset helps you with packaging and deployment during development, you'll eventually deploy the solution to a nondevelopment environment. So it's important to know the basic administrative tasks for SharePoint solutions and Features. Knowing how and when to upgrade solutions is also an important issue. SharePoint 2010 has new features that make the upgrading process easier and more efficient. Taking advantage of these features allows for more agile development and reduces server maintenance and downtime.

Sandboxed solutions in SharePoint make deployment easier and allow you to create custom applications in a controlled manner. Sandboxed solutions also introduce a new security scope for SharePoint applications with a limited security policy. Previous SharePoint versions had only one level where the application was fully trusted (deployed to the global assembly cache, or GAC) and one level in partial trust (deployed in the local web application bin folder, which required a lot of configuration). The level of security and type of deployment is determined by the needs and use of the application. This chapter discusses the various options using a set of examples.

7.1   Solution packages

All solutions, not just Web Parts, in SharePoint should be packaged as Windows Share-Point Solutions Package (WSP) files. These solution packages are compressed files containing all the files required for the solution and the Features that are bundled into the package. You add solution packages from a single point into a SharePoint farm and then deploy them out to all the servers in your farm.

A solution package most often contains one or more Features. A Feature can be scoped to different levels of the SharePoint farm depending on where it's going to be used. Features contain definitions for Web Parts, lists, content types, and all other SharePoint artifacts. A Feature can also contain property values that will be promoted to SharePoint. A Feature must be activated before you use it, and it can be deactivated to remove the functionality. Each Feature can contain a Feature receiver, also known as event receiver, which can be used to execute code during installation and activation.

Only trusted and safe Web Parts and controls can be used by SharePoint. Each package contains information about its containing Web Parts and controls and their trust level. During deployment, this trust level is applied to the web applications.

7.1.1   Windows SharePoint package files

WSP files are CAB compressed files containing all the files needed to install solutions into a SharePoint farm. So far in this book you've been using WSP files to deploy your solutions. Visual Studio 2010 automatically packages the Features and manifests to a WSP file and then deploys it into SharePoint when you press F5. When debugging is stopped, the WSP file is retracted from SharePoint (unless otherwise configured).

These packages are one of the key features of the SharePoint infrastructure and make the deployment of Features and applications an easy task, considering the complex environment. The WSP files are uploaded to the SharePoint configuration database, and when they're installed, the files are unpacked on each application and web server in the farm. When you add a new server to the SharePoint farm, SharePoint knows which packages are installed and unpacks them onto the new server, without you having to interact with the process. Compare this to many other applications and platforms where you manually have to copy the files onto several servers and make sure that they're in sync.

You can manually copy files into the SharePoint root folder and register the assemblies in the GAC (or build scripts that do it), but I don't recommend that approach.

Always use WSP packages to install your Features and solutions. If you manually add or edit files on the servers, your servers will eventually be out of sync and you'll have to troubleshoot the problem. Deploying the Features and files using WSP files ensures that you can deploy your solutions in a consistent manner and keep all servers in the farm in sync.

A WSP file contains a solution manifest that defines the contents of the package. It's this file that you're editing when you use the Package designer in Visual Studio. There can only be one package per project. If you rename the WSP file with a .cab extension, you can easily browse its contents using Windows Explorer. The solution manifest is the file called manifest.xml. It contains general information about the solution and references all items such as the Feature manifest, assemblies, and global resources.

Each Feature in a package is located in a subfolder in the package file and contains the Feature manifest. The Feature manifest is an XML file named feature.xml that you edit in Visual Studio using the Feature designer. The designer allows you to modify only parts of the Feature manifest. For more advanced configurations, you have the option to edit a file called *Feature*.Template.xml or use the Edit options on the Manifest tab in the Feature designer. The advanced configurations made in the Feature.Template.xml are merged with the data from the Feature Designer during the packaging process in Visual Studio.

The WSP files are created when you run or debug your projects in SharePoint. You can manually invoke the packaging by selecting Build > Package. When the packaging is done, the project output folder contains the WSP file.

The solution manifest also contains information as to whether the assemblies should be registered in the GAC or copied to the Web Application bin directory. (See section 7.4 for more details.) Referenced assemblies needed for the solution are also defined here.

7.1.2 SharePoint Features

SharePoint Features consist of a Feature manifest file defining the Feature. Each Feature must be located in its own subfolder of the {SharePoint Root}/TEMPLATE/ FEATURES folder. The Feature files from the solution packages are automatically extracted into those. The exception is the sandboxed solutions (which you'll read in section 7.3). Features can be scoped at different levels, as shown in table 7.1, and they must

Table 7.1 The Features are scoped to a specific level in SharePoint.

Level	Description
Farm (Farm)	The Feature is used by the whole farm. Administration is done in Central Administration.
Web application (WebApplication)	The Feature is used by a single web application. Administration is done in Central Administration.
Site collection (Site)	The Feature is used by a site collection. Administration is done on the root website.
Website (Web)	The Feature is used by a single website. Administration is done on the website.

be activated before you use them. Activation can be done from the web interface, using administrative commands, or automatically by SharePoint. When using Features with your Web Parts, the Features should always be scoped at the site collection level. This is because the Web Part Gallery is located at the site collection level.

FEATURE ACTIVATION

Activation of a Feature means that SharePoint reads the Feature manifest and goes through all the elements manifests within the Feature. These manifests are the actual content and actions that are applied to the scoped level. For instance, for a Web Part Feature the elements manifest contains a module that adds the Web Part controls description file to the Web Part Gallery. The elements manifests aren't activated when you install the solution unless you've specified automatic activation, which is default for and only works on farm- or web application–scoped Features.

> **NOTE**   When deploying solution packages from Visual Studio 2010, the Features will be activated by default. You can change this by editing the properties of the project and setting the Active Deployment Configuration option to No Activation.

Each Feature can also contain a Feature receiver. The Feature receiver is a class in an assembly that derives from the SPFeatureReceiver class and is used to programmatically perform actions on different events. This class has five event methods that are called on by SharePoint:

- FeatureActivated—Fired when the Feature is activated
- FeatureDeactivating—Fired when the Feature is deactivating
- FeatureInstalled—Fired when the Feature is installed
- FeatureUninstalling—Fired when the Feature is uninstalling
- FeatureUpgrading—Fired when the Feature is upgraded

The runtime filter sample in chapter 5 used a Feature receiver to modify the web.config file for the web application in which the Feature was activated. Feature receivers are a great way to perform actions that you can't do declaratively in the package, Feature, or elements manifests using the XML syntax. Feature receivers are compiled code and can do basically anything, and they can take advantage of the state and information in the currently targeted Feature scope.

You can add receivers to the Feature by right-clicking the feature in the Solution Explorer and selecting Add Event Receiver, as shown in figure 7.1. This will create a class under your Feature node that contains the receiver. By default, all methods are commented out and you need to uncomment those you're going to implement for use.

The Feature receivers have two methods that can be used when the solution is installed in the farm. These methods are fired after the installation of the Feature in the farm, and the methods are run on each server in the farm. The activation and deactivation methods are only run on one of the servers in the farm.

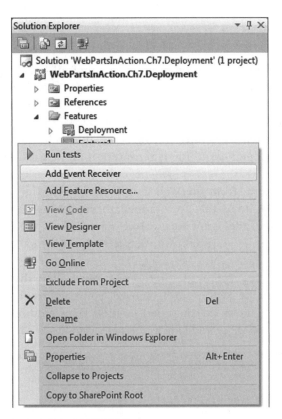

Figure 7.1 **Feature Event Receivers are added to a Feature by right-clicking the Feature in the Solution Explorer and selecting Add Event Receiver.**

FEATURE DEACTIVATION

When a Feature is deactivated, it fires the FeatureDeactivating method of the Feature receiver, but it doesn't undo the actions completed by the module statements in an elements manifest. For instance, the Web Part isn't removed from the Web Part Gallery. The reason that SharePoint doesn't remove the .webpart file is that it'd then remove any customizations made to the file. If you want to make sure that the .webpart file is removed from the Web Part Gallery, you have to implement a Feature receiver. Listing 7.1 shows you how.

Listing 7.1 Deactivation code to remove Web Parts from the gallery

```
public override void FeatureDeactivating(
    SPFeatureReceiverProperties properties) {

    SPSite site = properties.Feature.Parent as SPSite;
    if(site != null) {
        SPList gallery = site.RootWeb.GetCatalog(
            SPListTemplateType.WebPartCatalog);

        SPListItem webPart = gallery.Items.Cast<SPListItem>()
            .FirstOrDefault(w => w.Name == "DeploymentWebPart.webpart");

        if (webPart != null) {
            webPart.Delete();
```

```
        }
    }
}
```

The Feature receiver has one parameter, `properties`, containing information about the current Feature. Using that parameter, you get the current site collection. Using the root web `GetCatalog` method, you retrieve the Web part Gallery. Because the `Items` collection is a nongeneric collection and you're using LINQ, the collection is cast to `IEnumerable`. The first item matching the name of the Web Part controls description file defined in the elements.xml file is retrieved. If an item is found, it's deleted from the gallery.

This method of removing items from the Web Part Gallery works fine if you're interested only in removing the items that were added through the Feature. But because users can customize and add items to the Web Part Gallery, the filename might be changed or there might be multiple Web Parts defined in the gallery using the Web Part type. These Web Parts won't be deleted by this Feature receiver. To ensure that all Web Part control description files in the Web Part Gallery that use the type of the Web Part defined in the Feature are removed, you need to change the deactivation method. Listing 7.2 shows the modified method. This method iterates through all items in the Web Part Gallery and checks the type used by the Web Part.

Listing 7.2   Improved deactivation code for removing Web Parts from the gallery

```
public override void FeatureDeactivating(
    SPFeatureReceiverProperties properties) {

    SPSite site = properties.Feature.Parent as SPSite;
    if(site != null) {
        SPList gallery = site.RootWeb.GetCatalog(
            SPListTemplateType.WebPartCatalog);

        foreach (SPListItem item in                                    ❶ Iterate
            gallery.Items.Cast<SPListItem>().ToArray()) {                 all items

            SPFile file = item.File;
            using (XmlReader reader = XmlReader.Create(
                file.OpenBinaryStream())) {

                XDocument doc = XDocument.Load(reader);

                var type = from el in doc.Descendants()
                    where el.Name.LocalName == "type" &&             ❷ Read
                    el.Name.Namespace ==                                type
                        "http://schemas.microsoft.com/WebPart/v3"      from
                    select el.Attribute("name");                       XML

                if (type.Count() == 1) {
                    Type t = Type.GetType(type.First().Value);
                    if (t ==
                        typeof(DeploymentWebPart.DeploymentWebPart)) {
                        item.Delete();
                    }                            Compare type in  ❸
                }                                XML with Web
            }                                    Part type
```

```
            }
        }
    }
}
```

Instead of finding a Web Part control description file by name, this method iterates all items in the gallery ❶. For each item, it retrieves the SPFile object so that a stream can be opened and finally loaded into an XDocument object. The XDocument class is defined in the System.Xml.Linq namespace. To get the Type defined in the item, a LINQ to XML query is used that looks for the type element ❷ and returns the name attribute. The value of the attribute is used to create a Type object. If this type is the same as the type of the Web Part class ❸, the item is deleted.

This method allows for a more generic approach of removing Web Part control description files from the gallery and avoiding erroneous Web Part definitions. The Feature deactivator doesn't remove any Web Parts used on pages in the site collection; it just removes them from the Web Part Gallery. The downside of using deactivation code that removes the .webpart files is that any customizations done to the Web Part Control Description files will be lost.

FEATURE PROPERTIES

In many situations you need to have configuration data for your solutions and Web Parts. For example, you might need database connection strings, web service endpoints, or other types of information. SharePoint 2010 has support for promoting properties from a Feature property bag, which is a container to store key/value properties, to a website, folder, or list item, but not on lists. This property bag can be used to set default values for your Web Part. There's no support in Visual Studio for editing the property bags in a designer—you have to edit the Feature manifest XML file.

You add a property bag to a Feature by adding a new project item of the Empty Element type. You can add it to the project directly or to an existing SharePoint Project item such as a Web Part. The property bag is defined inside the Elements element as shown here:

```
<Elements xmlns="http://schemas.microsoft.com/sharepoint/">
  <PropertyBag
    ParentType="Web"
    RootWebOnly="True">
    <Property
      Name="FeedUrl"
      Type="string"
      Value="http://feeds2.feedburner.com/WictorWilen"/>
  </PropertyBag>
</Elements>
```

The property bag specifies that the properties should be promoted to the current SPWeb object and only on the root web. The property bag contains one or more properties, each of which has a name, a type, and a value.

When a Feature containing the element manifest is deployed and activated, it will add a new value to the property bag of the top-level web site of the site collection. The values of the property bag are retrieved using the `AllProperties` hash table object on the `SPWeb` object like this:

```
string url =
    SPContext.Current.Site.RootWeb.AllProperties["FeedUrl"] != null ?
        SPContext.Current.Site.RootWeb.AllProperties["FeedUrl"].ToString()
        : string.Empty;
```

Be cautious about what you store in these property bags. They can be accessed easily, even by sandboxed solutions. So don't store any confidential information such as passwords.

7.1.3   *Safe controls and the RequiresDesignerPermission attribute*

All Web Parts and controls that will be used in an ASPX page of SharePoint must be registered as a *safe control*. This is a security rule that's applied to each web application to avoid injections of malicious code.

Safe controls are registered in the web.config of each web application using the `SafeControl` element. The `SafeControl` entries are added to the web.config during deployment of a WSP package, and they're defined in the package manifest. Each Web Part will have its own `SafeControl` entry, by default.

```
<SafeControl
    Assembly="WebPartsInAction.Ch7.SafeControls, Version=1.0.0.0,
    Culture=neutral, PublicKeyToken=9b0d982a432f9891"
    Namespace="WebPartsInAction.Ch7.SafeControls.TheWebPart"
    TypeName="*"
    Safe="True"
    SafeAgainstScript="False" />
```

The `SafeControl` entry defines the assembly and namespace in which the Web Part exists. The `TypeName` attribute contains an asterisk character (*) by default, which indicates that all types within the specified namespace are considered safe. The `Safe` attribute must be set to `true`; the only reason you'd set it to `false` is to exclude certain types or namespaces.

The `SafeAgainstScript` attribute is new in SharePoint 2010 and is by default set to `false`. This attribute is used to prevent cross-site scripting (XSS), which is the term used when malicious attackers try to inject client script code into a web page. When the `SafeAgainstScript` attribute is set to `false`, only users with the Designer permission can insert the Web Part into a page or edit its custom properties. More specifically, the users need the *Add and Customize Pages* site permission, which the Designer permission level by default contains.

Users without the Designer permission can't edit custom properties and they won't see them in the tool pane (unless they're present in a custom Editor Part). If the property is accessible using an Editor Part, it's up to the developer to make sure that the user can't insert any malicious code. If a user without this permission level is trying to add a Web Part that isn't marked as safe, then they'll be presented with an error like the one in figure 7.2.

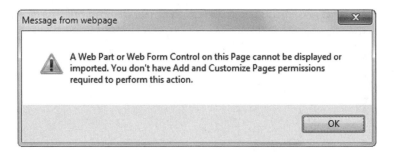

Figure 7.2
By default, users
with only Contributor
permissions aren't
allowed to add custom
Web Parts that aren't
specifically marked as
safe for scripting.

When the `SafeAgainstScript` attribute is set to `true`, users don't need the Designer permission to add the Web Part to a page or change it properties. Visual Studio automatically adds the necessary safe control information to the solution package when adding new Web Part SPIs to the project. To change the value of the `SafeAgainst-Script` tag, right-click the Web Part project item in the Visual Studio project and select Properties. In the Properties window, select the Safe Control Entries row and click the ellipsis button. This opens a dialog box where you can edit the `SafeControl` entry for this Web Part, as shown in figure 7.3. Change the value of the Safe Against Script property to True to mark the Web Part as safe against scripting. You can also use this dialog box to edit the other values in the `SafeControl` entry or add new ones.

To enhance the security of Web Parts that are marked as Safe Against Script, you can add a specific attribute called `RequiresDesignerPermission` to those properties that you still want to disable for nondesigners, as shown here. The attribute is defined

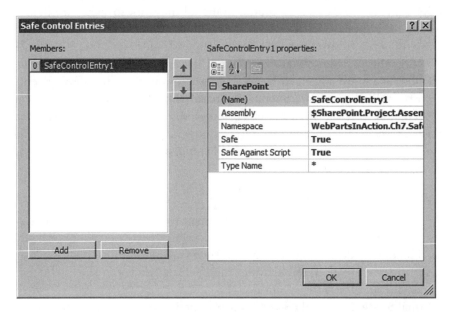

Figure 7.3   Use the Safe Control Entries dialog box to modify the Safe Control elements
of the package manifest. You can add and remove entries and edit their properties—for
instance, you can mark a Web Part as Safe Against Script.

in the `Microsoft.SharePoint.WebPartPages` namespace and in this sample this namespace has the alias of `SP`:

```
[Personalizable(PersonalizationScope.Shared)]
[WebBrowsable(true)]
[SP.RequiresDesignerPermission(true)]
public string Text {
    get;
    set;
}
```

The `RequiresDesignerPermission` attribute is used to indicate that this property can only be edited by those with Designer permission, even if the Web Part is marked as Safe Against Script in the web.config file. It's a good practice to use this attribute on all properties that accept text values and that are rendered in the Web Part to avoid cross-site scripting issues.

> **TIP** If you ever change the name of your Web Part (which you probably will do more than once), you also need to make sure that you update the Safe Control entry. Visual Studio doesn't automatically update the class name or namespace of the Safe Control entry.

7.2   *Deployment and activation*

Once you're done with your Web Parts and you've moved them into solution packages, you'll want to run them in a nondevelopment environment. Then the process of deploying the solutions in the test, staging, or production environment begins. You no longer have the ease of Visual Studio doing all the work for you with deploying and activating Features.

SharePoint 2010 uses PowerShell for administration, and this is a great improvement over the previous `STSADM` command. PowerShell allows you to execute operations that are more advanced and scripting and automate the deployment process. This isn't a book on PowerShell, but SharePoint 2010 requires you to have basic knowledge of it. If you want to get up to speed, I recommend *Windows PowerShell in Action, 2nd Edition,* by Bruce Payette (Manning, 2011). In this section, I'll introduce the necessary SharePoint 2010 PowerShell commands, called *cmdlets,* used to add and deploy solutions and activate Features.

7.2.1   *Solution deployment using PowerShell*

When Visual Studio is used to build and debug Web Parts, the deployment process is automated. The process can be configured using the deployment configurations in Visual Studio. By default, Visual Studio retracts the old solution if it's deployed before it adds the new solution and activates the Features when you start debugging. Once you're done, it retracts the solution.

Visual Studio isn't available on your production or test servers, so you have to do the deployment manually. The process can—and should be—scripted. You have a few options for making this deployment. You can use PowerShell or the `STSADM` command.

STSADM deployment

In SharePoint 2007, you used the STSADM command to add solutions. STSADM is a command-line tool used to configure and administer SharePoint. The tool is located in the {SharePoint Root}\bin folder. STSADM includes operations to perform administrative tasks in your SharePoint environment; some of these are available in Central Administration but most of them aren't. SharePoint 2010 hasn't removed the STSADM tool and it's still included to support compatibility across product versions. You can use the STSADM command to deploy solutions and activate Features.

PowerShell is the way to go with SharePoint 2010. Learning PowerShell is crucial whether you're an administrator or a developer. It can accomplish more tasks in more advanced ways than STSADM. When SharePoint 2010 is installed, it also installs a PowerShell snap-in for SharePoint. To use PowerShell for administering SharePoint, you can start either the SharePoint 2010 Management Shell or start PowerShell as normal and load the snap-in manually like this:

Add-PSSnapin Microsoft.SharePoint.PowerShell

Once the snap-in is loaded, you have access to all *cmdlets* in SharePoint. Deploying a solution requires that the WSP file is uploaded to the configuration database. The SharePoint cmdlet for uploading solutions is called *Add-SPSolution*. Installing a WSP is performed by invoking the cmdlet and passing the path to the WSP as an argument:

Add-SPSolution -Literalpath D:\install\WebPartsInAction.Ch7.Deployment.wsp

When the cmdlet is done, it returns the status of the operation, as shown in figure 7.4. The status includes the id of the solution and its deployment status. To retrieve a list of all installed solutions, use this command:

```
Get-SPSolution
```

Figure 7.4 PowerShell is the tool to use when you administer SharePoint. It can be used to view already installed solutions and deploy new ones.

PowerShell built-in help

Many cmdlets are available for SharePoint and they often have many parameters that you can take advantage of. PowerShell helps you write the commands—you can press the Tab key to access command completion and you can use the `get-help` cmdlet to search for or get help for a specific cmdlet.

Writing `get-help *spfeature*` will yield all commands related to Features and `get-help Install-SPFeature -detailed` will show you all the details about the `Install-SPFeature` cmdlet.

To remove a solution, you use the `Remove-SPSolution` cmdlet, but only solutions that aren't deployed can be removed this way. If you need to remove solutions that *are* deployed, you must specify the `-Force` parameter. The `-Force` parameter can, for instance, be used when you have exceptions thrown in your Feature uninstall receiver methods.

```
Remove-SPSolution -Identity visualwebpartproject.wsp -Force
```

> **NOTE**   There can be some confusion about the naming convention used in SharePoint. *Deploying* and *installing* is the same thing when it comes to solutions. *Deploy* is the term used in the interface (such as Central Administration), and *install* is the term used by PowerShell. The opposites are *retract* for the interface and *uninstall* in PowerShell. The same goes for Features. Features can be *activated* or *deactivated* in the web interface and *enabled* or *disabled* in PowerShell.

When the solution is uploaded into the farm, you must deploy it to use it. Deployment is accomplished using the `Install-SPSolution` cmdlet. This cmdlet takes a number of parameters. First, you need the name of your solution, which is the name of the WSP file. Because Web Parts are installed into a site collection, the name of the web application hosting the site collection is needed. The solution could be installed on all web applications by specifying the `-AllWebApplications` parameter, which includes Central Administration. But I recommend that you always specify which web applications you want to install your solutions in. For full-trust solutions, you must specify the `-GACDeployment` parameter so that installing the assembly in the GAC is allowed. Installation of a full-trust Web Part solution in a web application using a URL is done like this:

```
Install-SPSolution -Identity WebPartsInAction.Ch7.Deployment.wsp
   -WebApplication http://server/ -GACDeployment
```

This command will deploy the solution to the specified server and register the assembly in the GAC. The deployment can be verified using the `Get-SPSolution` cmdlet. To retract deployed solutions you use the `Uninstall-SPSolution` command like this:

```
Uninstall-SPSolution -Identity WebPartsInAction.Ch7.Deployment.wsp
   -WebApplication http://server -Confirm:$false
```

This command uninstalls the solution from the specified web application. The -Confirm:$false parameter is added to skip the confirmation prompt.

You can set the install and uninstall cmdlets to be executed at specific times. The examples presented so far are all performed immediately. Uninstallation and upgrades require that the application pools be recycled. This means that the web applications will be unavailable for a short period and current requests may be aborted. In scenarios when there are high availability requirements, all install and uninstall commands must be coordinated during specific support hours.

> **NOTE** All web applications in Microsoft Internet Information Services (IIS) need a process to execute in. These processes are called *application pools* and they can host one or more web applications. In SharePoint, the Central Administration website runs in its own application pool and the content web applications run in one or more application pools.

7.2.2 *Feature activation and deactivation*

When you're deploying or debugging SharePoint solutions from Visual Studio, the Features are by default automatically activated. When the solutions are installed on staging or production servers, you need to activate the Features manually. Features can be activated in the user interface and, depending on its scope, in different places, as you can see in table 7.1. They can also be activated and managed using PowerShell. As a developer, you wouldn't normally be the one responsible for deploying the solutions in the staging or production farms. But to make you aware of how administrators work with SharePoint and PowerShell, I'll give you a quick introduction to Feature management in SharePoint. Also, I find it helpful as a developer and architect to create scripts as an aid to the administrators and for myself.

To list all installed Features, use the Get-SPFeature cmdlet. This command will give you the name, id, and scope of all installed Features in the farm. Most often, you have many Features installed so you can use PowerShell features to search the output from a cmdlet:

```
Get-SPFeature |
    Where-Object {$_.DisplayName -match 'WebPartsInAction*'} |
    Format-List DisplayName
```

This command will retrieve all Features installed and then filter out those that begin with WebPartsInAction. The result will be printed as a list using the Format-List command with only the display name instead of the default table format. The pipe character (|) sends the result of the previous command into the next one. Studying PowerShell and using features like this can be valuable. You can call Get-SPFeature with different scope parameters to show only the activated Features in that scope. To get the currently activated Features on a specific site collection, use this command:

```
Get-SPFeature -Site http://server/
```

A Feature is activated using the `Enable-SPFeature` cmdlet. This cmdlet takes the name of the Feature and the URL where it should be activated. For Web Part Features, the URL should be the URL to a site collection:

```
Enable-SPFeature -Identity WebPartsInAction.Ch7.Deployment_Deployment
    -Url http://server/sites/team1
```

Deactivating a Feature is similar to activating it. To deactivate a Feature, use the `Disable-SPFeature` cmdlet:

```
Disable-SPFeature -Identity WebPartsInAction.Ch7.Deployment_Deployment
    -Url http://server/sites/team1
```

PowerShell can take a while to learn, but it will be all worth it in the end. The advanced functions take the administration experience to a whole new level. Suppose you have a large farm with thousands of site collections. Activating or deactivating site collection–scoped Features can be tedious work. With PowerShell, you can do it with a single line of instructions. The following snippet lists all enabled site collection–scoped Features on all site collections in all web applications in the farm that have a specific name:

```
Get-SPWebApplication |
Get-SPSite |
ForEach-Object { Get-SPFeature -Site $_} |
Where-Object {$_.DisplayName -match "WebPartsInAction*"}
```

This PowerShell command retrieves all web applications in the farm, excluding Central Administration, and then pipes those to the next command using the pipe character (|). The next operation retrieves all the site collections from the piped web application. For each of the site collections it finds, the command retrieves all enabled Features. The `$_` component is a local variable representing the current object in the pipeline. Only the ones matching the expression are returned. Note that `Get-SPSite` by default returns only 200 site collections, but you can change this limit by using the `-Limit` parameter. The command is split into several lines for easier reading, but you could write it on a single line.

> **NOTE** If you start building scripts for SharePoint using PowerShell, be aware that even in PowerShell you have to dispose of the objects. The SharePoint PowerShell snap-in has two commands to help you dispose of the objects correctly: `Start-SPAssignment` and `Stop-SPAssignment`. Use the built-in help to learn more about these cmdlets.

7.3   *Sandboxed solutions*

Sandboxed solutions were introduced in SharePoint 2010 to allow developers to create solutions and to make it easier to administer and control these solutions. Previous versions of SharePoint required that an administrator install the solutions, which often meant that applications had to be restarted. This, in turn, required a change ticket, which required someone to approve it, and so on. This process took time and often affected the creation of new solutions.

The sandbox in SharePoint allows site collection owners to create, deploy, and run their own solutions in a monitored and restricted sandbox. The resources and application failures in sandboxed solutions are measured, and a solution that exceeds its quota is automatically shut down. All this is done using the web interface, but adding a lot of solutions using the web interface isn't the best way. The SharePoint Power-Shell extensions provide commands that automate these tasks.

When the limitations of the sandbox are too strict, SharePoint offers a way to build proxies that run in full trust and that can be used by sandboxed solutions. These proxies can't be installed by the users; they must be installed as farm solutions and only administrators have control over them. You're going to change our previous RSS Web Part into a sandbox solution. You'll do this by removing the call in the Web Part to the external RSS feed and replacing it with a call to a full-trust proxy. The proxy that runs under full trust will then make the call to fetch the RSS feed and return it to the sandboxed Web Part.

7.3.1 What is sandboxing?

Sandboxed solutions, or user code solutions, are giving SharePoint a whole new level of extensibility. It allows site collection owners to build their own, download, or buy reusable solutions that can be used in the farm without involving administrators. These solutions can also be installed without incurring downtime for your web applications.

SharePoint Foundation has a service called *Microsoft SharePoint Foundation Sandboxed Code Service* in which all sandboxed solutions are executed. This process runs separately from the rest of SharePoint so any crashes or hiccups in the sandbox won't affect SharePoint. SharePoint communicates with the sandbox by using a proxy, and vice versa. The code executing inside a sandbox is deployed to the database but never ends up in the file system. The sandboxed worker process has restricted security policies. For instance, you aren't allowed to call web services or use custom database connections. You can add Web Parts, lists, workflows, and content types, and you can use event receivers in a sandboxed solution.

Sandboxed solutions are deployed into the Solution Gallery of a site collection. This also means that sandboxed solutions can only access information in the site collection to which it is deployed. To deploy a solution into the Solution Gallery, you go to Site Settings of the root web of the site collection and choose the gallery called Solutions. By selecting the Solutions tab in the Ribbon and clicking the Upload Solution button, you can upload a WSP package to the gallery. When the solution package is uploaded, it appears in the Solution Gallery; you can then select the solution and click Activate in the Ribbon to activate it (or Deactivate to deactivate the solution), as shown in figure 7.5. To be able to install sandboxed solutions, the user has to be a site collection owner, so not everyone is allowed to install sandboxed solutions.

SharePoint monitors all solutions running in the sandbox and logs counters such as CPU usage, thrown exceptions, and database queries. Each resource use is logged and assigned points, as shown in figure 7.5. When the total points from one or more solutions in one site collection reaches a certain threshold, the sandbox for the site

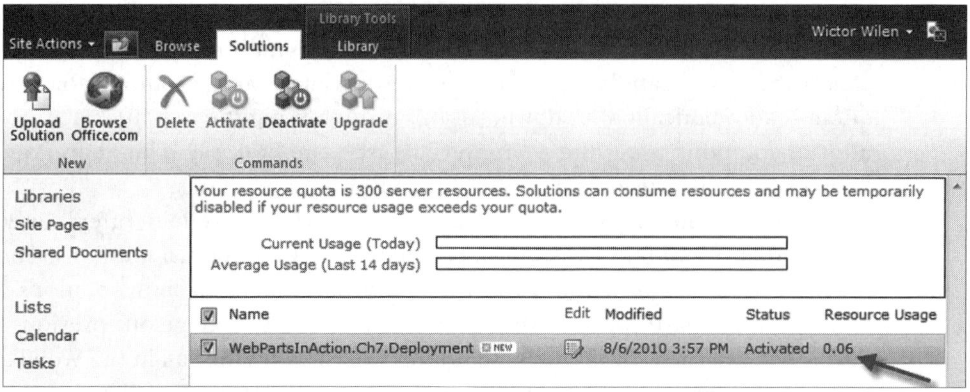

Figure 7.5   The Solution Gallery in a site collection is used to manage the sandboxed solutions. Solutions can be activated, deactivated, and upgraded, and the current resource use is shown for the entire site collection and each solution.

collection will be shut down and the users won't be able to use the solutions until the resource quota has been reset. The point quota is per day, so after 24 hours the solutions will be available once again. To prevent one single sandboxed solution from shutting down all the other solutions in the sandbox, it's crucial that you create solutions that don't throw unhandled exceptions, make unnecessary database calls, or perform other operations that count toward the resource quota.

7.3.2 *Configuring the sandbox*

The sandbox is controlled by the Sandboxed Code Service, described earlier. You start and stop this service by choosing Central Administration > System Settings > Manage Services on Server. To configure the service, choose Central Administration > System Settings > Manage User Solutions. Use the resulting configuration page to block user code solutions and specify load balancing for the Sandboxed Code Service.

The resource quotas for the sandboxed solutions are specified per site collection. To change the resource usage limit for a specific site collection, choose Central Administration > Application Management > Configure Quotas And Locks. Use the resulting page to set the maximum daily resource usage limit and the level of resource usage when a warning email should be sent to the site collection administrator. The quota templates used when creating site collections in SharePoint 2010 also contain the default values for the user code resource usage and the warning level.

PowerShell can be used to configure the Sandboxed Code Service. The Get-SPServiceInstance cmdlet retrieves the id and status of all SharePoint services:

```
Get-SPServiceInstance | format-list TypeName, Id, Status
```

This command lists all current service instances in the farm. You can start or stop using the Start-SPServiceInstance and Stop-SPServiceInstance, respectively. This command will stop the service with the specified id:

```
Stop-SPServiceInstance -Identity 6af4d5c3-6f8c-4f15-9a67-5b4c563bb0a6
```

7.3.3 *Deploying and installing sandboxed solutions*

You don't have to use the web interface to deploy user code solutions. The SharePoint PowerShell snap-in contains cmdlets for working with user code solutions. When deploying a user code solution on several site collections, you should use PowerShell scripting.

To list all installed user code solutions in a site collection, use the `Get-SPUserSolution` command. The command takes the URL to the site collection as a parameter:

```
Get-SPUserSolution -Site http://server/sites/site
```

This command only lists the sandboxed solutions within one site collection, but using command piping in PowerShell, you can combine a few SharePoint cmdlets to list all installed user code solutions in the farm:

```
Get-SPWebApplication | Get-SPSite | Get-SPUserSolution
```

The `Get-SPWebApplication` command will get all web applications, except Central Administration, and then pipe that to the `Get-SPSite`, which lists all site collections in the web application. Finally, all user code solutions for each site collection are printed.

Just as when installing farm solutions, the user code solutions have separate cmdlets. The `Add-SPUserSolution` is used to upload a WSP package to the Solutions Gallery and `Remove-SPUserSolution` removes it. Before removing any user code solutions, you need to deactivate them. Activation of user code solutions is done with `Install-SPUserSolution` and deactivation with `Uninstall-SPUserSolution`.

7.3.4 *Full-trust proxies*

Solutions built for the sandbox are limited due to the policy restrictions. If you try to access web services or databases from your sandbox solutions, you'll be denied. You have three options if you need access to information available outside the sandbox from your user code solutions:

- Install the solution as farm solution.
- Use Business Connectivity Services (BCS) to access external data.
- Create a full-trust proxy.

The first option is in many cases not an option at all (such as in hosted scenarios). If you don't have access to the server or are unable to install farm solutions, your only option is to use BCS to connect to the external systems. But if you're allowed to install farm solutions, full-trust proxies can be a good alternative. A full-trust proxy is an assembly that runs under full trust and is registered as a proxy with the Sandboxed Code Service. Sandboxed solutions can interact with the installed full-trust proxies and through them access external data. By making good decisions on what to install as full-trust proxies, you can minimize the amount of work spent on code reviews and server installation planning.

Let's take the example of the RSS Web Part from chapter 5 and turn it into a sandboxed Web Part. The RSS Web Part reads an RSS feed from an URL; that action isn't allowed in a user code solution, so you have to move that functionality to a full-trust proxy. First, create a new solution in Visual Studio based on the Empty SharePoint project template and choose to deploy it as a farm solution. A full-trust proxy contains proxy operations that are called by the sandboxed solutions. Create the proxy operations by adding a new class to the project that inherits from the `SPProxyOperation` class, available in the `Microsoft.SharePoint.UserCode` namespace. To pass arguments to the proxy operations, you need to create another class that inherits from the `SPProxyOperationArgs` class. Listing 7.3 shows the proxy operation arguments class.

Listing 7.3   Implementing the full-trust proxy operation arguments

```
[Serializable]
public class FeedOperationArgs : SPProxyOperationArgs {
    public FeedOperationArgs(string feedUri) {
        FeedUri = feedUri;
    }
    public string FeedUri {
        get;
        set;
    }
}
```

The proxy operation arguments class must be marked as serializable, and it inherits from the `SPProxyOperationArgs` class. A constructor is added that takes a string as an argument; that string is assigned to a public property. In this example, the string will represent the URL to the RSS feed that the Web Part is requesting.

The proxy operation will take an `SPProxyOperationArgs` object as an argument, which will be cast to the custom proxy operation argument. Listing 7.4 shows the implementation of the operation.

Listing 7.4   Implementation of the full-trust proxy operation

```
public class FeedOperation : SPProxyOperation {
    public override object Execute(SPProxyOperationArgs args) {
        if (args != null) {
            FeedOperationArgs feedArgs = args as FeedOperationArgs;
            if (feedArgs != null) {
                return XElement.Load(feedArgs.FeedUri).ToString();
            }
        }
        return null;
    }
}
```

The proxy operation inherits from the `SPProxyOperation` class and overrides the `Execute` method. This method is called by the sandboxed application using the proxy operation arguments. After casting the generic operation arguments into the custom arguments, the RSS is loaded using the `XElement` class, available in the `System.Xml.Linq` namespace; then the XML is returned as a string.

That completes our custom full-trust proxy; all you have to do now is register it with SharePoint. The best way is to add a new Feature to the project and set its scope to Farm level. Implement an event receiver for this Feature that will register the proxy when activated and unregister it when deactivated. This approach lets you easily manage the proxy from Central Administration. However, administrators can turn the proxy on or off as they like. To avoid that, you can hide the Feature and then make it available only for activation or deactivation using PowerShell or the STSADM command. In the event receiver, you have to implement the activation and deactivation methods, as shown in listing 7.5.

Listing 7.5 Registration and unregistration of the full-trust proxy

```
public override void FeatureActivated(
    SPFeatureReceiverProperties properties) {

    Type type = typeof(FeedOperation);
    SPUserCodeService userCodeService = SPUserCodeService.Local;
    userCodeService.ProxyOperationTypes.Add(
        new SPProxyOperationType(type.Assembly.FullName, type.FullName));   ← ❶ Register proxy operation
    userCodeService.Update();
}

public override void FeatureDeactivating(
    SPFeatureReceiverProperties properties) {

    Type type = typeof(FeedOperation);
    SPUserCodeService userCodeService = SPUserCodeService.Local;
    userCodeService.ProxyOperationTypes.Remove(
        new SPProxyOperationType(type.Assembly.FullName, type.FullName));   ← ❷ Remove proxy operation
    userCodeService.Update();
}
```

The FeatureActivated method gets the Type of the proxy operation class and retrieves the user code service. Using the service, it adds a new proxy operation type ❶, which takes the full name of the assembly and class as arguments. Finally, the method updates the user code service to reflect the new proxy operation type. The FeatureDeactivating method is similar but instead of adding the proxy it removes it ❷.

Once the Feature is activated, any user can create a sandboxed solution and access this full-trust proxy. To change the RSS Web Part, let's use the code from listing 5.2 and remove the feed loading and replace it with a call to the proxy. The code will look like listing 7.6.

Listing 7.6 Invoking the full-trust proxy from a Web Part

```
protected override void CreateChildControls() {                            ❶ Call proxy operation
    string xml = SPUtility.ExecuteRegisteredProxyOperation(   ←
        "WebPartsInAction.Ch7.SandboxFeedProxy, Version=1.0.0.0,
        Culture=neutral, PublicKeyToken=2dc5b379e872af76",                 ❷ Pass custom proxy operation arguments
        "WebPartsInAction.Ch7.SandboxFeedProxy.FeedOperation",
        new FeedOperationArgs(
            "http://feeds2.feedburner.com/WictorWilen")   ←
```

```
    ).ToString();

    XElement feed = XElement.Parse(xml);

    var items = feed.Descendants("item");
    foreach (var item in items) {
        Panel panel = new Panel();
        panel.Controls.Add(new HyperLink() {
            Text = item.Descendants("title").First().Value,
            NavigateUrl = item.Descendants("link").First().Value
        });
        this.Controls.Add(panel);
    }
    this.ChildControlsCreated = true;
}
```

To call the proxy, the SPUtility.ExecuteRegisteredProxyOperation method **❶** is called. This method takes the full assembly name and the class name of the proxy operation as arguments. These names must be exactly the same as the ones the proxy operation is registered with. The final argument **❷** is an object of the custom proxy operation argument. The method call will return an object that's converted to a string, which is finally parsed by the XElement class before the controls are built to show the feed in the Web Part.

You deploy the sandboxed Web Part just as you would any other sandboxed solution. Once you add it to a page, it will show the specified feed. Using full-trust proxies allows you to leverage fully trusted code to sandboxed solutions developers. And administrators will be grateful that you've used a Feature to turn the proxy on or off.

7.4   *Web application targeted solutions*

So far in this book you've deployed Web Parts as full-trust solutions or into the very limited sandbox. Previous versions of SharePoint didn't have a sandbox, and to deploy solutions under a more restricted security policy you deployed them into the web application's bin folder as a partial trust assembly. This is still a valid option if you need to have a security level that's not as strict as the sandboxed solution but not as fully trusted as farm solutions. Deploying partial trust solutions requires that you manually configure the security policy for your assembly using custom Code Access Security (CAS) policies. Although this approach can look like hard work at first, it's a well-documented process.

7.4.1   *Building solutions for web application deployment*

Visual Studio 2010 by default doesn't help you with building partially trusted solutions that are targeted for web application deployment. You should start a project by creating a farm solution in the SharePoint Configuration wizard. By default Visual Studio configures your assembly to be registered in the GAC. To change the assembly deployment target, select the project in the Solution Explorer and then press F4 to open the Properties window. This window contains a property called Assembly Deployment Target, as shown in figure 7.6. By default, it's set to GlobalAssemblyCache, but to deploy it

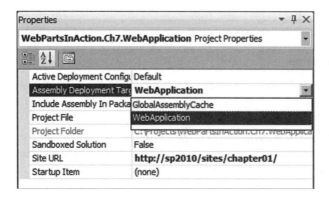

Figure 7.6 Use the Properties window to change the deployment target between full trust and partial trust solutions.

to the web application you must change the value to WebApplication. If you created a solution targeted for sandboxed deployment, you need to change the Sandboxed Solution property to False to enable the Assembly Deployment Target property.

The benefits of running Web Parts under partial trust are that doing so is more secure than running under full trust. Compared to sandboxed solutions (which have a fixed, limited security level), the security level of partial trust assemblies can be configured, which I'll discuss later. To get access to more functionality in a sandbox, you need to build full-trust proxies; that means you must install two different solutions. Another benefit is that deploying assemblies to the bin folder of the web application doesn't require that the application pool be recycled, thus reducing downtime. The disadvantage of partial trust solutions is that they require manual handling of CAS policies.

You can't use Visual Web Parts in partially trusted solutions. The ASP.NET Framework's `LoadControl` methods just don't allow partial trust.

> **NOTE** The Visual Studio 2010 SharePoint Power Tools, available for download through the Extension Manager, allow you to create a Visual Web Part that works without loading the user control from the file system.

Changing the deployment target for the assembly will change the XML for the Package project item. The `Assembly` node has an attribute called `DeploymentTarget` that reflects the value of the project property. When the deployment target is changed to WebApplication, Visual Studio also adds the `AllowPartiallyTrustedCallers` attribute to the AssemblyInfo.cs file. This attribute allows partially trusted assemblies to call your assembly.

Now add a Web Part, not a Visual Web Part, to this project and add a simple `Label` control to it like this:

```
this.Controls.Add(new Label { Text = "I'm deployed to the bin - yeah!"});
```

Then press F5 to build, package, and deploy the solution. Once the deployment is done, add the Web Part to a page and see that it works. To verify that your assembly is deployed to the web application's bin folder, open a Windows Explorer window and browse to c:\Windows\Assembly, which shows the contents of the GAC, and verify that your assembly isn't there. Then open the folder of the IIS website—normally c:\inet-pub\wwwroot\wss\VirtualDirectories\80\—and look for your assembly in the bin folder.

7.4.2 Code Access Security policies

The solution you just created now runs under the same security level as the web application. Farm solutions run under full trust, which means that any deployed code can do whatever it wants with your servers.

The security level of the web application is configured by the trust element in the web.config file and by custom Code Access Security (CAS) policies. By default, web.config defines the WSS_Minimal security level:

```
<trust level="WSS_Minimal" originUrl="" />
```

This is a default minimal level of security defined by SharePoint. The WSS_Minimal CAS policy is located in the {SharePoint Root}\Config\ and is called WSS_MinimalTrust.config. You shouldn't change this file or the other policy files. If you need to manually change the settings, make a copy of them and edit the copy. The WSS_Minimal trust level restricts the code from accessing the SharePoint object model and resources such as the file system and database connections.

CAS policies can be quite hard to maintain, and it isn't always obvious who's responsible for creating CAS policies: the developer or the administrator of the farm. Most often the developer creates the CAS policies, because few SharePoint administrators know how to read and interpret CAS policies. This essentially makes the CAS policies useless. The whole purpose of using such policies is that the administrator who owns the SharePoint farm sets the security level of the solution.

> **NOTE** The Sandboxed Code Service uses a CAS policy to define actions permitted by the user code solutions. The policy file for the service is located in the {SharePoint Root}\Config folder and is called wss_usercode.config.

7.4.3 Custom CAS policies

To test the CAS policies, let's change the Label control in our Web Part so that it prints the name of the current site. Change the Text property so that it looks like this:

```
this.Controls.Add(new Label {
    Text = "The name of this site is " + SPContext.Current.Web.Title }
);
```

This Label control will now output the name of the site, which is retrieved using the SPContext object. If you press F5 to deploy the solution and go back to the page where you previously added the Web Part (or create a new page with the Web Part), you'll see the SharePoint Error message page. If you've disabled the custom error page (see chapter 8), a SecurityException is thrown, with the following exception details:

```
System.Security.SecurityException: Request for the permission of type
    'Microsoft.SharePoint.Security.SharePointPermission,
    Microsoft.SharePoint.Security, Version=14.0.0.0, Culture=neutral,
    PublicKeyToken=71e9bce111e9429c' failed.
```

This exception is thrown because you're trying to use the SharePoint object model, which isn't allowed by the default minimal CAS policy. To allow the solution to execute this code, you must add a custom CAS policy to the solution.

A custom CAS policy is defined in the solution manifest for the package. Once deployed it's merged with the current policy of the web application. During installation, the trust level in web.config will be changed to WSS_Custom, which points to the merged policy file in {SharePoint Root}\Config. This custom policy file contains the default policy file and all merged custom CAS policies.

To add a custom policy to the solution, use the Package editor. In the Package designer, select the Manifest tab and then click Edit Options to bring up the editor. You can use the Package editor to add additional XML to the solution manifest, and the custom XML will be merged with the automatically generated XML and form the final solution manifest.

The custom CAS policy must contain the permission request that your application needs, in this example, that's `Microsoft.SharePoint.Security.SharePointPermission`. But the policies aren't inherited from the default policy, so you need to add all the policies needed to run the application. Listing 7.7 shows the custom CAS policy needed to run a Web Part that requires access to the SharePoint API. This XML is written into the Package Manifest template.

Listing 7.7   Custom CAS policies defined in the solution manifest

```xml
<?xml version="1.0" encoding="utf-8"?>
<Solution xmlns="http://schemas.microsoft.com/sharepoint/">
  <CodeAccessSecurity>
    <PolicyItem>                                    ❶ Define
      <PermissionSet                                  permission set
        class="NamedPermissionSet"
        version="1"
        Description="My permission set">            ❷ Add permission
        <IPermission                                  request
          class="AspNetHostingPermission"
          version="1"
          Level="Minimal"/>
        <IPermission
          class="SecurityPermission"
          version="1"
          Flags="Execution,ControlPrincipal,ControlAppDomain,
          ControlDomainPolicy,ControlEvidence,ControlThread"/>
        <IPermission
          class="Microsoft.SharePoint.Security.SharePointPermission,
          Microsoft.SharePoint.Security, Version=14.0.0.0, Culture=neutral,
          PublicKeyToken=71e9bce111e9429c"
          version="1"
          ObjectModel="true"/>
      </PermissionSet>
      <Assemblies>
        <Assembly
          Name="$SharePoint.Project.                      ❸ Add
                AssemblyFileNameWithoutExtension$"/>           assembly
```

```
        </Assemblies>
      </PolicyItem>
    </CodeAccessSecurity>
</Solution>
```

The custom CAS policy consists of policy item, which contains permission sets ❶. The permission set is of the type `NamedPermissionSet`, and it's given a description. For each requested permission, an `IPermission` element is added ❷. The first granted permission is `AspNetHostingPermission`, which is used to gain minimal access to ASP.NET. The `SecurityPermission` is used with a set of flags to grant security permissions. The last permission grant is the one needed to access the SharePoint API. The `ObjectModel` attribute grants access to the application using the CAS policy to access SharePoint using the object model. Finally, the permission set is given to one or more assemblies, in this case the current Web Part assembly ❸. The Visual Studio replaceable token is used here to insert the assembly filename.

Building custom CAS policies might be difficult at first because it involves using several different permission classes. I suggest that you start with a limited CAS policy, similar to the one discussed earlier, and then test the solution. The exceptions thrown usually give detailed information on which requested permission is required for the application to run.

Error in Visual Studio 2010 while deploying?

As of this writing, Visual Studio 2010 contains a bug that prohibits Visual Studio 2010 from deploying solutions with CAS policies. You'll get an error like this: "Error occurred in deployment step 'Add Solution': Property set method not found."

Fortunately there's a workaround for this error detailed in Microsoft Knowledge Base article KB2022463 (http://support.microsoft.com/kb/2022463). This article contains instructions on configuring Visual Studio to accept CAS policies. In future service packs of Visual Studio, this bug will likely be fixed.

7.5   Upgrading solutions

Very few applications never need an update. The easy way to upgrade is to remove and reinstall the application, which is done in SharePoint by retracting and redeploying the solution. A better approach is to use the built-in functionality to upgrade a solution. (Previous versions of SharePoint could also do this, but the functionality was of limited use.)

In application life-cycle management, it's good practice to use versioning of your code and assemblies. Due to annoying limitations and complicated workarounds, versioning of assemblies wasn't often used in SharePoint projects prior to SharePoint 2010. As you'll see in this section, this new version leverages native .NET features to make it easier to work with versioning in SharePoint.

This section also discusses how to handle updating of Web Parts when you've removed, added, or renamed properties.

7.5.1 *How to upgrade*

Upgrading solutions involves replacing the current solution with a new version. There are basically two ways to upgrade a solution:

- Upgrade
- Retract and redeploy

Depending on what has changed in your solution and the service level of your application, you can choose either approach. Retracting and redeploying a solution means that you completely remove the solution and its assemblies, Features, and files and once again apply them. SharePoint doesn't remove any information from the content databases so it's most often safe to use this method. On the other hand, because it removes files and Features, this method affects the state of the farm in a more serious manner than just upgrading the solution. You might also have to execute your Feature receivers once again, which could cause problems. Upgrading a solution is normally the quicker approach—and it works as long as you haven't added any new Features to the solution (if that's the case, you need to retract and redeploy).

You upgrade a solution using the PowerShell `Update-SPSolution` command. It's similar to the `Install-SPSolution` cmdlet but requires that you specify the solution file to upgrade with:

```
Update-SPSolution
    -Identity WebPartsInAction.Ch7.Deployment.wsp
    -Literalpath D:\install\WebPartsInAction.Ch7.Deployment.wsp
    -GACDeployment
```

Sandboxed solutions can be upgraded using the web interface. You have two options to accomplish this. The first is to deactivate the solution, then upload the solution again and finally activate it. A better approach (which also supports the upgrade actions discussed later) is to rename the package using the Package designer and upload the new solution file. SharePoint will detect that it's the same solution, unless you've changed the solution id. Then you can select the new item in the gallery and click Upgrade in the Ribbon to upgrade to the new solution.

For sandboxed solutions, there's also a corresponding PowerShell command called `Update-SPUserSolution`. This command has to follow an `Add-SPUserSolution` command, which uploads the new WSP file with the new name to the Solution Gallery.

```
Update-SPUserSolution
    -Identity WebPartsInAction.Ch7.Deployment.wsp
    -ToSolution WebPartsInAction.Ch7.Deployment2.wsp
    -Site http://server
```

7.5.2 *Upgrading Features*

SharePoint 2010 has support for you to add custom code or apply new element manifests when upgrading a Feature. This support is useful if you need to upgrade any items that were provisioned in previous versions. For instance, you might want to add a new Web Part to the gallery when upgrading from one version to another.

The Feature manifest has a new element in SharePoint 2010 called Upgrade-Actions. This element can be used to specify actions to perform when upgrading from one version to another. Listing 7.8 shows a sample when upgrading from version 1.0.0.0 – 1.5.0.0 to the new version.

Listing 7.8   Using the UpgradeActions element

```
<Feature xmlns="http://schemas.microsoft.com/sharepoint/">
  <UpgradeActions>                                              ❶ Define upgrade
    <VersionRange BeginVersion="1.0.0.0" EndVersion="1.5.0.0">     versioning range
      <ApplyElementManifests>
        <ElementFile Location="Elements2.xml"/>                 ❷ Apply new
      </ApplyElementManifests>                                    element
      <CustomUpgradeAction Name="RemoveOldWP">      Execute        manifest
        <Parameters>                                custom
          <Parameter Name="DeleteWebPart">          upgrade
            VersioningWebPart.webpart             ❸ action
          </Parameter>
        </Parameters>
      </CustomUpgradeAction>
    </VersionRange>
  </UpgradeActions>
</Feature>
```

This upgrade action will apply to the specified version range ❶. If the currently installed version is within that range, it will apply the specified element manifest ❷. The upgrade will also invoke a custom upgrade action called RemoveOldWP ❸ with a parameter.

The custom upgrade action is passed to the Feature receiver of the Feature. Specifically the FeatureUpgrading method is called with the name of the upgrade action and the specified parameters. Listing 7.9 shows an implementation for the upgrade action in the previous listing. This function can be used if you've changed your Web Part implementation so that you need to remove the old definitions from the Web Part Gallery.

Listing 7.9   Using the FeatureUpgrading method

```
public override void FeatureUpgrading(
    SPFeatureReceiverProperties properties,
    string upgradeActionName,
    System.Collections.Generic.IDictionary<string, string> parameters) {

    if (upgradeActionName == "RemoveOldWP") {              Check upgrade
        SPSite site = properties.Feature.Parent as SPSite; ❶ action
        if (site != null) {
            SPList gallery = site.RootWeb.GetCatalog(
                SPListTemplateType.WebPartCatalog);        ❷ Get parameter
                                                              value
            var itemsToDelete = parameters.Where(
                s => s.Key == "DeleteWebPart");
            foreach(var itemToDelete in itemsToDelete){    Find item ❸
                SPListItem item = gallery.Items.
                            Cast<SPListItem>().FirstOrDefault(
                            w => w.Name == itemToDelete.Value);
```

```
            if (item != null) {
                item.Delete();                    ◁──┐   Delete
            }                                    ❹    item
        }
    }
}
}
```

This upgrading action is quite similar to the `FeatureDeactivating` method in listing 7.2. The Feature upgrading method checks which upgrade action is passed ❶ to the method; if it's the correct one, it proceeds. It retrieves all parameters having the key value equal to `DeleteWebPart` ❷ and iterates over those. For each iteration, it checks the Web Part Gallery items for a Web Part with the specified name ❸ and if it finds a Web Part, the method deletes it ❹.

7.5.3 *Assembly redirection*

The .NET Framework uses assembly versioning to support running the same assembly but different versions side by side. It's a good practice to give the assemblies a version number and increment the version number as the assembly is patched and evolved. Having a version number in combination with source control can help you when you're troubleshooting your solutions.

The assembly version number is specified in the AssemblyInfo.cs file located under the Properties node in the Solution Explorer. The version is specified using an assembly attribute:

```
[assembly: AssemblyVersion("1.0.0.0")]
```

The version number is used for assembly full names in combination with the culture and public key token. Web Parts added to pages and stored in SharePoint store this full name of the Web Part class. If you change the version number of the assembly and replace the old assembly with your new one, then SharePoint won't find the Web Part. Because previous versions of SharePoint lacked good support for changing the version number, most solutions never changed the version number.

The .NET Framework has support for a method called *assembly redirection*. This method redirects assemblies within a certain version span to another version. For example, all requests to an assembly of version 1.0.0.0 to 1.5.0.0 are redirected to version 2.0.0.0. This assembly redirection is specified in the configuration file of the application (with SharePoint, it's web.config). You can do this manually by adding entries like these:

```
<runtime>
  <assemblyBinding>
    <dependentAssembly>
      <assemblyIdentity
        name="WebPartsInAction.Ch7.Upgrade"
        publicKeyToken="5bd2ee7eed22e9d1"
        culture="neutral" />
      <bindingRedirect
        oldVersion="1.0.0.0-1.5.0.0"
```

```
        newVersion="2.0.0.0" />
      </dependentAssembly>
    </assemblyBinding>
  </runtime>
```

In the configuration file under the `assemblyBinding` node, a new dependent assembly is added. This contains an assembly identity, which specifies the name, public key token, and culture for the assembly. The redirection contains the source version range and the target version.

With SharePoint 2010, the ability to create assembly redirection has been incorporated into the solution manifest. That way, you avoid manual editing of the configuration file and thus avoid creating inconsistency between servers. When an assembly gets a new version and you want to use assembly redirection, you open the solution manifest in the Package editor and choose to edit the manifest template. From the preview windows of the packaged manifest, copy the `Assemblies` node into the manifest template editor; then delete everything beneath the `Assembly` element and add the redirect as follows:

```xml
<?xml version="1.0" encoding="utf-8"?>
<Solution xmlns="http://schemas.microsoft.com/sharepoint/">
  <Assemblies>
    <Assembly Location="WebPartsInAction.Ch7.Upgrade.dll">
      <BindingRedirects>
        <BindingRedirect OldVersion="1.0.0.0-1.5.0.0"/>
      </BindingRedirects>
    </Assembly>
  </Assemblies>
</Solution>
```

The `Assembly` element only needs to contain the `Location` attribute. The `DeploymentTarget` attribute has been deleted because it will be added automatically and will be present in the merged manifest. The `BindingRedirect` element specifies the version span from which the redirection should start. The destination version is retrieved from the current version of the assembly.

NOTE You need to keep the old Safe Control entries in the web.config until you're sure that all the old Web Part instances have been updated.

Even though redirection is a great way to use versioning on your assemblies, proceed with caution. You can't make changes to the Web Part properties that make the old persisted values incompatible with the new version. If you change the type of a property, it can lead to unwanted results. Carefully plan your assembly redirections.

7.5.4 Upgrading Web Parts

If you make changes to your Web Part that make it incompatible with previous versions, such as renaming properties or changing how the property values are managed, you can't just change the assembly. All property values of a Web Part in SharePoint are serialized into the content databases, and an upgraded Web Part could potentially break if the serialized state is inconsistent with what's expected.

To upgrade a Web Part for which you've changed one or more properties, you have to implement the `IVersioningPersonalizable` interface. This interface contains a single method called `Load`, which is called whenever SharePoint detects one or more properties that exist in the database but not in the Web Part. Listing 7.10 shows a Web Part supporting the `IVersioningPersonalizable` interface and how it updates a property called `OldProperty` to the new property called `NewProperty`.

Listing 7.10   Upgrading a Web Part property

```
public class UpdateWebPart: WebPart, IVersioningPersonalizable {

    IDictionary _unknownProperties = null;

    public new void Load(IDictionary unknownProperties) {    ❶ Retrieve unknown
        _unknownProperties = unknownProperties;                 properties
    }

    [WebBrowsable(true)]
    [Personalizable(PersonalizationScope.Shared)]
    public string NewProperty {
        get;
        set;
    }

    protected override void OnInit(EventArgs e) {
        if (_unknownProperties != null) {
            foreach (DictionaryEntry  item in _unknownProperties) {
                if (item.Key == "OldProperty") {
                    this.NewProperty = item.Value.ToString();    ← Update
                    this.SetPersonalizationDirty();                new
                }                                                ❷ property
            }
        }
        base.OnInit(e);
    }
}
```

The Web Part derives from the `IVersioningPersonalizable` interface and implements the `Load` method. When the `Load` method is called, it stores the unknown properties into a local variable ❶. When the `OnInit` method is called, it checks whether any unknown properties exist. If there are unknown properties, the method will loop through them and look for a property called `OldProperty`. If `OldProperty` is found, the method copies the value of that property into the new property called `NewProperty` ❷. Once the new property is set, it calls the `SetPersonalizationDirty` method, which invalidates the Web Part and makes SharePoint save its personalization state.

> **TIP** If you're upgrading a SharePoint Web Part to an ASP.NET Web Part, you can use the `AfterDeserialize` method of the SharePoint Web Part implementation to update properties. When a Web Part has been updated from a SharePoint Web Part to an ASP.NET Web Part, the first time it's loaded it will be deserialized into a SharePoint Web Part and call the `AfterDeserialize` method. Then it will be serialized into the database as an ASP.NET Web Part.

7.6   *Summary*

This chapter covers deployment options and methods, and security considerations and implementations. It also introduced you to the world of PowerShell. I recommend that you learn PowerShell if you're unfamiliar with it, because it will make your SharePoint administration experience much better. Scripting your deployment allows for better application life-cycle management and ensures that you do the same thing for all environments.

You also learned the implications of various deployment options. Running applications in full trust is the easiest way to build powerful applications but requires that you and your administrators be in total control of the code that's being deployed. For better and detailed control of what the applications should be able to do, you can deploy them to the web application and use CAS policies to specify the security level. You and your power users can use sandboxed solutions to deploy applications; that way, your SharePoint farm is always safe and your applications are monitored. And you can extend the sandboxed solutions using full-trust proxies to leverage certain functionality to the user code solutions.

My recommendation is that you always start with sandboxed solutions. If you can do it in the sandbox, there's no reason to play anywhere else.

So far in this book you've focused on building Web Parts and deploying them into SharePoint farms. In the next couple of chapters I'll show you how to troubleshoot your Web Parts when the inevitable errors happen and how to get the most performance out of your Web Parts.

Tools for troubleshooting
and logging

8

This chapter covers

- Logging features in SharePoint
- Error and exception handling
- Debugging
- The Developer Dashboard
- Troubleshooting tools

In all projects, you'll eventually have to perform some sort of troubleshooting. Depending on your support personnel's troubleshooting skills and how the application is built, problems can be fixed before your users even notice them. Normally, a problem starts when a user receives an error and can't resolve it. The user then reports the error and the problem escalates to your support team. If the error can't be resolved by the support team, the troubleshooting will fall back on your developers or application management team. Without proper information from your support team, you'll have a hard time reproducing the incident. Building Web Parts that correctly handle errors and unexpected situations allows you to more quickly resolve any issues—hopefully the support team will even be able to resolve it before it ends up on your desk.

In large-scale scenarios with possibly hundreds of thousands of users, it can be difficult to track down a single problem by searching the log files of the application. SharePoint has solved this issue by using a unique id for each request. When an error occurs, SharePoint presents that id to the user, who can then send it to the support team using, for example, a screen dump. By giving your Web Parts the ability to be monitored and using the SharePoint logging facilities, you can cut down the time needed to find the source of problems. Once you've figured out where and how the error happened, you have to reproduce this error to devise a resolution. You need different tools, depending on the type of error.

If the error is in the code, you might have to reproduce the error in your development environment and eventually debug the code. Visual Studio 2010 is your primary development environment, and you can use it to step through each line of code until you isolate the problem.

Sometimes you need to debug your application in an environment where you don't have access to Visual Studio. For that purpose, SharePoint 2010 has a new feature called the Developer Dashboard, which shows detailed information about all exceptions and warnings on the current page. The dashboard can also be used to inspect the performance of each Web Part and its methods in a page—which is great when you need to optimize the application.

To avoid unnecessary support calls, it's crucial to build robust code that handles exceptions and helps users avoid unhandled errors. Well written and robust are valid criteria for all kinds of development, but a single Web Part can make a page or whole site fail if it doesn't handle exceptions correctly.

Visual Studio isn't the only tool you'll need when troubleshooting SharePoint and Web Parts. For specific scenarios, it may be important to have a JavaScript debugger if you don't have access to Visual Studio. And you may need to inspect what has been transferred between the client and server by using web proxy tools.

8.1   *Logging and error handling in SharePoint 2010*

SharePoint 2010 contains numerous features to enable you to troubleshoot your applications while developing or running in production. All requests to SharePoint are given a unique id, which can be used to trace a specific error message to a request. This number is called the *correlation id*. Depending on how you've configured Share-Point errors, warnings and information messages are logged to the SharePoint-specific trace logs and databases, or to the Windows Event Log. All of these log entries contain a correlation id, which allows you to combine logs from different sources to get a bigger picture of a specific error or warning.

The correlation id is new in SharePoint 2010. This unique value is shown on the default error page. The default error page never shows the exact error that the end users saw, but users can send the correlation id to the support team for further investigation. Any custom logging to the log files will also contain this specific id.

The trace logs, also called *Unified Logging Service (ULS)/ logs*, are a primary source when you're searching for exceptions and problems with your SharePoint installation. You can monitor these log files with external monitoring systems and search them by using simple text editing tools or PowerShell.

8.1.1   Introducing the correlation id

Errors can be shown in various ways in SharePoint. Unhandled errors and exceptions will eventually be displayed using the SharePoint error page (unless you've turned it off). This custom error page displays the following message: "An unexpected error has occurred." Although this error message doesn't help you with anything, SharePoint 2010 always displays a unique error id called the correlation id, as shown in figure 8.1. One of the reasons not to show the actual error message is that it can reveal too much of the actual code and call stack in the application and open it up for hacking attempts.

The correlation id is guaranteed to be unique for that particular error at that given time. It won't give any clues or help to an end user, but for an administrator this error message is important. An administrator can use the correlation id to look in the log files for the error message and source. Not only does SharePoint assign correlation ids to errors, but it also assigns every request and action a correlation id. This number is consistent over the whole farm and across service applications.

> **TIP**   If you want, you can customize the error page to provide your end users with more information or instruct them to send the error message to the support team. The error page is located in {SharePoint Root}/TEMPLATE/ LAYOUTS/ and is called error.aspx.

Figure 8.1   The default error page in SharePoint 2010 doesn't show any information about the error but instead shows a correlation id that you can use when searching for the error in the logs.

If an unhandled error occurs on a Web Part or Wiki page, a link to the Web Parts Maintenance page is provided. Click this link to inspect the Web Parts on the page and remove the ones that are failing.

8.1.2   *SharePoint trace logs*

Almost everything in SharePoint can be logged. SharePoint logs information to the *Unified Logging Service*, which stores the information in the file system under {SharePoint Root}\LOGS. These logs are called the ULS logs, or trace logs. All events can be logged to the trace logs, and some information is also logged to the standard Windows Event Logs. You configure what and how much to log in the trace and event logs in Central Administration > Monitoring > Configure Diagnostics Logging, as shown in figure 8.2.

The trace logs always contain the correlation id, and this number is preserved over multiple servers—for example, when service applications are invoked on other servers. That way, you can easily locate any errors. The log files are plain-text files and can be opened with any text editing tool, but it can be hard to search and get an overview of the events using those tools. Several tools that will help you search and monitor the log files are available for download. One tool I recommend is the ULS Viewer by Microsoft, which can be downloaded at http://code.msdn.microsoft.com/ULSViewer.

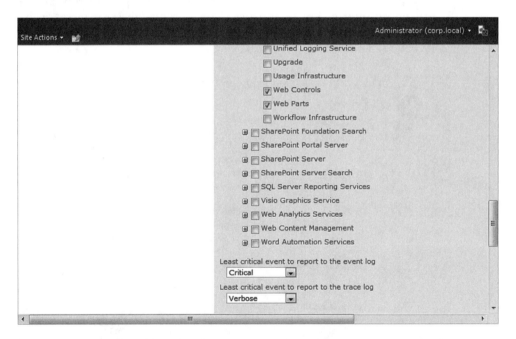

Figure 8.2   The logging levels for the trace and event logs is configured in Central Administration.

8.1.3 Searching the trace logs

The SharePoint PowerShell snap-in also has a set of commands that allow you to work with the trace logs. For example, you'll find the `Get-SPLogEvent` cmdlet useful when searching for errors using the correlation id. Assume that you have a Web Part that has failed in your production environment; your user reports the error to you but you only get the correlation id. You can either use one of the tools or this cmdlet to find out exactly what happened, if logging is enabled. To retrieve all logged information about a specific correlation id, use this PowerShell command:

```
Get-SPLogEvent |
Where{$_.Correlation -eq "a53ba71b-4231-4222-ac7e-4535dcf0c534"} |
Format-Table Category, Message -Autosize
```

The `Get-SPLogEvent` cmdlet returns records from all the trace log files on the current server. All records containing the specified correlation id are returned using the `Where` command. Finally, the category and message properties are formatted as an auto-sized table. The result of this command might look like figure 8.3, in which you see that there's an exception thrown by a Web Part.

If you need to use log files from multiple servers, use the `Merge-SPLogFile` cmdlet to merge all trace log files from all servers into a new local log file. The `Get-SPLog-Event` cmdlet can then be used on that new merged file to search for different records. Since the log files can grow to very large sizes I have found it very convenient to use the `New-SPLogFile` cmdlet. This cmdlet creates a new log file on demand. I use it in most of my scripts so that I can isolate the log events and have less information to search within.

In SharePoint 2010, some information is also logged to a specific log database, normally called WSS_Logging. If you have SharePoint 2010 Server, the trace logs are added to this database as well as to the log files on the disk. This allows you to query the database instead or even build a Web Part that takes the correlation id as input and outputs all the corresponding records.

Figure 8.3   Using PowerShell to search for logged events related to a specific correlation id makes it easier to find the source of any problems.

8.1.4 Custom logging to trace logs

The ULS has an API so that you can write customized records to the logs. This API is available both in SharePoint 2010 Foundation as well as in the Server editions. Writing to the trace log can be valuable for many reasons, such as generic logging and logging of handled exceptions.

To add custom logging to a Web Part project, use the `SPDiagnosticsService` class, which exists in the `Microsoft.SharePoint.Administration` namespace in the `Microsoft.SharePoint` assembly. This class has two interesting methods you can use when logging information:

- `WriteTrace()`—Writes to the SharePoint trace log
- `WriteEvent()`—Writes to the Windows event log and possibly to the trace log

Both methods have nearly the same signature but write to different locations. Writing to the Windows event log may be desirable if there are some serious errors that must be escalated to systems monitoring the event logs. Normally the SharePoint trace logs are the best way to go. Listing 8.1 shows how to write to the trace log and write the current correlation id in the Web Part. This can be a good practice if you'd like your users to report the correlation id if any errors occur so that you can find the source of the error.

Listing 8.1 Using the correlation id in custom error messages

```
[DllImport("advapi32.dll")]
public static extern uint EventActivityIdControl(      ❶ Importing
    uint controlCode,                                     method from
    ref Guid activityId);                                 advapi32.dll

public const uint EVENT_ACTIVITY_CTRL_GET_ID = 1;

protected override void CreateChildControls() {
    try {
        // code that throws an Exception
    }
    catch (FormatException ex) {
        SPDiagnosticsService diagSvc = SPDiagnosticsService.Local;
        diagSvc.WriteTrace(0,
            new SPDiagnosticsCategory("Exception",
                TraceSeverity.Monitorable,
                EventSeverity.Error),              ❷ Writing to
            TraceSeverity.Monitorable,               trace log
            "An exception occurred: {0}",
            new object[] {ex});
        Guid g = Guid.Empty;
        EventActivityIdControl(EVENT_ACTIVITY_CTRL_GET_ID, ref g);   ⟵
        this.Controls.Add(new Label {
            Text = string.Format(
                "An error occurred with correlation id {0}", g)
        });
    }                                                      Retrieving
}                                                          correlation id ❸
```

To get the current correlation id, the `EventActivityIdControl` method is imported ❶ from the advapi32.dll file. This Web Part throws an exception in the code, which is caught. To write to the trace log, the local diagnostics service is retrieved, and using the `WriteTrace` method ❷, the exception is logged. The first parameter is a custom id of the log record. The second parameter describes the category of the record and includes a name and the default throttling levels for the trace and event logs. The severity level of the current record is also supplied, as well as the error message with its optional parameters. The correlation id is retrieved by invoking the imported `EventActivity-IdControl` method ❸. The user is informed about the correlation id by adding a `Label` control to the Web Part.

Notice that the `SPDiagnosticsService` class used to write to the trace logs isn't available for use in sandboxed solutions. The imported method that acquires the correlation id isn't either allowed when running code in sandboxed solutions.

> **TIP** Microsoft Systems Center Operations Manager is monitoring software that can be used to monitor SharePoint using the ULS Logs.

8.1.5 Error handling in sandboxed solutions

If an unhandled exception occurs in a sandboxed solution, the exception is caught and handled by SharePoint. SharePoint then presents a more developer-friendly error message than the default error page. If debugging is enabled, then the error details can be shown, as you can see in figure 8.4.

All unhandled exceptions in sandboxed solutions are monitored and accounted for in the resource usage. This means that if the solution throws many exceptions, then the whole sandbox for the site collection eventually will be shut down, so handling the exceptions correctly is crucial for sandboxed solutions.

To log and monitor exceptions and other information, you need to create a logging mechanism of your own. You could create a full-trust proxy that uses the trace logging as described earlier. Another approach is to use the Business Connectivity Services

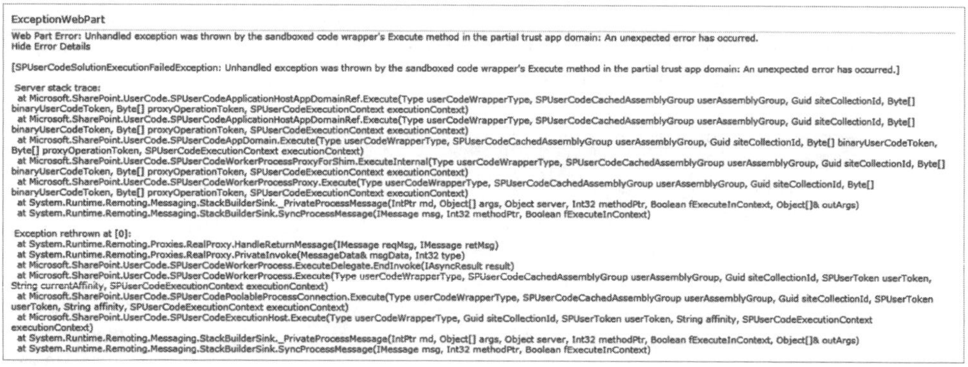
ExceptionWebPart
Web Part Error: Unhandled exception was thrown by the sandboxed code wrapper's Execute method in the partial trust app domain: An unexpected error has occurred.
Hide Error Details

[SPUserCodeSolutionExecutionFailedException: Unhandled exception was thrown by the sandboxed code wrapper's Execute method in the partial trust app domain: An unexpected error has occurred.]

```
 Server stack trace:
  at Microsoft.SharePoint.UserCode.SPUserCodeApplicationHostAppDomainRef.Execute(Type userCodeWrapperType, SPUserCodeCachedAssemblyGroup userAssemblyGroup, Guid siteCollectionId, Byte[] binaryUserCodeToken, Byte[] proxyOperationToken, SPUserCodeExecutionContext executionContext)
  at Microsoft.SharePoint.UserCode.SPUserCodeApplicationHostAppDomainRef.Execute(Type userCodeWrapperType, SPUserCodeCachedAssemblyGroup userAssemblyGroup, Guid siteCollectionId, Byte[] binaryUserCodeToken, Byte[] proxyOperationToken, SPUserCodeExecutionContext executionContext)
  at Microsoft.SharePoint.UserCode.SPUserCodeAppDomain.Execute(Type userCodeWrapperType, SPUserCodeCachedAssemblyGroup userAssemblyGroup, Guid siteCollectionId, Byte[] binaryUserCodeToken, Byte[] proxyOperationToken, SPUserCodeExecutionContext executionContext)
  at Microsoft.SharePoint.UserCode.SPUserCodeWorkerProcessProxyForShim.ExecuteInternal(Type userCodeWrapperType, SPUserCodeCachedAssemblyGroup userAssemblyGroup, Guid siteCollectionId, Byte[] binaryUserCodeToken, Byte[] proxyOperationToken, SPUserCodeExecutionContext executionContext)
  at Microsoft.SharePoint.UserCode.SPUserCodeWorkerProcessProxy.Execute(Type userCodeWrapperType, SPUserCodeCachedAssemblyGroup userAssemblyGroup, Guid siteCollectionId, Byte[] binaryUserCodeToken, Byte[] proxyOperationToken, SPUserCodeExecutionContext executionContext)
  at System.Runtime.Remoting.Messaging.StackBuilderSink._PrivateProcessMessage(IntPtr md, Object[] args, Object server, Int32 methodPtr, Boolean fExecuteInContext, Object[]& outArgs)
  at System.Runtime.Remoting.Messaging.StackBuilderSink.SyncProcessMessage(IMessage msg, Int32 methodPtr, Boolean fExecuteInContext)

 Exception rethrown at [0]:
  at System.Runtime.Remoting.Proxies.RealProxy.HandleReturnMessage(IMessage reqMsg, IMessage retMsg)
  at System.Runtime.Remoting.Proxies.RealProxy.PrivateInvoke(MessageData& msgData, Int32 type)
  at Microsoft.SharePoint.UserCode.SPUserCodeWorkerProcess.ExecuteDelegate.EndInvoke(IAsyncResult result)
  at Microsoft.SharePoint.UserCode.SPUserCodeWorkerProcess.Execute(Type userCodeWrapperType, SPUserCodeCachedAssemblyGroup userAssemblyGroup, Guid siteCollectionId, SPUserToken userToken, String currentAffinity, SPUserCodeExecutionContext executionContext)
  at Microsoft.SharePoint.UserCode.SPUserCodePoolableProcessConnection.Execute(Type userCodeWrapperType, SPUserCodeCachedAssemblyGroup userAssemblyGroup, Guid siteCollectionId, SPUserToken userToken, String affinity, SPUserCodeExecutionContext executionContext)
  at Microsoft.SharePoint.UserCode.SPUserCodeExecutionHost.Execute(Type userCodeWrapperType, Guid siteCollectionId, SPUserToken userToken, String affinity, SPUserCodeExecutionContext executionContext)
  at System.Runtime.Remoting.Messaging.StackBuilderSink._PrivateProcessMessage(IntPtr md, Object[] args, Object server, Int32 methodPtr, Boolean fExecuteInContext, Object[]& outArgs)
  at System.Runtime.Remoting.Messaging.StackBuilderSink.SyncProcessMessage(IMessage msg, Int32 methodPtr, Boolean fExecuteInContext)
```

Figure 8.4 Sandboxed solutions that fail don't show the default SharePoint error page. If debugging is enabled, the complete call stack is shown, which allows you to find the source of the exception. The stack traces are usually long for sandboxed solutions because several processes are involved.

(BCS) and log information to a custom database exposed as an external list. Note that if you start to log to a list or to a BCS source, you'll start consuming sandbox resource points, but less points than exceptions are accounted for.

8.2   *Debugging Web Parts with Visual Studio 2010*

Logging is most often used when your solutions are deployed to look at the application's behavioral history, even though the ULSViewer tool allows you to see the logging as it happens. To see your custom application in real time and step through the code to find the failing parts, debugging is extremely useful. Debugging is the most common way to find what's wrong with your code. Using the excellent debugging facilities in Visual Studio 2010, you can easily set a breakpoint in your code and run your application. When the breakpoint is reached, the execution is interrupted and you can step forward or inspect the values of objects and even change them. To debug a Web Part or any other piece of code, attach Visual Studio to a process on the server so that it can catch the debugging events. SharePoint normally uses the ASP.NET worker process to run the code. But sandboxed solutions are executed in their own process, and Feature receivers run in the SharePoint timer job process, which means that you might have to attach the debugger to other processes than Visual Studio by default attaches to.

8.2.1   *Attaching to processes*

The SharePoint Developer Tools for Visual Studio 2010 allows for easy debugging of Web Parts and other SharePoint solutions. When you press F5 or select Debug > Start Debugging, Visual Studio automatically attaches to the correct processes.

The first thing Visual Studio does is verify that debugging is enabled on the web application; if it's not, you'll receive a prompt asking if you want to enable it, as shown in figure 8.5.

Debugging is configured in the web.config file of the web application and when Visual Studio enables debugging, it changes three attributes in the file, as shown in table 8.1. These values can be changed manually as well. Remember to use this feature with caution in production environments because enabled debugging may slow down your application, and it will show detailed error messages to your users.

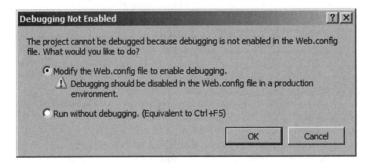

Figure 8.5   The first time a solution is debugged in a new web application using Visual Studio, you're asked to enable the debugging.

Table 8.1 The attributes used when changing to debug mode

Attribute	Description
`debug<configuration><system.web><compilation _` `debug="true|false"/>`	When set to true, debugging mode is enabled on the web application. The default value is false.

`mode`
`<configuration><system.web><customErrors _`
`mode="On|Off|RemoteOnly"/>`
	Sets the type of error page to use. The default value is On in Share-Point, which shows the Share-Point error page. When set to Off, it shows the default ASP.NET error page. If the value is RemoteOnly, then only local access to the site shows the ASP.NET default error page.

`Callstack`
`<configuration><SharePoint><SafeMode _`
`CallStack="true|false"/>`
	Indicates whether the call stack of the error should be shown. The default value is `false`. To show the detailed error messages, this must be set to `true`.

When `customErrors` is set to `Off` and the `CallStack` property is set to `true` in web.config, SharePoint will no longer show the friendly error message. It will instead show the ASP.NET error page, also known as the *Yellow Screen of Death*. This error page shows the exact exception and the call stack of the failing component, and you'll find it useful when troubleshooting Web Parts or other components.

Another way to start debugging is to attach to the processes manually. Use this approach if you'd like to debug an already running session. The SharePoint web application processes run in the standard ASP.NET worker w3wp.exe processes. To attach to a process using Visual Studio, select Debug > Attach To Process. Be sure that the Show Processes From All Users and Show Processes In All Sessions options are checked. Then select the w3wp.exe process to attach to and click Attach. There might be several w3wp.exe processes, and you can safely attach to all of them. Or you can use the IIS management console to find the process id of the application pool and then select the correct process.

> **TIP** If you need to retrieve detailed information about errors, such as line numbers and filenames in the production environment, distribute your code using debug built files. You should never use debug builds in production unless necessary.

8.2.2 *Debugging sandboxed solutions*

Sandboxed solutions aren't executed in the ASP.NET worker process w3wp.exe. Instead, they're executed in the special SharePoint Sandbox Code Service. Visual Studio is aware of this, and if you press F5 to run and debug your sandboxed solution, Visual Studio attaches to the correct process. The process that's used is named

SPUCWorkerProcess.exe, and you have to attach to this process if you manually attach Visual Studio to debug a sandboxed solution.

If you're debugging a sandboxed solution that uses a user code proxy, then this code is executed in the User Code Proxy service. This is a special service, named *SPUC- WorkerProcessProxy.exe,* that runs under full trust. You need to manually attach to this process when debugging user code proxy code.

8.2.3   *Debugging feature receivers*

Features are automatically activated by default in Visual Studio. You can change this behavior by editing the deployment configuration, discussed in chapter 3. Depending on how the activation/deactivation is done, you have to attach to different processes. If you have to debug the `FeatureActivated` or `FeatureDeactivating` methods from the web interface, attach to the ASP.NET worker process, w3wp.exe. And if you're enabling it using PowerShell, then you have to attach to the PowerShell.exe process.

Solution installation and uninstallation are accomplished using the SharePoint timer job. The `FeatureInstalled`, `FeatureUninstalling`, and `FeatureUpgrading` methods are executed by owstimer.exe. Notice that your breakpoints may not be hit immediately. You might have to wait a couple of seconds until the timer job starts and invokes the Feature receiver.

8.3   *The Developer Dashboard*

Visual Studio can help with troubleshooting, but normally debugging only works in the development environment. Once your application ends up in a nondevelopment environment, you can't set a breakpoint in your code to inspect the state of the application. You must have tools that you can use in production environments to show you how your application performs and behaves.

SharePoint 2010 contains a new monitoring feature called the *Developer Dashboard.* It's a special dashboard that can be enabled on pages; it shows all the current activity on a page, including timing, logs, warnings, and errors. By using the Developer Dashboard and by defining scopes in your code that can be monitored, you can identify which piece of your code is failing. In the following section, you'll learn how to work with the Developer Dashboard and how to incorporate logging into the dashboard by making your Web Parts aware of the monitoring facilities.

8.3.1   *Enabling the Developer Dashboard*

The Developer Dashboard isn't enabled by default in SharePoint 2010; you have to actively enable it. There's no functionality in the user interface for this feature out of the box, and you must use scripts or create custom code to enable it. The Developer Dashboard mode is set for the whole farm.

The easiest way to enable the Developer Dashboard is to use the `STSADM` command and use the `setproperty` operation. The operation is used to assign a value to the `developer-dashboard` property. This property can have one of three possible values and represents the mode of the Developer Dashboard:

- Off—The dashboard is never shown or available.
- On— The dashboard is always shown and accessible.
- OnDemand—The user can turn on the dashboard when it's needed.

The STSADM command has to be run from an elevated (Run as Administrator) command prompt or PowerShell window. You'll find the STSADM.exe file in the {SharePoint Root}\bin folder. The three different modes can be set like this:

```
stsadm.exe -o setproperty -pn developer-dashboard -pv on
stsadm.exe -o setproperty -pn developer-dashboard -pv off
stsadm.exe -o setproperty -pn developer-dashboard -pv ondemand
```

The first command turns on the Developer Dashboard and the second turns it off. The third command, which I recommend that you run on all your development farms, sets it to On Demand mode. When On Demand mode is configured, an icon will appear in the upper-right corner that users can click to open and close the Developer Dashboard, as shown in figure 8.6.

Figure 8.6 **When the Developer Dashboard is set to On Demand mode, users can turn the dashboard on and off by clicking the icon in the upper-right corner.**

The Developer Dashboard can be enabled through code as well. When configuring the dashboard through code, you have more options for the dashboard. The configuration is done using the SPDeveloperDashboardSettings class. The following code snippet shows how to set the Developer Dashboard in OnDemand mode and only make it available for users with full permissions on the current website:

```
SPDeveloperDashboardSettings settings =
    SPWebService.ContentService.DeveloperDashboardSettings;
settings.DisplayLevel = SPDeveloperDashboardLevel.OnDemand;
settings.RequiredPermissions = SPBasePermissions.FullMask;
settings.Update();
```

The current settings object for the Developer Dashboard is acquired from the web service of the content application. The settings are then configured, the mode is set to OnDemand, and the required permissions are set to full permissions. Finally, the settings object is updated to save the changes.

> **TIP** If you'd like to have a web interface for configuring all different parameters in the Developer Dashboard, you can download a solution package that adds configuration options for the Developer Dashboard in Central Administration. Download it from my blog at http://www.wictorwilen.se/Post/SharePoint-2010-Developer-Dashboard-configuration-feature.aspx.

8.3.2 Using the Developer Dashboard

The Developer Dashboard is a quick and useful tool to use when troubleshooting, working, and tuning your Web Parts. When the dashboard is set to be available at all times, it appears at the bottom of each page in SharePoint. And when you set it to On Demand, you can display it by clicking the Developer Dashboard icon in the upper-right corner.

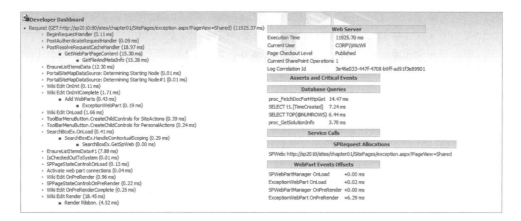

Figure 8.7   The Developer Dashboard in SharePoint 2010 shows the details of a specific request.

The Dashboard contains information about the current page and request. Figure 8.7 shows an example of how it might look.

The Developer Dashboard has a border in green, yellow, or red. A red border means that some of the monitored metrics have excessive values or that one or more critical events are logged. A yellow border indicates that the request took more than one second, and green indicates that the page was most likely successful. On the left side are all monitored events and method calls, including their execution time. This call tree is useful when you're looking for performance bottlenecks. The right column contains more information about the current request, including the total execution time, correlation id, and all database queries. If you click on one of the database queries, you'll get even more information about them.

8.3.3 *Using monitored scopes*

SharePoint 2010 introduces a new way to monitor custom applications. Using *monitored scopes* you can easily hook into the Developer Dashboard call tree and display your own operations. The standard call in the Developer Dashboard contains only the default events called by SharePoint, but a custom application most often contains more methods and classes that should be monitored.

Custom monitored scopes are created by instantiating a new object of the type SPMonitoredScope. This starts a new scope when created and ends the scope when you dispose of it. Figure 8.8 shows how custom scopes are added to a Web Part. A custom scope is added to the CreateChildControls method, and it calls two other monitored methods. By looking at the execution time, you can easily see which method performs slowly.

Listing 8.2 shows the code for realizing the custom scopes shown in figure 8.7. Notice that the usage pattern

Figure 8.8   The Developer Dashboard shows all the monitored scopes and their execution time. This allows you to locate the parts of the Web Part that can be causing a bottleneck.

is used to properly dispose of the SPMonitoredScope objects when the scope is over. Monitored scopes aren't supported in sandboxed solutions.

Listing 8.2   A Web Part using monitored scopes

```
public class SlowWebPart : WebPart {
    protected override void CreateChildControls() {
        using (SPMonitoredScope scope =
            new SPMonitoredScope("CreateChildControls")) {
            SlowMethod();
            FastMethod();
        }
    }
    private void SlowMethod() {
        using (SPMonitoredScope scope =
            new SPMonitoredScope("SlowMethod")) {
            System.Threading.Thread.Sleep(1200);
        }
    }
    private void FastMethod() {
        using (SPMonitoredScope scope =
            new SPMonitoredScope("FastMethod")) {
            System.Threading.Thread.SpinWait(10);
        }
    }
}
```

❶ Creates monitored scope

❷ Executes code

❸ Creates new monitored scope

❹ Creates new monitored scope

In the CreateChildControls method, a scope is created with the name of the method **❶**. Inside this scope the two methods are called **❷**. The first method creates another scope **❸** and then pauses the thread for 1.2 seconds. The second method also creates its own scope **❹**. As seen in figure 8.8, you can immediately identify where the code performs badly and where the call is coming from.

8.3.4   Logging using scoped performance monitors

Logging can be improved using custom *scoped performance monitors*. A custom monitor is a class deriving from the ISPScopedPerformanceMonitor interface. Monitors can be used to monitor and log actions in your custom code. For instance, you could use a monitor to log the number of calls made to a specific web service or a specific code that uses other expensive resources in the trace log. Each monitor can also have a threshold that's monitored by SharePoint. Classes implemented from this interface can be passed as arguments to a monitored scope.

To illustrate the use of a custom scoped performance monitor, let's create a simple monitor that increments a static value each time the monitor is used in a monitored scope. When the value exceeds a threshold, it should be logged to the trace logs. Listing 8.3 shows how to implement the custom monitor.

Listing 8.3   A custom scoped performance monitor

```
class CustomMonitor : ISPScopedPerformanceMonitor {
    static long s_counter = 0;

    public CustomMonitor() {
```

❶ Defines static counter variable

```
        Interlocked.Increment(ref s_counter);
    }
    public void Dispose() {
    }
    public string Description {
        get { return "Count the calls"; }
    }
    public string RenderValueForWeb() {
        return string.Format("Called {0} times", s_counter);
    }
    public string Name {
        get { return "CallCounter"; }
    }
    public object Value {
        get {
            return s_counter;
        }
    }
    public bool ValueIsExcessive {
        get {
            return s_counter > 5;
        }
    }
}
```

2 Increments counter when created

3 Returns actual counter value

4 Checks if value is excessive

The custom monitor class, which is derived from the `ISPScopedPerformanceMonitor` interface, instantiates a static counter variable **1**. The constructor, which is called each time the monitor is used, increments the value of the counter **2** in a thread-safe way. The `Description` property and the `RenderValueForWeb` method can't be used by custom applications and are only used by SharePoint managed monitors. The `Name` property is used when logging to the trace logs. To get the value of the monitor, the class returns the current value of the counter using the `Value` property **3**. SharePoint uses the `ValueIsExcessive` method **4** to ask the monitor if it has passed the threshold. In this sample, it should start logging when the monitor has been used more than five times.

This custom monitor is passed as an argument to a monitored scope, as shown in the following code snippet. The second required argument is a value for the maximum execution time. This value is converted into a specific scoped performance monitor that monitors the execution time of the scope. The default value is 100 milliseconds.

```
using (SPMonitoredScope scope =
    new SPMonitoredScope("Custom scope", 100, new CustomMonitor())) {
    // ...
}
```

If you run this code in a Web Part, the logging will start as soon as the monitor has been used more than five times. The logged information will look like this in the ULS logs:

```
Leaving Monitored Scope (Iterations). Execution Time=0.481799409360119
____CallCounter=7
____Execution Time=0.481799409360119
```

Each line starting with four underscore characters represents the value of one monitor. In this example, it's the custom monitor and the automatically created execution time monitor. If the SharePoint Foundation > Monitoring category is set to Verbose, the logging will occur even if the value isn't excessive. When writing to the log, all values from all active monitors are written regardless of which monitor had excessive values.

The Developer Dashboard configuration object also contains a property called AutoLaunch. If you've set the dashboard to On Demand mode and the Auto Launch property to true, then the Developer Dashboard will automatically appear if any critical events defined in SharePoint are logged.

8.3.5 Custom logging to the Developer Dashboard

When you're rendering a Web Part, SharePoint creates a top-level scope. One of the monitors that SharePoint adds to this scope is the SPCriticalCounter monitor. This monitor can be used to insert information into the Assert and Critical Events section in the Developer Dashboard. Figure 8.9 shows a custom entry written to the dashboard. By clicking on the logged entry in the dashboard, you display more information about the event. The information contains an event message and the current call stack.

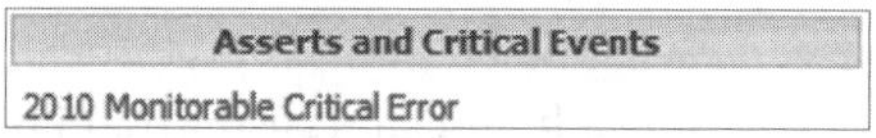

Asserts and Critical Events
2010 Monitorable Critical Error

Figure 8.9 Asserts and critical events are shown in the Developer Dashboard; you can click on them for more details.

To add custom entries to the Asserts and Critical Events section, use a static method of the SPCriticalCounter class. SharePoint will automatically add this monitor, together with a set of other monitors, when it receives a request. To add a custom entry to the Developer Dashboard, use the static AddDataToScope method of the SPCriticalCounter like this:

```
using (SPMonitoredScope scope = new SPMonitoredScope("Critical")) {
    SPCriticalTraceCounter.AddDataToScope(
        2010,
        "Critical Error",
        15,
        "An error occurred");
}
```

Using the static AddDataToScope method, a new entry is created. The first parameter is a custom tag id to identify the entry. The message shown in the Developer Dashboard is the category parameter of the entry, and the trace level is specified using an integer. The trace level corresponds to the internal Microsoft.SharePoint.Diagnostics.ULSTraceLevel enumeration. The value 15 corresponds to the Monitorable value. The last parameter contains the actual message. As of this writing, this enumeration isn't documented on MSDN, so you have to use the .NET Reflector tool to discern the actual values.

8.4 Custom error handling

Knowing how and when to catch exceptions is important. Always check your parameters for null before using them. Eventually exceptions will get thrown and just catching an exception and ignoring it won't make it easier to troubleshoot the application. That will only leave you and your users unaware of any problems. Not all exceptions should be caught—only catch exceptions that can be handled. Exceptions that can't be handled should instead fall through to SharePoint, which will eventually log the exception. There's a distinction between system exceptions and business logic errors. For instance, an Access Denied exception shouldn't always be handled; it can fall through to Share-Point, unless it's important for business logic to handle that exception. This isn't specific to SharePoint; it's good practice in all .NET development. In SharePoint with Web Parts it's important to do this correctly. A page in SharePoint can contain several Web Parts, and one single failing Web Part can make the whole page useless.

One common method is to use a generic `try-catch` block that will catch any exception just to avoid displaying error messages to the users. Although using a `try-catch` block could keep the solution from displaying unwanted errors or sensitive information, this method of catching all exceptions makes users unaware of what went wrong and they'll have problems resolving or reporting the error. Being unaware of what failed in business-critical applications can be fatal. Consider an application making a financial transfer that fails and the user doesn't notice what made it fail:

```
void button_Click(object sender, EventArgs e) {
    try {
        float amount = float.Parse(textBox.Text);
        TransferMoney(amount);
    }
    catch (Exception) {
        label.Text = "Transfer failed";
        return;
    }
    label.Text = "Succeeded";
}
```

This snippet is a response to a button click; it takes the value of a text box and parses it into a float value before it uses a method to transfer the amount of money. The generic `catch` statement will catch all kinds of exceptions and inform the user that the transfer failed—but not why. Even worse would be just catching the exception and not doing anything.

In this simple example, users won't know whether they entered an invalid value or the money transfer failed. A better approach is in this case to catch only exceptions of the type `FormatException`. All other exceptions will be let through to the SharePoint exception handling.

```
void button_Click2(object sender, EventArgs e) {
    try {
        float amount = float.Parse(textBox.Text);
        TransferMoney(amount);
    }
    catch (FormatException) {
        label.Text = "Invalid amount format";
        return;
```

```
    }
    label.Text = "Succeeded";
}
```

The procedure is the same as in the previous snippet; the text box value is converted to a float value and the float value is passed to the money transfer method. The `catch` statement only catches exceptions of the type `FormatException` and tells users that the value they entered is in the wrong format. Any other exceptions are unhandled and fall through to the SharePoint error page. This approach improves the overall experience and ensures that the severe exceptions from the submethod are logged.

SharePoint uses the default error page when unhandled exceptions fall through (see section 8.1.1). If you catch and handle exceptions in your code, you need to follow these best practices:

- Provide user-friendly messages.
- Avoid exposing sensitive information and data in error messages.
- Clean up resources in a correct way.
- Leave application in a consistent way.
- Log any errors that are unexpected and can't be handled by the user.
- Don't use exceptions to control the business logic.
- Rethrow exceptions that aren't handled.

If you can't follow these principles, leave the error handling to SharePoint. Take a look at listing 8.1, which catches an exception, logs the exception details, and displays an error message to the user.

Exception handling in sandboxed solutions is of particular interest, because any unhandled exceptions will count in the solution resource point usage. If a solution uses too many resources, the whole Solution Gallery for the site collection will be shut down. Because the SharePoint logging API isn't available in sandboxed solutions, you need to set a logging strategy for this. Consider creating a full-trust proxy for logging or log to a SharePoint list.

8.5   Other debugging tools

Everyone has their own set of tools and methodologies to troubleshoot web-based applications, and SharePoint is almost just like any other web application. You can most likely use the tools you're used to, but I'd like to highlight a few.

When troubleshooting the server-side code, Visual Studio is your primary tool along with the logging techniques we discussed earlier. ASP.NET developers have access to a built-in tracing tool in ASP.NET, and this tool can be used in SharePoint.

Even though Visual Studio 2010 is great for debugging JavaScript, there are alternatives such as the built-in tools in Internet Explorer or the Firebug extensions to Firefox. These tools, in combination with web proxy tools like Fiddler, can prove valuable when you're troubleshooting JavaScripts or when you need to inspect what's sent to SharePoint and what's sent back.

8.5.1   *ASP.NET tracing*

ASP.NET includes a method that lets you view diagnostic information about a page and the request. If you're an ASP.NET developer, you're familiar with it. In previous versions of SharePoint in which the Developer Dashboard didn't exist, this method was a good resource for troubleshooting. The tracing is written immediately following the page's output and contains tables with diagnostics information such as the following:

- Trace information and exact timings between the events
- Control tree containing all ids for all controls
- Information about the session and cookies
- Information about all header, form, and query string parameters

Some of the information overlaps with the Developer Dashboard, but if you need to get more information about, for instance, the form parameters passed to the page, you must enable the ASP.NET tracing.

The Developer Dashboard settings object (`SPDeveloperDashboardSettings`) contains a property called `TraceEnabled`. When this property is set to `true`, a link is inserted at the bottom of the Developer Dashboard. You click this link to turn on the ASP.NET tracing information, as shown in figure 8.10. Click the link again to turn off the ASP.NET tracing.

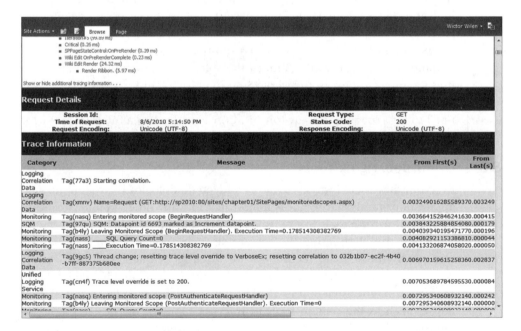

Figure 8.10   When ASP.NET tracing is enabled in the Developer Dashboard, the ASP.NET trace is shown at the bottom of the page.

8.5.2   *Internet Explorer Developer Tools or Firebug*

Tools for troubleshooting the client side of SharePoint are also important when developing and troubleshooting Web Parts. In chapter 4 I mentioned Internet Explorer 8/9 Developer Tools and the Firefox browser Firebug extension. Both of these tools have debugging capabilities that can help you figure out problems with JavaScript functions. Even though Visual Studio 2010 automatically attaches the debugger to Internet Explorer, when debugging the project you can only do it on a development machine. The client tools can be used on production servers directly without any installations. You can use these tools to set breakpoints in JavaScript and step through the code and watch variables and objects.

8.5.3   *Fiddler web proxy*

Another helpful tool that should be in your developer toolbox is Fiddler. Fiddler is a web debugging proxy that logs all HTTP traffic going from your development machine to any web server, local or remote. Use Fiddler to find problems or optimize your applications when they're running in production. It doesn't affect SharePoint at all; it just captures all traffic from the web browser to SharePoint. You can inspect all requests and responses to see exactly what data is transferred between the client and SharePoint. You can download Fiddler (for free) at http://www.fiddler2.com/ fiddler2/. Figure 8.11 shows how Fiddler looks when it catches all communication from the client to the server.

You can use Fiddler to manually send specific requests to the server. It also monitors the exact time and amount of data transferred. This information can be used to optimize your applications along with the timeline view, which shows the order and time it takes for all items requested by a page to get loaded.

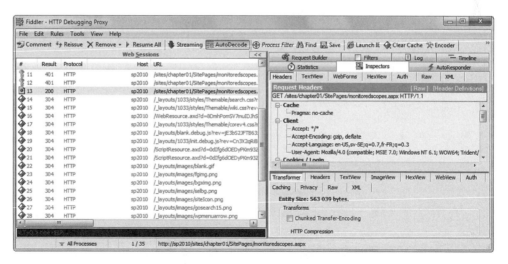

Figure 8.11   Fiddler inspects all outgoing and incoming web traffic.

8.6   *Summary*

This chapter explored both generic .NET and SharePoint-specific error handling. SharePoint is built on Microsoft .NET and ASP.NET, and you can use the same techniques for handling errors and troubleshooting them. SharePoint contains a set of out-of-the-box tools like the logging features and the Developer Dashboard tool that will prove valuable when you're troubleshooting Web Parts.

Many tools are available, including Visual Studio. We discussed a few of my favorites that I use both when developing Web Parts and when the Web Parts are running in a production environment. Hopefully this chapter will help you avoid some troubleshooting, but eventually we all end up with a Web Part that doesn't act as intended.

Programming and caching for performance

This chapter covers

- Programming for performance
- Using performance optimizations
- Querying SharePoint efficiently
- Understanding asynchronous Web Parts
- Using caching techniques

Performance is crucial! When you're using SharePoint's cool functionality to develop Web Parts, user controls, or other SharePoint artifacts, you'll likely build applications that consume server, client, and bandwidth resources. While in development mode, your Web Parts will run fine, but once they're in production, with more data and more users, your applications can degrade in performance. Personally, I'm a performance fanatic and like to achieve even the smallest optimization.

You can choose among several methods for improving performance. SharePoint is quite fragile and can be a performance killer if it's not programmed and handled correctly. You must know how to handle the SharePoint objects and know how to query correctly to get good performance. Several techniques can be used to improve the performance of the server-side executed code.

Caching is the next step to take once you've optimized your code. Caching allows the server to temporarily store already calculated or executed operations, thereby delivering them much faster to the client. SharePoint offers a number of configuration options to help you enhance performance.

9.1   *Programming for performance*

When thinking about performance, most developers consider how to optimize loops or reduce the number of local variables. Although such actions can improve performance, if the compiler doesn't already make those improvements, you need to look at the bigger picture. People have different opinions as to what performance is. Here are *a few of the common aspects:*

- Computational performance
- Object and memory usage
- Scalability
- Perceived performance

It can be hard to maximize the performance in all these areas. Depending on the type of application, the focus may shift between these aspects.

9.1.1   *Computational performance*

Computational performance is all about how fast code and algorithms are performed. Improving computational performance entails selecting the correct algorithms for your calculations and knowing how the application is designed in terms of classes, objects, and layers. The Developer Dashboard, used with the scoped monitors, is a great source for measuring computational performance.

9.1.2   *Object and memory usage*

Optimizing the object and memory usage might sound simple in managed code, but it's easy to fail at this task when working with SharePoint. The SharePoint objects such as `SPSite` and `SPWeb` contain references to COM+ objects, and each of these objects consumes quite a lot of memory. Later in this chapter, I'll show you how to handle these objects in a correct and safe way.

Following a design pattern and using a layered architecture will most likely result in many classes that will increase the memory footprint. To improve performance you might have to bend the rules to keep the number of objects down. On the other hand, bending the rules can also lead to code that's hard to understand and consequently more difficult to troubleshoot.

9.1.3   *Scalability*

Scalability is an application's ability to perform well under heavy loads or when processing a large amount of data. An application that performs well with just a few users may degrade in performance when stressed by many requests. The same goes with data; the application might perform well with small sets of data but perform poorly handling large amounts. A common mistake is failing to test the application thoroughly using relevant data and expected amounts of data. In the development and testing phases, you may use small numbers of users and small sets of data. But when running the application in production, the data and usage grows and performance degrades. A well-designed application is easier to scale out or up. Chapter 13 discusses design patterns that also are testable.

9.1.4 Perceived performance

In the Web Part world, *perception* may be the most important aspect of performance. It's about how the end users experience the performance of the application. SharePoint 2010 has improved perceived performance by using more Ajax-based functionality such as the dialog framework. Making long-running calls such as web requests may stall other Web Parts. This problem can be solved by making the Web Part asynchronous on the server side and the client. This metric is hard to measure and depends on many factors, such as the overall SharePoint performance, client browser, and client caching.

Perceived performance is also about testing. You need to test your solutions several times under different conditions using production data and realistic loads. It's not fun when the users or customers complain that their solution runs slowly and you know you didn't test it thoroughly.

9.2 Programming for performance in SharePoint

Building applications for SharePoint requires that you have a thorough understanding of the SharePoint objects and how they work. All the SharePoint data is stored in the content databases, so most of the commands use a database connection and query the database. These operations are larger than optimizing a `for` loop. Not handling these SharePoint objects can jeopardize the stability and performance of the SharePoint farm.

SharePoint 2010 introduces new techniques for querying data such as LINQ to SharePoint. Although such techniques might improve the development experience, they're not always the way to go when programming for performance. On the other hand, because LINQ to SharePoint uses the new CAML features that allow for relational queries, you can, in some situations, create a single query that targets multiple lists instead of having multiple queries. There are various ways to query SharePoint and each has its pros and cons.

Your Web Part might retrieve data from an external system that takes time to deliver a response or needs to wait on other processes to finish. This can cause your application to block execution for other Web Parts and thus slow down the response for the whole page. You can use asynchronous operations so that your Web Part isn't responsible for killing the performance of a page or a site.

Not all performance improvements are implemented in your server-side code. You should also seriously consider optimizing your JavaScripts, CSS files, and other resources.

9.2.1 *Proper handling of SharePoint objects*

If you've been working with SharePoint or participated in any SharePoint classes, you've probably heard that you must dispose the SharePoint objects such as SPSite and SPWeb. It's a common beginner's mistake not to dispose. Forgetting to dispose these objects might affect the stability of the whole server. The objects need to be disposed because they have references to the COM+ object, which won't be released automatically by the garbage collector. The COM+ objects contain connections to the SharePoint databases, and if not released, the server will unexpectedly recycle the application pool, or even worse, eventually run out of connections and refuse SharePoint access to the databases. The following snippet shows a correct handling of the disposable SPSite object:

```
SPSite site;
try {
    site = new SPSite("http://server");
    // ...
}
finally {
    site.Dispose();
}
```

Inside the try block, the SPSite object is created and used. The finally block is always executed, even if an exception occurs, and the object will always be disposed. These statements can be shortened with the using statement, which will do exactly the same thing:

```
using (SPSite site = new SPSite("http://server")) {
    // ...
}
```

The using statement will implicitly create try-finally blocks and correctly dispose the objects created in the using statement. All SPSite and SPWeb objects that are created by you must be disposed.

Instances of SPSite and SPWeb created by SharePoint—for instance, from the SPContext object—must not be disposed. They're shared by all Web Parts and controls in the current request and disposing these objects will dispose the current context and eventually cause exceptions in other Web Parts using the context. Reducing the number of SPSite and SPWeb objects allows for better scalability and a smaller memory footprint.

> **TIP** Microsoft has released a tool called the SharePoint Dispose Checker Tool, also known as SPDisposeChecker, which checks your compiled assemblies for problems related to failing to dispose the SharePoint objects and gives you an indication of common mistakes. You can include the tool in your Visual Studio postbuild scripts or add it to a code analysis rule set. You can download the tool here: http://code.msdn.microsoft.com/SPDisposeCheck. Use SPDisposeChecker with caution because it may report false positives.

9.2.2 *Make smarter queries to SharePoint*

Many Web Parts you'll build will query SharePoint for information from lists or sites. There are several ways to query SharePoint for information. The query will have different performance implications, depending on how it's done and which method you use. Creating the correct query is especially important when working with large lists. Next, I'll show you how to query a standard Tasks list for all items that have the status set to Completed.

QUERYING USING THE OBJECT MODEL

The easiest (but worst performing) way to query a SharePoint list is to iterate over the objects and check the fields for the data via the SharePoint object model. The following code snippet shows how to iterate over the Tasks list items using a `foreach` statement:

```
SPWeb web = SPContext.Current.Web;
SPList tasks = web.Lists["Tasks"];
foreach (SPListItem task in tasks.Items) {
    if (task["Status"].ToString() == "Completed") {
        Label1.Text += task.Title;
    }
}
```

The Tasks list is retrieved from the current `SPWeb` object before iterating over all items. To get the correct items, a string comparison is done on the `Status` field.

For a very small list, this code works fine, but as the list grows, this method will perform poorly. First, when iterating over the items in the list, the complete list item objects are retrieved from the database and read into memory. Second, the fields aren't strongly typed, which means you must programmatically convert the fields into the correct type. Doing this will also make your code more error prone.

QUERYING USING LINQ TO SHAREPOINT

SharePoint 2010 introduces a tool called *SPMetal* that can generate strongly typed objects of your lists and list items. The code generated by this tool allows you to use LINQ to query the SharePoint objects. You can more easily write queries and you don't have to be concerned with converting types.

> **NOTE** SPMetal is a tool that generates entity classes to provide an object-oriented way to work with the objects within a SharePoint site. The tool is available in SharePoint Foundation and is located in {SharePoint Root}\BIN (it's called SPMetal.exe).

The following code snippet shows how the previous object model listing is uses the entity classes generated by SPMetal and LINQ queries:

```
using (SPMetalDataContext context = new SPMetalDataContext(
    SPContext.Current.Web.Url)) {

    var tasks = from task in context.GetList<TasksTask>("Tasks")
                where task.TaskStatus == TaskStatus.Completed
                select task.Title;
```

```
    foreach (var title in tasks) {
        Label1.Text += title;
    }
}
```

To use the entity classes, you need a data context, which you create using the URL to current web site. A LINQ query is performed using the Tasks list, where all completed tasks are sorted out. Finally, all titles of these tasks are returned.

Using the entity classes (created by SPMetal) and LINQ, you can perform the query using strongly typed properties. This approach reduces the number of errors in the code. Behind the scenes, the LINQ query is converted to a CAML (Collaboration Application Markup Language) query that queries the database and returns only the items that match the query. This reduces the number of items in memory for this Web Part, and the query is faster than manually iterating the items. If the list contains a large number of items, this method is far better than the previous. To further improve performance, consider using the LINQ `Take(n)` method to return only the number of items that you really need.

The downside to using LINQ to SharePoint is that it requires that the LINQ runtime be loaded, which makes the first call slower compared to the succeeding ones. It also requires that more objects and classes be loaded into memory. If you're working with anonymous users, such as public-facing websites, you should know that LINQ to SharePoint doesn't currently support anonymous users in the RTM version. Cumulative updates for SharePoint have resolved this and it will work in upcoming service packs.

MANUALLY CREATING CAML QUERIES

The best way to query lists is to create the CAML queries manually—that is, create the same CAML that's created under the hood by the LINQ to SharePoint classes. CAML can be hard to learn at first, but in high-performance scenarios learning CAML can be worth the time. Visual Studio lacks good tools and support for building CAML queries, so it's easier to make mistakes than if you use the LINQ to SharePoint method.

> **TIP** The SharePoint `DataContext` object used in LINQ to SharePoint contains a property called `Log`. You can set this property to any `TextWriter` object such as the `Console.Out` or the return value from the `File.Create-Text` method. All queries executed in the `DataContext` will then be written to the `TextWriter` as CAML. You can use this logged CAML in your manual CAML queries.

The following code snippet demonstrates how to create the same query as earlier using a manual CAML query:

```
SPQuery query = new SPQuery();
query.Query = @"<Where><Eq><FieldRef Name='Status'/>          ❶ Creates
    <Value Type='Text'>Completed</Value></Eq></Where>";          CAML query

SPWeb web = SPContext.Current.Web;
SPList tasks = web.Lists["Tasks"];
```

```
SPListItemCollection items = tasks.GetItems(query);
```

← Gets items
② using query

```
foreach (SPListItem item in items) {
    Label1.Text += item.Title;
}
```

A CAML query is created by using an `SPQuery` object and then setting the `Query` property to the CAML query to be used ❶. The query object is used to return the items from the list ❷.

This approach is faster than the previous ones. But it's likely to take longer to develop the query, and you'll find that the opportunities to introduce errors into the code are greater than when you're using the LINQ to SharePoint approach. An alternative to `SPQuery` is the `SPSiteDataQuery`, which allows for cross-site queries.

9.2.3 *Asynchronous operations*

Using asynchronous operations to read data isn't often done in web applications (compared to client applications). That's because web applications are request-response based and the server-side execution has to wait for the asynchronous operation to complete before it delivers the response. This is true as long as there's one asynchronous operation going on at the same time. For example, think of the RSS Web Part from previous chapters; it's requesting the RSS feed from another server and waiting for that response. This operation can sometimes take a second or two. If there's one instance of the Web Part on the page, there's not much you can do about it. But what if there are several instances of the RSS Web Part (which is common in SharePoint where the end users build their own pages)? If the request for the RSS feeds is run synchronously, then the time to deliver the request will increase and consequently slow down the page, even though the server isn't doing any calculations.

A better approach is to run each request for the RSS feed asynchronously, which means that the requests will be executed in parallel. Then the time for rendering the page will be almost equal to the time of the longest-running RSS feed request.

To illustrate how to run operations asynchronously, let's modify our RSS Web Part. ASP.NET contains a method called `RegisterAsyncTask` for registering asynchronous tasks with the pages. This method registers a `PageAsyncTask` object that contains information about the task to be executed asynchronously. The registered asynchronous tasks are automatically called and synchronized after the `PreRenderComplete` event. To add the asynchronous functions to the RSS Web Part, add a new class called `RSSFeedAsyncTask` to our Web Part item, as shown in listing 9.1. This new class is responsible for handling the asynchronous events.

Listing 9.1 Asynchronous task for fetching an RSS feed

```
class RSSFeedAsyncTask{
    delegate void AsyncTaskDelegate();
    private AsyncTaskDelegate _asyncTaskDelegate;

    public delegate void AsyncTaskEnded();
    private AsyncTaskEnded _asyncTaskEnded;
```

```
private string _url;

public RSSFeedAsyncTask(string url, AsyncTaskEnded taskEnded) {
    _url = url;                                           Constructor taking    ❶
    _asyncTaskEnded = taskEnded;                          end delegate method
}

public IAsyncResult OnBegin(object sender,
    EventArgs e, AsyncCallback callback,
    object data) {
    _asyncTaskDelegate = new AsyncTaskDelegate(Execute);
    IAsyncResult result = _asyncTaskDelegate.BeginInvoke(
        callback, data);
    return result;                                        Asynchronous     ❷
}                                                         begin method

public void OnEnd(IAsyncResult result) {
    if (_asyncTaskEnded != null) {
        _asyncTaskEnded.Invoke();                         ❸  Asynchronous
    }                                                         end method
    _asyncTaskDelegate.EndInvoke(result);
}

public void OnTimeout(IAsyncResult result) {
    FeedData = new XElement("Timeout");
}

public void Execute() {                                   ❹  Method executed
    FeedData = XElement.Load(_url);                           asynchronously
    // System.Threading.Thread.Sleep(5000);
}

public XElement FeedData {
    get;
    protected set;
}
}
```

The class that handles the asynchronous task contains an asynchronous task delegate and a delegate to use once the task is done. This custom class has a constructor ❶ that takes the URL of the feed and a reference to the delegate method to use when the task is ended. Once the task is registered and ASP.NET decides to start executing the action, it will call the OnBegin method ❷. This method creates the asynchronous delegate for the Execute method that contains the code for requesting the feed and then starts the asynchronous call of the delegate. When the asynchronous call is done, the OnEnd method ❸ is called. This method invokes the AsyncTaskEnded delegate passed to the constructor before ending the asynchronous call. In case of timeouts, the class has a method called OnTimeout, which is called if the operation takes too long (the default is 45 seconds). The actual method that fetches the RSS stream is the Execute method, which makes the call just as in the synchronous version of the Web Part ❹. When testing and debugging the Web Part, consider inserting a sleep statement here so that you can see that it performs the actions in parallel. The property FeedData is used to set and retrieve the XML from the RSS feed.

What's left is to edit the control creation in the Web Part class. Listing 9.2 shows how the `CreateChildControls` method is altered and registers an asynchronous page task.

Listing 9.2 An asynchronous Web Part that fetches an RSS feed

```
private RSSFeedAsyncTask _asyncTask;
BulletedList _feedItems;

protected override void CreateChildControls() {
    if (string.IsNullOrEmpty(this.RssFeedUrl)) {
        HyperLink hl = new HyperLink();
        hl.NavigateUrl = string.Format(
            "javascript:ShowToolPane2Wrapper('Edit','129','{0}');",
            this.ID);
        hl.ID = string.Format("MsoFrameworkToolpartDefmsg_{0}", this.ID);
        hl.Text = "Click here to configure the Web Part";
        this.Controls.Add(hl);
        return;
    }

    _asyncTask = new RSSFeedAsyncTask(                      ❶ Create
        this.RssFeedUrl, feedFetched);                       asynchronous class

    PageAsyncTask pageAsyncTask = new PageAsyncTask(       ❷ Initialize
        _asyncTask.OnBegin,                                  asynchronous
        _asyncTask.OnEnd,                                    task
        _asyncTask.OnTimeout,
        "RSSFeedAsyncTask",
        true);                                             ❸ Register
                                                             asynchronous task
    Page.RegisterAsyncTask(pageAsyncTask);

    _feedItems = new BulletedList();
    _feedItems.DisplayMode = BulletedListDisplayMode.HyperLink;

    this.Controls.Add(_feedItems);
    this.ChildControlsCreated = true;                      ❹ Execute when
}                                                            asynchronous
                                                             task is done
private void feedFetched() {
    if(_asyncTask != null && _asyncTask.FeedData != null) {
        XElement feed = _asyncTask.FeedData;

        var items = feed.Descendants("item").Take(this.ItemCount);

        foreach (var item in items) {
            _feedItems.Items.Add(new ListItem() {
                Text = item.Descendants("title").First().Value,
                Value = item.Descendants("link").First().Value
            });
        }
    }
}
```

The previously shown asynchronous task, in listing 9.1, is defined as a private variable. The method that's changed is `CreateChildControls`. Instead of directly requesting the feed, an asynchronous object ❶ is created with the URL and the name of the method to run when the task is completed. A `PageAsyncTask` object is created ❷ with references to `OnBegin`, `OnEnd`, and `OnTimeout` methods, and this object is passed to the `RegisterAsyncTask` ❸ method of the ASP.NET page object. ASP.NET will then invoke all registered asynchronous tasks after the `PreRenderComplete` page event. The execution will continue without directly requesting the RSS feed, and you set up a `Panel` object to be used for adding the feed items. When the asynchronous task is finished, it will call the `feedFetched` ❹ method that was passed into the custom asynchronous task class constructor. This method checks that it contains data and then retrieves the RSS feed XML from the `FeedData` property. The control tree is built in the same way as it was in the `CreateChildControls` method of the synchronous Web Part, except that you now add the feed items to the `BulletedList` object in a separate method.

This technique is great to use when you have operations that can take a long time or that block other Web Parts from running. In this example, a web request was the bottleneck, but the issue can be other types of resources such as database calls, long-running calculations, or even synchronization with other Web Parts or controls.

You can register multiple asynchronous operations in your Web Part—for example, if you need to combine two RSS feeds into one and execute those requests in parallel. By default, ASP.NET executes all registered tasks after the `PreRenderComplete`, but you can also manually execute all the current registered tasks by calling the `ExecuteRegisteredAsyncTasks` method on the `Page` object. Note that this will synchronize all asynchronous tasks within the current scope or Web Part and will block other Web Parts from running until the task is complete. Also note that these asynchronous operations aren't available in sandboxed solutions.

These asynchronous operations were done on the server side. To improve the perceived performance, consider using asynchronous client-side operations using Ajax, which I'll discuss in the next chapter.

9.2.4 *Improve performance of resources*

Most likely your application will contain images, CSS files, JavaScript, and other resources that the clients will download. Downloading a lot of content not only affects bandwidth, it also reduces the performance of the web page rendering. By taking a look at all these resources, you can improve the overall performance of your SharePoint solution.

You can optimize JavaScript and CSS files by reducing whitespaces and redundant characters. You can find several tools available on the internet to help you with this. Optimizing your files will reduce the bandwidth used and the time needed to download the item.

> **TIP** Microsoft has released a JavaScript tool that minifies and optimizes your JavaScript files, called Microsoft Ajax Minifier 4. You can download it at http://aspnet.codeplex.com/releases/view/40584.

Another simple thing to do is to reduce the number of files. You can merge JavaScript and CSS files so that you have only one or just a few of each. For images it's a bit trickier but it can be accomplished in combination with *CSS sprites*. CSS sprites are CSS rules pointing out a specific area of a larger image. Instead of having multiple images, merge all your images into a composite image. Figure 9.1 shows how two images can be combined into one single image. The big benefit of this isn't the size of the resources but rather that it reduces the number of requests to the server. SharePoint extensively uses this approach for all images used in the Ribbon menu.

Figure 9.1 Using composite images instead of multiple images in combination with CSS sprites can improve the application performance and reduce the server load.

You can use CSS sprites to display only one of the images from the combined image. Do so by creating an HTML element or ASP.NET control that uses the image as a background image and then use CSS to specify the background position. Figure 9.2 shows a Web Part with a `LinkButton` control that uses a CSS sprite image using the left image in figure 9.1. When a user hovers the mouse over the `LinkButton` control, the image will be switched to the right image in figure 9.1 without loading a new image or changing the actual image used.

To create the `LinkButton` using the CSS sprite, you first need to combine the images and add the resulting image into the project. Then create a style declaration with the necessary CSS classes either directly in a Visual Web Part or preferably in a CSS file:

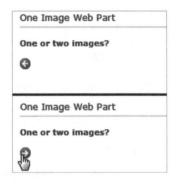

Figure 9.2 Using CSS sprites that show a specific part of a composite image in Web Parts will reduce the load on the servers and improve the performance of SharePoint. When you hover the mouse over the image in the figure, the image will change—not by loading a new image but by shifting the focus on the sprite image to show another part of it.

```
.linkButton
{
    width:17px;
    height:17px;
    display:block;
}
A.linkButton
{
        background: white
            url(/_layouts/Images/Back_Forward.png)
            -7px -11px;
}
A.linkButton:hover
{
    background: white
        url(/_layouts/Images/Back_Forward.png)
        -28px -11px;
}
```

❶ Defines Back sprite

❷ Defines Forward sprite

This snippet contains three CSS selectors. The first is a CSS class that defines the size of the control, which is the size of the icons in the image. Because a `LinkButton` creates an A tag, you also need to make it into a block element. The second class contains the default layout of the link button with a background image ❶. The background image is positioned so that only the left icon is shown. The last CSS class ❷ is used when the mouse cursor is positioned over the link using this class, and it uses the same image but another positioning.

To use these CSS classes, create a `LinkButton` control in your Web Part. This control should have the `CssClass` property set to `linkButton`:

```
<asp:LinkButton
    ID="linkButton"
    runat="server"
    CssClass="linkButton"
    Text=""/>
```

The CSS classes ensure that the correct image is used when users hover the mouse over the link button.

Improving performance of the application isn't all about coding smart—you need to look at the whole picture. When you're optimizing the resources of Web Parts tools such as Fiddler can be of great use. You can use such a tool to see the size of downloaded resources and the timeline when they're downloaded.

9.3 Caching techniques

One popular and effective technique for improving performance is caching. Caching means that data or objects are transparently saved so that future requests can be served faster. You can do this on the server side by storing already calculated answers or query results in the memory, or the web browser, so that the browser doesn't have to download the object again. Caching also means that users might not always see the latest information. If you require real-time data, caching may not be an effective option. Web Parts using long-running tasks or CPU-intensive operations may benefit from using caching.

ASP.NET provides several mechanisms for caching objects and data. SharePoint, which is built on top of ASP.NET, also has a set of methods for improving performance by using caching. The SharePoint caches are normally managed by SharePoint administrators and don't involve any programming tasks. It's a good practice to use caching and you should, as a developer, be aware of the different caching methods and techniques. Implementing caching in Web Parts may significantly improve performance for scenarios when you have time- or CPU-consuming operations. But doing so requires careful planning.

Instead of implementing caching in your Web Part, you can use the SharePoint built-in caches such as the BLOB cache and save you and your client development time. As a last resort, you can enable caching in Internet Information Services (IIS). IIS allows you to configure both server-side and client-side caching.

9.3.1 *ASP.NET caching*

Building custom cache mechanisms for multithreaded applications is hard work and something I don't recommend you do. Fortunately, ASP.NET provides a cache that has all the functionality you need. It's an in-memory cache that stores data in the memory of the local server and web application. This means that if you have multiple servers or web applications in your farm, the caches and possibly the information on the pages may be different for different users.

THE ASP.NET CACHE

The ASP.NET cache, which is defined in the `System.Web.Caching.Cache` class, stores cache data, in memory, using a key value and an object value. You add an object to the cache by specifying the name and the data:

```
HttpRuntime.Cache.Insert("key", data);
```

> **NOTE** you're using the `HttpRuntime.Cache` object instead of `HttpContext.Cache`. `HttpContext.Cache` requires that you run the code in the context of a web request whereas you can use `HttpRuntime.Cache` in any .NET application, including unit tests.

This code will insert the `data` object into the cache with the key value of `key`. The object will reside in the cache until removed or the application pool is recycled. Most often a cache is used to temporarily store objects and invalidate the cached value at specific times or when dependencies change. The ASP.NET `Cache` object offers functionality for adding time spans when the cache item should be invalidated and for connecting dependencies for invalidation. To insert a cache item that should live for 20 seconds, you have to specify a few more parameters as follows:

```
HttpRuntime.Cache.Insert(
    "key",
    data,
    null,
    DateTime.Now.AddSeconds(20),
    TimeSpan.Zero);
```

This code will add the item with a key and a value into the cache. The third parameter, which specifies any cache dependencies, isn't used here. The fourth parameter specifies the time when the cache is invalidated, which is the current time plus 20 seconds. The last parameter is used for sliding expiration and in this case it's set to 0. *Sliding expiration* means that the cache item will remain in the cache for at least that time span after the item was last accessed.

Cache dependencies are specific logical dependencies between items in the cache and the originating source item. For instance, data stored in a cache may be calculated from values in a file in the file system. When the file is changed, the cache item that's dependent on this file should be removed from the cache. ASP.NET contains cache dependencies for files, other items in the cache, SQL tables, or rows. You can even create your own cache dependencies by inheriting from the `CacheDependency` class defined in `System.Web.Caching`. To make a cache item dependent on a file, you must create a `CacheDependency` object and then insert the object into the cache like this:

```
CacheDependency dependency = new CacheDependency(fileName);
HttpRuntime.Cache.Insert("key", "value", dependency);
```

To access items in the cache, use the `Get` method of the `Cache` object. This method returns the item as an `object` (or `null` if the item isn't found in the cache):

```
object cacheItem = HttpRuntime.Cache.Get("key");
```

Objects will automatically be removed from the cache once its policies expire or any dependencies change. To remove items manually from the cache, you can use the `Remove` method with the cache item key as a parameter:

```
HttpRuntime.Cache.Remove("key");
```

ASP.NET PARTIAL CACHING

The ASP.NET runtime also contains functionality for partial caching. *Partial caching* means that you can cache single-user controls or a whole Web Part for a single page or for all pages. The partial caching is enabled on user controls declaratively in the user control using the `OutputCache` control directive or in the code-behind using the `PartialCaching` attribute. They both take a number of arguments that specify the cache duration and when to cache the control. To make a Visual Web Part cache its output for a minute, add the following directive to the top of the user control:

```
<%@ OutputCache Duration="60" VaryByParam="none"%>
```

This will make the Visual Web Part cached for 60 seconds for all pages where this Web Part is used. If you've previously worked with ASP.NET sites and used caching, you'll notice that this isn't how it works in ASP.NET. In plain ASP.NET sites with partially cached user controls, the item is cached per page, not all pages at once as in Share-Point. Keep this in mind: SharePoint caching is controlled by SharePoint on an application level and ASP.NET controls caching at the page or control level. Nevertheless, it can be useful for Web Parts that have static content that doesn't need to be updated often. Another pitfall with using partial caching is that it isn't cached per user; it's only cached once for all users. So you should never use partial caching in Web Parts if you're using the current user's credentials or information to render the content or when you're using personalization.

The parameters to the `OutputCache` directive can be used to control the cache, though. You can set the `VaryByParam` parameter to a custom value corresponding to the name of a query string parameter or forms parameter. This will make the control cache differently, depending on the value of the parameter. For example, the following code will result in different cached controls if the value of the query string parameter, `country`, is changed and the control depends on the value of the query string parameter:

```
<%@ OutputCache Duration="60" VaryByParam="country"%>
```

The `VaryByParam` can contain several parameters separated by commas if the control is dependent on several parameters.

If you need to cache the contents of controls, you should rely on the *SharePoint Server 2010 Output Cache.* This is a cache for full and partial caching of pages and controls when using the Publishing Infrastructure. This output cache is built on top of the ASP.NET caching mechanism and is enhanced with customizable caching profiles configurable through the web interface.

> **TIP** You can read more about output caching in SharePoint Server 2010 here: http://msdn.microsoft.com/library/aa661294.aspx.

9.3.2 Caching objects and structures

Caching items such as strings, integers, or other simple data types is easy to do with the ASP.NET cache. Once the cache item is invalidated, the item is removed from the cache—and eventually from memory by the garbage collector in .NET. But what about objects such as `SPSite` or `SPWeb` or other SharePoint objects that require manual disposal—can those objects be cached in the ASP.NET cache? The answer is no. You should never cache objects that require disposal, that have references to unmanaged code, or that aren't thread safe. Instead, create a custom thread-safe cache object and put it into the cache.

To demonstrate how to create a custom cacheable object, let's build a Web Part that shows statistics for all lists in a website. This Web Part will display a table containing all lists with the title, description, and the current number of items, as shown in figure 9.3. It will also be configurable with a custom property so that the caching can be turned on or off. You'll also use monitored scopes so that you can measure the difference in time using the Developer Dashboard for the noncached and cached Web Part.

List name	Description	Number of items
Announcements	Use this list to track upcoming events, status updates or other team news.	1
Cache Profiles	This system list was created by the Publishing Resources feature to store profiles for configuring caching in your site.	4
Calendar	Use the Calendar list to keep informed of upcoming meetings, deadlines, and other important events.	0
Content and Structure Reports	Use the reports list to customize the queries that appear in the Content and Structure Tool views	7
Customized Reports	This Document library has the templates to create Web Analytics custom reports for this site collection	0
Data		8
Documents	This system library was created by the Publishing feature to store documents that are used on pages in this site.	0
Form Templates	This library contains administrator-approved form templates that were activated to this site collection.	0
Images	This system library was created by the Publishing feature to store images that are used on pages in this site.	0
Links	Use the Links list for links to Web pages that your team members will find interesting or useful.	0
List Template Gallery	Make a template available for use in list creation by adding it to this gallery. The templates in this gallery are available to this site and all sites under it. Default list templates are not shown.	0
Long Running Operation Status		2
Master Page Gallery	Use the master page gallery to store master pages. The master pages in this gallery are available to this site and any sites underneath it.	54
Notification List		0
Pages	This system library was created by the Publishing feature to store pages that are created in this site.	1
Quick Deploy Items		0
Relationships List	A list created by Publishing Resources used to store Variations relationships.	1
Reporting Metadata	The Report Gallery stores the report types available to this site and all sites under it.	11
Reporting Templates	Use the Report Template Files library to store files used by the Report Template Gallery.	2

Figure 9.3 Building Web Parts that read data from SharePoint can be resource intensive; if possible, they should use caching to improve performance.

First, create a custom class that you'll use to store the list information in the cache. You can't add the SPList object to the cache because it's not thread safe. Your custom class should look like this:

```
class CacheData {
    public string Title;
    public string Description;
    public int ItemCount;
}
```

The class contains three public properties that are used to store the data that's going to be shown in the Web Part. Because the Web Part will display all lists in the site, a generic list object of the type List<Cachedata> will be the actual object stored in the cache.

The Web Part contains a configurable property called UseCaching that's used to determine whether the caching is enabled. The property definition is implemented like this:

```
[WebBrowsable(true)]
[Personalizable]
[WebDisplayName("Use cache")]
public bool UseCaching {
    get;
    set;
}
```

The statistics Web Part creates a table, iterates through all the lists, and adds a row for each one with its properties. It's all generated in CreateChildControls, as you can see in listing 9.3.

> **Listing 9.3   Web Part that displays all lists in a site and the number of items in each list**

```
protected override void CreateChildControls() {
    this.Controls.Add(new LiteralControl() {
        Text = "<h2>Site statistics</h2>"
    });

    Table table = new Table();
    this.Controls.Add(table);

    TableRow row = new TableRow();
    table.Rows.Add(row);

    row.Cells.Add(new TableHeaderCell() {
        Text = "List name", Width = Unit.Percentage(25)
    });
    row.Cells.Add(new TableHeaderCell() {
        Text = "Description"
    });
    row.Cells.Add(new TableHeaderCell() {
        Text = "Number of items", Width = Unit.Percentage(10)
    });

    if (UseCaching) {
        // see Listing 9.4
    }
```

❶ Creates table headings

❷ Checks if caching is enabled

```
    else {
        using(SPMonitoredScope scope =
            new SPMonitoredScope("Reading data from SharePoint")) {

            SPWeb web = SPContext.Current.Web;
            foreach (SPList list in web.Lists) {
                row = new TableRow();
                table.Rows.Add(row);

                row.Cells.Add(new TableCell() {
                    Text = list.Title
                });
                row.Cells.Add(new TableCell() {
                    Text = list.Description
                });
                row.Cells.Add(new TableCell() {
                    Text = list.ItemCount.ToString()
                });
            }
        }
    }
}
```

Iterates over all lists ①

Uses monitored scope ③

The Web Part creates the table and adds the necessary headings ① before checking whether the caching is enabled ②. If caching isn't enabled, the Web Part iterates over all lists ③ in the current website and produces the output.

If caching is enabled, the Web Part should regenerate the table using cached values of the list properties. Listing 9.4 shows how the caching is implemented.

Listing 9.4 Implementation of caching for the list statistics Web Part

```
using (SPMonitoredScope scope =
    new SPMonitoredScope("Reading data from Cache")) {

    List<CacheData> cachedData = HttpRuntime.Cache.Get("SiteStatistics")
        as List<CacheData>;

    if (cachedData == null) {
        cachedData = new List<CacheData>();

        SPWeb web = SPContext.Current.Web;
        foreach (SPList list in web.Lists) {
            CacheData cacheData = new CacheData() {
                Title = list.Title,
                Description = list.Description,
                ItemCount = list.ItemCount
            };
            cachedData.Add(cacheData);
        }
        HttpRuntime.Cache.Insert("SiteStatistics", cachedData, null,
            DateTime.Now.AddSeconds(20), TimeSpan.Zero);
    }
    cachedData.ForEach( cacheData => {
        row = new TableRow();
        table.Rows.Add(row);

        row.Cells.Add(new TableCell() {
```

Uses monitored scope

Retrieves item from cache ①

Checks if item was found ②

Creates new cached object ③

Adds objects to cache ④

Produces output ⑤

```
            Text = cacheData.Title
        });
        row.Cells.Add(new TableCell() {
            Text = cacheData.Description
        });
        row.Cells.Add(new TableCell() {
            Text = cacheData.ItemCount.ToString()
        });
    });
}
```

When caching is enabled, the Web Part will try to get the data from the cache ❶ using the specific cache key. If it doesn't find anything ❷, the Web Part will create a new object to add to the cache—in this case, a List<T> of the CacheData object defined earlier. The Web Part will iterate over all lists in the current site, create a new Cache-Data object for each list, and add values to it ❸. This object is then added to the list. When all objects are added to the list, the Web Part will insert the object into the cache ❹. Finally it creates the table using the newly created list or using the data fetched from the cache ❺.

Because you added monitored scopes to the Web Part, it's easy to compare the performance of the noncached and cached mode using the Developer Dashboard. When not using the cache, this is what's shown in the dashboard:

```
Reading data from SharePoint (14.09 ms)
```

After enabling the cache and reloading the page, this is what the Developer Dashboard shows:

```
Reading data from Cache (0.06 ms)
```

Quite an improvement! Note that this example uses the same static cache key for all users. In a real-world scenario the cache key should be user unique because the lists and their contents might be secured.

Although the HttpRuntime.Cache object is thread safe, your code might require a lock, using the C# lock keyword, if loading the data takes a lot of time. By using a lock, you prevent all incoming requests from loading the same data and causing excessive load on the server. If you use a lock, only the *first* incoming request loads the data and the subsequent requests wait for the loading to complete (for the lock to release) and then use the cached state, which the first request created.

9.3.3 Caching resources

For high-availability sites, it's necessary to cache JavaScript, Silverlight applications, CSS files, and images. These types of content are static and can benefit a lot from caching. For these resources, there are two types of caching:

- *Client-side caching*—Resources are cached on the client.
- *Server-side and BLOB caching*—The server caches items so that they aren't generated or fetched from the databases.
- These two types of caching can be used together for optimal performance.

CLIENT-SIDE IIS CACHING

In client-side caching, the web server tells the web browser that it can cache the requested item locally for a specific duration. The next request by the client for a page containing these resources won't require that the client request the cached resources.

Allowing the browser to cache the resources can improve the performance of your application and reduce the load on your servers. By default SharePoint enables content expiration in IIS for the _LAYOUTS, _WPRESOURCES, and CONTROLTEMPLATES folders. The default setting is 365 days. This means that when the browser requests information from these folders, it will cache the items in the local cache for 365 days or until the cache is cleared. Most browsers do send a request to the server for cached objects to see if it's been updated. If the object hasn't changed, the server will send an HTTP 304 response that tells the browser that it can use the object from the local cache. Note that this content expiration isn't set for the WPRESOURCES folder, which is used for web application scoped resources.

In addition, the content expiration isn't set on any items or content existing in the SharePoint content databases. To enable caching on these resources, you have to use the BLOB cache in SharePoint Server 2010, which I'll discuss in a moment.

Not only browsers take advantage of the client-side caching; other network performance enhancers such as WAN accelerators make use of it. Client-side caching can improve the performance of geo distributed installations.

TIP Another approach to improve the performance of applications is to use a content delivery network (CDN). A CDN is a service network that hosts resources instead of you having them on your network. These services are high performing and often geo distributed, and they take load off your network and servers. Microsoft has a CDN that hosts the ASP.NET Ajax and jQuery JavaScripts, which you can read more about here: http://www.asp.net/ajaxlibrary/cdn.ashx.

SERVER-SIDE IIS CACHING

You configure server-side caching in IIS by navigating to the site and path that you want to cache items in using IIS Manager. Then select the Output Caching feature in the Features View and click Add in the Actions menu to the right. A dialog box will open, as shown in figure 9.4. Here you specify the cache rules for the selected path.

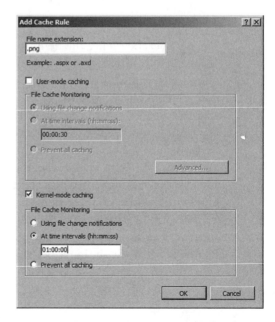

Figure 9.4   You can configure caching of files in IIS 7.0 using the Output Cache feature. This rule will cache all PNG files for one hour for a site using anonymous authentication.

Enter the filename extension for the files that you'd like to cache and then select a mode to use for caching. In the File Cache Monitoring section, choose the cache duration and then click OK to save the rule.

The major difference between Kernel mode and User mode is that in User mode the cache resides in the IIS worker process and in Kernel mode the cache resides in the kernel driver HTTP.SYS. Kernel mode can't be used on sites that require authentication or authorization, because those IIS features are User mode features.

SERVER-SIDE BLOB CACHING

In SharePoint a lot of content is stored in the content databases. To reduce the database load so that SharePoint queries the database for all requests to files that can be considered static, such as CSS files and images, you should configure SharePoint for caching. SharePoint Server 2010 contains a special cache called the BLOB cache, which caches the items on the file system instead. This functionality isn't available in SharePoint Foundation 2010.

The BLOB cache isn't enabled by default and requires that you make changes to the web.config file of the web application. The configuration of the cache is in the element called `BlobCache`. Here's the default configuration of the BLOB cache:

```
<BlobCache
    location="C:\BlobCache\14"
    path="\.(gif|jpg|jpeg|jpe|jfif|bmp|dib|tif|tiff|
    ico|png|wdp|hdp|css|js|asf|avi|flv|m4v|mov|mp3|mp4|
    mpeg|mpg|rm|rmvb|wma|wmv)$"
    maxSize="10"
    enabled="false" />
```

The BLOB cache caches the items in the file system and the path is specified using the `location` attribute. I strongly recommend that you store the BLOB cache on a separate disk for optimal performance. The `path` attribute specifies a regular expression that contains the extensions of the files to cache. The BLOB cache will store up to `maxSize` gigabytes (GB) of data in the cache. To enable the BLOB cache for the web application, set the `enabled` attribute to `true`.

By default the BLOB cache only caches the items on the server to reduce database load. If you'd like to enable caching of these objects on the client side, you need to add the `max-age` attribute. This attribute contains a numeric value that represents the number of seconds that the item should be cached on the client side.

The BLOB cache is probably the most efficient and easy way to enable caching of content in your SharePoint site and you should consider using it in all your projects. Remember that the setting is per web application.

9.4 *Summary*

Now that you've finished this chapter, I hope you'll enjoy performance optimizations as much as I do. You've seen that you have several options for improving the performance of your Web Parts, ranging from simple rules for handling and working with SharePoint to building your own caching. You need to take a look at the big picture and focus on the expensive parts first. Building custom caching can be hard work but worth it in the end. Whenever you're using expensive resources such as database connections, web requests, and services, consider caching the result. Just make sure that you don't forget the security aspects when caching. And as I stated earlier, use the built-in caching mechanisms when appropriate in SharePoint and keep it simple.

10
Dynamic interfaces in Web Parts

This chapter covers

- Understanding dynamic Web Parts
- Using JavaScript and jQuery to update the interface
- Introducing the SharePoint dialog framework
- Modifying the Ribbon
- Building context-aware Web Parts

Web pages have traditionally been built on the request-response methodology. You send a request for a web page and wait for a response containing the HTML. Each view requires that the server process and render all content, images, and scripts. This static process is slow. In recent years, browser technology has evolved and you can now create web pages that are dynamically and asynchronously updated. The combination of technologies, such as JavaScript, web services, Ajax, XML, and JSON, allows you to update only specific parts of a web page and make the experience more dynamic than ever before.

SharePoint 2010 uses the ASP.NET AJAX framework to build its interface. In this chapter, you'll take a look at some of the new user interface features that you can leverage in your Web Parts. The chapter begins by showing you how to make your Web Parts more dynamic using the ASP.NET Ajax framework and JavaScript. You'll also review the jQuery JavaScript library, which allows you to create clean, compact, and cross-browser compliant JavaScript code.

Next, you'll look at SharePoint-specific features such as the notification messages, the status bar, and the dialog framework. These simple features immediately make your Web Part more dynamic and user friendly.

One of the first things you'll notice in SharePoint 2010 is the context-aware Ribbon interface. Using XML code and JavaScript, you'll connect Web Parts to the Ribbon to add new tabs and controls.

10.1 Using Ajax and JavaScript in Web Parts

JavaScript and XML have made the web more accessible and interactive. The combination of these two, called Ajax, is what most people mean when they refer to the technology used to make websites dynamic. Ajax techniques allow you to retrieve information in an asynchronous way. The web page is displayed with placeholders that are asynchronously filled with content, which means the entire page doesn't have to reload for every single change. The same goes for Web Parts. A Web Part might initially contain a placeholder; after the page is rendered, it can asynchronously request information that fills that placeholder. In this way, you can change a page by updating just a Web Part. This is called a *partial update*.

> **NOTE** Ajax (Asynchronous JavaScript and XML) is a combination of browser and web techniques that makes it easy to create dynamic and interactive web applications. By using asynchronous requests on the client that sends JavaScript objects or data to the server, you achieve a dynamic experience. Although XML is in its name, sending XML back and forth isn't required. A common approach today is to use JavaScript Object Notation (JSON).

In ASP.NET, the use of Ajax has been implemented by Microsoft as a set of extensions to ASP.NET called ASP.NET AJAX Extensions. These extensions are used by SharePoint and you can use them in Web Parts to make them dynamic. Building dynamic Web Parts using ASP.NET AJAX Extensions (or in other ways) often requires that you use JavaScript to build the interface. A Web Part can register inline JavaScripts or use JavaScripts in external files.

One of the most popular and commonly used JavaScript libraries is the jQuery library. The jQuery library is often used in SharePoint to accomplish so-called *no-code solutions* but can also be used in Web Parts development. The use of jQuery simplifies JavaScript programming and at the same time maintains a cross-browser implementation.

10.1.1 Working with Microsoft ASP.NET AJAX Extensions

The Microsoft ASP.NET AJAX Extensions consist of a client framework with JavaScripts and a server framework with a set of controls. These extensions make it easy for

ASP.NET developers to enhance their web applications with dynamic interfaces. They use the same techniques and methods that they use in Visual Studio.

To use the extensions in a website, you must install the client and server framework and configure web.config accordingly. In previous versions of SharePoint this process had to be done manually or by using SharePoint Features that modified the web.config file and installed the components on all servers. SharePoint 2010 is based on ASP.NET 3.5, which includes the server and client ASP.NET AJAX framework. The web.config configuration elements are created by default, which makes it easier for you to use the Microsoft ASP.NET AJAX Extensions in any Web Part solution.

The most popular ASP.NET AJAX control is `UpdatePanel`. This control is similar to the standard `Panel` control but can be updated asynchronously. The `UpdatePanel` control has a set of asynchronous triggers that make the update panel reload.

To illustrate, let's continue to enhance the RSS Web Part that you've been building in the last few chapters. Add the button shown in figure 10.1. You'll use the button to refresh the RSS feed without reloading the entire page.

> **NOTE** Although I could show you how to do this in a Visual Web Part and use a declarative approach, I recommend using the programmatic approach. Even though you aren't using a Visual Web Part, this code won't work as a sandboxed Web Part. The `UpdatePanel` object requires the `ScriptManager`, which isn't accessible from the sandboxed worker process.

The first thing that you need to do is declare an `UpdatePanel` object and a `Button` in your Web Part class:

```
protected UpdatePanel updatePanel;
protected Button refreshButton;
```

These controls are declared in the class as `protected` so that they can be used in new Web Parts inheriting from this Web Part. The `CreateChildControls` method is implemented in listing 10.1; the method creates the update panel and the button. The feed isn't retrieved by this method (as in previous implementations of the RSS Web Part), but instead the feed retrieval is moved to the `OnPreRender` method.

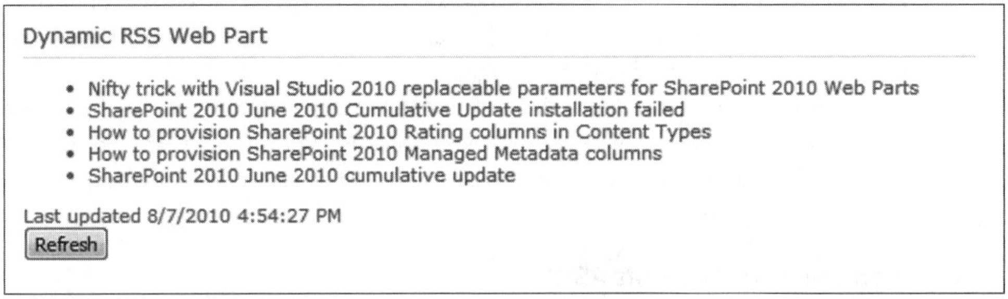

Dynamic RSS Web Part

- Nifty trick with Visual Studio 2010 replaceable parameters for SharePoint 2010 Web Parts
- SharePoint 2010 June 2010 Cumulative Update installation failed
- How to provision SharePoint 2010 Rating columns in Content Types
- How to provision SharePoint 2010 Managed Metadata columns
- SharePoint 2010 June 2010 cumulative update

Last updated 8/7/2010 4:54:27 PM

Refresh

Figure 10.1   The RSS Web Part has a button that makes a partial update of the page, refreshing only the contents of the specific Web Part.

Listing 10.1   Adding an `UpdatePanel` to the RSS Web Part

```
protected override void CreateChildControls() {

    if (string.IsNullOrEmpty(this.RssFeedUrl)) {
        HyperLink hl = new HyperLink {
            NavigateUrl = string.Format(
                "javascript:ShowToolPane2Wrapper('Edit','129','{0}');"
                , this.ID),
            ID = string.Format("MsoFrameworkToolpartDefmsg_{0}", this.ID),
            Text = "Click here to configure the Web Part..."
        };
        this.Controls.Add(hl);
        return;
    }

    updatePanel = new UpdatePanel();                    ← ❶ Creates UpdatePanel
    updatePanel.ID = "updatePanel";

    refreshButton = new Button() {
        Text = "Refresh",
        ID = "refreshButton",
        CssClass = "ms-NarrowButtonHeightWidth"
    };
    this.Controls.Add(refreshButton);                   ❷ Adds trigger to UpdatePanel

    updatePanel.Triggers.Add(new AsyncPostBackTrigger() {  ←
        ControlID = refreshButton.ID }                  ←
    );                                                  ❸ Connects button to trigger
    this.Controls.Add(updatePanel);

    this.ChildControlsCreated = true;
}
```

The `CreateChildControls` method makes the standard check to see if the `RssFeedUrl` property has a value. If it does, `CreateChildControls` creates an `UpdatePanel` object ❶. The button is then added to the control tree. It has no click event defined because you don't need to execute any specific code if it's clicked; you just need it to trigger an update. So you connect the button to the update panel using a trigger on the update panel. An `AsyncPostBackTrigger` ❷ is created that takes the control ID ❸ of the button as an argument. When the user clicks the button, this trigger will fire and a partial postback will occur. Finally, the `UpdatePanel` object is added to the control tree. This partial postback will only update the `UpdatePanel` in the user interface.

To retrieve the feed and also add information about when the feed last was retrieved, you add logic to the `OnPreRender` method. The implementation, in listing 10.2, looks quite similar to what you just did to render the RSS Web Part—with a few differences.

Listing 10.2   Modifying `OnPreRender` of the RSS Web Part

```
protected override void OnPreRender(EventArgs e) {
    XElement feed = XElement.Load(this.RssFeedUrl);

    var items = feed.Descendants("item").Take(this.ItemCount);

    foreach (var item in items) {
```

```
        Panel panel = new Panel();
        panel.Controls.Add(new HyperLink() {
            Text = item.Descendants("title").First().Value,
            NavigateUrl = item.Descendants("link").First().Value
        });

        updatePanel.ContentTemplateContainer.Controls.Add(panel);
    }
    updatePanel.ContentTemplateContainer.Controls.Add(
        new LiteralControl("Last updated "));
    updatePanel.ContentTemplateContainer.Controls.Add(
        new LiteralControl(DateTime.Now.ToString()));

    base.OnPreRender(e);
}
```

The feed is retrieved using the same methods you used earlier but the feed items are added to the `ContentTemplateContainer` control collection of the `UpdatePanel` object. This template container is dynamically refreshed in the web interface. Finally, two controls are added so that you can see the time when the feed was last retrieved.

If you now deploy and add the Web Part to a page, it will look like figure 10.1. Click the Refresh button and notice that only the update panel reloads, not the entire page.

The ASP.NET AJAX Extensions can do a whole lot more for your Web Part interfaces. For example, the extensions contain a `Timer` control that performs postbacks at regular intervals and an `UpdateProgress` control that shows status information about partial-page updates.

NOTE   The Microsoft Ajax extender controls enhance the client capabilities of standard ASP.NET controls. One common extender control library is the Ajax Control Toolkit, which is a community-supported extension from Microsoft. You can download the Toolkit from http://ajaxcontroltoolkit.codeplex.com/.

10.1.2 *JavaScripts in Web Parts*

JavaScript has evolved; once a web browser feature that made simple calculations or changes to the page, it's now a service that you can use to take load off the server. Most web applications built today rely heavily on JavaScript, and SharePoint is one of them. The ASP.NET AJAX Extensions use JavaScript to do partial postbacks and updates.

Using JavaScript in Web Parts is a great way to accomplish a dynamic interface that interacts with other items. There are two basic ways to add JavaScript to a Web Part: either using an external JavaScript (.js) file or using inline JavaScripts. Using external JavaScript files is what I recommend. They perform better because you can cache those files. Using inline JavaScript can make programming easier because you can generate the scripts dynamically.

I recommend that you use the `ScriptLink` control, mentioned in chapter 4, to add external JavaScript files to a Web Part. You can use `ScriptLink` as a control or add it to the control tree, or you can use one of its static methods to register a script. The following line shows how to register a custom script with a Web Part for the current page:

```
ScriptLink.Register(this.Page, "Custom.js", false);
```

The `ScriptLink` control ensures that the script element is used only once in the output. It also assumes that the JavaScript file is located in the Layouts folder. You can also tell the control to use a localized version of the JavaScript file by setting the third parameter to `true`.

The `ScriptLink` control isn't available in sandboxed solutions. Instead you have to inject the `<script>` tag manually and point it to a location in SharePoint where the JavaScript file is deployed. You should do this in the `RenderContents` method of the Web Part, as shown in the following snippet:

```
protected override void RenderContents(HtmlTextWriter writer) {
    string url = SPContext.Current.Web.Url + "/SiteAssets/script.js";
    writer.Write("<script type='text/javascript' src='"
        + url + "'></script>");
    base.RenderContents(writer);
}
```

The downside is that the script file will be loaded once for each Web Part instance. To add inline JavaScript code to a Web Part, you should use the `ClientScriptManager` object of the page. You can insert scripts declaratively in user controls or pages, but `ClientScriptManager` manages all scripts you add dynamically to the page. To add a script dynamically, you can choose among several methods depending on the situation. Each script has a key and a type that identifies the scripts and avoids duplicates. The `ClientScriptManager` is accessible from the sandbox, but any scripts registered won't be transferred from the sandbox.

Use `RegisterStartupScript` to insert a script that should execute when the page load is complete. A Hello World example of a startup script might look like this:

```
this.Page.ClientScript.RegisterStartupScript(
    typeof(MyWebPart),
    "helloworld",
    "alert('Hello World');",
    true);
```

This code will display a JavaScript alert dialog box with the text *Hello World* once the page is loaded and rendered. The last parameter tells `ClientScriptManager` that it should enclose the script with `script` tags. The `typeof` keyword is used instead of the `GetType` method of the current object to get the type of the object. This is the preferred approach and avoids double registrations of the scripts when the Web Part is subclassed.

> **TIP** You can avoid loading your JavaScript files multiple times in sandboxed Web Parts by loading them dynamically. One good way to achieve this is by using the SharePoint Script On Demand system, defined in the ECMAScript SP.SOD class. You can find more about it here: http://msdn.microsoft.com/en-us/library/ff410742.aspx.

When working with partial postbacks and partial updates, you can't use `ClientScriptManager`. The ASP.NET AJAX Extensions have their own script manager, called `ScriptManager,` to handle the partial updates. `ScriptManager` is very similar in operation to `ClientScriptManager`. For instance, if you need to run a script on every partial postback, use the `RegisterStartupScript` method of `ScriptManager` instead of the method with the same name of the `ClientScriptManager` control.

TIP If you're making your own master pages for SharePoint, include this `ScriptManager` object to ensure that Web Parts and other controls work as they should.

In SharePoint the `ScriptManager` object is defined in the master page directly after the form tag, which is a requirement for `ScriptManager`. The definition in the default SharePoint 2010 master page (v4.master) looks like this:

```
<asp:ScriptManager
    id="ScriptManager"
    runat="server"
    EnablePageMethods="false"
    EnablePartialRendering="true"
    EnableScriptGlobalization="false"
    EnableScriptLocalization="true" />
```

To get a reference to the `ScriptManager` from within a Web Part, you use the static method `GetCurrent`. This method accepts the current page as a parameter and returns the `ScriptManager` object or a null value as follows:

```
ScriptManager scriptManager = ScriptManager.GetCurrent(this.Page);
if (scriptManager == null) {
    scriptManager = new ScriptManager();
    this.Page.Form.Controls.AddAt(0, scriptManager);
}
```

The first call is to the `GetCurrent` method. If `ScriptManager` isn't found, `GetCurrent` creates it and dynamically adds it to the page. Use this approach whenever you're working with `ScriptManager`, because it saves you from exceptions in case the designers forgot to add the control to the master page. Notice how `ScriptManager` is added as the first control of the page's Form control.

NOTE The `ScriptManager` object for the current page can't be retrieved in a sandboxed Web Part. So, you can't use the `ScriptManager` or any dependent controls in a sandboxed Web Part.

10.1.3 *Working with jQuery*

One of the libraries you'll commonly use when working with JavaScript is the jQuery JavaScript library. jQuery allows you to write little yet effective JavaScript code and there are a great number of plug-ins to jQuery available. jQuery is now officially supported by Microsoft and included in Visual Studio 2010.

jQuery is a popular JavaScript framework and is often used in no-code solutions—solutions that don't require any server-side access. You'll find many resources on the internet for extending the SharePoint platform with jQuery. jQuery can be used to enhance your Web Parts, and you don't have to do any cross-browser adjustments.

> **About jQuery**
>
> jQuery is a popular open source cross-browser JavaScript library that's used as a building block to enhance the JavaScript and HTML experience.
>
> jQuery has a pluggable architecture and can be extended using plug-ins. Microsoft has adopted the jQuery library and is shipping it with Visual Studio.
>
> To learn more information about jQuery, visit http://jquery.com/.

You'll use jQuery to extend our RSS Web Part with a timer that automatically refreshes the RSS feed at regular intervals. You'll do this by including the jQuery library and one of the jQuery plug-ins. The jQuery version that you'll use is jQuery 1.4.2 and the plug-in is called jQuery.timers 1.2 (originally written by Blair Mitchelmore).

First, make sure that the jQuery JavaScript file is added to the SharePoint solution. As you know, you have basically two options: add it to the _Layouts folder or into a SharePoint library. For sandboxed solutions you only have the latter option. In this example, you're going to add all JavaScript files to the _Layouts folder. I prefer this approach when building farm solutions because it takes some load off the content databases and when I don't have to edit the JavaScript file (which could be a good reason to put the file in a SharePoint library).

In the RSS Web Part project, you add the SharePoint Layouts mapped folder; rename the automatically added folder to `DynRSSWebPart`. To this folder, add a new JavaScript file called `DynRSSWebPart.js` that contains custom JavaScript code. Also add the jQuery file (jQuery-1.4.2.min.js) and the timer plug-in file (jquery.timers-1.2.js) to the folder.

The auto-refresh of the feed should be configurable. Add a new property to the Web Part like this:

```
[WebBrowsable]
[WebDisplayName("Auto refresh")]
[Personalizable(PersonalizationScope.Shared)]
public bool AutoRefresh {
    get;
    set;
}
```

You'll use the `AutoRefresh` property in the `OnPreRender` method to determine if the refresh JavaScript timer should be added. Before including that check, you need to make sure that the JavaScript files are loaded by your Web Part using the `ScriptLink` control like this:

```
ScriptLink.Register(this.Page, "DynRSSWebPart/jquery-1.4.2.min.js", false);
ScriptLink.Register(this.Page, "DynRSSWebPart/DynRSSWebPart.js", false);
```

Add these statements to the `CreateChildControls` method. They ensure that the scripts are loaded only once and in the specified order. The timer plug-in JavaScript isn't added here—you'll do that only when the auto-refresh is enabled. You'll use these two scripts in later enhancements of the Web Part.

In the custom JavaScript file, you need a function (see listing 10.3) to invoke the timer that will refresh the feed at regular intervals. You'll create the JavaScript functions using JavaScript object literal notation—that is, you'll create a namespace that holds all the functions and variables. This best practice avoids function naming collisions and saves you a great deal of troubleshooting. In this case, you'll add an object literal to the window object only if it isn't already defined.

Listing 10.3 JavaScript with jQuery timer plug-in that updates the Web Part partially

```
if (!window.feeds) window.feeds = {

    feedTimer : function (id) {
        $(document).everyTime(5000, function () {
            __doPostBack($('#' + id + ' div:first')[0].id, '');
        }, 0);
    }
};
```

The feedTimer function takes an ID parameter that's the client ID of the Web Part. This function will create a timer using the jQuery Timers plug-in function everyTime, calling the inline function every 5,000 milliseconds. The function that's called in the inline function and making the partial postback is the ASP.NET __doPostBack JavaScript function. This function needs the client id of the UpdatePanel that will be partially updated. The client id of the UpdatePanel is retrieved using a jQuery selector. The $ function accepts a string that's the selector. The selector looks up the HTML element with the id of the Web Part and then takes the first child div element, which corresponds to the update panel. The id of the div element is passed as an argument to the __doPostBack function.

You could've passed the id of the UpdatePanel directly, and you could've used the ASP.NET AJAX Extensions timer control, which might have been more appropriate in this case. But I chose to use a jQuery plug-in to demonstrate the power of jQuery, jQuery plug-ins, and jQuery selectors—and you'll use more later. Using this approach, you don't have to write as much JavaScript code thanks to the efficiency of jQuery.

To connect the Web Part to the JavaScript and to invoke the function that creates the timer, you need to update the Web Part. In the OnPreRender method, after the code that writes the current time, add the following lines:

```
if (this.AutoRefresh){
    ScriptLink.Register(this.Page,
        "DynRSSWebPart/jquery.timers-1.2.js", false);
    this.Page.ClientScript.RegisterClientScriptBlock(
        typeof(DynRSSWebPart2),
        "AutoRefresh",
        string.Format("feeds.feedTimer('{0}');", this.ClientID),
        true);
}
```

If the `AutoRefresh` property is set to `true`, the jQuery timer plug-in script and a client script block are registered. The client script block calls the JavaScript function that's defined in the custom JavaScript file and calls the `feedTimer` function with the client id of the Web Part.

When this updated RSS feed Web Part is deployed, you can select to edit the Web Part, check the `AutoRefresh` property, and then apply the changes. You'll see that every 5 seconds it updates. Unless any new feed items appear in the feed, you'll at least notice that the last updated time will change.

Using automatically updatable Web Parts like this can impact your SharePoint installation and impress your users. Imagine having Web Parts on your front page that automatically update at regular intervals or when things change.

10.2 Using the SharePoint dynamic UI features

SharePoint 2010 has received a major facelift compared to its predecessors. The user interface is built with ASP.NET AJAX Extensions, as you saw in the previous section; it provides many dynamic features. Chapter 1 reviewed some of these features. Now, in this section I'll show you how to hook into a user interface API and use its features, such as adding notification messages to inform your users about your asynchronous operations or status bars that show errors and warnings.

If the Web Part needs to collect information from the user or show more details, the traditional way in SharePoint was to redirect to a custom application page. This made the user lose his or her current state and required that the pages be completely re-rendered. Using the new dialog framework, you can avoid this; instead, the previous application page is shown in a modal dialog window on top of the current page.

10.2.1 Notification messages and the status bar

In SharePoint 2010 you can add notifications to tell the user what's going on and to confirm operations that are asynchronous. Another great feature is the status bar, which shows status messages, warnings, and errors. Let's take a closer look at these new features.

ADDING NOTIFICATION MESSAGES TO THE RSS WEB PART

The last change you made to the RSS Web Part was to introduce asynchronous refreshing of the feed to avoid reloading the entire page. Unless the feed was changed, you could see that the Web Part was updated only by looking at the last updated time stamp. To improve this behavior and make it more apparent that the Web Part is actually refreshing the feed, you can use the SharePoint notification message, as shown in figure 10.2.

Figure 10.2 Notification messages can be used to inform the user about asynchronous events. This figure shows notification messages from the RSS Web Part.

You create a SharePoint notification message by invoking a JavaScript function defined in the SP.js JavaScript file, but you also need the CORE.js JavaScript file. These two files are normally included in the SharePoint master pages. The SP.UI. Notify.addNotification function allows you to add a new notification and SP.UI. Notify.removeNotification removes a notification. The notification message consists of an HTML string, and a Boolean value determines if the message should automatically disappear. Messages added are queued up and shown one after the other.

To add a notification to the RSS Feed Web Part that announces when the timer is automatically refreshing the feed, you need to add it to the JavaScript function. To do so, add a new line of JavaScript to the feed.feedTimer function so that it looks like this:

```
feedTimer : function (id) {
    $(document).everyTime(5000, function () {
        SP.UI.Notify.addNotification('Refreshing feed...');
        __doPostBack($('#' + id + ' div:first')[0].id, '');
    }, 0);
}
```

Every time the timer function is called and before the partial postback occurs, a notification message appears that informs the user that the feed is refreshing. To enhance it even further, you can add HTML with the SharePoint animated loading image like this:

```
SP.UI.Notify.addNotification(
'<img src="/_layouts/images/loadingcirclests16.gif"/> Refreshing feed...');
```

The SP.UI.Notify.addNotification takes two parameters: the first one is the HTML you want to show in the message and the second (optional) parameter is a Boolean value indicating if the message should automatically be removed. The function returns a unique id for the notification message, which can be used to remove it (using the SP.UI.Notify.removeNotification function).

ADDING A STATUS BAR TO THE RSS WEB PART

The status bar in SharePoint offers similar functionality as the notification message. The big difference is that notification messages are normally messages shown for a short period whereas the status bar messages are for more long-lived conditions.

Working with the status bar is also similar to working with notification messages. The status bar is defined in the SP.js JavaScript file and you access it using the SP.UI.Status JavaScript namespace. Status messages have a title and message as well as a priority color. The big difference compared to notification messages is that the status bar doesn't disappear after a few seconds and the status messages aren't queued. The status bar appears by default under the Ribbon menu and messages can be appended to the status bar or removed.

To demonstrate how to work with the status bar, let's introduce it into our RSS Feed Web Part. You'd like the status bar to appear and show if any feed fails to load. If there are several RSS Feed Web Parts on the same page, they'll use the same status bar, as shown in figure 10.3.

Figure 10.3 Use the status bar to give the users information, warnings, and error messages. In this figure, the status bar which appears in red on your screen ("Feed not found" in figure above) shows that errors have occurred in the RSS Web Part.

You're going to add a few new features to the JavaScript namespace that you added in listing 10.3. First you'll add two properties that will store the id of the status bar and an array of strings consisting of URLs of the feeds not found. Then you'll add the function that the Web Part will call whenever it finds a feed with an error. The code in listing 10.4 is added inside the window.feeds scope in listing 10.3.

Listing 10.4 Adding a status bar to the Web Part

```
statusId: null,
feedsNotFound : [],

feedNotFound: function (uri) {
    var html = 'Unable to locate the feed: <a href="' + uri +
        '">' + uri + '</a>. ';
    var title = 'Feed not found';
    if(this.statusId == null) {
        this.statusId = SP.UI.Status.addStatus(title, html, true);
        SP.UI.Status.setStatusPriColor(this.statusId, 'red');
        this.feedsNotFound[this.feedsNotFound.length] = uri;
    } else {
        var found = false;
        for(var i = 0; i < this.feedsNotFound.length; i++) {
            if(this.feedsNotFound[i] == uri) {
                found = true;
            }
        }
        if(!found) {
            this.feedsNotFound[this.feedsNotFound.length] = uri;
            SP.UI.Status.appendStatus(this.statusId, title, html);
        }
    }
}
```

The first property, statusId, represents the id of the current status bar that's used. The second, the feedsNotFound array, is used to store faulty feeds that have been added so a feed isn't added to the status bar more than once.

The feedNotFound function takes an argument with the URL of the feed that has a problem. If the statusId property has a null value, it'll create a new status bar and set its priority color to red and finally add the feed to the array. If a status bar already exists, the function checks if the feed has been added already to the array; if not, it'll append a message to the current status bar and add the URL to the array.

The priority color of the status bar can have one of the following values: Red, Green, Yellow, or Blue. You should use the appropriate color like this:

- Red—Indicates errors and exceptions
- Yellow—Used for warnings
- Blue—Used for help, notification, and information
- Green—Indicates a good status

The SP.UI.Status namespace also contains methods for updating and removing status bars using the status id.

Carefully plan when to use the status bar or notification messages. Using these features too much will clutter your interface. A combination of standard error messages in the Web Part and these dynamic features is probably the best solution.

10.2.2 *The dialog framework*

Dialog windows that appear when you're adding or editing list items are one of the most notable new features in SharePoint 2010. Using dialog windows is efficient for several reasons, such as enhanced user experience and a faster user interface.

Dialogs are created using the SharePoint JavaScript framework. The dialog framework is defined in SP.UI.Dialog.js and in the SP.UI.ModalDialog namespace. A modal dialog is created by calling the SP.UI.showModalDialog, which takes an SP.UI.DialogOptions object as an argument. The DialogOptions object defines the position, size, style, and behavior of the modal dialog.

Dialogs can be used for various tasks, such as showing information or requesting input from end users. The RSS Web Part is focused on retrieving an RSS feed and presenting it to users. To try the dialog framework and to improve the Web Part, let's extend the Web Part options menu with a new verb that opens a dialog for changing the RSS feed URL for the Web Part. To accomplish this, you need these components:

- A Web Part verb that invokes a JavaScript
- A JavaScript that opens the dialog
- A page that represents the dialog
- A hidden field in the Web Part that contains the URL
- Functionality to update the Web Part with the value from the hidden field

The page that will represent the dialog is built as an application page, which means that it's stored in the _Layouts folder. Add the page by right-clicking and selecting Add > New Item on the DynRSSWebPart folder that you created in the Layouts mapped folder. Then choose the Application Page item type and name it DynRSSDialog.aspx. The page will contain a text box for the feed URL and a button that saves and closes the dialog, as shown in figure 10.4.

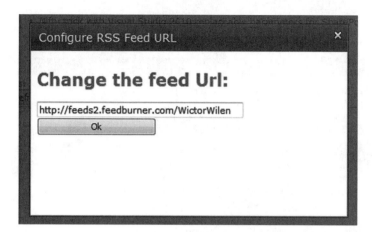

Figure 10.4 Modal dialogs can be created in SharePoint 2010 using the dialog framework. By using modal dialogs, you can provide a better end-user experience and a faster solution.

This code for the controls is added to the placeholder `PlaceHolderMain`:

```
<asp:Content ID="Main" ContentPlaceHolderID="PlaceHolderMain"
    runat="server">
<h1>Change the feed Url:</h1>
<asp:TextBox ID="feedUrl" runat="server" CssClass="ms-input"  Width="255"/>
<br />
<input id='ok' type='button' value='Ok' class="ms-ButtonHeightWidth" />
</asp:Content>
```

Both the text box and the button have received styling using standard SharePoint CSS classes. The text box contains the URL of the current feed of the Web Part; this value is set by passing the URL as a query string parameter to the application page:

```
protected void Page_Load(object sender, EventArgs e) {
    feedUrl.Text = Request.QueryString["url"];
}
```

The text box is filled with the value in the `Page_OnLoad` method in the code-behind of the page. The Web Part needs a hidden field that contains the currently configured URL for the RSS. It must be exposed as a hidden field so that you can access it through JavaScript. The hidden field control is defined in the class as a private member:

```
private HtmlInputHidden hiddenInput;
```

The reason that it's added as a private member is that it shouldn't be overridden if the Web Part is subclassed, compared to defining it as protected. The hidden field is added in the `CreateChildControls` method:

```
hiddenInput = new HtmlInputHidden() {
    ID = "HiddenFeedControl",
    Value = this.RssFeedUrl
};
this.Controls.Add(hiddenInput);
```

Now you can get the value of the RSS feed using JavaScript, but you need a way to save it back if the value of the hidden field is changed. You can accomplish this by overriding the OnLoad event on the Web Part. Listing 10.5 shows how to implement the update of the RSS feed.

Listing 10.5 OnLoad method that saves the RssFeedUrl property

```
protected override void OnLoad(EventArgs e) {
    if (this.hiddenInput != null &&
        !string.IsNullOrEmpty(this.hiddenInput.Value) &&
        (this.Page.IsPostBack || this.Page.IsCallback)) {

        if (hiddenInput.Value != this.RssFeedUrl) {         ❶ Indicate that
            if (this.WebPartManager != null) {                 state of Web Part
                this.SetPersonalizationDirty();                has changed
                SP.SPWebPartManager wpMgr = this.WebPartManager
                    as SP.SPWebPartManager;
                if (wpMgr != null) {
                    this.RssFeedUrl = hiddenInput.Value;
                    wpMgr.SaveChanges(wpMgr.GetStorageKey(this));
                }
            }                                                  Save the
        }                                                      changes ❷
    }
    base.OnLoad(e);
}
```

The OnLoad method starts by checking that the hidden field isn't null and that the current call is a postback or a callback so that it isn't saved on regular requests. Then OnLoad checks whether the value of the RSS feed has changed. If it has changed, then the method sets the personalization state to dirty ❶ to indicate to the Web Part Manager that it needs to save the state of the Web Part. Finally, the new value is set to the RSS feed URL and the Web Part Manager is used to save the Web Part ❷.

Now you need to create a dialog to accept the new RSS feed URL as input and then set the value of the hidden field. You must instantiate the dialog and show it using a JavaScript function. You add this function to the JavaScript object that you created earlier for the RSS Web Part. Listing 10.6 shows the function you should add to the window.feed object.

Listing 10.6 JavaScript function that creates and shows a modal dialog window

```
editFeed: function (id) {
    var options = {
        title: "Configure RSS Feed URL",              ❶ URL of
        url: "/_layouts/DynRSSWebPart/DynRSSDialog.aspx?url="   dialog
            + $('#' + id + ' input:first').val(),      source
        width: 400,
        height: 200,
        allowMaximize: false,
        showClose: true,
        dialogReturnValueCallback: function (result, target) {
            feeds.closeCallback(result, target, id)
        }
    }                                                  ❷ Show
    SP.UI.ModalDialog.showModalDialog(options);           dialog
}
```

The `editFeed` function takes a parameter that's the client id of the Web Part. It creates an object called `options`, which contains the properties and behavior of the dialog. Properties such as title, width, and height are configured. The URL property ❶ points to the application page that you created with the current feed URL as a parameter. The current URL is retrieved using a jQuery selector, which locates the first input field in the Web Part and takes the value from it. When the dialog is closed, a JavaScript should be invoked. You define this by setting the `dialogReturnValueCall-back`. This callback function is set to a new function that you'll define next; this function also takes the client id as input. Finally, the dialog is shown using the `showModalDialog` function ❷.

To close the dialog correctly, you need to add JavaScript to the button on the application page. This JavaScript will use a jQuery selector, so you add a `ScriptLink` control referring to the jQuery script:

```
<SharePoint:ScriptLink ID="jQuery" runat="server"
    Name="jquery-1.4.2.min.js" Localizable="false" />
<input id='ok' type='button' value='Ok' class="ms-ButtonHeightWidth"
    onclick='javascript:SP.UI.ModalDialog.commonModalDialogClose(
➡   SP.UI.DialogResult.OK,$("#<%=feedUrl.ClientID%>").val())'/>
```

The `onclick` attribute of the input element calls the `commonModalDialogClose` method with two arguments. The first one has a value of `SP.UI.DialogResult.OK`, which means that this is considered an OK click of the dialog, and the second one contains the value of the text box.

When the dialog closes, the callback function you defined when instantiating the dialog is invoked. The code that follows shows the `closeCallback` function and how it adds a notification message before updating the value of the hidden field:

```
closeCallback: function (result, target, id) {
    if (result == SP.UI.DialogResult.OK) {
        SP.UI.Notify.addNotification(
            '<img src="/_layouts/images/loadingcirclests16.gif"/>
            Saving Web Part...');
        $('#' + id +' input:first').val(target);
        __doPostBack($('#' + id + ' div:first')[0].id, '');
    }
}
```

The dialog callback checks if the result of the dialog was an OK value. If it was, then the callback shows a notification that the Web Part is being saved. This is a good spot for notification messages—telling the user that a value is saved in the background. The value of the new feed URL passed through the `target` argument to the method is put into the hidden field, which is found using a jQuery selector. Finally, it makes a partial post to the update panel that saves and refreshes the Web Part.

Before deploying and testing the Web Part, add a default value to the `ItemCount` property in the .webpart file:

```
<property name="ItemCount">5</property>
```

10.3 *Enabling a Web Part to use the Ribbon*

The ability to add and change functionality to the Ribbon is one of the great UI features of SharePoint 2010. Features, pages, controls, or Web Parts can add extensions to the Ribbon using *custom actions*. The extensions can be farm, site, all pages, or for a specific page or Web Part.

In this section you'll explore how to enable a Web Part to use the Ribbon in two ways. First, you'll make a Ribbon extension that appears whenever the Web Part is added to the page. This can be useful for functions that aren't tied to the specific Web Part instance on the page.

In the second sample, you'll take a look at something really interesting: making the Web Part contextual. This means that only when the Web Part is selected on a page will the Ribbon customizations appear. For instance, the out-of-the-box Media Web Part in SharePoint Server provides this capability. It adds a new Ribbon tab in which you can change the properties of that specific Web Part instance. You can use the Ribbon to edit Web Part properties instead of using custom Editor Parts. I'll show you how to do the same to your Web Parts.

Before continuing, I want to warn you about building Ribbon extensions and especially contextual ones. Creating a Ribbon extension requires a lot of XML coding. If you've worked with previous versions of SharePoint, you're familiar with this declarative approach. Visual Studio 2010 doesn't offer good support for building Ribbon extensions. In addition to writing XML code, you must be able to write quite a lot of JavaScript code. The JavaScript and XML code are sensitive to which ids you assign to items, so you need to build your Ribbon extensions carefully. Hopefully this chapter will make all this easier for you.

> **TIP** Customizing the Ribbon involves server-side code, JavaScript code, and manual XML editing. There are no good tools or templates in Visual Studio 2010 to make Ribbon customizations, but you can find samples and add-ons, such as the *SharePoint Ribbon Generator*, in the Visual Studio Online Extension gallery.

10.3.1 *Adding controls to the Ribbon*

The functionality that you'll add to the Ribbon in this section, is a new tab. This tab will appear in the Ribbon when you add the RSS Feed Web Part to the current page. The Ribbon tab will have a button that will refresh the feeds in all available RSS Feed Web Parts on the page. Figure 10.5 shows the customization.

Figure 10.5 You can extend the Ribbon with new tabs, groups, and controls that interact with SharePoint and Web Parts.

The first thing to do when building a Ribbon customization is to add a new Share-Point Project Item (SPI) to your project of the type Empty Element. This involves adding a new SPI to your project containing an empty Elements.xml file that will later contain the Ribbon customization. Ribbons are customized using the `CustomAction` element, which contains a `CommandUIExtension` element. Because the XML for adding a simple button is quite extensive, let's divide it into four sections:

- Defining the XML outline
- Defining the tab and button
- Defining the template
- Defining the Ribbon actions

The outline is the basic framework for building a Ribbon extension as shown in listing 10.7. There are three spots where you'll add the rest of the XML later. But before you delve into the details, I'll give you a few tips for customizing the Ribbon. First, you need to be careful when defining the ids of the various nodes in the Ribbon XML. SharePoint is very sensitive to this. Make sure that you don't reuse the same ids, and use only allowed alphanumeric characters separated by dots. Several of the ids will be converted into JavaScript namespaces and objects. Second, if you're deploying the Ribbon and testing and making changes to it, you must clear the browser cache, because a lot of the customizations are cached in the browser.

Listing 10.7 The basic outline of a Ribbon extension

```
<Elements xmlns="http://schemas.microsoft.com/sharepoint/">
    <CustomAction
        Id="WebPartsInAction.RssWebPart"                    ❶ Set custom
        Location="CommandUI.Ribbon">                           action location
        <CommandUIExtension>
            <CommandUIDefinitions>
                <CommandUIDefinition
                    Location="Ribbon.Tabs._children">       ❷ Add new
                    <!-- Tab -->                               Ribbon tab
                </CommandUIDefinition>                      ❸ Add new
                <CommandUIDefinition                           Ribbon
                    Location="Ribbon.Templates._children">     template
                    <!-- Template -->
                </CommandUIDefinition>
            </CommandUIDefinitions>                         ❹ Create Ribbon
            <CommandUIHandlers>                                actions
                <!-- Actions -->
            </CommandUIHandlers>
        </CommandUIExtension>
    </CustomAction>
</Elements>
```

The `CustomAction` element is used to define any custom interface actions. The Location attribute ❶ specifies that this custom action is a Ribbon extension with the CommandUI.Ribbon value. Following the `CustomAction` element is the `CommandUIExtension` element, which contains the `CommandUIDefinitions` that holds the Ribbon controls ❷

and the templates ❸. The `CommandUIHandlers` ❹ elements contain the definitions for the commands invoked by the Ribbon. In this sample, you use two `CommandUIDefini-`
`tion` elements. The first one contains the definition for the tab that will be added. By looking at the `Location` element, you can see that this definition is going to be added as a child node to the `Ribbon.Tabs` object. The second element contains the template that the tab will use. A template is used to determine the location of the controls within the tab for different scalings of the Ribbon. Scalings are used when the browser window is resized to allow the Ribbon to adapt to the space available to rendering controls. For instance when your browser window gets smaller you can make your Ribbon controls smaller or even group them. In this sample, you'll use only one template, which means that this Ribbon extension won't scale. Listing 10.8 shows the XML that defines the tab that should be added in the first `CommandUIDefinition` element in listing 10.7.

Listing 10.8   Adding a custom tab to the Ribbon

```
<Tab
    Id="WebPartsInAction.RssTab"
    Title="RSS Feeds"
    Description="RSS Web Part ribbon tab"
    Sequence="1000">
    <Scaling
        Id="WebPartsInAction.RssTab.Scaling" >                    Defines max
        <MaxSize                                                   scaling
            Id="WebPartsInAction.RssTab.Feeds.MaxSize"
            Sequence="10"                                       ❶ References
            GroupId="WebPartsInAction.RssTab.Feeds"                Group element
            Size="RSSTemplate1" />
        <Scale                                                     Defines
            Id="WebPartsInAction.RssTab.Feeds.CustomScaling"       custom scaling
            Sequence="20"
            GroupId="WebPartsInAction.RssTab.Feeds"
            Size="RSSTemplate1" />
    </Scaling>
    <Groups
        Id="WebPartsInAction.RssTab.Groups">
        <Group
            Id="WebPartsInAction.RssTab.Feeds"
            Title="RSS Feeds"
            Description="RSS Feed Web Part"
            Sequence="100"                                      ❷ References custom
            Template="Ribbon.Templates.RSSTemplates">             Ribbon template
            <Controls
                Id="WebPartsInAction.RssTab.Feeds.Controls">
                <Button
                    Id="WebPartsInAction.RssTab.Feeds.Refresh"
                    LabelText="Refresh feeds"
                    TemplateAlias="ctrl1"
                    Image16by16="/_layouts/images/rsswebparticons.png"
                    Image16by16Left="0"
                    Image16by16Top="-32"
                    Image32by32="/_layouts/images/rsswebparticons.png"
```

```
                    Image32by32Left="0"
                    Image32by32Top="0"
                    Command="WebPartsInAction.RefreshCommand"/>
            </Controls>
        </Group>
    </Groups>
</Tab>
```

References custom
action command ❸

The `Tab` element defines the tab that you'll add to the Ribbon; it has a title and description. All elements in the XML must have an `Id` attribute. Omitting this attribute will result in the Ribbon failing to render properly. The `Sequence` attribute defines the order of the control. The first element under the `Tab` element is the `Scaling` element, which defines how this tab should handle scaling. The Ribbon automatically scales when the browser window is resized. For this tab, you define two sizes. The `Scale` and `MaxSize` elements have a `Size` attribute that determine which layout from the Ribbon templates to use. In this case they both share the same template, so no scaling will occur. Each scaling element must have a `GroupId` ❶ element that references the group to scale. The `Groups` element defines the different groups within this tab. Here, only one `Group` element is used. The `Template` ❷ attribute specifies the id of the Ribbon template you want to use (you'll define that shortly). Each group has a set of controls defined under the `Controls` element. The `Button` control you'll use to refresh all feeds uses the `LabelText` attribute for the text and a set of image attributes to set the image to be used. The `TemplateAlias` is used to match the position in the Ribbon template. There are two images: one 16x16

pixels and the other 32x32 pixels. Which image the button will use depends on the scaling. The images are rendered using CSS sprites, so each image has a `top` and a `left` value. You can see the image used in this sample in figure 10.6. The `Command` ❸ attribute is the name of the command to be executed when the user clicks the button.

Our next task is to create the template that's referenced by the scaling, group, and controls. The template is placed in the second `CommandUIDefinition` element in listing 10.7. Listing 10.9 shows how to build the template. You can use several templates for scaling the Ribbon, but because this tab contains only one button, that won't be necessary.

Figure 10.6 You should use CSS sprites, which use images combined into one image file, when adding images to controls in the Ribbon to improve performance and reduce request load on the server.

Listing 10.9 Defining a Ribbon group template

```
<GroupTemplate
    Id="Ribbon.Templates.RSSTemplates" >
    <Layout
        Title="RSSTemplate1"
        LayoutTitle="RSSTemplate1" >
        <Section
            Alignment="Top"
```

❶ Used by the
Group element

❷ Used by Size
attribute in scaling

```
            Type="OneRow" >
            <Row>
                <ControlRef
                    DisplayMode="Large"
                    TemplateAlias="ctrl1" />
            </Row>
        </Section>
    </Layout>
</GroupTemplate>
```

3 **Used by
controls**

Each template is contained in a `GroupTemplate` element that has an id **1** that's used by the `Template` attribute on the `Group` element in listing 10.8. There can be multiple `Layout` elements where each has a unique `LayoutTitle` **2** attribute that's used by the scaling elements (`Scale` and `MaxSize`). The `Layout` contains sections that have `Row`s or `Strip`s. A `Row` or a `Strip` contains `ControlRef` elements, which are placeholders for the controls. Each `ControlRef` element has a `DisplayMode` that determines the layout of the control. You have to pay attention to which `DisplayMode` is used with which control. Not all controls support all display modes. The `TemplateAlias` **3** attribute specifies the name of the control reference and is used by the controls in the Ribbon.

> **NOTE** You should always create your own group templates and not reference templates from other projects or the out-of the box Ribbon. This will ensure that the template is loaded when referenced by your controls.

The last part of the Ribbon XML defines the action that's executed when a user clicks the button. For simple actions, this can be defined in XML, but for more advanced operations a custom Page Component JavaScript is needed, as you'll see in the next sample. The command is defined as follows and the `CommandUIHandler` elements are placed in the `CommandUIHandlers` element in listing 10.7:

```
<CommandUIHandler
    Command="WebPartsInAction.RefreshCommand"
    CommandAction="javascript:feeds.refreshAll()"/>
```

Each `CommandUIHandler` has a `Command` attribute that contains the name referenced by the `Command` attribute of the control. The `CommandAction` attribute defines the command to be executed. In this case it invokes a JavaScript method. The JavaScript method is added to the JavaScript namespace that you created earlier:

```
refreshAll: function () {
    SP.UI.Notify.addNotification('Refreshing feeds...');
    $(".feedWebPart div:first").each(function () {
        __doPostBack($(this)[0].id, '');
    });
}
```

The method will display a notification message and then use jQuery to find all elements that have the CSS class `feedWebPart` and then the first `div` in that HTML element. Using the id of each of those `div` elements, it'll make a partial update. To add the CSS class to the RSS Feed Web Part, add the following to the `CreateChildControls` method of the Web Part:

```
this.CssClass = "feedWebPart";
```

There's one more thing to do before you can see the Ribbon: configure the Web Part to show the Ribbon when it's added to a page. In the `CreateChildControls` method, add the following:

```
SPRibbon current = SPRibbon.GetCurrent(this.Page);
if (current != null) {
    current.CommandUIVisible = true;
    current.MakeTabAvailable("WebPartsInAction.RssTab");
}
```

This code retrieves the current instance of the Ribbon. If the Ribbon is available, the code will make sure that the Ribbon is visible and then make our RSS Feed tab available. The `MakeTabAvailable` method requires that the `Microsoft.Web.CommandUI.dll` be added as a reference to the project. This assembly is found in {SharePoint Root}\ISAPI.

Now you're all set to build and deploy. Add two or more RSS Web Parts to a page and configure them. Click the Refresh Feeds button in the custom Ribbon tab and watch the times in the Web Parts change.

You can use the same method to add Ribbon customizations to a page using delegate controls, traditional server or user controls, or even add Ribbon controls directly to a custom page. Ribbon customizations aren't specific to Web Parts. In the next sample, you'll look at a Ribbon customization that's for Web Parts only.

> **TIP**   Full reference of the Server Ribbon Schema can be found in the Share-Point 2010 SDK at the Microsoft MSDN site: http://msdn.microsoft.com/library/ff458369.aspx. The default Ribbon in SharePoint 2010 is defined in the CMDUI.XML file, located in {SharePoint Root}\Template\Global\Xml. I suggest you look at that one to get inspiration and ideas for your own Ribbon customizations.

10.3.2 *Making a Web Part context aware*

The previous sample added a custom Ribbon tab to a page when a Web Part appeared on the page. This customization was quite generic and not only applicable to Web Parts. But what if you'd like to add to the Ribbon a custom tab that's tied to a Web Part? That way, when the Web Part is selected the Ribbon extensions become available. This is called a *context-aware Web Part* and is used, for instance, by the Media Web Part in SharePoint 2010 Server. When that Web Part is selected, the media options appear in the Ribbon.

I'll show you how to make the RSS Web Part context aware. When the Web Part is selected, a new contextual Ribbon tab will appear and allow you to edit the feed URL from the Ribbon instead of using the Editor Part. The Ribbon XML is built in much the same way as the previous approach, with just a few changes. The JavaScript is more

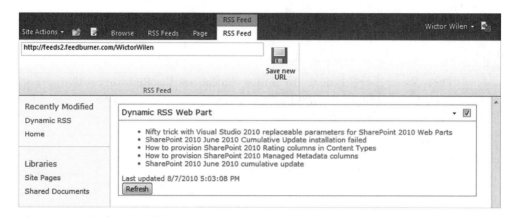

Figure 10.7   Ribbon tabs can be made contextual so that they're visible only when specific Web Parts are selected.

complex and you need to make more edits to the Web Part code. The result will look like figure 10.7.

BUILD THE RIBBON XML

The first thing to do is to add a new Empty Element SPI to the project that will contain the XML for the contextual tab. The XML is much like the previous one, but you have to change the `Location` attribute of the `CommandUIDefinition` so that the new tab is added to the contextual groups of the Ribbon like this:

```
<CommandUIDefinition Location="Ribbon.ContextualTabs._children">
    <!-- Tab -->
</CommandUIDefinition>
```

Instead of adding a `Tab` element, you add a new contextual group using the `ContextualGroup` element and in that group you add the tab. Listing 10.10 shows how the contextual group, tab, and controls are built.

Listing 10.10   Creating a contextual group containing a Ribbon tab

```
<ContextualGroup                                    ◁─┐  Defines contextual
    Id="WebPartsInAction.ContextualTabGroup"          ❶  group
    Color="Orange"                          ◁─┐  Sets
    Sequence="2000"                            ❷  contextual tab color
    Title="RSS Feed"
    ContextualGroupId="RSSFeedContextualTabGroup"
    Command="RssWebPart.ContextualGroupCommand">
    <Tab
        Id="WebPartsInAction.RssContextualTab"
        Title="RSS Feed"
        Description="RSS Web Part contextual Ribbon tab"
        Sequence="1000"
        Command="RssWebPart.TabCommand">
        <Scaling Id="WebPartsInAction.RssContextualTab.Scaling" >
            <MaxSize
```

```
                    Id="WebPartsInAction.RssContextualTab.Feed.MaxSize"
                    Sequence="10"
                    GroupId="WebPartsInAction.RssContextualTab.Feed"
                    Size="RSSTemplate1" />
                <Scale
                    Id="WebPartsInAction.RssContextualTab.Feed.CustomScale"
                    Sequence="20"
                    GroupId="WebPartsInAction.RssContextualTab.Feed"
                    Size="RSSTemplate2" />
            </Scaling>
            <Groups Id="WebPartsInAction.RssContextualTab.Groups">
                <Group
                    Id="WebPartsInAction.RssContextualTab.Feed"
                    Title="RSS Feed"
                    Description="RSS Feed Web Part Options"
                    Sequence="100"
                    Template="Ribbon.Templates.ContextualRSSTemplates"
                    Command="RssWebPart.GroupCommand">
                    <Controls
                        Id="WebPartsInAction.RssContextualTab.Feed.Controls">
                        <TextBox
                            Id="WebPartsInAction.RssContextualTab.Feed.URL"
                            ToolTipTitle="URL of feed"
                            Width="400"
                            TemplateAlias="ctrl1"
                            QueryCommand="RssWebPart.URLQueryCommand"
                            Command="RssWebPart.URLCommand"
                            Sequence="1"/>
                        <Button
                            Id="WebPartsInAction.RssContextualTab.Feed.Save"
                            LabelText="Save new URL"
                            TemplateAlias="ctrl2"
                            Image16by16="/_layouts/images/rsswebparticons.png"
                            Image16by16Left="0"
                            Image16by16Top="-80"
                            Image32by32="/_layouts/images/rsswebparticons.png"
                            Image32by32Left="0"
                            Image32by32Top="-48"
                            Sequence="2"
                            Command="RssWebPart.SaveCommand"/>
                    </Controls>
                </Group>
            </Groups>
        </Tab>
    </ContextualGroup>
```

3 Uses second template

4 Defines text box

5 Declares function to fill text box

6 Defines button

7 Declares save function

The ContextualGroup element ❶ encapsulates the tabs in this ribbon customization; it has a title and a color ❷. The Tab element follows the contextual group, looking the same as in the previous sample. The Scaling element also looks the same, except that the custom Scale element in this sample uses a second template ❸. After the Scale element comes the Groups element, and then the Group element, which contains the controls. For this contextual tab, a TextBox element ❹ contains the URL of the RSS feed. The text box uses a QueryCommand attribute ❺ to define the function that will be called when the tab is activated or changed. This command will later be implemented using a custom page component instead of a `CommandUIHandler`. The last element is the `Button` element ❻, which will save the value from the text box to the selected Web Part. The `Command` attribute ❼ for the button will be handled by a JavaScript function in the page component.

Several other elements in listing 10.10 have the `Command` attribute. This attribute is needed to enable those parts of the Ribbon even though there's no code or logic behind those commands. For instance, the text box would never call the `QueryCommand` function if there were no `Command` functions defined.

The Ribbon template for this contextual tab will use two different templates, instead of just one as in the previous Ribbon sample. Listing 10.11 shows the `GroupTemplate` element of the contextual Web Part group.

Listing 10.11   Ribbon template with two layouts

```
<GroupTemplate Id="Ribbon.Templates.ContextualRSSTemplates" >
    <Layout
        Title="RSSTemplate1"
        LayoutTitle="RSSTemplate1" >                              ❶ Defines max
        <Section                                                     size template
            Alignment="Top"
            Type="OneRow" >
            <Row>
                <ControlRef
                    DisplayMode="Medium"
                    TemplateAlias="ctrl1" />
                <ControlRef
                    DisplayMode="Large"
                    TemplateAlias="ctrl2" />
            </Row>
        </Section>
    </Layout>
    <Layout
        Title="RSSTemplate2"
        LayoutTitle="RSSTemplate2" >                              ❷ Defines custom
        <Section                                                     scale template
            Alignment="Top"
            Type="OneRow" >
            <Row>
                <ControlRef
                    DisplayMode="Medium"
                    TemplateAlias="ctrl1" />
                <ControlRef                                       ❸ Displays small
                    DisplayMode="Small"                              button
                    TemplateAlias="ctrl2" />
            </Row>
        </Section>
    </Layout>
</GroupTemplate>
```

The `GroupTemplate` contains two `Layout` elements. The first ❶ is used when the Ribbon uses the max size scaling. The second one ❷ is used when the browser window is resized and the max size template doesn't fit in the browser. The only difference in this case is that the button, which uses the `ctrl2` TemplateAlias, will be displayed using a small image ❸ when using custom scaling instead of a large image.

CREATE A PAGE COMPONENT

When building more advanced logic for the various Ribbon commands, you can use a page component. A *page component* is a custom JavaScript object that's inherited from a base `Page Component` object. The `Page Component` object exposes several methods that can be used to make the Ribbon more dynamic.

You create a page component by building a JavaScript object. For that you need to add a new JavaScript file to the project. Name the file `RSSRibbon.js` and add it to the Layouts mapped folder. The page component is implemented in listing 10.12. The JavaScript object model in SharePoint extensively uses the ASP.NET AJAX framework, and if you're familiar with those JavaScripts, you'll recognize several parts of this implementation.

Listing 10.12 The page component required for the contextual Web Part

```
Type.registerNamespace('RssWebPart');              ←❶ Registers namespace

RssWebPart.CustomPageComponent = function (         ❷ Creates object
    webPartPageComponentId) {                          constructor

    this._webPartPageComponentId = webPartPageComponentId;
    RssWebPart.CustomPageComponent.initializeBase(this);
}
RssWebPart.CustomPageComponent.prototype = {
    init: function () {
    },                                              ❸ Returns available
    getFocusedCommands: function () {               ←   focused commands
        return ['RssWebPart.SaveCommand',
            'RssWebPart.URLQueryCommand',
            'RssWebPart.URLCommand',
            'RssWebPart.ContextualGroupCommand',
            'RssWebPart.TabCommand',
            'RssWebPart.GroupCommand'];
    },                                              ❹ Returns global
    getGlobalCommands: function () {                ←   commands
        return [];
    },                                              ❺ Checks if command
    canHandleCommand: function (commandId) {        ←   can be handled
        var cmds = this.getFocusedCommands();
        for (var i = 0; i < cmds.length; i++) {
            if (cmds[i] == commandId) {
                return true;
            }
        }
        return false;
    },
    handleCommand: function (commandId, properties, sequence) {
        if (commandId === 'RssWebPart.URLQueryCommand')     ❻ Sets value of
            properties['Value'] = $('#' + this.getId() +        Web Part to
                ' input:first').val();                          Ribbon control
            return true;
```

```
        }
        if (commandId === 'RssWebPart.SaveCommand') {                    ➐ Saves
            SP.UI.Notify.addNotification('Saving Web Part...');              Web Part
            $('#' + this.getId() + ' input:first').val(
                $('#WebPartsInAction\\.RssContextualTab\\.Feed\\.URL').
                val());
            __doPostBack($('#' + this.getId() +
                ' div:first > div:first')[0].id, '');
            return true;
        }
    },
    getId: function () {
        return this._webPartPageComponentId;
    },
    isFocusable: function () {
        return true;
    }
}                                                                 ➑ Registers class as
RssWebPart.CustomPageComponent.registerClass(                        page component
    'RssWebPart.CustomPageComponent',
    CUI.Page.PageComponent);
```

First, a new namespace is registered ❶; this one is called `RssWebPart`. This namespace is then used to contain the page component, which is called `CustomPageComponent` ❷. Objects in JavaScript are defined using the `function` keyword, and this function is also its constructor. This definition will store a local variable containing the id of the page component, which is unique for each Web Part. One page component object is created per Web Part. Finally, the constructor calls its base object, which will be configured later. To define methods on the JavaScript object, you use the `prototype` keyword. You define the `init` method that's used to initialize the object but in this case does nothing. Then you define the `getFocusedCommands` function ❸. This function returns an array of names of the Ribbon commands that should execute when the control has focus. The `getGlobalCommands` function ❹ also returns an array of commands, but these commands are executed regardless of focus. The `canHandleCommand` ❺ function takes a command as an argument and decides whether the command can be executed. For this example, all focused commands can be executed.

If the command can be handled, then it will be invoked using the `handleCommand` function. This function is where the action takes place in the page component. The function takes the command as a parameter, and then depending on which command is called, the page component executes different code. When the tab gets the focus, it will call the command defined in the `QueryCommand` attribute of the text box. This command retrieves the value from the hidden field, which you previously created in the Web Part, and sets that value into the `properties` argument object ❻. The Ribbon uses this `properties` object to set the value of the text box control. When the user clicks the save button, the command of that `Button` element is called ❼. This command will get the value from the text box and put it into the hidden field. All other commands defined in the `getFocusedCommands` aren't handled specifically.

The `getId` function returns the current id of the page component instance. The `isFocusable` function always returns `true` and tells SharePoint that the contextual group can get focus.

The final task is to register this object as a class using the ASP.NET Ajax `register-Class` function ❽. This function takes the name of the class and the base object (`CUI.Page.PageComponent`) from which it will inherit logic. You've just overridden a few of the base object methods, but there are more, such as `yieldFocus` and `recieve-Focus`, which can be used to execute code when the contextual group yields or receives focus.

> **TIP** The documentation of Page Components is, at the time of writing this book, very sparse but can be found at http://msdn.microsoft.com/library/ff408634.aspx.

To connect the RSS Web Part, the contextual Ribbon tab, and the page component, you need wiring code. First, create a JavaScript that instantiates a new page component using the unique Web Part Component Id for the Web Part. For this you'll use a new JavaScript object called `pageComponentFactory`. This object is made to handle instances when you use `UpdatePanel` controls on the page. When a Web Part with a page component gets partially updated, SharePoint will re-create all the page components on the page. The Ribbon will then lose the connection to the page components and stop working. It's here that the `pageComponentFactory` comes to the rescue and makes sure that the page components aren't recreated during a partial update by storing the reference between the page component and the Web Part.

You add the `pageComponentFactory` object to the same JavaScript file, although you could move it to a separate JavaScript file so that you could reuse it more easily. Listing 10.13 shows the implementation of the `pageComponentFactory` object.

Listing 10.13 The `pageComponentFactory` object

```
function pageComponentFactory(webPartPageComponentId,      ❶ Creates
    componentClass, jsFile, jsFilePath) {                     pageComponentFactory

    this.webPartPageComponentId = webPartPageComponentId;
    this.pageComponent = null;
    this.jsFile = jsFile;
    this.jsFilePath = jsFilePath;
    this.componentClass = componentClass;                  ❷ Defines add
    this.add = function () {                                  function
        if (typeof SP.Ribbon.PageManager.get_instance().
            getPageComponentById(webPartPageComponentId) ==
            'undefined') {

            pageComponent = new RssWebPart.CustomPageComponent(
                webPartPageComponentId);

            SP.Ribbon.PageManager.get_instance().
                addPageComponent(pageComponent);
        }
    }
```

```
}
pageComponentFactory.prototype = {                          ❸ Defines register
    register: function () {                          ◄──┘      function
        SP.SOD.registerSod(this.jsFile, this.jsFilePath);
        SP.SOD.executeFunc(this.jsFile, this.componentClass, this.add);
    }
}
```

The `pageComponentFactory` constructor ❶ takes four arguments. The first is the id of the Web Part component and the second is the class that was registered. The last two parameters are the name and location of the JavaScript file where the page component is registered. The object contains one local method called add ❷, which instantiates the page component if there isn't already a page component with the specific id created. Then it adds the page component to the SharePoint Ribbon Page Manager.

The JavaScripts in SharePoint contain a set of functions called *Script On Demand* (*SOD*). These functions allow you to register JavaScript files as they're loaded and notify registered functions to execute when they're loaded. The second method of the page component factory is the `register` ❸ function. The `register` function is the first method called; it will register the JavaScript file using the `SP.SOD.registerSod` function and then connect the page component class and method to it using the `SP.SOD.executeFunc` function. Once the JavaScript file is loaded by SharePoint, it will execute the function specified in the last parameter, in this case the add function.

> **TIP**   More information about the Script On Demand functions in Share-Point 2010 can be found in the SharePoint 2010 SDK; http://msdn.micro-soft.com/library/ff410742.aspx.

To use this page component factory, you add a function to the JavaScript file. This function will be called from the Web Part using the page component id that will be used for the Web Part:

```
function createRssRibbon(webPartPageComponentId) {
    return new pageComponentFactory(webPartPageComponentId,
        'RssWebPart.CustomPageComponent',
        'DynRSSWebPart/rssribbon.js',
        '/_layouts/DynRSSWebPart/rssribbon.js');
}
```

This function takes the id of the Web Part page component as parameter and then creates a new `pageComponentFactory` object specifying the class and the JavaScript. When the `register` method is called on the returned `pageComponentFactory` object, it will wait for the RSSRibbon.js file to load; the method then invokes the add method, as in listing 10.13.

You have one more thing to add to the custom JavaScript file (RSSRibbon.js): the code that informs the SOD Manager that the file is loaded. This has to be added to the end of the JavaScript file:

```
SP.SOD.notifyScriptLoadedAndExecuteWaitingJobs(
    "DynRSSWebPart/rssribbon.js");
```

CONNECTING THE WEB PART TO THE PAGE COMPONENT

Now that you have all the necessary JavaScript code for the contextual Web Part, it's time to modify the Web Part so it can connect to the Ribbon and page component. The first thing that you need to do is make the Web Part class implement the `IWeb-PartPageComponentProvider` interface. This interface contains one property that returns information about the current Web Part Ribbon status. When the Web Part Manager adds the Web Parts to the page, it queries for this interface; if it's found on a Web Part, the Manager will retrieve the contextual and page component information from the Web Part and register the associated Ribbon tabs. Modify the class definition of the Web Part so that it looks like this:

```
public class DynamicRSSWebPart : WebPart, IWebPartPageComponentProvider
```

Then right-click on the newly added interface and select Implement Interface > Implement Interface. This adds the property of the `IWebPartPageComponentProvider` interface to the Web Part. Change the implementation so that it looks like listing 10.14.

Listing 10.14 Implementing the `IWebPartPageComponentProvider` interface

```
public WebPartContextualInfo WebPartContextualInfo {
   get {
      WebPartContextualInfo contextInfo = new WebPartContextualInfo();

      contextInfo.ContextualGroups.Add(new
         WebPartRibbonContextualGroup() {                    ❶ Sets id of
                                                               Contextual Group
         Id = "WebPartsInAction.ContextualTabGroup",
         VisibilityContext = "WebPartsInAction.CustomVisibilityContext",
         Command = "RssWebPart.ContextualGroupCommand"
      });
      contextInfo.Tabs.Add(new WebPartRibbonTab() {           ❷ Sets id
         Id = "WebPartsInAction.RssContextualTab",              of Tab
         VisibilityContext = "WebPartsInAction.CustomVisibilityContext"
      });
      contextInfo.PageComponentId = SPRibbon.              ❸ Sets id of current
         GetWebPartPageComponentId(this);                    Web Part
      return contextInfo;
   }
}
```

The property returns a `WebPartContextualInfo` object. This object contains a list of `WebPartRibbonContextualGroup` objects, which are the contextual groups associated with the Web Part specified using the `Id` attribute ❶. The object also contains the associated tabs defined by a list containing `WebPartRibbonTab` objects using the `Id` of the tab ❷. The `VisibilityContext` property used by both objects must be unique. Finally, the `PageComponentId` property ❸ is set using the built-in function of the `SPRibbon` class to get the unique id for the page component.

Now the Web Part Manager is aware that this is a Web Part with a page component and it has added the contextual group and tab to the Ribbon. It doesn't yet have the information about the page component and JavaScripts. The JavaScripts are registered in the `CreateChildControls`:

```
ScriptLink.RegisterScriptAfterUI(this.Page,
    "CUI.js", false, true);
ScriptLink.RegisterScriptAfterUI(this.Page,
    "SP.Ribbon.js", false, true);
ScriptLink.RegisterScriptAfterUI(this.Page,
    "DynRSSWebPart/RssRibbon.js", false);
```

Three JavaScripts registrations are added. The first to be registered is CUI.js, which contains the base definition for the page component. Next the SP.Ribbon.js file is registered. This file contains the Ribbon Page Manager that's used by the page component factory. Finally, the custom JavaScript file for the RSS Feed Web Part is added; this file contains the page component. The two first JavaScripts are SharePoint JavaScripts, but you've added them here so you're sure that they're loaded.

All that is left is to create the Page Component in the Web Part. You create the page component by using a JavaScript that calls the `createRssRibbon` function in the JavaScript file. To invoke this function, use the `ScriptManager` to register a new startup script in the `OnPreRender` method:

```
ScriptManager.RegisterStartupScript(this.Page,
    typeof(DynamicRSSWebPart),
    "RssWebPartPageComponent" + this.ClientID,
    string.Format("SP.SOD.executeOrDelayUntilScriptLoaded(" +
        "function(){{createRssRibbon('{0}').register();}}," +
        "'DynRSSWebPart/rssribbon.js');",
        SPRibbon.GetWebPartPageComponentId(this)),
    true);
```

This registration will add a new script for each Web Part that's executed once the RSRibbon.js file is loaded. It will then call the `createRssRibbon` function using the unique Web Part page component id.

It took a lot of code, both XML, JavaScript, and server-side C#, to finish this contextual Web Part, but now it's ready for a test drive. Build the project and deploy it to your SharePoint site; then add a few of the Web Parts to the page and configure them using the contextual tab. Each time you select a new RSS Web Part on the page, the page component will retrieve the value from the hidden field and populate the text box. And when you click the save button, it will copy the value from the text box to the Web Part hidden field. Then the page component makes a partial update that saves the new value of the feed URL and updates the Web Part.

10.4 *Summary*

By using all the dynamic features—such as the built-in notifications and dialogs, the Ribbon framework, and ASP.NET AJAX extensions—you can make your Web Parts more user-friendly and more Web 2.0-ish.

You must have knowledge of JavaScript to be able to build dynamic Web Parts, and I recommend that you learn how to use jQuery as well. Using jQuery in combination with the plug-ins allows you to build JavaScript code quickly and you don't have to worry so much about browser compliancy.

In this chapter you did a combination of server-side and client-side programming using JavaScript, jQuery, XML and C#. In the next chapter you'll continue exploring JavaScript and also create a Web Part using Silverlight.

11

The Client Object Model and Silverlight Web Parts

This chapter covers

- The Client Object Model and Web Parts
- The Silverlight Web Part
- Custom Silverlight Web Parts

Browsers have become increasingly more powerful, allowing developers to build rich user interfaces with JavaScript and plug-ins such as Silverlight and Flash. The combination of rich clients and web services enables applications to take some load off the servers and even perform tasks not possible on the servers. A benefit for power users is the ability to add custom functionality to applications without access to the server. JavaScript and Silverlight in combination with SharePoint sandboxed solutions is the way to go when you have your SharePoint hosted or if you can't install solutions directly onto the server in any other way.

In previous SharePoint versions, external applications had the option of interacting with SharePoint using web services only. These web services were poorly documented, loosely typed, and hard to work with. A new concept called the *Client Object Model* lets external applications work with SharePoint 2010 using a client runtime and API. The Client Object Model doesn't replace the old web services (which still remain) but makes it easier and more efficient to work with the Share-Point object model remotely.

Silverlight is a technology that Microsoft is pushing hard, and SharePoint comes with a Silverlight Web Part out of the box. Silverlight applications can make the user interface more interactive and rich, and it allows developers to be more creative when building applications. This chapter shows you how to work with the Client Object Model and Silverlight to create a rich experience for your end users.

11.1 The Client Object Model

One of the most innovative new features of SharePoint 2010 is the Client Object Model. It's a completely new approach to working with SharePoint for remote clients. Previously, remote clients used SharePoint web services, a limited and tedious task for developers. The Client Object Model offers a client-side API that comes in three flavors: one for managed .NET code, one for Silverlight applications, and a JavaScript variant.

You can use the Client Object Model to accomplish many SharePoint tasks, but for Web Parts, its use is limited. The client-side API for Web Parts lets you add, move, and delete Web Parts on a page and change some default properties, such as the title. There's no way to access the custom properties or methods on a Web Part. If you need to do this kind of customization with remote clients, you have to add your own remote API to SharePoint. Other parts of the Client Object Model allow you to access larger portions of SharePoint's features and APIs.

Web Parts built using the SharePoint Web Part implementation have had their own client-side JavaScript library called Web Part Page Services Components (WPSC), which enabled client-side Web Part interactions. This JavaScript library still exists in Share-Point for backward compatibility only with SharePoint 2003 and SharePoint 2007.

11.1.1 What is the ECMAScript Client Object Model?

The Client Object Model is Microsoft's response to user requests for more and better web services in SharePoint. Instead of building new web services, Microsoft built a whole new API using a subset of the standard SharePoint API. The Client Object Model is an API that's supposed to run where access to the server API isn't possible. The client API is similar to the server API, but it's limited to using objects from the site collection (SPSite) level and down—which means that it's easier to learn and understand the model than to learn a set of new web services.

The Client Object Model consists of three APIs that are very similar:

- A managed client API for Microsoft .NET Framework code
- A Silverlight 2.0+ client API for Silverlight applications
- An ECMAScript client API for web browser–based JavaScript applications

NOTE ECMAScript (ECMA-262) is the standardization (ECMA International) of JavaScript.

The Client Object Model uses a client runtime proxy that communicates with a Windows Communication Foundation (WCF) service. The service is located at /_vti_bin/client.svc. To communicate, the client proxy sends batched XML commands and the WCF services respond with a result formatted using JavaScript Object Notation (JSON). Because all commands are batched together and the JSON notation is a compact form, the Client Object Model bandwidth use is kept to a minimum.

Creating Client Object Model applications using a managed .NET client requires references to Microsoft.SharePoint.Client.dll and the Microsoft.SharePoint.Client.Runtime.dll. These files are located in the {SharePoint Root}\ISAPI folder. The Silverlight API uses two other assemblies as reference: Microsoft.SharePoint.Client.Silverlight.dll and Microsoft.SharePoint.Client.Silverlight.Runtime.dll. These files are located in {SharePoint Root}\TEMPLATE\LAYOUTS\ClientBin. To use the ECMAScript Client Object Model, you need to copy or reference the following JavaScript files that are located in the {SharePoint Root}\TEMPLATE\LAYOUTS folder:

- SP.js
- SP.Core.js
- SP.Ribbon.js
- SP.Runtime.js

Each of those JavaScript files has a debug version that includes IntelliSense support. Use the debug files when you've enabled debugging in the web application (using the web.config file as described earlier in this book). The debug and release versions differ in such a way that the release versions are minified JavaScript files and the debug files contain readable and debuggable code. The debug versions have the following names:

- SP.debug.js
- SP.Core.debug.js
- SP.Ribbon.debug.js
- SP.Runtime.debug.js

The JavaScript files are normally an out-of-the-box feature added to all pages using the SharePoint master pages. If you intend to create a custom web page that uses a custom master page, use the SharePoint `ScriptLink` control, described in chapter 4, to add these JavaScript files to your pages.

11.1.2 *Working with the Client Object Model and Web Parts*

The Client Object Model is fairly limited when it comes to working with Web Parts. Basic operations such as adding and removing Web Parts can be done as well as changing some default properties of the Web Part. There's no access to custom Web Part properties.

You can use the Client Object Model to remotely add Web Parts to pages or inspect pages for closed or hidden Web Parts. The Client Object Model API differs a bit from the server object model. All Web Part functionality is in the `Microsoft.SharePoint.Client.WebParts` namespace. Three classes are of interest to us for this discussion:

- `LimitedWebPartManager`—Imports and adds Web Parts
- `WebPartDefinition`—Provides move, remove, and change state operations
- `WebPart`—Provides information about the Web Part

ADDING A WEB PART USING THE CLIENT OBJECT MODEL

The `LimitedWebPartManager` object is used to add new Web Parts to a page by first importing a Web Parts control description XML file and then adding it to a page and zone. To create an application that adds a Web Part to a page, you create a console application using Visual Studio 2010. Be sure to set the .NET Framework to version 3.5. Then add Microsoft.SharePoint.Client.dll and the Microsoft.SharePoint.Client.Runtime.dll, found in the {SharePoint Root}\ISAPI folder, as references to the project. Listing 11.1 shows how a Web Part is loaded from a Web Parts description file and then added to a page using the Client Object Model.

Listing 11.1 Adding a Web Part to a page using the Client Object Model

```
using (ClientContext context = new ClientContext("http://server")) {

    Web web = context.Web;
    File file = web.GetFileByServerRelativeUrl("/SitePages/Test.aspx");
    LimitedWebPartManager wpMgr = file.GetLimitedWebPartManager(
        PersonalizationScope.Shared);                          Retrieves Web ❶
                                                               Part Manager
    WebPartDefinition webPartDef = wpMgr.ImportWebPart(
        System.IO.File.ReadAllText("Content_Editor.dwp"));
    wpMgr.AddWebPart(webPartDef.WebPart, "Left", 1);           ❷ Executes
                                                                  query
    context.ExecuteQuery();
}
```

When working with the Client Object Model, you always start by acquiring a client context (`ClientContext`) to the site. Using this context, the `Web` object is retrieved and from that a specific page. The Client Object Model `Web` object corresponds to the server API `SPWeb` object. The `LimitedWebPartManager` object is then retrieved from the file object ❶. The Web Part is created by first importing a Web Parts control description file, exported from a page, for instance. This results in a `WebPartDefinition` object that's then added (using the `LimitedWebPartManager`) to a specific zone on the page. So far, everything is done on the client side and the server isn't yet updated. Not until it calls the `ExecuteQuery` ❷ method of the client context object is the command sent to the server. All commands are batched together and executed on the server only when the `ExecuteQuery` method is invoked. This allows you to make several additions and changes before making the changes permanent. Note that the batch jobs aren't transactional.

MODIFYING A WEB PART USING THE CLIENT OBJECT MODEL

In the Client Object Model, the only Web Part properties that you can access are the following:

- `Title`
- `Subtitle`
- `Hidden`
- `TitleUrl`
- `IsClosed`
- `ZoneIndex`

This means that you can't do more than add a Web Part and then change its title or inspect for closed or hidden Web Parts in the pages. To change the title of a Web Part, the approach is similar to our previous example. Listing 11.2 shows how to retrieve all Web Parts on a page and then make all titles uppercase.

Listing 11.2   Modifying Web Parts using the Client Object Model

```
using (ClientContext context = new ClientContext("http://server/")) {

    Web web = context.Web;
    File file = web.GetFileByServerRelativeUrl("/SitePages/Home.aspx");
    LimitedWebPartManager wpMgr =
        file.GetLimitedWebPartManager(PersonalizationScope.Shared);

    context.Load(wpMgr.WebParts,                          ❶ Loads all
        webParts => webParts.Include(                        Web Parts
            webPart => webPart.WebPart.Title));    ❷ Loads only
                                                      Title property
    context.ExecuteQuery();

    foreach (WebPartDefinition webPartDef in wpMgr.WebParts) {
        WebPart webPart = webPartDef.WebPart;
        webPart.Title = webPart.Title.ToUpper();   ❸ Saves
        webPartDef.SaveWebPartChanges();              changes
    }
                                      ❹ Persists
    context.ExecuteQuery();              changes
}
```

Just as in the previous sample, the client context is created first and then the file and Limited Web Part Manager are retrieved. In this case you're only interested in the titles of the Web Parts, so you tell the Client Object Model to load all Web Parts on the page ❶ and then only include the `Title` properties of those objects ❷. Then the `ExecuteQuery` method is called so that it fetches the information from the server of the Web Parts to work with. All Web Parts are iterated over and their title is changed to uppercase and saved ❸ before calling `ExecuteQuery` ❹ once again to persist the changes.

This sample required two calls to the `ExecuteQuery`: one to load the Web Parts and one to save the titles. Requesting the titles of the Web Parts minimizes the network traffic and potentially speeds up the application.

What about Web Part Page Services Components in SharePoint 2010?

The Web Part Page Services Component (WPSC) Object model is a JavaScript component that delivers client-side functionality to Web Parts and Web Part pages. It was used in previous versions of SharePoint and still exists for backward compatibility. The WPSC could make changes to and listen to events from Web Parts using JavaScript.

The WPSC is only available for SharePoint Web Parts derived from the old Web Part base class (`Microsoft.SharePoint.WebPartPages.WebPart`). Because Microsoft discourages the use of the old Web Part implementation, they don't recommend you use WPSC either. Instead, use the Client Object Model, ASP.NET Ajax, or other dynamic JavaScript libraries such as jQuery.

11.2 *Silverlight Web Parts*

Silverlight is a rich client technology that allows you to do even more than is possible with just HTML, JavaScript, and the Client Object Model. SharePoint 2010 supports Silverlight out of the box. It's used sparsely in the default user interface but can be enhanced with custom Silverlight applications using the Silverlight Web Parts. Share-Point Foundation has a generic Silverlight Web Part that you can use to add any Silverlight application to a Web Part page. Silverlight in combination with the Client Object Model is a great way to develop SharePoint solutions. It allows developers to build their applications and package them as sandboxed solutions, which means that they can install them without access to the SharePoint servers. This is great both for custom on-premise solutions as well as for hosted SharePoint solutions such as Office 365 and SharePoint Online 2010. Silverlight allows developers to be more creative with the user interface and introduce new and richer interfaces.

In this section, I'll show you how to create a Silverlight application using the Silverlight SDK that uses the Client Object Model to read information from SharePoint. The Silverlight application will first be deployed using the out-of-the-box Silverlight Web Part and then using a custom Web Part. I'll show you how to customize the default Silverlight Web Part and use various packaging options in Visual Studio. Custom Silverlight Web Parts allow developers to lock down the ability for users to change which Silverlight application they want to use and make it easier to add preconfigured Silverlight Web Parts to the Web Part Gallery.

NOTE Silverlight isn't available for all platforms, so you have to carefully plan whether to use Silverlight. Silverlight is currently available for all major browsers on Windows and Mac OS X.

11.2.1 *SharePoint Silverlight Web Part*

SharePoint Foundation contains a Web Part for Silverlight applications out of the box. This Web Part is found in the *Media and Content* Web Part category, as you can see in figure 11.1. The Silverlight Web Part can be used to show custom Silverlight applications and only requires you to specify the source of the Silverlight XAP file.

Figure 11.1   The SharePoint Silverlight Web Part is available in all SharePoint editions and can be used to add Silverlight applications to your pages. You'll find the Silverlight Web Part in the Media and Content category in the Web Part Gallery.

Once you've added the Silverlight Web Part to the page, the Web Part will ask you to enter the URL where the Silverlight XAP file is located. The URL can be a local URL in your SharePoint farm or a remote URL where the Silverlight application is hosted by someone else. You can easily edit the export mode settings of a configured Silverlight Web Part and then export it to use in your applications.

Using Silverlight in combination with SharePoint allows you to build a richer user interface that you can't achieve using standard HTML, CSS, and JavaScript. Silverlight has great support for rich media and streaming, and SharePoint Server has a configurable Silverlight-based Media Web Part out of the box.

11.2.2 *Building a Silverlight SharePoint application*

To illustrate the Silverlight Web Part, I'll show you how to build a simple Silverlight application that uses the Client Object Model. The application retrieves the number of tasks in a Tasks list and displays the number on the screen, as shown in figure 11.2.

Silverlight applications are built using Visual Studio 2010 with the Silverlight SDK, which is a separate download. After you've downloaded Silverlight SDK 4 and installed it on your development machine, create a new project using the Silverlight Application template. After you enter the name of your project, the New Silverlight Application wizard asks you to optionally create a website that hosts the Silverlight application and the Silverlight version to use. Because this application will be hosted in SharePoint, you don't need a website and you should select Silverlight Version 4. Click OK to create your project.

> **NOTE**   To create Silverlight applications you need the Microsoft Silverlight 3/4 Tools for Visual Studio. This is a free download at http://msdn.microsoft.com/Silverlight/.

Visual Studio will create a solution containing two XAML (Extensible Application Markup Language) files: one named App.xaml, which is the actual application, and a second file named MainPage.xaml, which is the Silverlight user interface/control. Double-click on the MainPage.xaml file to open the Silverlight designer. Then use the Toolbox in Visual Studio to drag and drop a new `Label` control onto the Silverlight control. Next, use the Properties window to set the value of the Content property to `Task Count`. Add another label and change the Content property to ??, and then set its text size to 24.

When this is done, resize the whole control so that the two labels fit nicely. The Silverlight application should look something like that shown in figure 11.3.

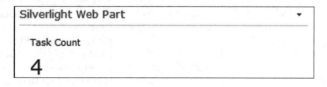

Figure 11.2   The Silverlight Web Part configured to use the Task Count Silverlight application, which shows the number of tasks in the Tasks list of the current site.

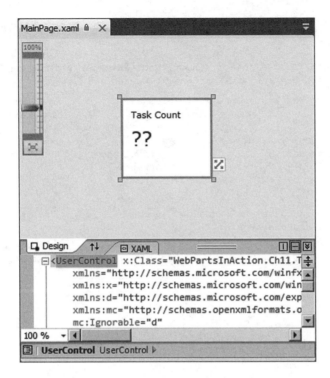

Figure 11.3 The Silverlight XAML designer in Visual Studio 2010 makes the design of the Silverlight application easy.

The Silverlight designer in Visual Studio creates the XAML code, which you can see by switching to the XAML view in Visual Studio. You can edit the XAML code directly instead of using the designer, if you prefer.

Now it's time to write the code that retrieves the number of tasks from the current Tasks list in the site. You'll use the Client Object Model for Silverlight, and for that you need to add the Silverlight Client Object Model reference assemblies. These assemblies are located in {SharePoint Root}\TEMPLATES\LAYOUTS\ClientBin\ and are called Microsoft.SharePoint.Client.Silverlight.dll and Microsoft.SharePoint.Client. Silverlight.Runtime.dll, respectively. Add these two files as references in the Silverlight project.

This application should load the tasks as soon as the control is loaded, so you need to add a code-behind file to the Silverlight control. On the Designer surface, click on the gray area surrounding the control and then press F4, or open the Properties window. The Properties window has two tabs: Properties and Events. Select the Events tab and locate the Loaded event. Double-click on the event name to create the stub code for that event in the code-behind file. Visual Studio will automatically give it the name `UserControl_Loaded`. Once that is done, the code-behind file will open and the cursor will be positioned in the new event method. You'll use this method to load the tasks from the Tasks list using the Client Object Model. Listing 11.3 shows how to implement the retrieval of the tasks.

Listing 11.3   Silverlight code using the Client Object Model to retrieve tasks

```
List tasks;

private void UserControl_Loaded(object sender, RoutedEventArgs e) {          ◄─┐
    using (ClientContext context = ClientContext.Current) {

        tasks = context.Web.Lists.GetByTitle("Tasks");              Defines
                                                                    shared variable ❶
        context.Load(tasks);

        context.ExecuteQueryAsync(            ❷ Executes
            requestSuceeded,                     asynchronous
            requestFailed);                      method

    }
}

private void requestSuceeded(object sender,
    ClientRequestSucceededEventArgs e) {

    Dispatcher.BeginInvoke( () => {                          ❸ Updates user
        label2.Content = tasks.ItemCount.ToString();    ◄─┘    interface
    });
}

private void requestFailed(object sender,
    ClientRequestFailedEventArgs e) {

    Dispatcher.BeginInvoke( () => {
        label2.Content = "??";
    });
}
```

This code requires that the namespace `Microsoft.SharePoint.Client` be added as a using statement so you can access the Client Object Model API. All queries to the Client Object Model are done asynchronously in Silverlight, in contrast to the .NET sample you looked at earlier. This forces you to declare the `tasks` variable, representing the Tasks list, to be declared as a class variable ❶. In the `UserControl_Loaded` method, the current client context is retrieved and then the Tasks list is fetched using the title of the list. When the list has been loaded into the context, it queries asynchronously for the information. The `ExecuteQueryAsync` ❷ method takes two event handlers as parameters. The first one points to a method that's going to be executed if the query is successful, and the second if the query fails. The succeeded event handler, `requestSuceeded`, will update the content of the label in the control with the count of tasks in the Tasks list ❸. The failure event handler, `requestFailed`, just writes two question marks to indicate that it couldn't retrieve the number of tasks.

The two event handler methods use `Dispatcher.BeginInvoke` to execute delegates that update the `Label` controls. The delegates are executed asynchronously on the UI thread. Trying to update the user interface controls directly from the succeeded or failed event handlers would result in an exception because these methods execute on a separate thread.

NOTE   Silverlight is a multithreaded application and the only thread that can update the user interface is the UI thread.

The resulting Silverlight Application Package has the .xap extension (pronounced ZAP). You'll reference this file in the Silverlight Web Part. Because you didn't create a web project to host the Silverlight application, upload the XAP file to SharePoint, preferably to a document library. Open up a SharePoint site and browse to Shared Documents and choose to upload a new document. Select the XAP file from your project (located in the bin\debug folder if you're using a debug build) and then upload the file. Right-click the newly uploaded file and select Copy Shortcut to copy the URL to the Silverlight application.

Create a new Web Part page or Wiki page and add the Silverlight Web Part to the page. When the Web Part asks for the URL to the Silverlight application package, paste the URL you just copied from the document library and click OK. The Silverlight Web Part will load your Silverlight application and display it, as shown in figure 11.2.

TIP If you want to debug a Silverlight application using Visual Studio while the application is running in SharePoint, you must enable Silverlight debugging. To do that, open the project's Properties window and click the SharePoint tab (on the left side). Make sure that the Enable Silverlight Debugging check box is checked. When that option is enabled, you won't be able to debug JavaScript using Visual Studio.

11.2.3 Input parameters to the Silverlight Web Part

There are often situations where you need to configure the Silverlight applications with different input parameters. Properties are passed to the Silverlight application through a text property called Custom Initialization Parameters, which can be found under the Other Settings Web Part property category, as shown in figure 11.4.

The Custom Initialization Parameters property consists of a comma-separated list of keys and values that will be sent to the Silverlight application. You can retrieve these parameters from the Silverlight application using a dictionary object. This dictionary object is accessible in the Application_Startup event of the Silverlight applications. To use the parameters or send them to the Silverlight control, you need to modify that event. The following code demonstrates how to extract the dictionary from the startup event arguments and then retrieve the properties:

Figure 11.4 The editor pane of the Silverlight Web Part allows you to set the Silverlight application using the Configure button and supply custom initialization parameters to the application using the text field.

```
private void Application_Startup(object sender, StartupEventArgs e) {

    IDictionary<string, string> parms = e.InitParams;

    string listId = parms.ContainsKey("ListId")
        ? parms["ListId"].ToString() : null;
```

```
        int itemId = parms.ContainsKey("ItemId")
            ? int.Parse(parms["ItemId"]) : 0;

        this.RootVisual = new MainPage() {
            ListId = listId,
            ItemId = itemId
        };
    }
}
```

In this sample, the application expects that two parameters will be passed with the Custom Initialization Properties, as shown in figure 11.4: `ListId` and `ItemId`. The properties dictionary is retrieved from the `StartupEventArgs` object passed to the event. Each initialization property is stored in this dictionary and is retrieved and stored in local variables. These variables are then sent to the `MainPage` object. This object represents the Silverlight application control, which has been extended with two public properties that accept the values from the initialization properties.

11.2.4 *Packaging the Silverlight Web Part*

To improve the experience for the end user, you can bundle the Silverlight application into a SharePoint solution package and preconfigure the Silverlight Web Part. First, add a new Empty SharePoint project to your current solution. Choose to deploy this solution as a sandboxed solution.

In the SharePoint project, add a new Module SharePoint project item. Once you create the project item, remove the sample.txt file that's automatically added. Right-click the project item, select to add an existing item, and then browse to your XAP file and select it to add it to the project. Open the elements.xml file and edit it so that it looks like the following listing.

Listing 11.4   Elements.xml file provisioning the Silverlight application package

```
<Elements xmlns="http://schemas.microsoft.com/sharepoint/">
  <Module
    Name="TaskCountApp"
    Url="Shared Documents">
      <File
        Path="TaskCountApp\WebPartsInAction.Ch11.TaskCount.xap"
        Url="TaskCountApp/WebPartsInAction.Ch11.TaskCount.xap"
        Type="GhostableInLibrary" />
  </Module>
</Elements>
```

The `Url` attribute of the `Module` element must be manually edited in the elements.xml file to correspond to the name of the library where you want to deploy your XAP file. Doing so deploys the files to the Shared Documents library instead of a custom folder. The `File` element is automatically added when you add a new or an existing item to this project item. Make sure that you add and set the `Type` attribute to `GhostableInLibrary`, because you're deploying a file to a document library. GhostableInLibrary allows SharePoint to keep a reference to the file in the file system instead of in the content database, which improves performance.

When you build and deploy this solution, it will add the Silverlight XAP file. That file can be used in any Silverlight Web Part by referencing the XAP file. The problem is that whenever the Silverlight application is changed in your Visual Studio solution or when the build target is changed, you need to read the XAP file to the module in the SharePoint project from the output of the Silverlight project.

A better approach is to use a *project output reference* on the SharePoint Project item. First remove the XAP file from the SharePoint project; you won't use this manually added file anymore. Then, right-click on the Module item (or select it and press F4) and click the ellipsis icon on the Project Output References property. The Project Output References dialog box opens. Click the Add button to add a new reference. In the Project Name property of the new reference item, select the project name for the Silverlight project and as Deployment Type select ElementFile, as you can see in figure 11.5.

After adding the Project Output Reference, the elements.xml file is updated with a File element looking exactly the same as you wrote. However, this time the XAP file isn't added to the project; instead it's added during the packaging processes of the SharePoint solution package. In addition, the XAP file will always be the latest version and thus will use the correct build version. Try it by building and deploying the solution, then navigate back to the page where you added the Silverlight Web Part. Edit the Web Part and its properties so that the path to the Silverlight application points to the newly deployed XAP file.

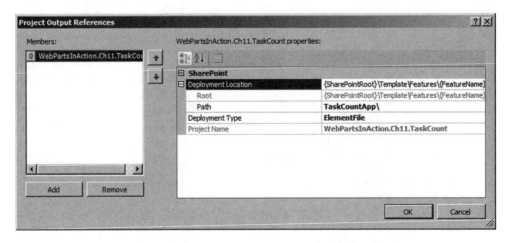

Figure 11.5   To include output files from other Visual Studio projects, use the Project Output References dialog box. Here you can add the output from a Silverlight project into a SharePoint project and add the XAP file as an ElementFile**.**

11.2.5 *Preconfiguring the Silverlight Web Part*

Not all users are comfortable selecting XAP files and editing the parameters in the Silverlight Web Part. To make it easier for end users to use the Silverlight Web Part, preconfigure the Silverlight Web Part and deploy it to the Web Part Gallery.

You add a preconfigured Web Part to the Visual Studio solution by adding a second Module item to the SharePoint project; don't forget to remove the sample.txt file from the new project item. To add the Web Parts control description file, either write one or even better, export the Silverlight Web Part. To export the .webpart file, you first need to enable export on the Silverlight Web Part. By default, the export mode of the Silverlight Web Part is set to Do Not Allow. Edit the Web Part and change the Export Mode setting in the Advanced category to Export All Data, and then save the Web Part. Use the Web Part options menu to export the Web Part to your local drive. The exported Web Part will contain all settings you configured prior to exporting it.

Go back to Visual Studio and select to add an existing item to the Web Part Module you just created. Add the exported .webpart file and give it a meaningful name, such as `TaskCountWebPart.webpart`, instead of using the default filename, as shown in figure 11.6.

The `File` element is automatically added to the elements.xml file. Open the .webpart file, locate the `Title` property, and change the default value; then change the `ExportMode` property so that it can't be exported:

```
<property
    name="Title"
    type="string">
    Task Count Web Part
</property>
<property
    name="ExportMode"
    type="exportmode">
    None
</property>
```

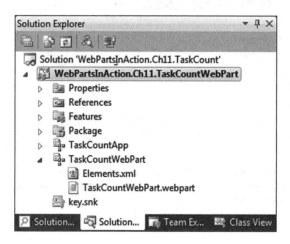

Figure 11.6 **Preconfigured Web Parts can be added to a Visual Studio solution using an Empty SharePoint Project Item and then be deployed to the farm.**

Finally, make sure that the .webpart file is deployed to the Web Part Gallery. Edit the elements.xml file so that it looks like listing 11.5.

Listing 11.5   The element manifest that provisions the Silverlight Web Part

```
<Elements xmlns="http://schemas.microsoft.com/sharepoint/">
  <Module
    Name="TaskCountWebPart"
    List="113"
    Url="_catalogs/wp">
      <File
        Path="TaskCountWebPart\Silverlight_Web_Part.webpart"
        Url="Silverlight_Web_Part.webpart"
        Type="GhostableInLibrary">
          <Property
            Name="Group"
            Value="Web Parts in Action"/>
      </File>
  </Module>
</Elements>
```

The first thing to edit is the `Module` element; the `List` and `Url` attributes have to be configured so that the `Module` is targeting the Web Part Gallery. Second, add the `Type` attribute to the `File` element and remove the folder name from the `Url` attribute. Finally, add a `Property` element to the `File` element and configure the element to set the Group property of the Web Part.

Before deploying the solution, make sure that the Feature of the SharePoint project has its Scope set to Site. Because this Feature is deploying the Web Part to the Web Part Gallery, you can't use the default Scope value (which is Web). When the solution is deployed, the Task Count Web Part can be found in the Web Part Gallery under the category you specified in the element manifest. The Web Part is now preconfigured with the Silverlight application that's deployed with the Feature.

11.2.6 *Custom Silverlight Web Part*

The previous example allowed you to bundle the Silverlight application with a preconfigured Silverlight Web Part, which made it easier for end users to use the Silverlight application. Because you're using the out-of-the-box Silverlight Web Part, users can still modify the Web Part's properties, such as the initialization parameters, and modify which Silverlight application to use. There are situations where you don't want your users to configure the Silverlight application and therefore you'd like to remove the ability to configure the source to the Silverlight XAP file or the initialization parameters. Unfortunately, the Silverlight Web Part is sealed so you can't subclass it and remove the custom Editor Part that provides the ability to configure the XAP URL. So, you have to create your own Silverlight Web Part from scratch. This also gives you benefits such as creating a better experience for the administrators using Web Part properties, instead of using the Custom Initialization Parameters.

Before building the new Silverlight Web Part, add an error check in the Silverlight application, which checks whether the `ClientContext` is `null` before proceeding. The check is implemented in the `UserControl_Loaded` method so that it looks like this:

```
private void UserControl_Loaded(object sender, RoutedEventArgs e) {
    using (ClientContext context = ClientContext.Current) {
        if (context == null) {
            Dispatcher.BeginInvoke(() => { label2.Content = "--"; });
            return;
        }
        tasks = context.Web.Lists.GetByTitle("Tasks");
        context.Load(tasks);
        context.ExecuteQueryAsync(requestSuceeded, requestFailed);
    }
}
```

Checks if ClientContext is available ❶

When `ClientContext` is equal to `null`, you write two dashes in the `Label` control and exit the method. ❶ `ClientContext` will be set to `null` if the Silverlight application can't acquire the client context—for instance, when you run the application outside of SharePoint.

You create the new Silverlight Web Part by adding a new Web Part project item to the solution's SharePoint project. This Web Part will add the necessary HTML code and reference the XAP file without allowing users to change the Silverlight application. Listing 11.6 shows the `CreateChildControls` method of the new Silverlight Web Part.

Listing 11.6   A custom Silverlight Web Part

```
protected override void CreateChildControls() {
    Panel ctrlHost = new Panel() {
        ID = "silverlightControlHost"
    };

    var objectControl = new HtmlGenericControl("object");
    objectControl.Attributes.Add("data",
        "data:application/x-silverlight-2");
    objectControl.Attributes.Add("type", "application/x-silverlight-2");
    objectControl.Attributes.Add("width", "100%");
    objectControl.Attributes.Add("height", "100%");

    objectControl.Controls.Add(createParam("source",
        SPContext.Current.Site.Url +
        "/Shared%20Documents/TaskCountApp/" +
        "WebPartsInAction.Ch11.TaskCount.xap"));

    objectControl.Controls.Add(createParam("background",
        "white"));

    objectControl.Controls.Add(createParam("minRuntimeVersion",
        "4.0.50401.0"));

    objectControl.Controls.Add(new LiteralControl("Install Silverlight!"));

    ctrlHost.Controls.Add(objectControl);
```

```
        this.Controls.Add(ctrlHost);
}

private static HtmlGenericControl createParam(string name, string value) {
        var param = new HtmlGenericControl("param");
        param.Attributes.Add("name", name);
        param.Attributes.Add("value", value);
        return param;
}
```

The `CreateChildControls` method creates a new `Panel` object that will host the Silverlight application. Then an `object` element is created, using the `HtmlGenericControl` that represents the Silverlight application. This `object` needs a set of parameters that are defined with `param` elements. The `param` elements are created using the `createParam` helper method. The `source` parameter references the Silverlight XAP file and in this case is hardcoded.

When you build and deploy the project into Share-Point, you can add the new Silverlight Web Part to a page. There's no need to specify the XAP file, and it can't be modified. The Web Part will look like the one shown in figure 11.7. As you can see, the Silverlight application writes two dashes in the control. That indicates that it can't acquire the client context from within the Silverlight application. In a moment you'll learn how to overcome this issue.

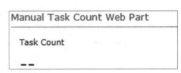

Figure 11.7 By default Silverlight can't use the Client Object Model in custom Web Parts—they need to be initialized with the proper parameters.

Using this method, you can add custom Silverlight applications as long as they aren't using the Client Object Model. To be able to use the Silverlight Client Object Model, the client runtime has to be initialized and this isn't done in our custom Silverlight Web Part. In the next section you'll learn how to initialize the client context so that you can build custom Silverlight Web Parts that can interact with SharePoint.

11.2.7 Enabling custom Silverlight Web Part interaction with SharePoint

So that your custom Silverlight Web Part can use the Client Object Model and get the current client context, you need to initialize the Client Object Model client runtime when instantiating the Silverlight application. The SharePoint Silverlight Web Part derives from an abstract class called `ClientApplicationWebPartBase` that exists in the `Microsoft.SharePoint.WebPartPages` namespace. This abstract class contains the logic necessary to send initialization information to the Silverlight application.

The `ClientApplicationWebPartBase` class can't be used in sandboxed solutions, so the first thing you need to do is change your SharePoint project to be deployed as a full-trust solution. Do so by setting the Sandboxed Solution property to False in the project's Properties window. Then modify the declaration of the custom Silverlight Web Part class so it looks like this:

```
public class ManualTaskCountWebPart : ClientApplicationWebPartBase
```

Next, add a new `param` element to the Silverlight object element in the `CreateChild-Controls` method. This `param` element is called `initParams` and is a string containing the necessary parameters that the Client Object Model needs to initialize. These parameters may be the current URL or the Form Digest token and timeout. The parameters are generated by the `GetInitParams` method of the `ClientApplication-WebPartBase`; here's the code you need to add to your Web Part:

```
objectControl.Controls.Add(
    createParam(
        "initParams",
        GetInitParams()));
```

Now when you deploy this Web Part into SharePoint, you can use it as expected. The Silverlight application can now get the client context and the number of tasks in the Tasks list because the Client Object Model runtime is correctly initialized. There's also no way for the end user to change the Silverlight application that the Web Part uses.

The Silverlight Application XAP file is deployed to a document library, and users with necessary permissions on that library can change the Silverlight application. Deploy the XAP file to the Layouts folder so users can't change it.

> **TIP**   If you want to learn more about the Form Digest token and security validation in SharePoint, read the following article at MSDN: http://msdn.microsoft.com/library/ms472879.aspx.

11.3   *Summary*

The Client Object Model and Silverlight allow you to create rich SharePoint applications. You can think out of the box when it comes to the user interface. Using Silverlight to create graphs or animations can greatly enhance the user experience for any SharePoint site.

The SharePoint 2010 sandbox has its limitations; you can't, for instance, call web services from a sandboxed Web Part. Silverlight, on the other hand, is executed on the client, can be used in a sandboxed Web Part and used to call web services to overcome the sandbox limitations.

The Client Object Model can be used in Silverlight, JavaScript, or .NET applications. The JavaScript Client Object Model is something that you'll likely use when building Ribbon extensions or when you need to build non-Silverlight-based sandboxed Web Parts. For administrative remote operations or when you have other ASP.NET-based applications, you can use the .NET Client Object Model. For example, if you build solutions in Windows Azure, use the .NET Client Object Model to communicate with your SharePoint farms.

Making Web Parts mobile 12

This chapter covers

- SharePoint mobile interface
- Control adapters
- Mobile controls

Over the last few years, the use of mobile devices has exploded. You use mobile phones to read your email and browse the web at work, on the bus...pretty much everywhere. A combination of new and innovative devices and a well-established high-speed mobile network allows you to access information wherever you are. SharePoint 2010 has built-in support for mobile devices that makes the interface adapt to the various devices used to browse a SharePoint site. Using specifically created page views optimized for smaller screens and touch-enabled devices, you can now use SharePoint everywhere on nearly all devices. These views are also optimized to reduce network traffic.

In this chapter we'll take a look at the mobile interface of SharePoint 2010 and see how you can configure the mobile experience for Web Part pages and Web Parts. Not all Web Parts can be used in mobile devices; you can use only those with specific control adapters that create a mobile interface for the Web Part. I'll show you how to create and deploy control adapters in a consistent and reusable way.

12.1 *SharePoint 2010 mobile interface*

SharePoint 2010 allows users to access SharePoint from a wide variety of browsers and devices. Using a phone or tablet device, you can access nearly all information in SharePoint. It's not only accessible; you can also add or update information and even view Office documents using the mobile view of Office Web Apps.

The mobile interface in SharePoint supports Web Part pages and Wiki pages as well as lists, views, and list items. Web Parts can be used in mobile pages if they have a control adapter that optimizes the Web Part for mobile views. SharePoint has support for a few of the out-of-the-box Web Parts and you can also build your own control adapters. Depending on the capabilities of the browser and device, the mobile user interface may look differently. SharePoint uses a file called the *browser definition file* to keep track of the various devices and their ability to optimize the mobile experience.

12.1.1 *Using the mobile SharePoint 2010 interface*

SharePoint 2010 is delivered with an out-of-the-box mobile interface for mobile or small screen devices. The mobile interface is optimized to fit on small screens and reduce the amount of data transferred over the network. The ASP.NET framework includes features that can detect which device is used and, using that information, can adapt the SharePoint interface for that device. SharePoint is aware of the capabilities of the device, such as whether it has a built-in phone or whether it can handle JavaScript. For instance, when SharePoint recognizes a touch-enabled screen, it renders the mobile interface with additional padding that makes links and buttons respond to a finger tap. Figure 12.1 shows a blog post rendered on a Windows 7 Phone device using the mobile view of a site. You can also see that the blog post

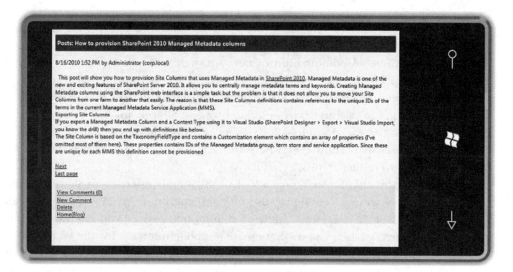

Figure 12.1   A Windows 7 Phone that uses the mobile interface to read a blog post. The blog post is paginated so that only a minimal amount of information is transferred for each request.

viewed is paginated automatically. This is a default optimization designed to reduce the data transferred to the device.

Some devices (or browsers on devices) support the default SharePoint interface. The default interface isn't optimized for small screens or touch gestures, which may make the interface less usable when working with information. Even though the device might support the default SharePoint interface, you might want to speed up the access while on slower networks and to reduce the traffic and roaming costs. To access the mobile pages using a full browser or on a device that supports the full interface, append `mobile=1` to the query string, like this:

```
http://server/SitePages/Page.apx?mobile=1
```

12.1.2 Page, form, and Web Part support

Almost all pages and sites can be shown using the mobile interface. The mobile pages are specific application pages stored in {SharePoint Root}\TEMPLATE\LAYOUTS\

MOBILE\. Depending on what type of page is requested in the mobile interface, different files from this folder are used to convert the page into a mobile representation. For instance, the mblwp.aspx page is used to convert a Web Part page into a mobile Web Part page, and mblwiki.aspx is used for Wiki pages. Once a user requests a Web Part page from the device using the default URL, the user is redirected to the mblwp.aspx page with the target page passed as a `QueryString` parameter.

The mobile interface also has full support for viewing lists and items as well as editing and adding items. Figure 12.2 shows a user adding a new announcement to an Announcement list. Lists can have specific views that are optimized for mobile device access.

Both Wiki and Web Part pages can be displayed in the mobile interface. All content will be shown, including rich text content in the Wiki pages, all depending on the capabilities of the device. Web Parts on the pages can also be shown if they support a mobile interface. As I mentioned earlier, only Web Parts with a mobile control adapter can be shown. Later in this chapter I'll show you how to build your own control adapters.

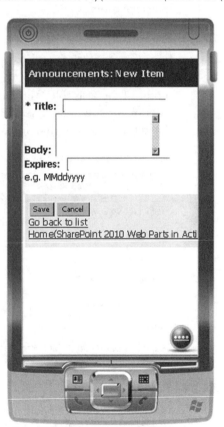

Figure 12.2   All lists in SharePoint can be accessed from the mobile interface. The mobile forms also allow users to add new or edit existing items.

For Wiki content pages, all Web Parts with mobile support are shown on the page. But for Web Part pages, you can configure exactly which Web Parts will be shown in the mobile interface. To determine which mobile Web Parts are visible on a Web Part page, click the Page tab in the Ribbon menu and choose the Edit Mobile Page button in the Page Actions group, as shown in figure 12.3.

Figure 12.3   The Web Parts in the mobile view of a Web Part Page can be configured. You can specify the order and which Web Parts to show.

The Edit Mobile Page option allows you to configure the default mobile settings for this page, and the Edit Mobile Personal Page option allows you to customize your own personalized mobile page. The mobile interface of a Web Part page ignores the Web Part zones. The Web Parts are listed in the order that they appear on the page. Using the Edit Mobile Page option, you can customize the order of the Web Parts for the specific page if the order should differ from the default interface order.

12.1.3   Supported mobile Web Parts

Web Parts, by default, aren't supported in mobile pages; to show them, you need to create one control adapter per Web Part. SharePoint 2010 has control adapters for only a subset of the available Web Parts. You can create control adapters for your own Web Parts or for the default Web Parts; we'll explore this in the next section. Table 12.1 shows the Web Parts that are available in mobile pages by default.

Table 12.1   Web Parts that by default can be used in mobile Web Part pages

Web Part	SharePoint SKU
XSLT List View Web Part	SharePoint Foundation
List View Web Part	SharePoint Foundation
Image Web Part	SharePoint Foundation
Whereabouts Web Part	SharePoint Foundation
RSS Viewer Web Part	SharePoint Server
Business Data Item Web Part	SharePoint Server
Business Data Item Builder Web Part	SharePoint Server

12.1.4   Supported devices

SharePoint 2010 supports a wide range of mobile devices, ranging from Windows Mobile, Windows Phone, Blackberry, to iPhone, as well as tablet devices such as the iPad, as shown in figure 12.4. Depending on the capabilities of the device and browser, the full SharePoint 2010 user interface or the specific mobile interface will appear. No configuration is needed to enable the mobile device support. For devices

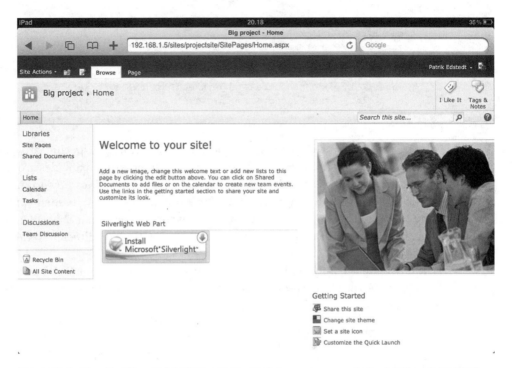

Figure 12.4   Browsing SharePoint 2010 using an iPad gives you access to the full SharePoint 2010 interface instead of the mobile version. Notice that the Silverlight Web Part doesn't show the Silverlight application.

such as Windows Mobile 6.5 or iPhone, the mobile interface is shown by default; for Windows Phone 7 or iPad, the default SharePoint interface is used.

12.1.5   *Browser definition files*

Since version 2.0 of ASP.NET, the ASP.NET runtime has used a file called the browser definition file, by default named *compat.browser* in SharePoint, to determine the capabilities of browsers and devices. For instance, this file might specify whether the device is a mobile device, whether it supports JavaScript, or whether it can initialize a phone call. When ASP.NET receives a request, it uses the user agent information in the header of the request to look up the browser specifics in the .browser file. The .browser file exists in the App_Browser folder of each web application, and you can configure it with new devices and capabilities to fit your needs.

The .browser file is an XML file that consists of browser elements that correspond to a specific platform, browser, or browser version. For instance, the iPod Safari browser is defined like this:

```
<browser id="iPodSafari" parentID="AppleSafari">
    <identification>
      <userAgent match="iPod" />
      <userAgent match="Mobile" />
```

```
    </identification>
    <capabilities>
      <capability name="isMobileDevice" value="true" />
      <capability name="canInitiateVoiceCall" value="true" />
      <capability name="optimumPageWeight" value="1500" />
      <capability name="requiresViewportMetaTag" value="true" />
      <capability name="supportsTouchScreen" value="true" />
    </capabilities>
  </browser>
```

The `browser` element contains a unique `id` element for the specific browser and optionally a parent browser `id` element for inheritance of capabilities from other defined `browser` elements. The `identification` element defines how to match the specific browser, and the `capabilities` element contains all the defined capabilities of the browser. The `isMobileDevice` property is the property that SharePoint checks to see whether or not the device is going to be automatically redirected to the mobile interface.

You can use the information in the file during runtime in your Web Part to detect the capabilities of the current browser. Do this by using the `HttpBrowserCapabilities` object, like this:

```
HttpBrowserCapabilities caps = Request.Browser;
string s1 = "Type of Browser: " + caps.Type;
string s2 = "Is current browser a crawler: " + caps.Crawler;
string s2 = "Has touch capabilities: " + caps["supportsTouchScreen"];
```

Some of the browser capabilities are available as strongly typed properties of the object, and some are available through the `indexer` property. Using these capabilities during runtime can help you make decisions as to how to render a specific Web Part or enable certain features. For instance, you could adapt the size of buttons, images, or links.

> **TIP** Microsoft provides updates to the .browser file using the ASP.NET CodePlex project, which you can find at http://aspnet.codeplex.com/. The latest release (http://aspnet.codeplex.com/releases/view/41420) is targeted for ASP.NET 4 but the download includes instructions on how to use the updated files with ASP.NET 3.5.

SharePoint Server 2010 adds a specific browser definition file called *compat.moss. browser* instead of modifying the default compat.browser file. This file contains the control adapters for the SharePoint Server Web Parts.

12.2 *Mobile Web Part adapters*

You can also create your own mobile views of your Web Parts by leveraging features in the ASP.NET infrastructure. ASP.NET supports alternate renderings of controls through control adapters. A control adapter is a specific registered control that allows you to modify the output of another control without any changes to the original control. By using a custom browser definition file, you can create and register a control adapter for the

Silverlight-based Task Count Web Part (which you built in the previous chapter). This adapter will provide an alternate rendering for mobile devices, as shown in figure 12.5, because most mobile devices don't support Silverlight (at least when this book was written).

12.2.1 Create a mobile adapter

To provide the alternate rendering of the Silverlight-based Task Count Web Part, the first thing you need to do is build a new control adapter. Building this adapter doesn't require any changes to the original Web Part and therefore you can create a new empty SharePoint project. The project has to be a farm solution because registering the control adapter requires that you edit the compat. browser file or add a new custom browser definition file. (The latter is preferred because updates to SharePoint or ASP.NET might overwrite the original files.)

Control adapters for Web Parts derive from the WebPartMobileAdapter, which is based on the generic control adapter class ControlAdapter object. The first thing to do is to add a new class file to the project and give it a name. I recommend that the name always end with MobileAdapter; in this example, name the class TaskCountMobileAdapter.

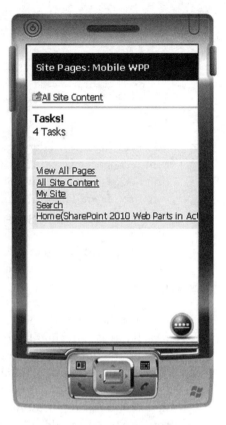

Figure 12.5 Control adapters are used to create a mobile representation of a Web Part. The Windows Mobile 6.5 phone in this figure shows the number of tasks from the Task Count Web Part using text rather than the Silverlight application.

Once you create the class, you need to create the alternate interface, using the code in the following listing (see figure 12.5).

Listing 12.1 A control adapter for the Task Count Web Part

```
[Guid("95bd5e48-0771-4f32-9ff8-1877b6deaa6d")]
public class TaskCountMobileAdapter: WebPartMobileAdapter {     ❶ Detailed
                                                                    view
    protected override void CreateControlsForDetailView() {
        SPWeb web = this.Web;
        SPList list = web.Lists.TryGetList("Tasks");
        if (list != null) {
            SPMobileLabel heading = new SPMobileLabel() {
                Text = "Tasks",
                BreakAfter = true
            };
            heading.Font.Bold = BooleanOption.True;
            this.Controls.Add(heading);
```

```
            this.Controls.Add(new SPMobileLabel() {
                Text = string.Format("{0} Tasks", list.ItemCount) }
            );
        }
    }
    protected override void CreateControlsForSummaryView() {
        base.CreateControlsForSummaryView();
    }
}
```

2 Summary view

To create the control adapter, set the `TaskCountMobileAdapter` class to inherit from the `WebPartMobileAdapter` class. First, you need to add the `Guid` attribute to the class. This isn't necessary for the control adapter to work but will make it easier to deploy, which you'll see later. The `Guid` attribute requires that you include the `System.Runtime.InteropServices` namespace in the class. You can generate the globally unique identifier (GUID) using the Guidgen tool found in Visual Studio under the Tools menu. Then, to provide the alternate rendering for the control, you must override a few methods. You don't have to override all the methods in the `WebPartMobileAdapter`, just those necessary for your alternate view. In this example, two methods are overridden: `CreateControlsForDetailView` **1** and `CreateControlsForSummaryView` **2**. The first one

contains the detailed view of the mobile interface. It retrieves the number of tasks in the Tasks list and uses the `SPMobileLabel` control to write out a heading and the number of tasks. The `SPMobileLabel` is a `Label` control optimized for mobile interfaces. To use the mobile controls, you also need to add a reference to the System.Web.dll and the System.Web.Mobile.dll in the project. In the second overridden control, the base implementation is called; this overridden method could be left out but I'm using it here to show the difference between the two.

> **NOTE** To generate a GUID, use the Guidgen tool available in Visual Studio. If that tool isn't installed, you can browse to http://www.guidgen.com/ to get a GUID. Never handcraft your GUIDs on your own; always use a tool so that it's guaranteed to be globally unique.

The summary view is what the user sees by default when browsing to a page. The default implementation of the `CreateControlsForSummaryView` shows the name of the Web Part and an icon that the user can click to display the detailed view, as shown in figure 12.6. In this case it might

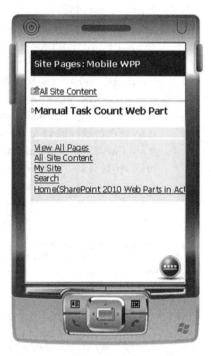

Figure 12.6 The Task Count Web Part, using the summary view of the control adapter. Clicking the icon in front of the Web Part title switches to the detailed view shown in figure 12.4.

be more appropriate to have the summary view call the detailed view method and show the same interface. That would allow the user to see the number of tasks directly instead of having to click the icon.

The `WebPartMobileAdapter` contains a set of helper methods and properties that you can use to build the mobile interface. Table 12.2 shows some interesting properties and methods.

Table 12.2 Important methods and properties in Mobile Web Part adapters

Method or property	Description
`CreateWebPartIcon()`	Creates an `Image` control with the current Web Part icon, optionally linked to the summary or detailed view of the Web Part
`CreateWebPartLabel()`	Creates a `Label` control with the title of the Web Part
`DetailViewPageUrl`	The URL to the detailed view of the Web Part
`SummaryViewPageUrl`	The URL to the summary view of the Web Part
`ItemBulletIconUrl`	A URL to a bullet icon that's used when the adapter needs to render a bulleted list

12.2.2 Register a mobile adapter

So far you've only created the control adapter—you haven't yet registered it for use in mobile web pages. To register control adapters, you modify the existing com-pat.browser file or add your own .browser file to the App_Browsers directory. You simply add `adapter` elements to any of the `browser` elements in the file. The `adapter` element contains information about the control adapter and the control (Web Part) that the adapter will replace when rendering the mobile view.

You can add a control adapter to one or more specific browsers or add a generic control adapter. Generic control adapters have the `refID` attribute on the `browser` element set to `default`. For this project, you'll add a generic control adapter in a custom .browser file.

CREATE THE CUSTOM BROWSER DEFINITION FILE

To add a custom browser definition file to the project add an Empty Element SPI to your project. Rename the elements.xml file to `customAdapters.browser` (or delete it and add a new .browser file). This empty element doesn't need any elements manifest; it's just there so that the .browser file will be copied to the feature folder in the SharePoint root. Edit the file so that it looks like this:

```
<browsers>
  <browser refID="default">
    <controlAdapters>
      <adapter
        controlType="WebPartsInAction.Ch11.TaskCountWebPart.
➥         ManualTaskCountWebPart.ManualTaskCountWebPart,
➥         WebPartsInAction.Ch11.TaskCountWebPart,
```

```
➡          Version=1.0.0.0, Culture=neutral,
➡          PublicKeyToken=6c2febfebf1839cd"
       adapterType="
➡          $SharePoint.Type.95bd5e48-0771-4f32-9ff8-1877b6deaa6d.FullName$,
➡          $SharePoint.Project.AssemblyFullName$" />
     </controlAdapters>
   </browser>
</browsers>
```

The custom browser definition file defines one adapter for the Silverlight Task Count Web Part, created in the previous chapter. The control to replace is specified in the controlType attribute and the adapter is specified in the adapterType attribute. Both the control and adapter require that the full name of the class and assembly be specified. But you don't have to enter the full class and assembly name of the adapter; the adapterType attribute uses the Visual Studio 2010 replaceable parameters, which are replaced by Visual Studio during the packaging process with the correct values. By using these replaceable tokens, you'll save a lot of typing.

The replaceable token for the full class name has the format of $SharePoint. Type.<Guid>.FullName$ token, where <Guid> is the lowercase representation of the Guid attribute on the adapter that you previously added. By default, Visual Studio doesn't parse .browser files for these tokens, so you need to make a small change to the project file (.csproj) in Visual Studio. Right-click on the project in the Solution Explorer and select Unload Project. Visual Studio will unload the project and you'll see a gray icon next to your project name. Right-click the project node once again and select Edit WebPartsInAction.Ch12.Mobility.csproj (or whichever name you gave your project). Visual Studio will now display the XML for your project file. Before the Import element that contains the SharePoint targets file, create a new PropertyGroup element or add the following to any existing PropertyGroup element:

```
<TokenReplacementFileExtensions>browser</TokenReplacementFileExtensions>
```

This code will make Visual Studio replace all tokens in all files ending with .browser. You can add any file extension you like here; just be sure to separate them with semicolons. By default, Visual Studio parses files with the extensions .ascx, .aspx, .dwp, .webpart, and .xml. Right-click the project node in Visual Studio once again and select Reload Project to go back to editing your project.

> **TIP**   For full reference of all available replaceable parameters in Visual Studio, refer to http://msdn.microsoft.com/library/ee231545.aspx.

The Solution file will not add the file to the App_Browser folder of the web applications when deployed; it will only be added to the SharePoint Root. You could manually copy or edit the customAdapters.browser file in the App_Browsers folder for each web application on each server to add the control adapter. But I don't recommend that you manually copy or edit the .browser file because it's hard to maintain consistency over all web applications in the farm. A better approach is to create a timer job in SharePoint that creates the file or makes the change in the existing file for you on all the web applications. You can use a similar timer job to remove the control adapter from the .browser file.

To make the registration process more seamless (and to make it a reusable solution), I'll show you how to create a timer job that registers the mobile control adapter in your solution. This timer job will be invoked when a feature is activated or deactivated. Failing to remove the control adapters from the .browser file when removing the control adapter assembly will cause the entire SharePoint application to break and throw exceptions.

When you add a custom browser definition file, SharePoint, or rather ASP.NET, won't automatically pick that up. ASP.NET caches a compiled version of the browser definition files and only empties that cache when already compiled and existing .browser files are changed. This means that if you update the compat.browser or compat.moss.browser file, ASP.NET will recompile the browser definitions. To force ASP.NET to recompile custom browser definition files, you have two options. The first is to empty the cache by deleting all files from the Temporary ASP.NET Files directory located under c:\Windows\Microsoft.NET\Framework64\v2.0.50727\. The second alternative, which I'll show you in this example, is to change the last edited time on the default compat.browser so that ASP.NET thinks that the file has been updated and thus recompiles all browser definition files.

CREATE THE TIMER JOB

A timer job is a task that is asynchronously executed by the SharePoint Timer Service. Creating timer jobs is a great way to schedule repetitive jobs or long-running operations. The timer job can be set to run on all servers or only on specific servers.

TIP For more information about timer jobs, read the following article on MSDN: http://msdn.microsoft.com/library/ms468237.aspx.

To create the timer job that you'll use to add the custom browser definition file, first add a new class to the project; assign the class the name `BrowserDefinitionTimerJob`. This class should inherit from the `SPJobDefinition` class. The timer job will copy a custom browser definition file from the feature folder in the SharePoint root to the App_Browsers directory of the web application. To create the timer job, you must define the constructors and timer job information, such as the name and description, as shown in listing 12.2.

> **Listing 12.2 Timer job definition that installs the control adapter**

```
[Guid("C721BF4D-F892-45B2-A098-B9610F85A2FD")]
public class BrowserDefinitionTimerJob: SPJobDefinition {
    public BrowserDefinitionTimerJob()
        : base() {
    }

    public BrowserDefinitionTimerJob(string name,
        SPWebApplication webApplication) :
        base(name, webApplication, null, SPJobLockType.None) {
```

```
    }

    public override string DisplayName {
        get {
            return "Add custom browser definition file";
        }
    }

    public override string Description {
        get {
            return "Copies a custom browser definition file
to the App_Browsers directory";
        }
    }
}
```

The timer job has two constructors: the default without parameters and a second one that accepts a name and an SPWebApplication object. Because the browser definition file is a web application–level file, this timer job has to be run on each web application. The constructor calls the base implementation constructor with SPJobLockType set to None, which ensures that this job is run on all front-end servers for the specified web application. DisplayName and Description are used to provide information to the administration interface in the Central Administration website.

To complete the timer job, you have to implement the Execute method, which does the work when the timer job is triggered. Listing 12.3 shows the code that copies the browser definition file into the App_Browsers folder of the web application.

Listing 12.3   The Execute method of the timer job

```
public override void Execute(Guid targetInstanceId) {          ❶ Get timer job
    bool add = (bool)this.Properties["add"];                       property

    foreach (SPUrlZone zone in Enum.GetValues(typeof(SPUrlZone))) {
        if (this.WebApplication.IisSettings.Keys.Contains(zone)) {

            string path = this.WebApplication.IisSettings[zone].Path +
                @"\App_Browsers\customAdapters.browser";
                                                               Build custom  ❷
                                                               .browser path
            if (add) {
                if (!File.Exists(path)) {
                    string sourcePath = SPUtility.GetGenericSetupPath(
                        @"TEMPLATE\FEATURES\WebPartsInAction.Ch12.
                        Mobility_MobileAdapter\Browser\
                        customAdapters.browser");              ❸ Copy
                    File.Copy(sourcePath, path);                 .browser file

                    string compatPath =
                        this.WebApplication.IisSettings[zone].Path +
                        @"\App_Browsers\compat.browser";

                    File.SetLastWriteTime(compatPath, DateTime.Now);
                }                                              Update
            }                                                  compat.browser ❹
            else {
                if (File.Exists(path)) {
```

```
                              File.Delete(path);
                }
            }
        }
    }
```

The Execute method is executed for each web application for which this timer job is created. The same timer job will be used both for addition and removal of the browser definition file, and that's configured using timer job properties ❶. Because a web application can be extended to different zones, you need to iterate over all the available zones that are used by the SharePoint web application and for each create the path for the new .browser file ❷. Using the GetGenericSetupPath method of the SPUtility class, the path to the feature and the source .browser file is created, and then the file is copied to the destination folder (App_Browsers) ❸. Finally, the last write time is changed on the compat.browser file so that ASP.NET is forced to recompile all browser definition files. ❹ Because the same timer job is used for deleting the custom browser definition file, the last branch just deletes the file from the App_Browsers directory.

Now that the timer job is defined, you need to create an instance of it. Do so by adding a new Feature to the project and creating a Feature receiver class that will configure the timer job for addition during activation and removal when deactivated.

Add a new Feature to the project and set its scope to WebApplication. Remember that you register the adapters on a web application basis. To add the Feature receiver, right-click the Feature and select Add Event Receiver. Add a constant to the Feature receiver class that contains the name of the timer job, like this:

```
public const string jobName = "browser-definition-timer-job";
```

To instantiate the timer job in the activation method, uncomment the FeatureActivated method. Enter the following code to create and schedule the timer job instance in the FeatureActivated method:

```
SPWebApplication webApplication = properties.Feature.Parent
    as SPWebApplication;

BrowserDefinitionTimerJob newJob = new BrowserDefinitionTimerJob(
    jobName, webApplication) {
        Schedule = new SPOneTimeSchedule(DateTime.Now)
};
newJob.Properties.Add("add", true);
newJob.Update();
```

The timer job instance is created using the constant name and the web application that the feature is activated on. A one-time schedule is used to schedule the job for running immediately. Because it's a one-time scheduled job, you don't have to take care of removing the job—that's done automatically after the job has executed successfully. Before the timer job is saved, add a parameter called add with the value true, which tells the timer job that it should add the new browser definition file, as shown in listing 12.3.

> **TIP** Timer jobs are executed by the SharePoint Timer Service. If you're making changes to the timer job in your solution, you need to restart that service, because it caches your assembly. Do so by executing the following PowerShell command: `restart-service sptimerv4`. To debug timer jobs you need to attach the Visual Studio debugger to the owstimer.exe process.

For the removal of the adapters, follow the same procedure: uncomment the `Fea-tureDeactivating` method. And instead of configuring the timer job for addition, specify that it should remove the browser definition file:

```
newJob.Properties.Add("add", false);
```

CREATE THE SAFECONTROL ENTRY FOR THE ADAPTER

There's one thing more you should do to before deploying the solution: add safe control entries for the adapters. You can do this by using the SharePoint Developer Tools in Visual Studio. Select the SPI node containing the customAdapters.browser file, which you created earlier, in the Solution Explorer. Right-click the SPI node and select Properties. In the Properties window click the ellipsis button next to the Safe Control Entries property to open the Safe Control Entries dialog box. Click the Add button and modify the Namespace property so that it has the namespace of the mobile adapter, as shown in figure 12.7.

All that's left is the testing. Build and deploy your solution and you should be able to browse the Web Part pages where you added the Silverlight-based Task Count Web Part using a mobile browser. Or you can append `mobile=1` to the query string in your browser and see that there's a mobile version of the Web Part, as shown in figure 12.6.

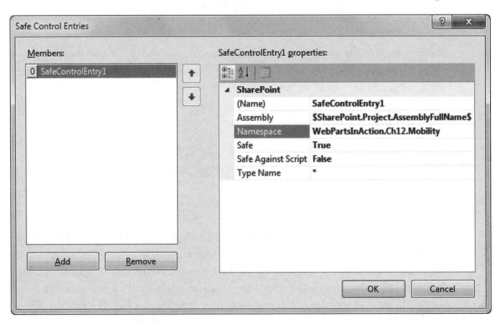

Figure 12.7   The Safe Control Entries property of SharePoint Project Items in Visual Studio 2010 allows you to easily add new safe Control entries.

History

Job Title	Server	Web Application	Duration (hh:mm:ss)	Status	Completed
Scheduled Approval	SP2010	SharePoint - 80	0:00:00	Succeeded	8/16/2010 2:12 PM
Scheduled Approval	SP2010	SharePoint - 80	0:00:00	Succeeded	8/16/2010 2:12 PM
Add custom browser definition file	SP2010	SharePoint - 80	0:00:00	Succeeded	8/16/2010 2:12 PM
Content Type Subscriber	SP2010	SharePoint - 80	0:00:01	Succeeded	8/16/2010 2:12 PM
Scheduled Unpublish	SP2010	SharePoint - 80	0:00:00	Succeeded	8/16/2010 2:11 PM
Scheduled Approval	SP2010	SharePoint - 80	0:00:00	Succeeded	8/16/2010 2:11 PM

Figure 12.8   Check the Monitoring section in the Central Administration for the status of the timer jobs.

You can also go to Central Administration and select m > Review Job Definitions > Job History. There you'll see (after a few seconds) that the timer job has successfully been executed, as shown in figure 12.8.

To test the activation and deactivation, in Central Administration choose Application Management > Manage Web Applications and select the web application that you're going to test the Feature receiver on. Then choose Manage Features to activate and deactivate the web application–scoped feature, as shown in figure 12.9.

Figure 12.9   The control adapters are deployed as web application–scoped Features and are activated and deactivated from Central Administration.

If you make updates to the project, and specifically the timer job, you have to manually restart the timer service, because it keeps a reference to the assembly. To restart the SharePoint timer service, use the following PowerShell command:

```
Restart-Service sptimerv4
```

12.3   Mobile controls

Rather than adapting all your controls to the Web Part interface, you can take advantage of the set of mobile controls that comes out of the box with SharePoint and ASP.NET. The ASP.NET assembly `System.Web.Mobile.dll` contains several useful mobile controls representing most of the default ASP.NET web controls in the `System.Web.UI.MobileControls` namespace. These controls take advantage of the various browser capabilities such as JavaScript, touch, and phone support. Table 12.3 describes some of the available mobile controls.

Table 12.3   Sample ASP.NET mobile controls

Control	Description
Calendar	A calendar control optimized for mobile view.
Image	Displays an image based on the characteristics of the device.
List	Renders a list that can use pagination.
PhoneCall	For devices with phone capabilities, this control renders a link that invokes a phone call. For other devices, the phone number is displayed.

SharePoint also has its own mobile controls specifically designed for SharePoint. These controls are defined in `Microsoft.SharePoint.dll` in the namespace `Microsoft.SharePoint.MobileControls`. Most SharePoint controls and fields have a corresponding mobile control. Table 12.4 explains some of the mobile controls available in SharePoint.

Table 12.4   Sample ASP.NET mobile controls

Control	Description
SPMobileDispFormNavigation	Renders a link to the display form for a list item
SPMobileHomePageNavigation	Renders a link to the home page of the site
SPMobilePeoplePickerForm	Renders a people picker control
SPMobileThumbnail	Renders a thumbnail for an image list item

For a Web Part that shows the name of the page editor with an option to contact the editor, the contact option would normally consist of an email link for use with standard browsers. With a mobile adapter, you can add the phone number, which the user can click to invoke the phone function of the mobile phone. The default Web Part would show an email link, as you can see in figure 12.10.

This Web Part overrides the `Create-ChildControls` method like this:

Figure 12.10   The Page Author Web Part in the standard web interface shows a link that you can click to contact the author via email.

```
protected override void CreateChildControls() {
    SPFile file = SPContext.Current.File;
    SPUser author = file.Author;
    this.ChromeType = PartChromeType.None;
    this.Controls.Add(new HyperLink() {
```

```
        Text = "Page author: " + author.Name,
        NavigateUrl = "mailto:" + author.Email
    });
}
```

For this Web Part, you can create a control adapter that uses the mobile controls to render a phone call–enabled link using the `PhoneCall` mobile control. For browsers with phone support, it will render as shown in figure 12.11. If users click the link, they'll be taken to the phone interface of the device with the phone number automatically entered. If phone support isn't enabled for the device, the phone number will be printed on the screen instead.

The mobile adapter for this Web Part is implemented as follows. Only the `Create-ControlsForSummaryView` method is overridden:

```
protected override void CreateControlsForSummaryView() {
    SPFile file = SPContext.Current.Web.GetFile(
        this.Page.Request.QueryString["Url"]);
    SPUser author = file.Author;

    this.Controls.Add(new SPMobileLabel() {
        Text = "Page author: " + author.Name
    });

    this.Controls.Add(new PhoneCall() {
        Text = "Call author",
        PhoneNumber = "555-123456"          ◁————
    });
}
```

Replace with appropriate User Profile property ❶

Because this is a mobile page representation of the original Web Part page, the `SPFile` object must be retrieved using the `Url QueryString` parameter. Two controls are added: the an `SPMobileLabel` control and a `PhoneCall` control. ❶ The `SPMobileLabel` control and other mobile controls have a *weight*. The weight of the controls is used to determine pagination of mobile web part pages. You can set the `Weight-less` property of the `SPMobileLabel` control to `true` to exclude the control from the pagination calculation. The `PhoneCall` control is a standard ASP.NET control that renders the phone number on the device differently, as explained earlier, depending on the device's capabilities.

Figure 12.11   The control adapter for the Page Editor Web Part renders a phone call supported link for devices with phone support instead of a link that sends an email.

12.4   Summary

Building mobile support for your Web Parts can significantly affect the availability of your SharePoint solutions. Even though many devices support the full SharePoint interface, the mobile network bandwidth is limited in some places and the roaming costs for mobile devices are quite high. The mobile SharePoint interface can reduce costs by generating content and Web Parts that require less bandwidth.

The control adapters you built in this chapter use a timer job and a Feature receiver to deploy the control adapters and the browser definition files to the web applications. Although it might seem like a lot of steps, once you have done this you can reuse the solution for all your mobile adapters.

In the next chapter we'll take a look at Web Part development from a design principles perspective and you'll learn how to make testable and configurable solutions.

13
Design patterns and testability

This chapter covers

- Design patterns
- Dependency injection
- Model-View-Presenter pattern
- Unit-testing

Design patterns and testability have unfortunately been a low priority for many SharePoint developers. Their focus, instead, has been on understanding the platform and the tools, which until now has been quite a challenge. It's not that SharePoint developers aren't interested in building nicely designed and well-tested solutions; it's that they lack knowledge of design patterns or are too cautious to get involved with using a pattern.

This chapter introduces design patterns in general and shows you how to design your Web Parts to improve

- Testability
- Separation of concerns
- Reusability

There's one pattern that fits perfectly into the way Web Parts work and interact with the surrounding environment; it's called the Model-View-Presenter (MVP) design pattern. This pattern allows developers and architects to separate the data model and domain from the business logic and presentation layers and provides a better way to reuse the application logic. You can also apply other design patterns to SharePoint projects. For instance, the Model-View-ViewModel (MVVM) pattern is often used when building rich Silverlight applications.

By using a service provider and service repository called the service locator, you can enhance the flexibility of your applications by providing multiple implementations of the different layers in the application. Using registered services in the application also facilitates the reuse of code and components, and the amount of code you have to maintain decreases.

If you build your Web Parts using a pattern such as MVP, you can take advantage of unit-testing to test the code. Visual Studio 2010 contains efficient tools for testing code using unit-tests; you'll learn more about that in section 13.4.1.

Much of what I discuss in this chapter, such as the MVP pattern and the service locator, is also recommended by the Microsoft Patterns & Practices group. You'll also use some of the tools and services that the Microsoft Patterns & Practices group has built to allow for more maintainable and testable code.

13.1 Design patterns

Design patterns are an abstract term, and some developers love using them—and some don't. Design patterns have evolved over time, and some are tied to specific technologies whereas others are generic. Because this chapter is about design patterns and specifically the MVP pattern (which I discuss in the next section), this section covers the key features required to successfully implement the MVP pattern. One feature, loose coupling, makes application component implementations less dependent on one another. Loose coupling is important for dependency injection, a method used to insert dependency objects during runtime.

13.1.1 What are design patterns?

Software design patterns are guidelines and templates that describe how to solve a problem. Design patterns aren't a new thing; they've been around since the early ages of software engineering. A design pattern provides a proven and tested pattern for use when architecting and developing applications. Each design pattern tries to solve one or more problems and can be technology specific. It's important to understand that a design pattern isn't a component that you use or include in your application. A design pattern is more of a guideline on how to write the code. Design patterns start from different approaches. Some focus on the code's structure whereas others focus on the application's behavior. The naming conventions and terms used in design patterns are also a common language among developers, which makes it easy to discuss and document systems without going into details.

Design patterns offer several benefits when you're building and designing software. The reuse of the same pattern within a solution helps you understand the solution design, and it allows for better collaboration because everyone on the team is aware of the methodology.

As I mentioned earlier, many SharePoint developers generally haven't used software design patterns when building SharePoint applications. The lack of tools supporting a good development environment has put the focus on other things instead. Until recently, there has been no guide or official best practices documentation in this area for SharePoint development. The Microsoft Patterns & Practices group only mentioned SharePoint in a few pages in the *Microsoft Application Architecture Guide, 2nd Edition* (Microsoft Press, 2009). Since then, they've expanded their guidance for SharePoint and now have documentation, sample applications, and libraries.

Microsoft Patterns & Practices group

The Microsoft Patterns & Practices group is a team of experts and architects from Microsoft and other external organizations who focus on guidance and practices for developers. They continuously build and improve guidance, documentation, and sample implementations for Microsoft technologies.

The Patterns & Practices group is currently on their second SharePoint guide. You can find more information about this group at http://msdn.microsoft.com/practices/ and http://spg.codeplex.com.

13.1.2 *Loose coupling*

Several design patterns are based on loosely coupled objects. A *loosely coupled system* refers to a system where the objects and components aren't directly dependent on one another. Loosely coupled objects are connected through an interface; the dependent class uses the interface to communicate to the concrete services. The opposite of a loosely coupled system is a *tightly coupled system.*

Figure 13.1 shows a tightly coupled application where ClassA directly calls ClassB. There's no way to replace or edit ClassB without recompiling and changing the system.

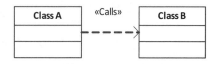

Tightly coupled systems are hard to test, change, and maintain because of the dependencies between the components. It's also harder to build tightly coupled systems in teams and to split the systems into separate parts or domains.

Figure 13.1 In a tightly coupled application, the classes are directly referencing each other. This makes the classes dependent on each other and makes it harder to replace classes and layers.

In a loosely coupled system, ClassA doesn't directly depend on ClassB. Instead, it uses a contract or an interface that defines the coupling. Figure 13.2 shows how ClassA depends on an interface, in this example, IService. This interface is used by both ClassB1 and ClassB2, which can be hosted in the same solution or in another

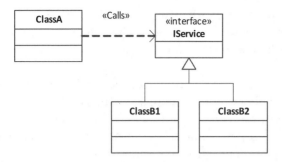

Figure 13.2 **In loosely coupled systems, the dependent class uses an interface to communicate with its services. This arrangement allows for easier updates of the services, even during runtime, and a clear separation of layers in the application.**

one. ClassA doesn't know anything about the implementation of ClassB1 or ClassB2. You can edit or replace ClassB1 or ClassB2 and even add new objects that implement the IService interface without recompiling ClassA.

Changes to the IService interface would require that you modify all classes. This is where planning and specification become important. Building loosely coupled systems tends to involve more planning but it does allow for easier management.

Loosely coupled systems are modular and simple to test. Because the objects don't directly reference one another, you can isolate them for unit-testing. This testing method is also known as *white-box* testing. Unit-testing is focused on testing the object itself and not how it interacts with other objects. This approach allows for a more agile development process, and you can apply practices such as *test-driven development (TDD)*, where you start writing the unit-tests before you implement the object itself. The opposite of white-box testing is black-box testing, where you test the whole system without any knowledge of the internals of the system.

13.1.3 *Dependency injection*

Dependency injection has become one of the most popular patterns when building loosely coupled systems. Because the loosely coupled system uses an interface as the contract for its services and modules, you can inject the implementation you want to use at runtime. The best way to describe dependency injection is by an example. Assume you have an interface that describes a car engine:

```
public interface IEngine {
    int GetSpeed();
    void IncreaseSpeed();
    void DecreaseSpeed();
}
```

This IEngine interface describes the functionality of the car engine but not how it works, how fast it accelerates, and so forth. An implementation of an engine would derive from the IEngine interface like this:

```
public class FastEngine: IEngine {
    int _speed = 0;
    public int GetSpeed(){
        return _speed;
```

Inherit from
❶ IEngine interface

```
    }
    public void IncreaseSpeed () {
        _speed += 2;
    }
    public void DecreaseSpeed () {
        _speed = _speed > 1 ? _speed-2 : 0;
    }
}
```

Different cars have different engines, which means that you can have several implementations of the IEngine interface ❶. A fast car could be implemented as follows:

```
public class FastCar {
    readonly IEngine _engine;
    public FastCar() {
        _engine = new FastEngine();
    }
    public void Start() {
        while(_engine.GetSpeed() < 100) {
            _engine.IncreaseSpeed();
        }
    }
}
```

In the constructor of the FastCar class, the FastEngine implementation of the IEngine
interface is injected. That way, you provide a great deal of flexibility to use different
engines using the same car implementation by just changing the constructor. It's worth
mentioning here that the private engine declaration is *immutable*. Set the private engine
variable as readonly, which means that it can only be set during the class construction.

> **TIP** If you're interested in reading more about designing large testable and
> modular applications, check out *Dependency Injection, Design Patterns Using
> Spring and Guice*, by Dhanji R. Prasanna (Manning, 2009).

13.2 The Model-View-Presenter pattern

There's one design pattern that fits nicely into Web Part development more than others: the Model-View-Presenter (MVP) pattern. This pattern has been used since the
early 1990s. In 2006, Martin Fowler split MVP into two separate patterns: the *Passive
View* and the *Supervising Controller*. The MVP term is still widely used and implies one of
the two updated patterns.

Building Web Parts using the MVP pattern differs from what you may be used to.
If you've been in the ASP.NET business, you might be familiar with the Model-View-
Controller (MVC) pattern, from which MVP is derived. An MVP-based Web Part
requires additional coding and a separation of the business logic from the WebPart
class implementation. That way, the work can be distributed among team members,
and it allows for better testing of the layers independently.

13.2.1 The Passive View pattern

The MVP pattern is a user interface design pattern that decouples the user interface
(View) from the business logic (Presenter) and from the domain/data layer (Model).

The different pieces can be tested individually with or without one another and optionally using mock (fake) objects.

The MVP pattern not only makes unit-testing easier but also facilitates code reuse. For instance, the same Model and Presenter can be used for different user interfaces, such as a Web Part, a page, or a Silverlight application. In addition, decoupling enables different developers to build different pieces, independently. That way, you can use the appropriate type of developer for the right task; user interface developers can build the views, and so on.

The basics of the MVP pattern is that the View is responsible for the user interface and is defined using an interface that acts as a contract for the Presenter. All actions in the user interface are forwarded to the Presenter, which is responsible for updating the View through the interface. The presenter uses the Model to access the domain, data, or underlying systems.

The Passive View variation of the MVP pattern is the cleanest version of the two. As you can see in figure 13.3, the View forwards user actions to the Presenter, which updates the View through the interface. The Presenter uses information from the Model to update the View. The Presenter optionally responds to events fired in the Model if the Model is updated by someone other than the Presenter. The View is totally unaware of the Model.

This decoupled pattern allows you to test the Presenter and Model independently. As always, the user interface is difficult to unit-test, but the Presenter can be replaced with a mock object that makes it easier to manually test the interface.

TIP   To test the user interface of a SharePoint application you can use the Coded-UI tests available in Visual Studio Premium or Ultimate editions.

Compared to a user interface component built using a single class, this pattern introduces a higher level of complexity, both in number of files and method calls. But at the same time, early testing and a clear separation of layers means that errors are discovered earlier in the process.

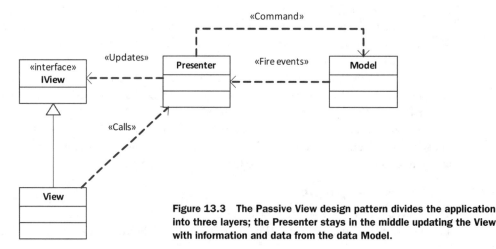

Figure 13.3   **The Passive View design pattern divides the application into three layers; the Presenter stays in the middle updating the View with information and data from the data Model.**

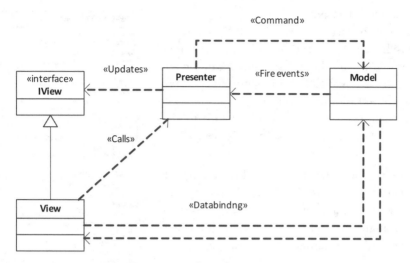

Figure 13.4   The Supervising Controller pattern is similar to the Passive View pattern but allows the View to make simple calls and data binding to the Model.

13.2.2 *The Supervising Controller pattern*

Another variation of the MVP pattern is the *Supervising Controller.* It differs from the Passive View in that the View is allowed to do simple data binding to the Model but isn't allowed to make changes to it (see figure 13.4).

The Supervising Controller makes the Presenter easier to implement because it doesn't need to move all data from the Model to the View. One of the main goals for this variation is to make the coding easier, but it reduces the testability of the solution. It's also sometimes less difficult to maintain solutions built using the Supervising Controller because smaller changes in the user interface don't require that the Presenter be modified.

13.2.3 *MVP and Web Parts*

The MVP design pattern is a perfect match for Web Parts. The way that the Presenter is communicating with the View allows for a clear separation of the business logic and the interface components. Reusing code is also a key factor here. By using the same Model and/or Presenter for several Web Parts, you'll find the development cycle is faster and more failsafe.

I'll show you how to build a Web Part using the Passive View variant of the MVP pattern for a Web Part that lists all the available Lists in the current site. This is a very simple Web Part that uses a single Web Part class and just a few lines of code. To show you the benefits of using the Passive View pattern, I'll explain each part of the code. Finally, I'll take the pattern one step further by decoupling the Model and preparing it for isolated testing and for use with a service locator.

BUILDING AN MVP WEB PART

To build a Web Part, you use the MVP pattern in Visual Studio 2010 and the SharePoint Developer Extensions. You can choose to build a sandboxed Web Part or deploy it as a farm solution. The Web Part that you'll build next will display all the available lists within a site and provide a link to the default view of each one, as shown in figure 13.5.

THE VIEW

The first thing you'll define after adding a new Web Part to your solution is the View interface. This interface will be the contract that the Presenter uses to update the View. The View interface, IListsView, is implemented as follows:

```
public interface IListsView {
    IEnumerable<ListInfo> Lists {
        get;
        set;
    }
}
```

The Lists property defined in the interface returns an enumerator with ListInfo objects. The ListInfo object is a class that contains the name (Title) of a list and its default view URL (Url). The reason that a custom class is used instead of the

SiteListsWebPart
Announcements
Cache Profiles
Calendar
Content and Structure Reports
Customized Reports
Data
Documents
Form Templates
Images
Links
List Template Gallery
Long Running Operation Status
Master Page Gallery
Notification List
Pages
Quick Deploy Items
Relationships List
Reporting Metadata
Reporting Templates
Reusable Content
Shared Documents
Site Assets
Site Collection Documents
Site Collection Images
Site Pages
Solution Gallery
Style Library
Suggested Content Browser Locations
Tasks
TaxonomyHiddenList
Team Discussion
Theme Gallery
Variation Labels
Web Part Gallery
wfpub
Workflow Tasks

Figure 13.5   A Web Part based on the Passive View pattern displaying links to all lists within a SharePoint site

SharePoint SPList object is that this approach decouples the View and the Presenter from SharePoint and allows for easier testing. The ListInfo class is defined like this:

```
public class ListInfo {
    public string Title {
        get;
        set;
    }
    public string Url {
        get;
        set;
    }
}
```

THE MODEL

The Model can be implemented in several ways; it can be a SharePoint object, a data context, or something else. For instance, the Model could be the SPListCollection object in this example. But the best solution is to create a service model that encapsulates the data layer. In your Lists Web Part, a service class called ListsService is created that provides the operations needed to the Presenter:

```
class ListsService {
    public IEnumerable<ListInfo> GetLists() {
        SPWeb web = SPContext.Current.Web;
        List<ListInfo> listInfo = new List<ListInfo>();
        foreach (SPList list in web.Lists) {
            listInfo.Add(new ListInfo() {
                Title = list.Title,
                Url = list.DefaultViewUrl
            });
        }
        return listInfo;
    }
}
```

This Model implementation provides a method called `GetLists`, which returns a collection of `ListInfo` objects. The Presenter uses this method to set the state of the View.

THE PRESENTER

The Presenter is the glue that connects the data provided by the Model to the View. In the MVP pattern, the Presenter interacts with the View implementation through the interface. You create the Presenter like this:

```
public class ListsPresenter {
    protected readonly IListsView _view;

    public ListsPresenter(IListsView view) {
        _view = view;
    }
    public void LoadLists() {
        ListsService service = new ListsService();
        _view.Lists = service.GetLists();
    }
}
```

The Presenter contains a reference to the `IListsView` interface through a protected variable. The variable is set as `readonly`, which means that it's immutable and can only be set in the constructor of the class. The constructor of the Presenter accepts the View interface to keep the reference. This method of injecting a dependency is called *dependency injection;* specifically this is *constructor injection* because you insert the dependencies in the constructor. The `LoadLists` method, which is the business logic, uses the service class (Model) to retrieve the lists and finally updates the View through the internal property.

You can define all the code classes and interfaces in the same or a separate assembly. It all depends on how you'll reuse the code in your solution.

THE WEB PART

In this MVP implementation, the Web Part is the implementation of the View. That is, the Web Part class will inherit from the `IListsView` interface like this:

```
public class SiteListsWebPart : WebPart, IListsView
```

The `IListsView` interface contains a single property, `Lists`. This property needs to be implemented in the Web Part:

```
public IEnumerable<ListInfo> Lists {
    get;
    set;
}
```

Then all that's left is to build the user interface. Do so using the `CreateChildControls` method of the Web Part:

```
protected override void CreateChildControls() {
    ListsPresenter presenter = new ListsPresenter(this);
    presenter.LoadLists();

    foreach (ListInfo listInfo in this.Lists) {
        this.Controls.Add(new HyperLink() {
            Text = listInfo.Title,
            NavigateUrl = listInfo.Url
        });
        this.Controls.Add(new LiteralControl("<br/>"));
    }
}
```

First, this code creates an instance of the `ListsPresenter` and passes the Web Part (the View) as an argument to the constructor. Then the `LoadLists` method of the Presenter is called. Because the Presenter is responsible for updating the View, it will populate the `Lists` property of the Web Part. Finally, the interface is built by iterating over the `Lists` collection objects, which creates the list of links to the lists.

From a practical perspective, you can now see how you can benefit from using this pattern. For instance, you can have several developers building the various parts. The person building the View can use a fake Presenter to avoid waiting for completion of the real Presenter. The developer building the Presenter can use the same approach with the Model. The different parts also are decoupled, so you can unit-test most of the code.

DECOUPLING THE MODEL FROM THE PRESENTER

The current design ties the Model to the Presenter because the `LoadLists` method instantiates the Model and uses the methods directly. By changing the Model class to inherit from an interface that expresses the Model's functionality, you can decouple the implementation of the Model from the Presenter:

```
public interface IListsService {
    IEnumerable<ListInfo> GetLists();
}
```

Once that's done, you edit the `ListsService` class definition so that it inherits from the new Model interface as follows:

```
class ListsService : IListsService
```

Now there's a contract for how the Model is implemented, through the interface, and you can use dependency injection to provide multiple Models to the same Presenter and View. For instance, the current `ListsService` Model returns all lists within a site. If you need another Model, called `LibraryService`, that returns all document libraries, you can create a new Model implementation that has a `GetLists` method like this:

```
public IEnumerable<ListInfo> GetLists() {
    SPWeb web = SPContext.Current.Web;
    List<ListInfo> listInfo = new List<ListInfo>();
    foreach (SPList list in web.GetListsOfType(SPBaseType.DocumentLibrary))
    {
        listInfo.Add(new ListInfo() {
            Title = list.Title,
            Url = list.DefaultViewUrl
        });

    }
    return listInfo;
}
```

You must modify the Presenter implementation to support the dependency injection. Simply add a new local variable to the Presenter class and modify the constructor to support injection of the Model:

```
class ListsPresenter {
    protected readonly IListsView _view;
    protected readonly IListsService _model;

    public ListsPresenter(IListsView view) {
        _view = view;
        _model = new ListsService();
    }

    public void LoadLists() {
        _view.Lists = _model.GetLists();
    }
}
```

The `IListsService` is stored as an immutable variable in the Presenter class. The constructor is modified so that it sets the injected View and then creates one of the Model implementations. Finally, the `LoadLists` method is modified to use the Model interface instead of creating a Model class, as the previous implementation did. By using this pattern with decoupled objects, you can easily replace, change, or duplicate almost any part of the Web Part without affecting the other parts. Using the Visual Studio 2010 class diagram designer, the solution looks like figure 13.6.

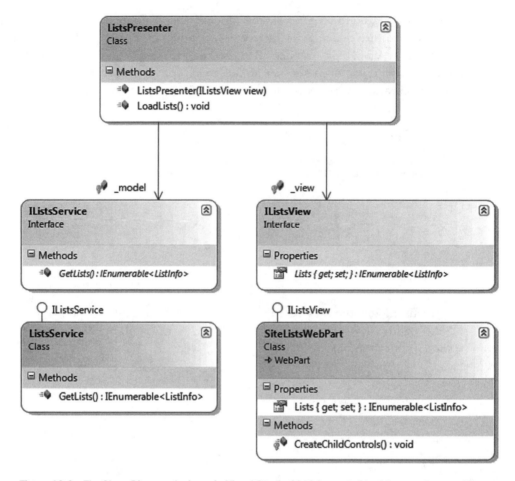

Figure 13.6   The Class Diagram designer in Visual Studio 2010 is a great tool to use when working with decoupled objects to visualize the system design.

13.3   *SharePoint Service Locator*

In a fully decoupled system, you want to write code that isn't dependent on the concrete implementation of the classes. To accomplish this goal, you can use a repository that stores mappings between the service interfaces and the service implementations. A service locator is such a repository; it handles registrations of types and maps them to one or more implementations.

The Microsoft Patterns & Practices group has created a base *service locator* implementation and a specific service locator for SharePoint. The *SharePoint Service Locator* allows developers to store different type-mappings at different levels in SharePoint, such as farms or site collections. That way, your service can use different Models or Views depending on where it's located or depending on what features have been enabled at the current level.

13.3.1 Service locators

The problem with this implementation of the Web Part is that you're referencing a Model implementation in the code of the Presenter. To switch to another Model, the Web Part must be compiled and redeployed to SharePoint—not a very flexible solution. It's also hard to test the Presenter in isolation using unit-tests because it depends on the Model, as you can see in figure 13.7. If you'd like to dynamically switch between different Model implementations, you need to provide logic for that.

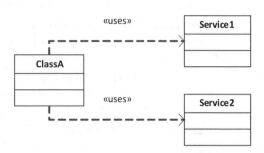

Figure 13.7   Using multiple services for a class requires custom code that handles the request for the correct service during runtime.

A service locator is a central repository that contains references to services and the different implementations of the services. Services are registered in the service locator, and classes can query the service locator for a specific service to get an instance of it, as you can see in figure 13.8.

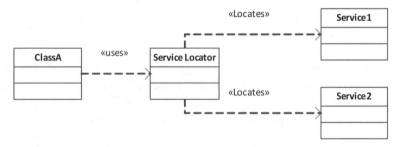

Figure 13.8   Using a service locator allows for dynamic changes during runtime of services. The service locator is a shared service within the application that handles registration and location of services.

Services are registered in the service locator using an interface or a key-value and a reference to its implementation. The classes using the service locators use the interface or key to query for the implementation of the service and the service locator decides which implementation to use at runtime.

The service locator preferably has a persistent storage but can also be populated during application initialization. The locator allows the application to locate a service during runtime and use it. Adding new services might not always require that the code be recompiled because the classes only depend on an interface or a key.

13.3.2 Use the SharePoint Service Locator

The SharePoint Service Locator provides functionality to register a service using an interface and an optional key value and functionality to locate an implementation of a registered interface. In this section, you'll learn how to modify the Web Part you built using the MVP pattern to use the locator to find the implementation of the Model.

ADDING SHAREPOINT SERVICE LOCATOR REFERENCES

To use the SharePoint Service Locator, you need to download its implementation from the Patterns & Practices group SharePoint Codeplex site at http://spg.codeplex.com/. The implementation contains the source code required to build the assembly for the locator. Once you've built the SharePoint Service Locator, you'll need to add references to the assemblies in your SharePoint project. Right-click References in the Solution Explorer in Visual Studio and select Add Reference. Browse to location where the Share-Point Service Locator assemblies are located and choose to add them. The files are called Microsoft.Practices.ServiceLocation.dll and Microsoft.Practices.SharePoint.Common.dll. The first of the assemblies is a general service locator implementation. The second contains the SharePoint-specific implementation as well as other useful components for SharePoint development, such as logging and configuration.

> **NOTE** The SharePoint Service Locator can be used in the sandbox, but then services can only be located from the site collection level. To provide access to farm-level registered services, a proxy solution is provided as an alternative.

To include the referenced assemblies in the SharePoint Solution package, you must add them to the package manifest. Do so by editing the package in Visual Studio and selecting the Advanced tab. Click Add > Add Existing Assembly in the designer to open a dialog box. Here you can select an assembly and click OK to add the assembly to the package. Add both of the referenced assemblies. Make sure that the Deployment Target is set to *GlobalAssemblyCache*. These assemblies will now be registered in the Global Assembly Cache when the solution is deployed in the farm.

> **TIP** If you're going to use the SharePoint Service Locator in many solutions, create a separate farm solution that registers the locator in the Global Assembly Cache.

REGISTERING THE MODEL WITH THE SERVICE LOCATOR

The services in the SharePoint Service Locator are typically registered when a feature is installed or activated. The SharePoint Service Locator supports registration of services at both the site collection level and the farm level. A site collection–registered service has precedence over a farm-registered service.

UPDATING THE PRESENTER

To decouple the Presenter from the Model, you have to modify the constructor of the Presenter. You do this by modifying the constructor and adding a second constructor to the `ListsPresenter` class:

```
public ListsPresenter(IListsView view): this (view, new ListsService()) {
}

public ListsPresenter(IListsView view, IListsService model) {
```

```
    _view = view;
    _model = model;
}
```

The first constructor calls the second constructor but still creates an instance of the `ListsService` object. This constructor is kept so that the View implementation doesn't break. The second constructor takes both the View and the Model as parameters.

REGISTERING THE MODEL

You must register the Model in the SharePoint Service Locator before using it. I recommend that you use a Feature receiver to do this. Registering farm-scoped features requires that they be registered using a Farm Administrators account. This means that you can't enable and disable the features using the web user interface in a site collection. You can perform farm-scoped registrations in one of three ways:

- Using hidden features enabled by PowerShell
- Using the `FeatureInstalled/FeatureUninstalling` events of the Feature event receiver
- Using a farm-scoped feature

To register the `ListsService` Model for the Web Part, add a new event receiver to the Web Part feature. Then implement the `FeatureInstalled` and `FeatureUninstalling` like this:

```
public override void FeatureInstalled(
    SPFeatureReceiverProperties properties) {

    IServiceLocator serviceLocator =
            SharePointServiceLocator.GetCurrent();
    IServiceLocatorConfig serviceLocatorConfig =
        serviceLocator.GetInstance<IServiceLocatorConfig>();

    serviceLocatorConfig.
        RegisterTypeMapping<IListsService, ListsService>();
}
public override void FeatureUninstalling(
    SPFeatureReceiverProperties properties)

    IServiceLocator serviceLocator =
            SharePointServiceLocator.GetCurrent();
    IServiceLocatorConfig serviceLocatorConfig =
        serviceLocator.GetInstance<IServiceLocatorConfig>();

    serviceLocatorConfig.RemoveTypeMappings<IListsService>();
}
```

To register the service with the locator at the farm level, a user with farm administrator privileges must register the service during the installation of the solution. Both `FeatureInstalled` and `FeatureUninstalling` use the static method `GetCurrent` of the `SharePointServiceLocator` object to retrieve the current service locator. The service locator configuration object is also a service registered with the service locator, and you locate it by using the `GetInstance` method using the `IServiceLocatorConfig` interface. When an instance of the service locator configuration object is retrieved, the

RegisterTypeMapping method is used to register the ListsService. This is done by providing the interface of the service and an implementation of the service. The uninstall method removes all registrations of a specific service using the RemoveTypeMappings method.

USING THE SERVICE LOCATOR IN THE VIEW

The only task remaining is to use the service locator in the implementation of the View and inject the Model into the Presenter. Modify the CreateChildControls method of the Web Part to use the SharePoint Service Locator:

```
protected override void CreateChildControls() {
    IServiceLocator serviceLocator = SharePointServiceLocator.GetCurrent();
    IListsService service = serviceLocator.GetInstance<IListsService>();

    ListsPresenter presenter = new ListsPresenter(this, service);
    presenter.LoadLists();

    foreach (ListInfo listInfo in this.Lists) {
        this.Controls.Add( new HyperLink() {
            Text = listInfo.Title,
            NavigateUrl = listInfo.Url
        });
        this.Controls.Add(new LiteralControl("<br/>"));
    }
}
```

Just as in the Feature receiver, you retrieve the SharePoint Service Locator using the GetCurrent method. Rather than retrieving the configuration service, the configured mapped type for IListsService is retrieved using the GetInstance method. The service instance is injected to the constructor of the ListsPresenter together with the current Web Part. That is, both the Model and the View are injected into the Presenter.

If you deploy the Web Part and add it to a page, you'll see that it looks exactly the same as before. You haven't changed the Web Part's appearance—you've just decoupled the Presenter from both the Model and the View and made it possible to switch to different implementations of the Model.

REPLACING THE MODEL AT RUNTIME

To add a second Model implementation, replacing the previous one, and add that as a service to the service locator, you add a new feature to the project. The feature must be scoped to Farm, if the service is to be registered at farm level, to avoid access denied exceptions. Add a Feature receiver to the new feature and, in the FeatureActivated method, register the LibraryService, which you created earlier. Instead of displaying all lists, the Web Part shows only document libraries. Figure 13.9 shows how the Web Part might look like when the LibraryService is used instead of the ListsService.

SiteListsWebPart

Customized Reports
Documents
Form Templates
Images
List Template Gallery
Master Page Gallery
Pages
Reporting Templates
Shared Documents
Site Assets
Site Collection Documents
Site Collection Images
Site Pages
Solution Gallery
Style Library
Theme Gallery
Web Part Gallery
wfpub

Figure 13.9 By supplying an alternative Model to the Site Lists Web Part, you modify its appearance to show libraries instead of lists without editing the View or Presenter classes.

You use the `RegisterTypeMapping` to register the new service. The registration will replace any previous type mapping:

```
serviceLocatorConfig.RegisterTypeMapping<IListsService, LibraryService>();
```

This code replaces the current type mapping in the service locator with the new `LibraryService`. In the `FeatureDeactivating` method, add the following to restore the original service implementation:

```
serviceLocatorConfig.RegisterTypeMapping<IListsService, ListsService>();
```

When the updated solution is deployed to SharePoint, the farm-scoped feature is automatically activated and the document libraries are shown. To display the lists again, the farm-scoped feature has to be deactivated in Central Administration or via PowerShell. The SharePoint Service Locator caches all type mappings, and the application pools need to be recycled. You can do this by executing the `IISRESET` command.

Figure 13.10 shows how the Visual Studio class designer visualizes the Web Part, interfaces, and services after adding the new Library service. Notice how the Presenter now allows for injection of the Model through its constructor.

If you'd like to specify which model to use during runtime, the SharePoint Service Locator supports naming the registered interfaces. You can then use the `GetInstance`

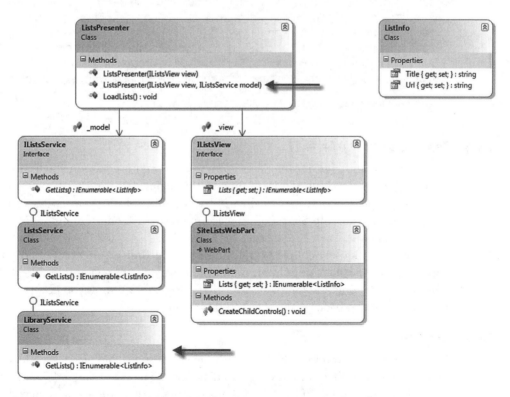

Figure 13.10   Adding the injection of the Model into the Presenter's constructor allows you to implement multiple Models to be used by the same Presenter and View.

method of the service locator to retrieve the instance using the interface and the registered name. The service locator also contains a method for retrieving all registered services for a specific interface called `GetAllInstances`. You could use this method to create a Web Part where the end user chooses, via an Editor Part, which service to use.

> **TIP**   To recycle the application pools from the Visual Studio 2010 interface, install the CKS:DEV extensions using Visual Studio 2010 Extensions Manager. Then choose Tools > CKSDEV > Recycle All SharePoint Application Pools to recycle the application pools. Download it through the Visual Studio Extension Manager.

The farm-scoped feature can now be used to switch between the two Model implementations. While working in teams, this can be useful. For instance, one developer might be working on the Presenter and View and another developer on the Model. The developer working with the Presenter implementation can then use a mock Model service until the final Model service is complete.

Microsoft's Unity Application Block

Microsoft's Unity Application Block is a dependency injection container that has become widely popular. It's powerful but can be quite complex for beginners. Unity is supported on different platforms such as web, desktop, and Silverlight. If you're familiar with the Unity Application Block or if your company uses Unity in other applications, it might be good idea to use Unity in your SharePoint projects as well. The SharePoint Service Locator `GetCurrent` method returns `IServiceLocator`, which can be replaced with any custom service locators, such as a Unity service locator.

You can download Unity at http://unity.codeplex.com/.

13.4   Testing Web Parts

Just as with design patterns, the SharePoint world hasn't used automatic testing to the same degree as developers using other technologies. It's very hard to test components and applications automatically in SharePoint. And it's even harder to test the components outside the SharePoint environment because most components rely on the environment.

By building loosely coupled applications, you'll find it much easier to take the application or specific components out of their original context and test them. Visual Studio contains tools and templates for unit-testing, and I'll show you how to use these tools to test the Web Part you've built in this chapter.

13.4.1   Unit-testing

Unit-testing is a method in which you test the smallest testable piece of code, called a unit. The foundation for unit-testing is that by having small tests that independently test parts of the code you'll find errors and mismatches early in the software development cycle. Not only do unit-tests examine the code, but they can also serve as specifications of the code and are often used as a check for requirements. For instance, *test-driven development* starts with writing the unit-test before writing the code that's going to be tested, which also requires you to have the basic requirements and functional specification agreed upon before starting.

Unit-testing also allows for better refactoring of the code and lets you track any changes that would potentially break your solution when you're modifying the source code. Keeping the unit-test small enables the tests to run quickly so that they can be included in all builds without slowing down the developers.

Unit-testing relies heavily on mock or fake objects during the tests. Mock objects are simulated objects that mimic the behavior of the real objects. For instance think of a data model object that reads from a SharePoint list and returns the title of the list; a mock object for this model object could return a hardcoded string for testing purposes. By using loosely coupled objects and dependency injection, you'll find it easier to create the tests.

13.4.2 Creating a test project

Visual Studio 2010 has built-in support for creating test projects containing automatic and manual test items. The test tools in Visual Studio contain a complete suite for building tests and analyzing those results, including code coverage, profiling, and test impact.

The Web Part that you've been building in this chapter is designed for testability, and to create tests for it you need to add a new test project to the solution. Do so by creating a new project in Visual Studio, selecting the Test Project template, and adding it to the current solution. A default Unit-test project item is added to the project; you can remove this test item.

You can add many types of test project items to a test project, as shown in figure 13.11. Most of the project items are focused on unit-testing, and you can create unit-tests

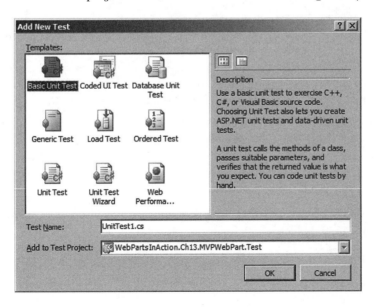

Figure 13.11 Visual Studio 2010 allows developers and testers to select from many different test project items, ranging from custom tests, to unit-tests, to fully automated interface tests.

manually from scratch or use a wizard. You can even combine your unit-tests into a composite test. Not everything can be tested using unit-tests, and there are project items for recording actions to test user interfaces.

> **NOTE** Not all types of tests are available in all editions of Visual Studio 2010. For more information, see http://www.microsoft.com/visualstudio/products.

13.4.3 *Mock objects*

Before creating the tests for the Web Part, you need to create the mock objects. Mock objects serve as fake objects that are injected into the code to be tested. For instance, the `ListsService` class (the Model) used by the `ListsPresenter` class (the Presenter) relies on the code running inside a SharePoint environment. Because the Web Part is designed using dependency injection, this is an easy task to perform. Instead of injecting the `ListsService` class when testing the `ListsPresenter`, you can inject a mock object inheriting the `IListsService` interface. The mock object, called `MockModel`, is added to the test project and implemented like this:

```
class MockModel: IListsService {
    public IEnumerable<ListInfo> GetLists() {
        List<ListInfo> dummy = new List<ListInfo>();
        dummy.Add(new ListInfo(){
            Title = "Title 2",
            Url= "http://test1/"
        });
        dummy.Add(new ListInfo(){
            Title = "Test 2",
            Url= "http://test2/"
        });
        return dummy;
    }
}
```

The `MockModel` implements the `IListsService` interface and provides an implementation of the `GetLists` method. In the `GetLists` method, a fake list of `ListInfo` objects is created.

The same is done for the View of the Web Part. A mock object called `MockView` that inherits from the `IListsView` interface is also added to the test project:

```
class MockView: IListsView {
    public IEnumerable<ListInfo> Lists {
        get;
        set;
    }
}
```

All this mock object requires is that an implementation of the `Lists` property be done. These two mock objects allow for testing the complete implementation of the Presenter.

Unit-testing the Model of the Web Part—that is, the `ListsService` or `Library-Service`—is harder. You can't create fake objects of the `SPWeb` or the `SPList` objects.

Fortunately, certain products on the market allow for mocking SharePoint objects that during runtime of the tests replace the SharePoint objects with fake objects. Microsoft Research has released a power tool for Visual Studio called *Pex and Moles*. This is an isolation and white-box testing framework in which Pex automatically generates unit-tests. Moles is an advanced framework that uses the code profiler API to intercept calls to any dependencies and then replace that dependent object with a fake object. You can download Pex and Moles from the Visual Studio Extension Manager and read more about them at http://research.microsoft.com/pex.

13.4.4 *Test the Web Part*

By now, everything is set up for creating the unit-tests of the Web Part. To add a unit-test using the Create Unit-tests wizard, select Add > Unit-test on the test project. In the dialog window that appears, select the class or classes for which you want to create automatic tests, as shown in figure 13.12, and click OK.

For this example, on the Create Unit-tests screen select the `ListsPresenter` class, which is the class that will be used for this test case. Once you click OK, the wizard will add a new file to the test project called ListsPresenterTest.cs. This new file contains the stub methods for the unit-tests. For the `ListsPresenter`, the test class will contain three tests: two for the two constructors and one for the `LoadLists` method.

Each test method is suffixed with `Test` and has the `TestMethod` attribute. The `TestMethod` attribute allows Visual Studio to pick up all unit-tests within the classes and project and identify them as tests.

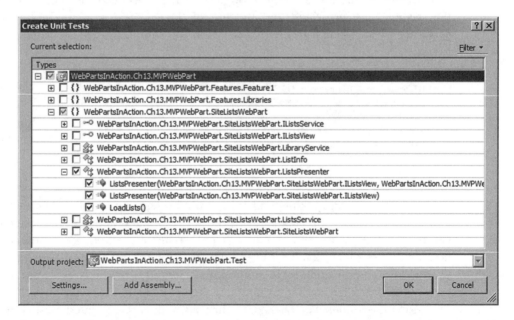

Figure 13.12   The Create Unit-tests wizard generates stubs for the test methods, to which you then add the test logic.

Let's take a look at the first constructor test. When the wizard creates the test, it looks like this:

```
[TestMethod()]
public void ListsPresenterConstructorTest() {
    IListsView view = null; // TODO: Initialize to an appropriate value
    IListsService model = null; // TODO: Initialize to an appropriate value
    ListsPresenter target = new ListsPresenter(view, model);
    Assert.Inconclusive("TODO: Implement code to verify target");
}
```

To complete the test, you have to modify this method so that it tests the constructor of the ListsPresenter. The View and the Model interfaces that are going to be injected into the ListsPresenter constructor are defined as null; these two have to be initialized with the mock objects. Then the ListsPresenter is created with these mock objects, and the result has to be evaluated. You must change the assertion to verify that the returned object from the constructor isn't null. After you make these changes, the test should look like this:

```
[TestMethod()]
public void ListsPresenterConstructorTest() {
    IListsView view = new MockView();
    IListsService model = new MockModel();
    ListsPresenter target = new ListsPresenter(view, model);
    Assert.IsNotNull(target);
}
```

Now, the test method is ready for testing. The same procedure has to be repeated for the second constructor test and the test of the LoadLists method. The second constructor test is similar to the first one, and you should change the LoadLists test to this:

```
[TestMethod()]
public void LoadListsTest() {
    IListsView view = new MockView();
    IListsService model = new MockModel();
    ListsPresenter target = new ListsPresenter(view, model);
    target.LoadLists();                                          ❶ Method
    Assert.IsNotNull(view.Lists);                                  to test
    Assert.IsTrue(view.Lists.Count() == 2);
}
```

This test of the LoadLists method creates the Presenter using the View and Model mock objects. As you can see, the first three lines of the test define what's tested in the constructor test. A unit-test should test only a single method, ❶ if possible, and because there's already a test for the constructor, it's not tested here. After calling the LoadLists method (which is the method that's tested), the Lists object of the Mock-View object is verified so that it's not null. Remember the Presenter object filled the View using the Model. The MockModel that was built earlier created a list containing two items, and they're also tested as the last part of the test.

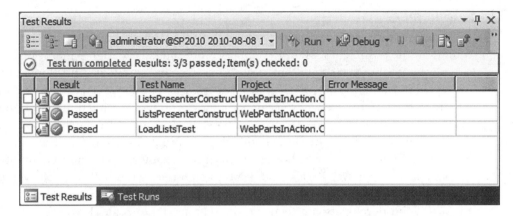

Figure 13.13 Use the Test Results window to inspect the status of the test runs and to get more information about failed tests.

It's now time to run the tests. Do so by selecting Tests > Run > All Tests in Solution in Visual Studio. Visual Studio will open the Test Results window, and you can follow the test's progress. Once all tests are finished, you can see the results in the Test Results window, as shown in figure 13.13, and eventually check and fix failed tests. In this example, all tests passed successfully.

If you have an edition of Visual Studio 2010 (such as Visual Studio 2010 Ultimate) that supports code coverage, you can enable that feature to inspect the parts of the source that were tested. Figure 13.14 shows that the current tests fully cover the Lists-Presenter class in the Web Part.

Hierarchy	Not Covered (Blocks)	Not Covered (% Blocks)	Covered (Blocks)	Covered (% Blocks)	
□ 🗄 administrator@SP2010 2010-08-08...	82	91.11 %	8	8.89 %	
□ 🗄 WebPartsInAction.Ch13.MVPW...	82	91.11 %	8	8.89 %	
⊞ { } WebPartsInAction.Ch13.M...	10	100.00 %	0	0.00 %	
⊞ { } WebPartsInAction.Ch13.M...	12	100.00 %	0	0.00 %	
□ { } WebPartsInAction.Ch13.M...	60	88.24 %	8	11.76 %	
□ 🔧 LibraryService	18	100.00 %	0	0.00 %	
⊸🔧 GetLists()	18	100.00 %	0	0.00 %	
□ 🔧 ListsPresenter	0	0.00 %	8	100.00 %	
⊸🔧 .ctor(class WebPar...	0	0.00 %	3	100.00 %	
⊸🔧 .ctor(class WebPar...	0	0.00 %	2	100.00 %	
⊸🔧 LoadLists()	0	0.00 %	3	100.00 %	
⊞ 🔧 ListsService	18	100.00 %	0	0.00 %	
⊞ 🔧 SiteListsWebPart	24	100.00 %	0	0.00 %	

Figure 13.14 The Code Coverage tool in Visual Studio lets you see exactly what parts of the code executed during the tests.

13.5 *Summary*

If you're new to design patterns and unit-testing, I hope that this chapter opened your eyes to the possibilities. Many developers put testing and design patterns on the low-priority list. But you should now realize that it's not as hard as it first looks and that testability should be on your high-priority list. By using the MVP pattern, you make it easier to test your code and you can test large portions of it using unit-tests. If the Web Parts are continuously tested, you get fewer errors and bugs, which means you can focus on creating new stuff instead of fixing old problems.

The SharePoint Service Locator used in this chapter allows you to have different backends of your Web Parts, which leads to high reusability. It also enables you to put the right person on the right task; the GUI expert can build the user interface and the SharePoint developers can focus on the data model or logic. If you like the Share-Point Service Locator, consider looking into the other SharePoint assets provided by the Patterns & Practices group, such as the Hierarchical Configuration Manager and the SharePoint Logger.

In the next chapter, I'll show you how to connect your Web Parts. Web Part connections allows you to build composite applications consisting of multiple Web Parts that can communicate with each other.

Part 3

Dashboards and connections

P art 3 is divided into two chapters, which are focused on how to make Web Parts communicate and interact which each other to create new or more advanced solutions. Chapter 14 gives you all the details you need to start building Web Parts that can be connected to other Web Parts. Connected Web Parts can send information from one Web Part, called the provider, to one or more consumer Web Parts.

The final chapter, 15, will show you how to build complete and ready-to-go Web Part pages with connected Web Parts. You'll learn how to package, deploy, and provision these pages using solution packages. Once you've finished reading this chapter, you will know a lot about Web Parts in SharePoint 2010 and you should be ready to build new master pieces.

Connecting Web Parts

This chapter covers

- Web Part connections
- The consumer/provider model
- Standard SharePoint connection interfaces
- Filter Web Parts

Up to now you've focused on one Web Part at a time, but in this chapter I'll show you how to get your Web Parts to work together. By creating connections, you ensure that one Web Part can communicate with other Web Parts using specific *contracts*. For instance, say you have a Web Part containing a list of orders; when a user selects one of the orders, another Web Part shows its details. Connected Web Parts are often used in dashboards and reporting scenarios in which you'd like to "slice and dice" the information. You can configure the connections in code or directly in the user interface without any coding (which allows end users to create their own applications or mashups using different Web Parts).

Nearly all out-of-the-box Web Parts in SharePoint support connections in one way or another. In addition, if you're fortunate to be working with the Server edition of SharePoint, you get a whole bunch of filter Web Parts that you can use to filter the information in your Web Part pages.

In this chapter, you'll learn how to create both Web Part connection providers and consumers using custom connection contracts as well as the default connection types defined in SharePoint. I'll show you how to combine Web Part connections with ASP.NET Ajax techniques to make the connections and updates more dynamic. In addition, you'll look at filter Web Parts, specialized Web Parts that you can use to filter the contents of other Web Parts.

14.1   *Introducing Web Part connections*

Web Part connections are one of the core fundamentals of the Web Part infrastructure. Connecting Web Parts allows your end users to build rich and advanced applications using the various Web Parts that exist in their SharePoint installation.

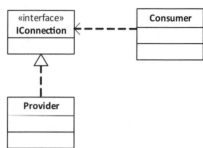

A Web Part connection always has one provider side and one consumer side. The providers send information to one or more consumers that use this information to filter or show more information. Here's an example: You can connect one Web Part containing data read from a database to another Web Part showing a chart representing that data. The chart isn't directly connected to the database; instead, that Web Part retrieves the data through the connection.

Figure 14.1   The provider Web Part implements an interface that acts as a contract for the connection. The consumer Web Part uses this interface to retrieve or exchange information with the provider.

The concept of connecting Web Parts is built on the principle that there are providers and consumers. A *provider* Web Part is one that provides information to *consumers*. A Web Part can have either of these roles, or both. Not all consumers can consume information from all providers—each connection needs a contract that both the consumer and provider understand. This contract is defined using an interface that's implemented by the provider and used by the consumer, as you can see in figure 14.1.

A provider Web Part can provide its interface to multiple consumers, and consumers can use connections from several providers, as figure 14.2 illustrates. But a consumer can't consume the same interface from multiple providers. In advanced scenarios where a consumer is both a consumer and a provider,

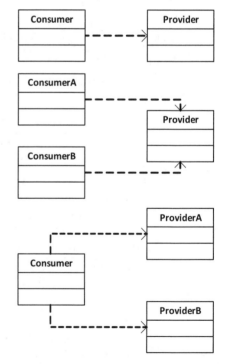

Figure 14.2   Web Parts can be connected in many ways, depending on how the connection endpoints are configured.

the Web Part can forward the information to a second consumer that's chaining the result.

Web Part connections aren't specific to SharePoint; they're defined in ASP.NET 2.0. Web Parts were a part of SharePoint prior to ASP.NET 2.0, and connections existed during the pre–ASP.NET 2.0 era. The technique was similar and used an interface as the contract, but otherwise the actual connection was very unlike the method used today. The pre–ASP.NET 2.0 Web Part connection had one thing that ASP.NET 2.0 connections don't have: client-side connections using JavaScript. Client-side connections can be replaced using ASP.NET 2.0 Ajax, which you'll learn about in section 14.3.3.

Connections can only be made between Web Parts with compatible interfaces on the same Web Part page and if both the consumers and providers exist in Web Part zones (including the Wiki Web Part zone). Previous versions of SharePoint allowed Web Parts to be connected across page boundaries. The ASP.NET implementation of Web Part connections didn't implement this feature out of the box.

14.2 Connecting Web Parts

One of the great things with Web Part connections is that end users can make the connections themselves. They can use the SharePoint web interface or use a rich client application such as SharePoint Designer. Web Part connections in the SharePoint interface are designed to be easy to use and configure.

Connected Web Parts can be used in many different scenarios. Let's return to our earlier example in which you have a list of orders in one Web Part and a second Web Part that shows the details of a specific order. By connecting your Web Parts, you build a dynamic interface. You can have even more Web Parts involved in your connections. In this example, you could connect to another Web Part that shows customer details so that when a user selects an order both the details of the order and information about the customer are shown.

14.2.1 Connecting using the web interface

Web Parts can be connected using the web interface in SharePoint. You do so by selecting Edit Web Part in the Web Part options menu to enter edit mode and open the Web Part's property pane. Click the options menu again and select the Connections option. The Connections submenu is dynamic and depends on what consumer and provider endpoints the current Web Part exposes and whether there are compatible Web Parts on the page (see figure 14.3).

By selecting a connection type and then the target Web Part, you'll connect your Web Parts. Depending on the type of the connection, an optional pop-up window will ask you to provide the connection with further details, such as which parameter or property to retrieve or send values to. You'll see this in action a bit later in the chapter. Once the connection is established, a check mark appears beside the current connection. Depending on the implementation of the Web Parts, there might be multiple connections.

Figure 14.3   Using the Web Part options menu, you can create Web Parts connections.

To disconnect Web Parts from one another, you use the same procedure. Select the current connection (the one with the check mark). If the connection is configurable, the pop-up window will allow you to change the settings, or you can choose to remove the connection. If you can't configure the connection, you'll simply see a dialog box asking you to confirm the disconnect.

14.2.2 *Connecting using SharePoint Designer*

SharePoint Designer is another option available to you when you're working with Web Part pages and configuring Web Parts and connections. When you're editing a page in SharePoint Designer and you select a Web Part, the Ribbon menu will display the contextual Web Part Tools tab. This tab contains a group called Connections that you can use to add new connections or manage existing ones. Figure 14.4 shows the dialog box that appears when you click Manage Connections. This dialog box lets you add, modify, and remove connections of the selected Web Part.

The SharePoint Designer interface is a great complement to the web interface, especially when you're building complex dashboards with a lot of connections. The connections configuration wizards in SharePoint Designer are more helpful and intuitive than the corresponding ones in the web interface.

Figure 14.4   SharePoint Designer 2010 can be used to configure Web Part connections. The rich interface in SharePoint Designer makes the connection experience easier.

14.2.3 *Connection permissions*

If for some reason you don't want to allow users to create Web Part connections, an administrator can disable that capability. Web Part connections might slow the performance down somewhat, due to the extra processing needed when transferring information between Web Parts and filtering them. But most often you don't want to prohibit users from using Web Part connections.

You configure these permissions on a per–web application basis in Central Administration. Click Application Management and then select Manage Web Applications. Choose your web application and then click Web Part Security in the Ribbon. This opens the dialog box shown in figure 14.5. The first option, Web Part Connections, allows you to turn on or off your users' ability to create connections for the specified web application.

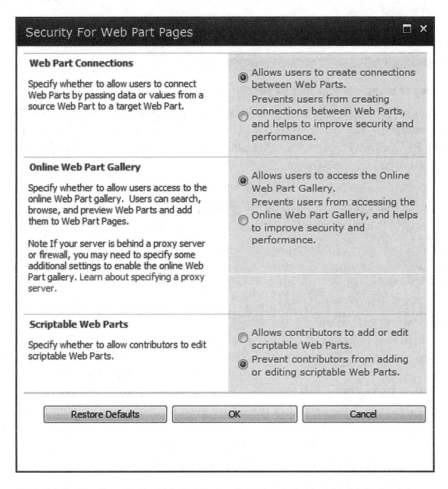

Figure 14.5 The Security For Web Part Pages dialog box in Central Administration lets you enable or disable the functionality for connecting Web Parts.

14.3   Creating connectable Web Parts

Building Web Parts that can be connected requires that you either create a provider Web Part or a consumer Web Part—and in many cases you create both ends. Each provider–consumer connection has a contract that tells the consumer what it can expect to receive from the provider. The provider and consumer communicate using an interface, the contract, which the provider Web Part exposes. The consumer Web Part uses this interface to retrieve information from the provider.

You can create custom interfaces for your own providers and consumers or use any of the default connection interfaces. There's a huge benefit to using the default interfaces because they're compatible with several of the out-of-the-box Web Parts in SharePoint. (See appendix A for a comprehensive list of Web Parts and their connection interfaces.) In this section, I'll show you both ways: custom interfaces and the default interfaces.

In addition, I'll describe how to combine the ASP.NET Ajax framework with Web Part connections. This approach allows you to make your dashboards perform better without reloading the page completely.

14.3.1   Connect using custom interfaces

The first technique you'll explore is creating a custom connection defined by a custom interface. You use this type of connection when you don't need to connect your Web Parts with Web Parts from SharePoint or third-party applications. To create a custom connection, you need to

- Define a connection interface, which is the connection contract
- Create a provider Web Part, implementing the interface
- Create a consumer Web Part, using the interface

For this example, you'll continue to build on the RSS Web Part used in previous chapters and make it into a consumer Web Part. The RSS Web Part will be connected to a provider Web Part that provides a URL to the RSS Web Part. You'll create a new Web Part that will serve as the provider.

DEFINE THE CONNECTION INTERFACE

To build this solution, you need to create a new SharePoint project based on the Empty SharePoint Project template. Be sure to select to deploy the project as a farm solution; Web Part connections can't be used with sandboxed solutions. First, Add a new Web Part to the project and give it the name `FeedInputWebPart`.

The connection interface you'll create must be able to send a URL from one Web Part to another. The URL will be exposed from the interface as a property with the string type. Add an interface item to the newly created Web Part and name the interface `IUrlConnection`. This interface will be the contract of the connection, and it will have a single property called `Url`, like this:

```
public interface IUrlConnection {
    string Url {
        get;
    }
}
```

Note that the interface is defined as `public`. This is necessary so that SharePoint (the Web Part Manager) and other Web Parts outside your project can access it. This interface has a single property that will contain the URL and is read-only; there's no need to be able to write back the value in this case.

CREATE THE PROVIDER

When you've defined the interface, it's time to build the provider Web Part. This Web Part will have a text input control and a button, as shown in figure 14.6.

The user interface for this Web Part is built in the `CreateChildControls` method. You can build this Web Part using a Visual Web Part if you prefer, but doing so would require the extra plumbing between the user control and the Web Part. The code that generates the interface should look like this in a standard Web Part:

```
protected TextBox url;

protected override void CreateChildControls() {
    HtmlGenericControl fieldset = new HtmlGenericControl("fieldset");
    HtmlGenericControl legend = new HtmlGenericControl("legend") {
        InnerText = "Enter feed URL:"
    };
    fieldset.Controls.Add(legend);

    url = new TextBox();
    fieldset.Controls.Add(url);

    Button button = new Button() {
        Text = "Submit"
    };

    fieldset.Controls.Add(button);

    this.Controls.Add(fieldset);
}
```

The `TextBox` containing the URL is defined as a `protected` class property. You'll need that property later when you add the connection interface to this Web Part. This Web Part uses the `fieldset` and `legend` HTML elements to encapsulate the text box and button. All these controls are then added to the controls collection.

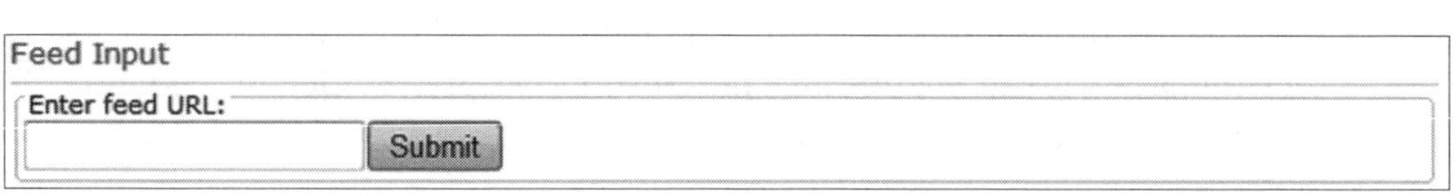

Figure 14.6   A provider Web Part that accepts a text input—in this example a URL to an RSS feed—and sends the value of the text box to any connected Web Part consumers

Once you've built the user interface, it's time to let the provider Web Part implement the connection interface. Do so by adding the interface to the provider class definition:

```
public class FeedInputWebPart : WebPart, IUrlConnection
```

Now that the interface is defined for the class, you need to implement the property. You can either right-click on `IUrlConnection` in the class definition and select Implement Interface or you can write the code yourself. The `Url` property implementation should return the value of the text box:

```
public string Url {
    get {
        return url.Text;
    }
}
```

There's one more thing that you need to do in order to turn this into a provider Web Part: create a method in the Web Part that returns the connection interface and mark that method as a connection provider endpoint:

```
[ConnectionProvider("Feed url")]
public IUrlConnection SetFeedConnection() {
    return this;
}
```

The attribute `ConnectionProvider` informs the Web Part Manager on the page that this Web Part has a provider connection endpoint and that the parameter is the name for it, which will be shown in the interface when connecting the Web Part. You can give the method any name, but it must return the interface; because the Web Part implements the interface, the current object (`this`) is returned.

The `ConnectionProvider` attribute always requires that you specify a name for the connection point. This name will be used in the SharePoint user interface to identify the connection. If you have multiple connection provider endpoints in your Web Part, you also have to supply an `ID` parameter that uniquely identifies the endpoint.

By default, a provider connection point can be used to connect to multiple consumers. You can change this by setting the named property called `AllowsMultiple-Connections` to `false` in the `ConnectionProvider` attribute.

BUILD THE CONSUMER

As the consumer Web Part in this sample, you'll build a new RSS Web Part. This Web Part is similar to the RSS Web Part that you built in chapter 5. First, add a new Web Part to the project and give it the name `RssWebPart`. Add two properties, as you did for the Web Part in chapter 5. These properties are the default URL and the default number of items retrieved from the feed:

```
[WebBrowsable]
[Personalizable(PersonalizationScope.Shared)]
[WebDisplayName("RSS feed Url")]
[WebDescription("Enter the Url to the RSS feed")]
public string RssFeedUrl {
```

```
        get;
        set;
}
[WebBrowsable]
[Personalizable(PersonalizationScope.Shared)]
[WebDisplayName("Items to show")]
[WebDescription("The number of RSS feed items to show")]
public int ItemCount {
        get;
        set;
}
```

These properties are used as default values for the RSS feed and the number of items to retrieve. The `RssFeedUrl` will be used when the Web Part isn't connected to a provider Web Part. To initialize the value of the `ItemCount` property, use the following constructor:

```
public RssWebPart() {
        this.ItemCount = 5;
}
```

This constructor will ensure that the default value for the number of items retrieved is 5. You could set the default value in the .webpart file instead, if you prefer.

To render the feed items as links in the Web Part, you'll implement a separate method. The method is declared as `private` and looks like this:

```
private void renderFeed() {
        if (string.IsNullOrEmpty(this.RssFeedUrl)) {
            return;
        }

        XElement feed = XElement.Load(this.RssFeedUrl);

        var items = feed.Descendants("item").Take(this.ItemCount);

        BulletedList bulletedList = new BulletedList();
        bulletedList.DisplayMode = BulletedListDisplayMode.HyperLink;

        foreach (var item in items) {
            bulletedList.Items.Add(new ListItem(
                item.Descendants("title").First().Value,
                item.Descendants("link").First().Value));
        }
        this.Controls.Add(bulletedList);
}
```

The `renderFeed` method is essentially just a copy of what you used in chapter 5 in the `CreateChildControls` method. If the `RssFeedUrl` property isn't set, it quits the method; otherwise, it creates a `BulletedList` object, which shows a link for each feed item, and then adds the bulleted list to the Web Part child controls collection.

The consumer Web Part needs a consumer connection endpoint, and you implement that in a similar way. First add a new method that takes the connection interface as a parameter and mark it with the `ConnectionConsumer` attribute. The code should look like this:

```
IUrlConnection _provider;

[ConnectionConsumer("Feed Url", "feed")]
public void GetFeedConnection(IUrlConnection provider) {
    _provider = provider;
}

internal bool IsConnected() {
    return _provider != null;
}
```

First, a local property called _provider is defined and used to store a reference to the connection interface. The instance of that connection interface is set in the GetFeed-Connection method, which is the connection consumer endpoint. The attribute has two parameters; the first one is the display name for the connection and the second one an ID for the connection. The ID is optional at this point, but it's required if the Web Part will have more than one connection consumer endpoint (and you'll soon add more). Finally, you add an internal method that checks whether the Web Part is connected. This method will be used to ensure that the Web Part doesn't use the connection if it's not set.

If you deployed this project now, the provider and consumer can be connected, but because you haven't as yet added any code in the RSS Web Part that uses the connection, you won't see any results of the connection. To use the connection interface, you have to consider the order of events in a Web Part (see chapter 4). Figure 14.7 shows a part of the event flow of the Web Part when connections are involved.

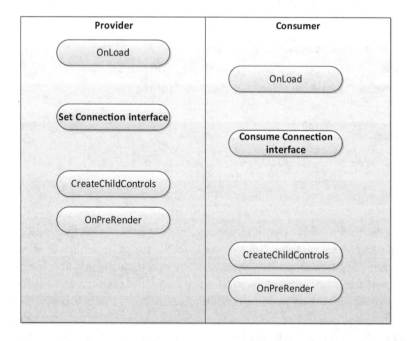

Figure 14.7   The Web Part Manager connects Web Parts during a page load (HTTP GET) immediately after the OnLoad event and before the CreateChildControls event.

During an HTTP GET request, the provider connection method is called after the OnLoad events of both the consumer and provider. Directly after retrieving the provider connection, the connection consumer method is called to establish the connection. Once the connection is established, the CreateChildControls method is invoked.

For a postback event, when an event is triggered in the provider Web Part, the event flow differs just as discussed in chapter 4 (see figure 14.8). The CreateChild-Controls method is now invoked before the OnLoad event and the connection methods are invoked after the postback events.

The Web Part connections aren't connected until just before the OnPreRender method. This means that you can't use CreateChildControls to render the links of the feed. Instead you use the OnPreRender method to render the parts of the interface that are dependent on the connection. Before rendering the interface, the URL has to be retrieved from the connection:

```
protected override void OnPreRender(EventArgs e) {

    if (IsConnected()) {
        this.RssFeedUrl = this._provider.Url;
    }

    renderFeed();

    base.OnPreRender(e);
}
```

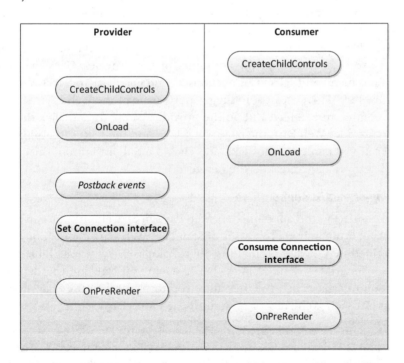

Figure 14.8 Web Part connections are established after the postback events during a postback (HTTP POST) and immediately before the OnPreRender event.

Figure 14.9   To connect the Feed Input connection provider with the RSS Web Part, select Connections in the Web Part options menu, and then select the name of the connection and finally the name of the Web Part.

The OnPreRender method checks whether the Web Part is connected to a provider by using the IsConnected method. If it's connected, then the method sets the RssFeedUrl property to the value of the Url property of the interface. The list of links to the feed items is then rendered using the renderFeed method.

The ConnectionConsumer attribute that defines the consumer connection point must have a name. As in the previous sample, an ID must be used if the Web Part has more than one connection consumer point. Just as with the ConnectionProvider attribute, the AllowsMultipleConnections property can be used to specify whether the connection point supports multiple providers. For a connection consumer point, the default value is false, which means it supports only a single provider.

Now it's time to build, deploy, and connect the Web Parts. Once you've deployed the solution to SharePoint, navigate to a page or create a new one and then add both the provider Web Part and the consumer Web Part to the page. Then click Edit Web Part in the Web Part options menu so that the Web Part enters Edit mode. To connect the Web Parts, you can use either the consumer or the provider. Click the provider Web Part options menu and select Connections > Send Feed Url To > RSS Web Part, as shown in figure 14.9. Then click OK in the property pane of the Web Part.

If you now enter an RSS feed URL in the provider Web Part and click the Submit button in the provider Web Part, the page will reload and the feed URL will be sent to the consumer. If you enter another URL and click the Submit button, the consumer Web Part will again reload and show the new feed.

14.3.2   *Connect using standard connections*

To be able to connect to the out-of-the-box Web Parts in SharePoint, you can't use custom interfaces. Fortunately there's a set of standard Web Part connection provider interfaces defined in ASP.NET 2.0 that the SharePoint Web Parts use. Table 14.1 lists the connection interfaces defined by ASP.NET. When you can, use the default Web Part connection interfaces because they allow you to connect to the SharePoint Web Parts, such as List View Web Parts or even third-party Web Parts.

> **NOTE**   You might see references to interfaces such as ICellProvider, ICellConsumer, and IFilterConsumer when looking at Web Part connections. These are interfaces used by the SharePoint implementation of Web Part connections before ASP.NET 2.0. These interfaces are now obsolete and shouldn't be used.

Table 14.1 Standard connection provider interfaces

Interface	Usage
IWebPartField	Transfers a single field of data
IWebPartRow	Transfers one row of data (multiple fields)
IWebPartTable	Transfers one table of data (multiple rows)
IWebPartParameters	Transfers a single field of data based on a parameter

I'll show you how to use some of these connection provider interfaces by modifying the RSS Web Part and then connecting it to a standard list Web Part that shows a Links list, where the Links list will be the provider. When a link in the Web Part is selected, that link will be used to retrieve the feed in the RSS Web Part, as shown in figure 14.10.

Figure 14.10   By using the built-in connection interfaces, you can connect custom Web Parts to the out-of-the-box Web Parts such as List Web Parts. Notice the Select column in the List Web Part; it appears when a List Web Part is acting as a provider Web Part.

CONNECT USING IWEBPARTROW

The IWebPartRow default connection provider interface allows a provider Web Part to send a row of data to a consumer Web Part. There's a benefit to using this interface in a Web Part. For instance, say the SharePoint XSLT List View Web Part provides that interface, inherited from the Data Form Web Part. Using an XSLT List View Web Part (which is used to display lists in SharePoint), you can easily retrieve feeds from a Links list into the RSS Web Part.

First you need to add the consumer connection endpoint to the RSS Web Part. You can use the endpoint you created in the previous section; remember that you set an ID on it that allows for more than one endpoint. The IWebPartRow consumer connection endpoint is implemented as follows:

```
IWebPartRow _row;

[ConnectionConsumer("Row", "row")]
public void GetRowData(IWebPartRow row) {
    _row = row;
}
```

This endpoint is marked with the `ConnectionConsumer` attribute, and it takes the `IWebPartRow` interface as the parameter. The connection interface is stored in a local variable. You also need to update the `IsConnected` method so that the Web Part can be connected through this endpoint:

```
internal bool IsConnected() {
    return _provider != null || _row != null;
}
```

The updated `IsConnected` method checks whether the Web Part is connected to the custom interface or if it uses the `IWebPartRow` connection.

The default connection interfaces in ASP.NET don't use properties to transfer the data between Web Parts, as in our example custom connection. Instead, they use callback methods. The provider interfaces contain methods that you send in a callback method from the consumer. You have to modify the `OnPreRender` method as follows:

```
protected override void OnPreRender(EventArgs e) {

    if (IsConnected()) {
        if (this._provider != null) {
            this.RssFeedUrl = this._provider.Url;        ❶ IUrlConnection
        }                                                   connection
        else if (this._row != null) {
            this._row.GetRowData(getRowData);            ❷ IWebPartRow
        }                                                   connection
    }
    renderFeed();
    base.OnPreRender(e);
}
```

After you've made those changes, `OnPreRender` will first check whether the Web Part is connected to the custom interface ❶, and if that's the case, it will use that connection. Otherwise, it will check whether it's connected using the `IWebPartRow` connection ❷. If that's the case, the method calls the `GetRowData` method of the provider with a callback method `getRowData`, defined here:

```
private void getRowData(object rowData) {
    DataRowView dataRow = rowData as DataRowView;
    if (dataRow != null) {
        foreach (PropertyDescriptor property in this._row.Schema) {
            if (property.Name == "URL") {
                SPFieldUrlValue value =
                    new SPFieldUrlValue(dataRow[property.Name].ToString());
                this.RssFeedUrl = value.Url;
                return;
            }
        }
    }
    this.RssFeedUrl = null;
}
```

The `getRowData` callback method accepts an object that's converted into an object of the type `DataRowView`. If the cast is successful, it'll iterate over all property descriptors found in the `Schema` property of the `IWebPartRow` interface. The `Schema` contains information, such as the name and type, about all columns in the row. When a column with the name "URL" is found in the row, this Web Part assumes that it's a URL column. The column is transformed into a SharePoint `SPFieldUrlValue` object. From this object the `Url` property is retrieved and put into the Web Part `RssFeedUrl` property. If no column called "URL" is found, it sets the feed URL to `null`.

That's all you need to connect the custom RSS Web Part to a standard SharePoint Links list. Deploy the solution and go to your site. Use an existing Links list or add a new one, and then fill the list with a few links to RSS feeds. When you've done that, create a new page and add the Links list to that page and then the RSS Web Part. Click Edit Web Part on the Links list options menu; then once again in the options menu of the Web Part, select Connections > Send Row of Data To > RSS Web Part. Click OK in the edit pane of the Web Part. Now the Links list is connected to the RSS Web Part and you can see that the Links list has a new column called "Select." If you click the Select icon on any of the rows, the RSS Web Part displays the contents from the URL of that selected row in the Lists Web Part, as shown previously in figure 14.10.

CONNECT USING IWEBPARTPARAMETERS

The third connection type that I'll show you is an alternative to the `IWebPartRow` when you need to select a list column to send to the consumer during the connection. The interface you'll use for this is called `IWebPartParameters`. This approach is better than iterating over the columns in the row as in the previous sample because it doesn't depend on a specific hardcoded name of the column.

The connection provider interface requires that the consumer tell the provider which field or fields to send to the consumer. You must add the connection endpoint to the RSS Web part and mark it as a connection consumer endpoint:

```
IWebPartParameters _parameters;

[ConnectionConsumer("Parameters", "parameters")]
public void GetRowParameters(IWebPartParameters parameters) {

    PropertyDescriptorCollection pdc =
        new PropertyDescriptorCollection( new PropertyDescriptor[]{
            TypeDescriptor.CreateProperty( this.GetType(),          Creates
                "RssUrl",                                            property
                typeof(string))                                   ❶ descriptor
    });

    parameters.SetConsumerSchema(pdc);

    _parameters = parameters;
}
```

This implementation differs from the previous ones because it's not just storing the value of the connection endpoint. In this case you need to inform the provider Web Part about the property (or properties) that you'd like it to provide to your consumer. You do so by creating a `PropertyDescriptorCollection` that consists of `Property-Descriptor` objects. In this example, the property you need is a string to set the feed

URL. You create that property description using the `CreateProperty` method of the `TypeDescriptor` object ❶, using the current Web Part type, the name (RssUrl), and the type of property. The collection of property descriptors is then used with the `Set-ConsumerSchema` method of the connection provider interface before the connection instance is stored to a local variable.

Using the property descriptors and the configuration of the connection, the provider Web Part will know which property to send to the consumer. The connection configuration is determined when the connection is established in the user interface.

Before modifying the `OnPreRender` method to support this new connection endpoint, you have to update the `IsConnected` method once again. It'll now check whether the Web Part is connected to any of the three connection endpoints:

```
internal bool IsConnected() {
    return _provider != null || _row != null || _parameters != null;
}
```

You then update the `OnPreRender` method so that it'll retrieve the feed URL from the new parameterized connection:

```
protected override void OnPreRender(EventArgs e) {

    if (IsConnected()) {
        if (this._provider != null) {
            this.RssFeedUrl = this._provider.Url;
        }
        else if (this._row != null) {
            this._row.GetRowData(getRowData);
        }
        else {
            this._parameters.GetParametersData(        ❶ IWebPartParameters
                getParametersData);                       connection
        }
    }
    renderFeed();
    base.OnPreRender(e);
}
```

Just as with the `IWebPartRow` connection, the `IWebPartParameters` connection calls a method in the provider, passing a local callback method called `getParametersData` ❶. This callback method now knows the name of the property to retrieve and the correct feed URL can safely be retrieved:

```
private void getParametersData(object rowData) {
    IDictionary dictionary = rowData as IDictionary;
    if (dictionary != null) {
        SPFieldUrlValue value =
            new SPFieldUrlValue(dictionary["RssUrl"].ToString());
        this.RssFeedUrl = value.Url;
        return;
    }
    this.RssFeedUrl = null;
}
```

The getParametersData method takes an object as an argument and that argument is cast into an IDictionary object containing the parameters. Using the SPFieldUrlValue class, the "RssUrl" parameter is retrieved and the value of that parameter is set into the Web Part RssFeedUrl property. This implementation is easier and safer because you can specify the property that you need. Note that this sample requires that the parameter passed have the name "RssUrl"; in your implementations you should check for the correct parameter names.

To connect the Links list and the RSS Web Part, you deploy the solution and go back to the page where you previously added the Links Web Part and the RSS Web Part. Remove the current (IWebPartRow) connection by editing one of the Web Parts, and then select Connections > Send Row of Data To > RSS Web Part. SharePoint will display a pop-up window that asks you if you'd like to remove the connection. Click OK to remove it.

To connect the Web Parts using the IWebPartParameters interface, start with the consumer Web Part. Select Connections > Get Parameters From > Links from the options menu of the RSS Web Part. In the resulting dialog box, select URL from the Provider Field Name drop-down list and RssUrl from the Consumer Field Name drop-down list, as shown in figure 14.11. Click Finish to configure the connection and then click OK to save and close the edit pane of the Web Part.

If you instead choose to create the connection using the provider, select Connections > Send Row of Data To > RSS Web Part. SharePoint will then detect that there's both an IWebPartRow connection and an IWebPartParameters connection available. The Configure Connection dialog box will appear and you must choose the connection type; Get Row From or Get Parameters From, as previously shown in figure 14.3. If you select the latter of the two, you'll then be required to choose the fields.

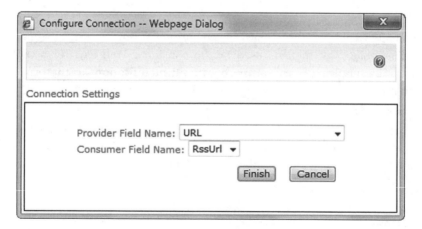

Figure 14.11 Some Web Part connection interfaces require that you configure the connections. If necessary, SharePoint will show a dialog box that asks you to configure the connection.

14.3.3 *Ajax and Web Part connections*

When you use a connected Web Part to filter a consumer, the page will make a post-back to update the values for just the consumer. Because SharePoint now supports ASP.NET Ajax out of the box, you can use update panels in the Web Parts. That's a simple way to improve the performance of the page or dashboard: it makes SharePoint update only the Web Parts instead of the whole page.

PROVIDER AND INTERFACE CHANGES

To learn how to use Ajax and dynamically updating Web Parts, you'll take the consumer and provider Web Parts, update the connection interface, and add an update panel to the consumer. First, let's update the connection interface. The provider must be able to send information to the consumer (in addition to the URL) indicating that it contains a control that can be used for asynchronous operations:

```
public interface IUrlConnection {
    string Url {
        get;
    }

    Control AsyncTrigger {
        get;
    }
}
```

This version has a new property called `AsyncTrigger` that returns a `Control` object. This object is the trigger of the asynchronous update. You must modify the original provider Web Part so that it supports this new property from the interface:

```
public Control AsyncTrigger {
    get {
        return _button;
    }
}
```

The implementation of the `AsyncTrigger` property returns the current `_button` object. This object will then be used by the consumer Web Part for asynchronous operations. By supplying it as a property without modifications to the provider Web Part, you make it optional for the consumer Web Part to use the property.

CONSUMER CHANGES

In the consumer Web Part, there are three changes you must include to make it update asynchronously. The first change is to override the `CreateChildControls` method and add an `UpdatePanel` object to the consumer:

```
protected UpdatePanel updatePanel;

protected override void CreateChildControls() {
    updatePanel = new UpdatePanel();
    this.Controls.Add(updatePanel);
    base.CreateChildControls();
}
```

The UpdatePanel is declared as a protected property in the Web Part class. In the CreateChildControls it's created and added to the child controls collection. This UpdatePanel object is then used by the renderFeed method in the consumer. Instead of adding the BulletedList (which shows the RSS feed items) to the Web Part child controls collection, it's added to the template container of the UpdatePanel, like this:

```
BulletedList bulletedList = new BulletedList();
bulletedList.DisplayMode = BulletedListDisplayMode.HyperLink;

foreach (var item in items) {
    bulletedList.Items.Add(new ListItem(
        item.Descendants("title").First().Value,
        item.Descendants("link").First().Value));
}
updatePanel.ContentTempalteContainer.Controls.Add(bulletedList);
```

This allows the feed items to be updated when the UpdatePanel is asynchronously updated. All that you've changed is that the RSS feed items are now contained within an update panel. Any clicks on the button will still invoke a full postback.

The final modification is to edit the OnPreRender so that it registers the Control object provided from the connection interface as an asynchronous postback control. You accomplish this by using the ScriptManager object in the OnPreRender method:

```
protected override void OnPreRender(EventArgs e) {
    if (IsConnected()) {
        if (this._provider != null) {
            ScriptManager scriptManager =
                ScriptManager.GetCurrent(this.Page);
            if (scriptManager != null) {                           ❶ Register
                scriptManager.RegisterAsyncPostBackControl(            asynchronous
                    _provider.AsyncTrigger);                           postback control
            }
            this.RssFeedUrl = this._provider.Url;
        }
        else if (this._row != null) {
            this._row.GetRowData(getRowData);
        }
        else {
            this._parameters.GetParametersData(getParametersData);
        }
    }
    renderFeed();

    base.OnPreRender(e);
}
```

If the consumer Web Part is connected using the IUrlConnection interface, the current ScriptManager is retrieved. If the ScriptManager is found, it's used to register ❶ the control (AsyncTrigger) from the connection interface as an asynchronous postback control. This operation converts the functionality of the button into an asynchronous operation.

If you deploy the solution now, connect the Web Parts using the custom connection interface, enter a URL to a feed, and click the Submit button, you'll see that the consumer Web Part updates without refreshing the whole page. This simple change to the Web Parts and the connection interface is a small but efficient way to make the user interface of connected Web Parts and SharePoint faster.

14.4   Filter Web Parts

Filter Web Parts are provider Web Parts used to filter the information in other Web Parts. For instance, a filter Web Part might define a date range that's used by another Web Part to filter its contents. SharePoint Server Enterprise is delivered with a set of filter Web Parts that you can use with your consumer Web Parts. Or you might create custom filter Web Parts to add new filtering functionality to your SharePoint installation. If you're working with SharePoint Foundation or SharePoint Server, you have no filter Web Parts at all by default, and you might find it worth your time to add your own.

14.4.1   Default filter Web Parts

A filter Web Part is a special kind of provider. Its sole purpose is to serve as a filter for another Web Part. Only the Server version of SharePoint 2010 contains filter Web Parts out of the box. Most of them are quite easy to implement on your own, if you need them in SharePoint Foundation. Table 14.2 shows the filter Web Parts in Share-Point Server.

Table 14.2   Out-of-the-box filter Web Parts in SharePoint Server Enterprise 2010

Name	Description
Business Data Connectivity Filter	Filters a Web Part using values from the Business Data Connectivity service
Choice Filter	Filters a Web Part using a list of values entered by the page author
Current User Filter	Sends a user id to a Web Part
Date Filter	Filters a Web Part with a selected date
Filter Actions	Synchronizes two or more filter Web Parts
Page Field Filter	Filters a Web Part based on metadata of the Web Part Page
PerformancePoint Filter	Filters PerformancePoint Web Parts
Query String Filter	Filters a web part using Query String parameters
SharePoint List Filter	Filters a Web Part using a list of values
SQL Server Analysis Server Filter	Filters a Web Part with values from a SQL Server Analysis Server cube
Text Filter	Filters a Web Part using a value entered by the user

All of these Web Parts (except the Business Data Connectivity and PerformancePoint filter Web Parts) are defined in the `Microsoft.Office.Server.FilterControls.dll` assembly, which is installed in the global assembly cache in a SharePoint Server installation.

14.4.2 Web Part transformers

Before you dig into how the filter Web Part works, I want to explain the concept of Web Part transformers. Web Part transformers are used to connect two Web Parts with incompatible connection endpoints and translate the data. For instance, a transformer can be used to transform an `IWebPartRow` provider endpoint to an `IWebPartField` consumer endpoint.

The transformers derive from the abstract `WebPartTransformer` class defined in the `System.Web.dll` assembly and are a part of the ASP.NET framework. To create a Web Part transformer, you need to create a new class that derives from the transformer base class and returns the connection interface for the type you're transforming to. Listing 14.1 shows how to implement a transformer that transforms an `IWebPartField` connection provider to our custom `IUrlConnection` interface.

Listing 14.1 Transforming `IWebPartField` endpoint to `IUrlConnection` endpoint

```
[WebPartTransformer(typeof(IWebPartField), typeof(IUrlConnection)]
public class FieldToUrlTransformer:
    WebPartTransformer, IUrlConnection {

    protected IWebPartField _provider;
    protected string _url;

    public override object Transform(object providerData) {
        _provider = (IWebPartField)providerData;
        return this;
    }

    public string Url {
        get {
            this._provider.GetFieldValue(getFieldValue);
            return _url;
        }
    }

    private void getFieldValue(object fieldValue) {
      _url = fieldValue.ToString();
    }
}
```

The `FieldToUrlTransformer` class inherits from `WebPartTransformer` and the `IUrlConnection` interface is marked with the `WebPartTransformer` attribute. This attribute defines which connection type the transformer can transform from and which connection type the transformation results in. To transform the interfaces, the `Transform` method must be overridden; in this case it stores the from provider in the local variable. The `Url` method of the `IUrlConnection` interface uses the provider callback method to get the value from the `IWebPartField` provider, thus converting from `IWebPartField` to the `IUrlConnection` provider.

To use a transformer, you must register it in the web.config of the web application. You do so in the `webParts` section using the `transformers` element. Add each transformer using an `add` element:

```
<webParts>
    <transformers>
        <add name="FieldToUrlTransformer"
            type="WebPartsInAction.FieldToUrlTransformer, ... "/>
    </transformers>
</webParts>
```

The `name` attribute is a unique name for the transformer and the `type` attribute contains the transformer type. Creating custom transformers is rarely done, especially if you're using SharePoint Server, but using them can simplify development when building advanced dashboards. Transformers can be useful if you're working with third-party Web Parts with incompatible connection contracts.

NOTE Don't manually make changes to the web.config files. Use the `SPWeb-ConfigModification` classes or a similar approach to provision your changes throughout your farm.

SharePoint Server 2010, by default, adds all the needed transformers for the filter Web Parts in the web.config file. The following are the default transformers registered in a SharePoint 2010 Server installation. The assembly where the transformer is defined appears within parentheses:

- `TransformableFilterValuesToFilterValuesTransformer` (`Microsoft.SharePoint`)
- `TransformableFilterValuesToParametersTransformer` (`Microsoft.SharePoint`)
- `TransformableFilterValuesToFieldTransformer` (`Microsoft.SharePoint`)
- `TransformableFilterValuesToEntityInstanceTransformer` (`Microsoft.SharePoint.Portal`)

For an Enterprise installation of SharePoint, the following transformers are also added:

- `TransformableBIDataProviderToFilterValuesTransformer` (`Microsoft.PerformancePoint.Scorecards.WebControls`)
- `TransformableBIDataProviderToWebPartParametersTransformer` (`Microsoft.PerformancePoint.Scorecards.WebControls`)
- `TransformableBIDataProviderTransformer` (`Microsoft.PerformancePoint.Scorecards.WebControls`)

These transformers are used by PerformancePoint Services Web Parts, and by building custom filter Web Parts, you can enhance the feature set of PerformancePoint Services dashboards.

Figure 14.12 Using the SharePoint defined interfaces for connections allows you to create filter Web Parts that can be connected to almost any Web Part.

14.4.3 *The ITransformableFilterValues interface*

All filter Web Parts in SharePoint use the `ITransformableFilterValues` interface. This interface was specifically created for Web Part transformers in SharePoint. The default transformers are used to transform from this interface to the interfaces used by the default consumer Web Part in SharePoint. If you build your Web Parts using the default interfaces, which I discussed earlier, you can take advantage of the filter Web Parts. This interface is defined in `Microsoft.SharePoint.dll` in the `Microsoft.SharePoint.WebPartPages` namespace.

To build your own filter Web Part that could be used by the default SharePoint Web Parts, you need to make your provider Web Part implement the `ITransform-ableFilterValues` interface. In the project with the connectable RSS Web Part, add a new Web Part project item called `CustomFilter`. This will be a filter Web Part with a drop-down list containing a few RSS feeds (see figure 14.12). By selecting an item from the drop-down list, you can update the RSS Web Part.

Listing 14.2 shows the full implementation of the filter Web Part. Notice that the `ITransformableFilterValues` interface is prefixed with `SPWPP`. This is because the interface exists in the same namespace in which the SharePoint `WebPart` class is declared. To avoid conflicting class names, you employ a `using` statement:

```
using SPWPP=Microsoft.SharePoint.WebPartPages;
```

This custom filter implements the five different properties of the interface and exposes the interface as a connection provider.

Listing 14.2 A filter Web Part that uses the `ITransformableFilterValues` interface

```
public class CustomFilter : WebPart, SPWPP.ITransformableFilterValues {
    protected DropDownList _dropDown;

    protected override void CreateChildControls() {
        _dropDown = new DropDownList();
        _dropDown.Items.Add(new ListItem("Wictor Wilén",
            "http://feeds.feedburner.com/WictorWilen"));
        _dropDown.Items.Add(new ListItem("SharePoint Team Blog",
            "http://blogs.msdn.com/sharepoint/rss.xml"));
        _dropDown.AutoPostBack = true;
        this.Controls.Add(_dropDown);
    }

    public bool AllowAllValue {
        get { return true; }
    }
```

```
public bool AllowEmptyValue {
    get { return false; }
}
public bool AllowMultipleValues {
    get { return false; }
}
public string ParameterName {
    get { return "Url"; }
}
public ReadOnlyCollection<string> ParameterValues {
    get {
        EnsureChildControls();
        string[] values = new string[] {_dropDown.SelectedValue};
        return new ReadOnlyCollection<string>(values);
    }
}
[ConnectionProvider("Feed filter",
    "ITransformableFilterValues",
    AllowsMultipleConnections = true)]
public SPWPP.ITransformableFilterValues SetConnectionInterface() {
    return this;
}
}
```

The `CreateChildControls` method of the filter Web Part adds a `DropDown` control to the controls collection. This drop-down list is filled with two different RSS feeds. To avoid adding a button to apply the filter, you set the drop-down to `AutoPostBack` when it's changed. The `AllowAllValue`, `AllowEmptyValue`, and `AllowMultipleValues` properties are set to default values in this implementation. The `ParameterName` property returns the parameter name of this filter, and `ParameterValues` returns a single value in this case, which is the value of the selected item in the drop-down. To make the Web Part into a provider, the `ITransformableFilterValues` interface is returned by the `SetConnectionInterface` method. Notice how it's also set to support multiple consumers.

Once you deploy the project, you can connect the custom filter Web Part to the RSS Web Part and see how the feed item changes when you switch feeds using the drop-down list. Using this technique with filter Web Parts, you can enhance the use of your Web Parts as well as the out-of-the-box ones.

14.5   Summary

Web Part connections are powerful and can enhance the user experience. They can make different Web Parts interact with one another, and users can filter and customize potentially large amounts of information. Connectable Web Parts can be used to provide new functionality to existing and even the out-of-the-box Web Parts. Web Part connections allow power users to use existing Web Parts in combination with other Web Parts to build new applications. In the next, and last, chapter, you'll build full configurable dashboards.

Building
pages and dashboards

In the previous chapter, I showed you how to build Web Parts that you can connect so that they can exchange information. Users can combine various Web Parts and connect them to build dashboards and pages. For instance, a user might build a customer relationship management (CRM) dashboard by connecting a SharePoint list of customers, Web Parts that read information from a backend system, and filter Web Parts. But not all users can or want to build their own Web Part pages with Web Parts and connections. In many cases, it's better to build ready-to-go dashboard pages and then allow users to fine-tune them. Building deployable dashboard solutions is a good idea if you plan to reuse the pages or dashboards multiple times.

In this chapter, we'll take an in-depth look at Web Part pages and zones. You'll learn how to add and configure pages with Web Part zones and package them into solutions. Then we'll look at the control that orchestrates the Web Part pages: the Web Part Manager. Finally, I'll show you ways to package and deploy dashboards.

15.1   Working with pages

I think that Web Parts are one of the most important and interesting things in Share-Point, but Web Parts wouldn't be useful if you had no place to put them. Web Parts are added to pages and Web Part zones. Specifically the site pages, compared to application pages, are of interest because it's in those pages that end users can customize Web Parts. Web Part pages have one or more zones that contain the Web Parts. These zones can be configured in several ways and control how the Web Parts within them can be customized.

The glue that holds the Web Parts, pages, and zones is the Web Part Manager. This control is responsible for the connections between Web Parts and ensures that the customized values of the Web Part are persisted to the content databases. Developers can programmatically customize Web Parts using the Web Part Manager, which is useful when you're dynamically creating Web Part pages.

15.1.1   Pages and Web Part zones

In the first chapter of this book, I introduced you to the various kinds of pages in SharePoint, such as site, publishing, and application pages. Most pages in SharePoint are site pages that contain text, images, Web Parts, and Web Part zones. These pages are normally added to a document library or similar library, and users with the appropriate permissions can add and edit them. A dashboard (which is just another name for a page that uses connected Web Parts) is a site page with one or more Web Part zones.

In many situations you need to supply your users with a preconfigured page or dashboard instead of just giving them the puzzle pieces (the Web Parts). In this section I'll show you how to build a SharePoint project using Visual Studio and you'll see how to deploy pages into a site page library.

ADDING PAGES TO SHAREPOINT

There are many ways to add new pages to SharePoint. Your options vary, depending on the type of page you're going to deploy. In chapter 10 you learned how to deploy application pages. In this chapter the focus is on site pages and especially Web Part pages.

Although you could use the SharePoint API to add pages using a Feature receiver, the easiest way is to use a declarative approach and deploy the pages using a `Module` element in a Feature. You do this by creating a new SharePoint project using Visual Studio and adding a new item of the type Module. You can use a sandboxed or a farm solution (more on this later in the chapter). You then remove the sample.txt file that's included in the Module SPI by default. To add the site page, you need to add a new ASPX page to this module. Unfortunately, Visual Studio doesn't offer a project item for site pages. So here are your options:

- Export a page from SharePoint Designer 2010
- Manually create an ASPX site page or Wiki page or copy from out-of-the-box pages in SharePoint root
- Download extension project items, such as the CKS:DEV, which contains a Basic Site Page SPI

The first option is useful if you want to customize the page using a rich editor. Pages can be created and edited in SharePoint Designer and then exported as ASPX files. First, select the file in a site page library in SharePoint Designer. Then in the Manage group of the Pages Ribbon tab, select the Export File option, as shown in figure 15.1. Although this approach works well, the code that's exported into the file contains a lot of SharePoint Designer code and attributes, which may clutter the code (and is useless in this case).

To import the page into the Module project item in Visual Studio, right-click the item and select Add > Existing Item; then select the ASPX file that you exported using SharePoint Designer. Visual Studio automatically modifies the elements.xml file to include the new file.

NOTE When exporting a site page from SharePoint Designer, you'll see two attributes in the Page directive: `meta:webpartpageexpansion` and `meta:progid`. These two tags instruct SharePoint to automatically customize the pages.

The second approach requires that you write all the code yourself or, better still, make a copy of the default SharePoint Team Site page. You can copy this file, called default.aspx, from {SharePoint Root}\TEMPLATE\SiteTemplates\sts\. Add the page using Add > Existing Item. (When adding pages throughout the rest of this chapter, you'll use this method.)

To add a site page based on the Wiki page (which allows you to add Web Parts into the Wiki contents instead of in just Web Part zones), you follow the same procedure but use another source page. You'll find the source page for Wiki pages (called wkp-std.aspx) in {SharePoint Root}\TEMPLATE\DocumentTemplates\.

The final approach is to use an extension project item such as the Basic Site Page from the CKS:DEV Visual Studio extension. I recommend that you download this extension because it'll increase your productivity and it contains a useful set of features and project items.

The elements.xml file that defines how the pages are deployed into SharePoint automatically updates itself when you're adding new pages to the Module project item. By default, the `Module` element creates a folder in the root of the SharePoint site where it's deployed. This folder isn't accessible from any navigation in the SharePoint

Figure 15.1 Use SharePoint Designer 2010 to create and edit Web Part pages and then export them to a file that can be imported to a Visual Studio project.

user interface, and these folders can't be configured for versioning, security, and more. A better way is to deploy the page into a new or an existing document or site pages library. Do so by adding the Url attribute to the Module element; this attribute specifies the root URL of the deployment as follows:

```
<Module
    Name="PageDeployment"
    Url="SitePages">
<File
    Path="PageDeployment\Page.aspx"
    Url="PageDeployment/Page.aspx" />
</Module>
```

The Url attribute of the Module element specifies the root where the files are deployed (SitePages). Each File element represents a file to be deployed, and its Url attribute specifies the filename and (optionally) a folder. In this case the Page.aspx page will be deployed to folder called PageDeployment. To deploy the file's Site Pages root, remove the folder name from the Url attribute of the File element as follows:

```
<File
    Path="PageDeployment\Page.aspx"
    Url="Page.aspx" />
```

The File element contains more attributes, such as the Type, which you can set to Ghostable or GhostableInLibrary. Only use GhostableInLibrary on libraries where you store pages, files, and documents that can benefit from versioning, check-in, and check-out. The benefit of setting File to either of those values is that SharePoint will keep the files cached in memory and any updates to the original file in the file system will be reflected. Not specifying the File attribute puts the file in the database only, and you can't benefit from caching or updates to the original file. Another important attribute is IgnoreIfAlreadyExists, which you can set to true or false. If you specify this attribute as true, SharePoint ignores any existing file during the file provisioning. The best practice when deploying content files and Web Part pages into a library is to use these attributes. The following code shows the modified elements manifest (elements.xml) with the Type and IgnoreIfAlreadyExists attributes configured:

```
<Elements xmlns="http://schemas.microsoft.com/sharepoint/">
    <Module
        Name="PageDeployment"
        Url="SitePages">
        <File
            Path="PageDeployment\Page.aspx"
            Url="Page.aspx"
            IgnoreIfAlreadyExists="TRUE"
            Type="GhostableInLibrary" />
    </Module>
</Elements>
```

CONFIGURING WEB PART ZONES

The foundation of a Web Part page or dashboard is the zones that contain Web Parts. The zones allow users to add, move, and configure Web Parts, and they determine the basic layout of the page. Even though Web Parts can be added to areas outside a zone, only Web Parts within the zones, called dynamic Web Parts, can be configured and customized. Static Web Parts can only be updated by customizing the file using Share-Point Designer in Advanced Editing mode or by editing and redeploying the feature.

You add a Web Part zone to a page using the `WebPartZone` control, defined in the `Microsoft.SharePoint.WebPartPages` namespace. This control is a SharePoint-specific Web Part zone that derives from the ASP.NET Web Part zone. In Share-Point 2010 there are two types of Web Part zones: the standard Web Part zone and the new Wiki-based zone (which allows mixing of wiki content and Web Parts).

The Team Site page that you used earlier to add a new page in the Module project item uses two Web Part zones defined in a table. The first one (the left one) looks like this:

```
<WebPartPages:WebPartZone
    runat="server"
    FrameType="TitleBarOnly"
    ID="Left"
    Title="loc:Left" />
```

In addition to the `runat` attribute, the zone has three parameters. `FrameType` defines how the frame of the zone should be rendered. Normally you set this parameter to `TitleBarOnly`. The `ID` attribute is important, not only because the zone needs a unique ID, but also because it's used to reference the zone when programmatically adding Web Parts to the zone. Also, it's this `ID` that the Web Part uses to connect to the zone. The `Title` attribute is also important, because it's the name of the Web Part zone and is used when adding new Web Parts to the page through the Web Part Gallery. If you remove a zone that contains Web Parts, these Web Parts will still be stored in the database and can't be removed until you add the zone back or create a new zone with the same `ID` as the removed zone.

There are a few other attributes that you should know about that you can use when configuring or adding zones. One of the most important is `LayoutOrientation`. This attribute specifies whether the Web Parts are displayed horizontally or vertically in the zone. Table 15.1 lists some of the attributes that you can use when designing Web Part pages.

Table 15.1 Web Part Zone properties

Property	Description
AllowCustomization	Boolean value indicating whether users are allowed to customize the shared mode of Web Parts in the zone.
AllowLayoutChange	Boolean value indicating if a user can add, close, remove, or change specific layout properties of Web Parts in the zone.
AllowPersonalization	Boolean value indicating if users are allowed to personalize the Web Parts in the zone.
Title	The title of the Web Part. The property accepts localization strings.
LayoutOrientation	Determines the layout orientation of the Web Parts in the zone. Its value can be Horizontal or Vertical.

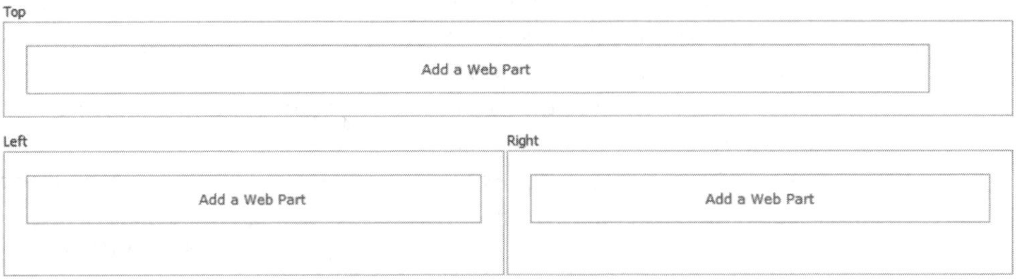

Top

```
                        Add a Web Part
```

Left   Right

```
        Add a Web Part                                    Add a Web Part
```

Figure 15.2   Web Part zones are positioned in the ASPX pages and are preferably positioned using DIV elements and CSS classes.

The Web Part zone controls have numerous properties that can be used to format the zones. Normally you shouldn't use these properties but should instead rely on the SharePoint standard layout and design.

To build a page that has one zone that's horizontally oriented and two zones with vertical aligned Web Parts, as shown in figure 15.2, remove all markup in the asp:Content element named PlaceHolderMain of the Web Part page.

The default markup of the Team Site Web Part page uses tables to arrange the Web Part zones, but we'll use DIV elements instead in this implementation. Listing 15.1 shows how the PlaceHolderMain should look like after you add the DIV elements and Web Part zones.

Listing 15.1   Three Web Part zones positioned using DIV elements and CSS

```
<asp:Content ContentPlaceHolderId="PlaceHolderMain" runat="server">
<style type="text/css">                          ◁──┐  Add custom
#wrapper {                                        ❶  CSS styles
    width:100%;
    margin:0 auto;
}
#left {
    float:left;
    width:50%;
}
#right {
    float:right;
    width:50%;
}
</style>
                                                 ❷  Build interface using
<div id="wrapper">                               ◁──┘  DIV elements
    <div id="top">
        <WebPartPages:WebPartZone
            runat="server"
            FrameType="TitleBarOnly"
            ID="Top"
            Title="loc:Top"
            LayoutOrientation="Horizontal"/>
```

```
        </div>
        <div id="left">
            <WebPartPages:WebPartZone
                runat="server"
                FrameType="TitleBarOnly"
                ID="Left"
                Title="loc:Left"
                LayoutOrientation="Vertical"/>
        </div>
        <div id="right">
            <WebPartPages:WebPartZone
                runat="server"
                FrameType="TitleBarOnly"
                ID="Right"
                Title="loc:Right"
                LayoutOrientation="Vertical"/>
        </div>
    </div>
</asp:Content>
```

To use DIV elements for the layout of the page, you need to add custom CSS styles ❶. In this case the CSS elements are added inline in the site page, instead of using a custom CSS file (which might have been more appropriate). Then the user interface is built using a set of DIV elements ❷ with unique IDs that map to the CSS styles. In the inner DIV elements, the WebPartZone controls are added. The top one uses horizontal orientation and the other two use vertical.

> **TIP** If you want to change the HTML that the Web Part zones are omitting, you can create a custom control adapter for the WebPartZone control, just as you did for the mobile controls in an earlier chapter.

15.1.2 *The Web Part Manager*

The Web Part Manager is the control that makes the Web Part pages work. It's responsible for everything relating to Web Parts and zones, such as loading and storing the customized state and layout of the Web Part. The Web Part Manager allows Web Parts to be connected to one another.

SPWEBPARTMANAGER

In addition to handling all zones, Web Parts, connections, and events on the page, the Web Part Manager is responsible for storing and retrieving the current customized or personalized state of all Web Parts. SharePoint uses the SPWebPartManager, which derives from the ASP.NET WebPartManager control.

The SPWebPartManager control is added to the master page, and normally you don't need to use it directly, unless you're building custom master pages. In the v4.master master page, used by SharePoint 2010, the SPWebPartManager is added just below the form control and the ScriptManager control:

```
<WebPartPages:SPWebPartManager id="m" runat="Server" />
```

The `SPWebPartManager` can be accessed from code using a static method. This method requires that you have access to the `HttpContext` and a page. For instance, in a Web Part or control, the current manager is retrieved like this:

```
SPWebPartManager manager =
    SPWebPartManager.GetCurrentWebPartManager(this.Page);
```

You can use the SharePoint Web Part Manager to create Web Parts from a list using the `CreateWebPartFromList` static function or to add new Web Parts to the page. `SPWebPartManager` also lets you connect Web Parts or verify whether Web Parts can be connected.

THE SPLIMITEDWEBPARTMANAGER

The `SPWebPartManager` control is a complex control and requires that an `HttpContext` object exist. To make it easier to work with Web Parts programmatically, there's an object called `SPLimitedWebPartManager`. This control provides you with a limited but useful set of Web Part operations without requiring an `HttpContext` object, as in Feature receivers or timer jobs. The `SPLimitedWebPartManager` also exposes a subset of its functionality through the Client Object Model, as you saw in chapter 11, but it's not available in sandboxed solutions.

You use the `SPLimitedWebPartManager` when you need to modify properties of a Web Part during runtime and save its state, or when you add new or connect existing Web Parts on a page. To update and save a property of a Web Part, you can use `SPLimitedWebPartManager` in an application page, web service, or a dialog window.

Assume that you have a Web Part with a property called `Data` and that you'd like to update the property when the user clicks a button in the Web Part. To do so, add a button click event handler like this:

```
button.Click += (s, e) => {
    using (SP.SPLimitedWebPartManager wpMgr =        ◁── ❶ Must be disposed correctly
        SPContext.Current.File.GetLimitedWebPartManager(
            PersonalizationScope.Shared)) {

        CustomWebPart wp = wpMgr.WebParts[this.ID] as CustomWebPart;
        if (wp != null) {
            wp.Data = tb.Text;
            wpMgr.SaveChanges(wp);
        }
    }
};
```

The button click event is defined as a lambda expression and the `SPLimitedWebPart-Manager` is retrieved ❶ by getting the current `SPFile` object from the `SPContext` object. The current file is the page where the Web Part exists. When instantiating the `SPLimitedWebPartManager` object, you need to specify which personalization scope to use (Shared or User); in this case the Shared scope is used. By using the `ID` of the Web Part, you ensure that the correct Web Part is retrieved from the collection of Web Parts in the `SPLimitedWebPartManager`. Finally, the `Data` property is set and the Web Part is saved using the `SaveChanges` method.

15.2 *Deploying dashboards*

Now that you know how Web Parts, zones, and connections work, it's time to put them all together into a dashboard. A dashboard is essentially a Web Part page with a set of connected Web Parts. It could be a reporting page that reads information from a line-of-business system where the users can filter and slice the information dynamically. Typically a dashboard page contains one or more connection providers and a set of connection consumer Web Parts. The consumer Web Parts can be lists or graphs, or they can present other relevant information.

You can build and deploy dashboards in several ways. Which method you'll use depends on the situation. You can create a complete dashboard by using a declarative approach where you define the page, Web Parts, and connections using XML. Or you can programmatically provision the Web Parts and connections on a page, perhaps using external dependencies. The dashboard can be a preconfigured Web Part page that your end users can extend and configure, or it can be a static dashboard that can't be configured. You can even deploy dashboards as a part of the site-creation procedure.

15.2.1 *Deploying using a Feature*

The first way to deploy a Web Part page or dashboard is to use a declarative approach, without any compiled code. By using a Module in a Feature, you can create a page, including its Web Parts and connections.

I'll show you how to deploy a Web Part page that will contain a Web Part zone and two connected Web Parts. You'll use the Web Parts from the previous chapter, as shown in figure 15.3. First you need to create a new Empty SharePoint project. For this first sample, you can select to deploy your solution as a sandboxed solution. Also make sure that the solution from chapter 14 is deployed to SharePoint. Remember that Visual Studio, by default, retracts solutions after running and debugging solutions unless you explicitly tell it to deploy the solution.

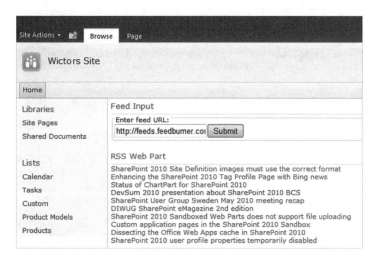

Figure 15.3 A page can be installed prefilled with Web Parts and connections to make it easier for end users to configure their sites.

Add a new Module to the project, remove the sample file, and then add a new Web Part page (by copying the Team Site Web Part page as shown earlier). Give it the name `default.aspx`. Modify the `PlaceHolderMain` so that it contains one Web Part zone called Main; the code looks like this:

```
<asp:Content ContentPlaceHolderId="PlaceHolderMain" runat="server">
    <WebPartPages:WebPartZone
        runat="server"
        FrameType="TitleBarOnly"
        ID="Main"
        Title="loc:Main"
        LayoutOrientation="Vertical"/>
</asp:Content>
```

Make sure that the page is provisioned to a Site Pages library and configure it as described earlier in the elements manifest file. The following code copies the default.aspx page into the Dashboard1 subfolder in the Site Pages library:

```
<Elements xmlns="http://schemas.microsoft.com/sharepoint/">
    <Module
        Name="Dashboard1"
        Url="SitePages">
        <File
            Path="Dashboard1\default.aspx"
            Url="Dashboard1/default.aspx"
            Type="GhostableInLibrary"
            IgnoreIfAlreadyExists="TRUE"/>
    </Module>
</Elements>
```

To add Web Parts to the file that's provisioned using the Module item, use an element called `AllUsersWebPart`. This element is added as a child to the `File` element, and it contains the contents of a Web Part controls description file (the .webpart file), as shown in listing 15.2. You can either copy the contents of a .webpart file from a Visual Studio project or select to export a preconfigured Web Part, save it to disk, and then copy the contents from that file. The connection between the Web Parts is done using another element called `WebPartConnection`.

Listing 15.2   Declarative provisioning Web Parts on a page

```
<File
    Path="Dashboard1\default.aspx"
    Url="Dashboard1/default.aspx"
    Type="GhostableInLibrary"
    IgnoreIfAlreadyExists="TRUE">                      ➊ First Web
<AllUsersWebPart                                          Part
        WebPartZoneID="Main"
        WebPartOrder="0"
        ID="FeedInput">
        <![CDATA[
            <webParts>
            <webPart xmlns="http://schemas.microsoft.com/WebPart/v3">
```

```
                <metaData>
                <type name="WebPartsInAction.Ch14.Connections.
                    FeedInputWebPart.FeedInputWebPart,
                    WebPartsInAction.Ch14.Connections, Version=1.0.0.0,
                    Culture=neutral, PublicKeyToken=8b0f149932984439" />
                <importErrorMessage>Cannot import this Web Part.
                </importErrorMessage>
                </metaData>
                <data>
                <properties>
                <property name="Title" type="string">Feed Input</property>
                </properties>
                </data>
                </webPart>
                </webParts>
        ]]>
    </AllUsersWebPart>
    <AllUsersWebPart                        ❷  Second
        WebPartZoneID="Main"                    Web Part
        WebPartOrder="1"
        ID="RSSWebPart">
        <![CDATA[
                <webParts>
                <webPart xmlns="http://schemas.microsoft.com/WebPart/v3">
                <metaData>
                <type name="WebPartsInAction.Ch14.Connections.
                    RssWebPart.RssWebPart,
                    WebPartsInAction.Ch14.Connections, Version=1.0.0.0,
                    Culture=neutral, PublicKeyToken=8b0f149932984439" />
                <importErrorMessage>Cannot import this Web Part.
                </importErrorMessage>
                </metaData>
                <data>
                <properties>
                <property name="ItemCount" type="int">10</property>
                <property name="Title" type="string">RSS Web Part</property>
                </properties>
                </data>
                </webPart>
                </webParts>
        ]]>
    </AllUsersWebPart>                       ❸  Web Parts
    <WebPartConnection                          connection
        ConsumerID="RSSWebPart"
        ProviderID="FeedInput"
        ConsumerConnectionPointID="feed"
        ProviderConnectionPointID=""
        ID="Connection"/>
</File>
```

The `File` element contains two `AllUsersWebPart` elements: the Feed Input Web Part ❶ and the RSS Web Part ❷. Both specify that the Web Parts are placed in the zone called `Main` using the `WebPartZoneID` attribute. The `WebPartOrder` element specifies the order of the Web Parts in the zone using an integer starting with 0. Both Web Parts are also given a unique ID. The inner value of the `AllUsersWebPart` element is a `CDATA` element used to specify the definition, the .webpart file contents, of the Web Parts. The first Web Part is the custom Web Part provider you built in chapter 14 and the second is the RSS Web Part from the same chapter. Both Web Parts have their `Title` specified in the `CDATA` element, and the RSS Web Part also has the `ItemCount` property defined.

> **NOTE** I use the fully qualified name of the Web Parts and its assemblies in this sample since they exist in another Visual Studio project. If the Web Parts exist in the same project as the page provisioning Module, then you should use the Visual Studio replaceable tokens instead of the fully qualified names.

The Web Parts are connected using the `WebPartConnection` element ❸. This element connects two Web Parts using the IDs specified in the `AllUsersWebPart` elements with the `ConsumerID` and `ProviderID` attributes. It's also necessary to specify the names of the connection endpoint for the consumer (using `ConsumerConnectionPointID` and `ProviderConnectionPointID`), because it has several endpoints. Finally, the connection needs an ID.

The dashboard is now ready to be deployed. This deployment works with the sandbox because the Web Parts used and connected are deployed using a farm solution. Press F5 to deploy and debug your solution. Then go to the Site Pages library and locate the dashboard under the Dashboard1 folder. Enter a URL in the Feed Input Web Part and see how the connected RSS Web Part is updated.

> **TIP** Microsoft recommends that a Web Part page not contain more than 25 Web Parts (open or closed) for performance reasons.

15.2.2 *Deploying using a Feature receiver*

Another option to deploy a dashboard with configured Web Parts is to use a Feature receiver and the `SPLimitedWebPartManager`. (You can't use this option in sandboxed solutions.) The benefit of this approach is that you can debug the provisioning of the dashboard, which isn't possible using the declarative approach. Another benefit of using a programmatic approach is that you can define the layout of the dashboard depending on the runtime state of the site.

To build this solution you can either create a new project that's deployed as farm solution or change the previous project from a sandboxed solution to a farm solution. The easiest way to change the old project is to select the project in the Solution Explorer, press F4, and toggle the value for Sandboxed Solution to False.

I'll show you how to create the same dashboard with the connected Web Part as in the previous section but this time using a Feature receiver. Start by adding a new Module to the project; give it the name `Dashboard2` and then add a Web Part page. Modify it as you did earlier so that it has one Web Part zone called `Main`. Update the elements.xml file so that your page is deployed into the Site Pages library and to a subfolder called `Dashboard2`, and that the name of the file is default.aspx. Once you've completed these steps, you need nothing more to the Module project item.

TIP When creating a dashboard in a solution that's deployed as fully trusted, you can create your own Web Part page implementation by overriding the `Microsoft.SharePoint.WebPartPages.WebPartPage` class. This allows you to add your custom code-behind to the Web Part page.

You add the Feature receiver that will do all the work in this scenario to the project by right-clicking on the Feature and selecting Add Event Receiver. When Visual Studio has added the necessary files and configuration, the event receiver file will be opened in Visual Studio. Uncomment the `FeatureActivated` method. It's in this method that you'll add the code shown in listing 15.3, which will populate the Web Part page with the Web Parts and connections. Before writing the code, add a reference to the project built in chapter 14 so that the Web Part classes can be used in this project.

Listing 15.3 Programmatically provisioning Web Parts on a page

```
public override void FeatureActivated(
    SPFeatureReceiverProperties properties) {
    SPWeb web = properties.Feature.Parent as SPWeb;                          // Get file ❶
    if (web != null) {
        SPFile file = web.GetFile("SitePages/Dashboard2/default.aspx");
        using (SP.SPLimitedWebPartManager wpMgr =
            file.GetLimitedWebPartManager(PersonalizationScope.Shared)) {    // Get limited ❷
                                                                             // Web Part Manager
            wpMgr.WebParts.Cast<WebPart>().ToList()
                .ForEach(wp => wpMgr.DeleteWebPart(wp));

            RssWebPart rssWebPart = new RssWebPart {
                ID = "RssWebPart",
                Title = "RSS Reader",
                ItemCount = 5
            };
            FeedInputWebPart feedInput = new FeedInputWebPart {
                ID = "FeedInput",
                Title = "Feed input"
            };
            wpMgr.AddWebPart(feedInput, "Main", 0);
            wpMgr.AddWebPart(rssWebPart, "Main", 1);                         // Connect ❸ Web Parts

            SP.SPWebPartConnection connection =
                new SP.SPWebPartConnection {
                ConsumerID = "RssWebPart",
                ProviderID = "FeedInput",
                ConsumerConnectionPointID = "feed",
                ProviderConnectionPointID = "",
                ID = "connection"
            };
            wpMgr.SPWebPartConnections.Add(connection);

            wpMgr.SaveChanges(rssWebPart);                                   // Save Web ❹ Parts
            wpMgr.SaveChanges(feedInput);
        }
    }
}
```

The code in the Feature receiver retrieves the current site (SPWeb) and the file using the path ❶. The namespace alias SP is used for `Microsoft.SharePoint.WebPart-Pages` to avoid conflicting `WebPart` definitions. Using the file object (SPFile), the current `SPLimitedWebPartManager` object is retrieved ❷. Note that the use of the `SPLimitedWebPartManager` is scoped in a `using` statement so that it's safely disposed at the end of the call. To make sure that Web Parts aren't added many times to the page if the Feature is repeatedly activated, all Web Parts are removed from the page, using the LINQ statement. Once that's done, the RSS Web Part is created and initialized. The same is done for the Feed Input Web Part. When the objects are created, they're added to the zone on the page using the `SPLimitedWebPartManager` method `AddWebPart`. This method takes the Web Part, the name of the zone, and the position as arguments. Next up is to connect the Web Parts; this is done using a `SPWebPartConnection` object ❸. This object works similarly to the `WebPartConnection` element in the previous sample. It needs the IDs of the provider and the consumer as well as the names of the connection endpoints and an ID of the connection itself. This connection object is added to the collection of connections in the Web Part Manager. The last thing that's needed to complete the dashboard is to save the Web Parts using the `SaveChanges` method of the `SPLimitedWebPartManager` ❹.

When you deploy this project solution, it will look like and work exactly the same as the previous dashboard, defined using the declarative method. The benefit of this approach is that you can debug the provisioning and add Web Parts and connections dynamically. And the downsides are that you need to reference the assemblies where the Web Parts are defined and you can't deploy the solution into the sandbox.

15.2.3 Static dashboards

The two dashboards you've created are built as Web Part pages that users can further customize or personalize. In some cases you might prefer to deploy a static dashboard or page with connected Web Parts. Web Parts can be connected when they're static, but a static Web Part can't be connected to a dynamic Web Part. To create a static dashboard you basically have two options: lock down the Web Part zones of a dashboard page or deploy all Web Parts and connections as static.

To lock down a Web Part zone for editing, you can use the Web Part zone attributes specified in table 15.1. The following Web Part zone would prohibit users from adding new Web Parts, personalizing the Web Parts, and making layout changes:

```
<WebPartPages:WebPartZone
    runat="server"
    FrameType="TitleBarOnly"
    ID="Main"
    Title="loc:Main"
    LayoutOrientation="Vertical"
    AllowPersonalization="False"
    AllowLayoutChange="False"/>
```

The `AllowPersonalization` and `AllowLayoutChange` attributes are both set to `False` to prohibit users from personalizing and editing the layout of the Web Part zone. In this example, the `AllowCustomization` property is not set to `False`, which would've been appropriate in this case. The reason this attribute isn't used is that when Share-Point loads the page for the first time it needs to store the values of the Web Parts into the database; if `AllowCustomization` is set to `False` this can't be done and you'll receive an exception. If you need to set `AllowCustomization` to `False`, you can edit the page in SharePoint Designer and customize it, which will save the contents to the database.

The other way to create a static dashboard is to not use Web Part zones and add the Web Parts directly to the page. Web Parts are essentially ASP.NET web controls and can be added to any page. When Web Parts are added out of a zone, they're called static and can't be modified or customized by users. But users with appropriate permissions can still use SharePoint Designer to modify the page.

Instead of adding the Web Parts to the element manifest, you add the Web Parts to the page that's provisioned through the Module. First, add the page directives to register tag prefixes for the Web Parts:

```
<%@ Register
    Tagprefix="RSS"
    Namespace="WebPartsInAction.Ch14.Connections.RssWebPart"
    Assembly="WebPartsInAction.Ch14.Connections, Version=1.0.0.0,
➥   Culture=neutral, PublicKeyToken=8b0f149932984439" %>
<%@ Register
    Tagprefix="FI"
    Namespace="WebPartsInAction.Ch14.Connections.FeedInputWebPart"
    Assembly="WebPartsInAction.Ch14.Connections, Version=1.0.0.0,
➥   Culture=neutral, PublicKeyToken=8b0f149932984439" %>
```

These directives register the two tag prefixes RSS and FI and the corresponding namespaces and assemblies for the two Web Parts. Using the tag prefixes, you can add the Web Parts directly to the ASPX page:

```
<FI:FeedInputWebPart
    runat="server"
    id="FIWP"/>
<RSS:RssWebPart
    runat="server"
    id="RSSWP"
    ItemCount="10"/>
```

This code will add the Feed Input Web Part and the RSS Web Part to the page and configure the RSS Web Part to retrieve 10 items from its feed. The Web Parts can't be connected as you did before using the `WebPartConnection` element in the declarative dashboards using the `SPLimitedWebPartManager` in the event receiver. In this case the `SPWebPartManager` control, defined in the master page, must be used, but achieving this would require code to connect them during runtime. Fortunately there's a proxy control, called `SPProxyWebPartManager` (this control can't be used in the sandbox), that the Web Part Manager uses to handle static connections. To create the static connection between the Web Parts, use the following code:

```
<WebPartPages:SPProxyWebPartManager
    runat="server"
    id="ProxyWebPartManager">
    <SPWebPartConnections>
        <WebPartPages:SPWebPartConnection
            ID="connection"
            ConsumerConnectionPointID="feed"
            ConsumerID="RSSWP"
            ProviderConnectionPointID=""
            ProviderID="FIWP">
        </WebPartPages:SPWebPartConnection>
    </SPWebPartConnections>
</WebPartPages:SPProxyWebPartManager>
```

The `SPProxyWebPartManager` control contains a collection of `SPWebPartConnection` objects, the same kind of object used when adding connections to the `SPLimitedWebPartManager`. The connection consumer and provider and their endpoints are specified as before. Once the `SPProxyWebPartManager` code is added to the page, you can deploy it using a Module project item containing the ASPX file. When the page is used in Share-Point, users can't edit or customize the Web Parts. The approach of employing static Web Parts and connections can also be used when you're deploying an application page.

15.2.4 *Dashboards with a sandboxed Web Part*

So far you've learned how to build dashboards using fully trusted Web Parts, but what about a sandboxed dashboard with a sandboxed Web Part? Creating a sandboxed dashboard involves using a single sandboxed Web Part in a Web Part page. No connections are used here because sandboxed Web Parts can't be connected using ASP.NET 2.0 connections.

> **NOTE** For sandboxed Web Part pages you need to use the `WebPartPage` class. You can't create custom code-behind classes for pages in the sandbox.

Just as with previous dashboards, the solution should consist of a Module project item that contains a Web Part page. If you added the Sandboxed Web Part to the `AllUsersWebPart` element specifying the type and assembly, SharePoint would throw an exception like this:

```
Web Part Error: Cannot import this Web Part.
```

This exception is thrown because the dashboard tries to reference a fully trusted Web Part with that name, and the Web Part specified only exists in the sandbox. To resolve this issue, you need to make a little modification to the Web Part control description in the `AllUsersWebPart` element. First, go to the Web Part Gallery, select to edit the sandboxed Web Part, and then click the View XML button in the Ribbon. Finally, save the XML file. Open the file and notice that a new element called `Solution` has been added as a child element to the `metaData` element, like this:

```
<Solution
    SolutionId="242e1187-5478-4ccc-9358-dff4d1188d56"
    xmlns="http://schemas.microsoft.com/sharepoint/" />
```

This element specifies that this Web Part belongs to a solution in the Solution Gallery of the site collection—that is, a sandboxed Web Part. The value in the `SolutionId` attribute is the ID of the Solution Package. By adding this to the Web Part definition in the `AllUsersWebPart`, you can successfully deploy the dashboard. You can also find this ID from the properties of the Package Editor. The `AllUsersWebPart` should look like this after you add the `Solution` element:

```
<AllUsersWebPart WebPartZoneID="Body" WebPartOrder="0" ID="SandboxedWP">
<![CDATA[
    <webParts>
    <webPart xmlns="http://schemas.microsoft.com/WebPart/v3">
    <metaData>
    <type name="WebPartsInAction.Ch15.SBDashboard.          ❶ Replaceable
                SandboxedWebPart.SandboxedWebPart,              parameter for
                $SharePoint.Project.AssemblyFullName$" />       assembly name
    <importErrorMessage>$Resources:core,ImportErrorMessage;
    </importErrorMessage>
    <Solution                                        ❷ Replaceable parameter
        SolutionId="$SharePoint.Package.Id$"              for solution ID
        xmlns="http://schemas.microsoft.com/sharepoint/" />
    </metaData>
    <data>
    <properties>
    <property name="Title" type="string">SandboxedWebPart</property>
    <property name="Description" type="string">My WebPart</property>
    </properties>
    </data>
    </webPart>
    </webParts>
]]>
</AllUsersWebPart>
```

The definition of the `AllUsersWebPart` element looks the same as for the fully trusted dashboards, with the difference that the `Solution` element is added to the Web Part control description. Visual Studio replaceable parameters are used for the assembly in the `type` element ❶ and for the solution ID in the `Solution` element ❷ to avoid manually entering them.

When this dashboard is deployed, it'll show the sandboxed Web Part and users can modify it. You can mix sandboxed and already deployed fully trusted Web Parts in your sandboxed dashboards.

To create a static sandboxed dashboard, you need to use another approach. The Web Part must be wrapped in a special Web Part called `SPUserCodeWebPart`. The `SPUserCodeWebPart` is a fully trusted Web Part that acts as a proxy for a sandboxed Web Part and serializes information to and from SharePoint to the sandbox. The user code Web Part looks like this when placed directly on an ASPX page:

```
<WebPartPages:SPUserCodeWebPart
    ID="SandboxWP"
    runat="server"
    Title="Sandboxed WebPart"
```

```
AssemblyFullName="$SharePoint.Project.AssemblyFullName$"
SolutionId="$SharePoint.Package.Id$"
TypeFullName="WebPartsInAction.Ch15.SBDashboard.
        SandboxedWebPart.SandboxedWebPart" />
```

The `SPUserCodeWebPart` has three properties used to locate the wrapped sandboxed Web Part. `SolutionId` identifies the solution, and `TypeFullName` and `AssemblyName` identify the Web Part.

15.2.5 *Deploying using a site definition*

If you're building reusable portals and sites, you've probably been creating, or at least looked at, site definitions. Site definitions are the basis for all sites in SharePoint, and they serve as a template for the sites. They contain, for example, the default activated features and one or more modules that are provisioned when a site is built on a site definition. In SharePoint 2010 the concept of Web Templates are introduced. Web Templates are quite similar to Site Definitions but offer more flexibility and sandbox support. Web Templates should be considered before Site Definitions because they're supported in SharePoint Online, and Site Definitions aren't.

The topic of building site definitions could fill a few chapters on its own and there are many opinions on how and when to use them. For our purposes here, it's important to know that you can provision dashboards directly in a site definition using one of the following options:

- Deploy the dashboard as a module in the site definition
- Deploy the dashboard as a feature in the site definition
- Deploy the dashboard feature to the sites using the site definition with feature stapling
- Use a provisioning provider as a part of a site definition

Let's take a look at the options starting at the top. The first option is to use a Module in the onet.xml file of the site definition. This is exactly the same procedure I've shown you a few times in this chapter. For the `File` elements in the `Module` elements, you add `AllUsersWebPart` elements that contain the Web Parts you want to provision. An easy and fast solution! The downside relates to the nature of site definitions; once the site definition is deployed and in use, modifying the site definition is no longer supported. So this approach doesn't fit very well into an agile development methodology. For Web Templates, this option is not available.

The second alternative is slightly better. Instead of adding the Web Parts directly to the site definition onet.xml file, you create a Feature containing a dashboard and reference that Feature from the onet.xml file. For a web-scoped Feature the code could look like this:

```
<WebFeatures>
    <Feature ID="2c2fd31b-d7c1-4e19-8981-8595f4da781d"/>
</WebFeatures>
```

When a site based on this site definition is provisioned, it'll automatically activate the feature with the ID specified in the Feature element. Using this approach allows you to update the dashboard Feature in a supported way. This option is also valid for Web Templates. But what if you want to add your dashboard to an already existing site definition, perhaps one of the out-of-the-box site definitions? I've already told you that you aren't allowed to modify existing site definitions. But then, you can take advantage of something called *feature stapling*.

Feature stapling is a way to add Features to an already existing site definition or Web Template. This is done by creating a specific stapler Feature that contains information about which Feature to staple onto which site definition. To create a stapler Feature, you need to create a new Feature that's scoped at the farm level and then add an element manifest containing FeatureSiteTemplateAssociation elements:

```
<Elements xmlns="http://schemas.microsoft.com/sharepoint/">
    <FeatureSiteTemplateAssociation
        Id="2c2fd31b-d7c1-4e19-8981-8595f4da781d"
        TemplateName="STS#0"/>
    <FeatureSiteTemplateAssociation
        Id="2c2fd31b-d7c1-4e19-8981-8595f4da781d"
        TemplateName="DashboardSiteDefinition#0"/>
</Elements>
```

The Feature containing this element manifest would staple the Feature with the specified Id onto the default SharePoint Team Site (STS#0) and to a custom site definition called DashboardSiteDefinition with configuration 0. For all new sites created with any of those site definitions, the specified Feature would automatically be activated. Sites that are already created won't benefit from the Feature stapling and the Feature must be activated manually or through code.

The final option, using a provisioning provider, allows you to programmatically add Web Parts and perform other logic operations in code that's executed after the site is fully provisioned. Provisioning providers are only available for Site Definitions in SharePoint Server and are a part of the publishing infrastructure. A provisioning provider is a class derived from the SPWebProvisioningProvider class, and it's specified in the site definition using the ProvisioningClass and ProvisioningAssembly. The same rules apply here; you can't change the site definition once it's in use but you can update the provisioning provider.

15.3 *Summary*

This was the final chapter of this book and I hope you enjoyed the ride as much as I have. Even though this chapter didn't mention all the amazing things that can be done using Web Parts, it showed you how to combine several of the Web Part techniques to build a complete solution. Providing your end users with prebuilt dashboards is one thing that can greatly enhance the SharePoint experience and make users feel more comfortable with it if they aren't used to the technology.

By now you should be thinking that you know everything about Web Parts. If you read and understand this book you know a great deal, but not everything. SharePoint is such a complex and amazing product and there are very few folks around the world who know every detail about it. I've intentionally left a few things out because they're either seldom used or too specific for this book. Perhaps I'll find more time and space to write about them in the future!

appendix
Out-of-the-box Web
Parts in SharePoint 2010

This appendix lists details of the out-of-the-box Web Parts in SharePoint 2010. The Web Parts are divided into three main stock-keeping units (SKUs): SharePoint Foundation 2010, SharePoint Server 2010 Standard, and SharePoint Server 2010 Enterprise.

Each Web Part has the following information:

- Title
- Description
- Assembly—Identifies in which assembly the Web Part is defined.
- Class—Shows the full name of the Web Part class.
- Web Part Type—Indicates which base Web Part Type the Web Part is derived from: SharePoint or ASP.NET.
- Group—Shows the group that the Web Part is added to in the Web Part Gallery, if applicable.
- Filename—Shows the name of the Web Part control description file (.dwp or .webpart) in the Web Part Gallery.
- Sealed—Indicates whether or not the Web Part is sealed.
- Feature—Provides the name of the Feature where the Web Part is added to the gallery, if applicable. The actual .webpart/.dwp file might exist in a different feature that's activated using dependencies.
- Provider Connections—Lists the connection provider interfaces of the Web Part.
- Consumer Connections—Lists the connection consumer interfaces of the Web Part.

There are literally hundreds more Web Parts in SharePoint than listed here. Web Parts not listed either aren't intended for custom use or aren't available to users from the user interface.

NOTE All titles and groups are written as called in the English language pack of SharePoint.

A.1   *SharePoint Foundation 2010 Web Parts*

These Web Parts are available in SharePoint Foundation.

Content Editor	
Allows the author to enter rich text content	
Assembly	Microsoft.SharePoint
Class	Microsoft.SharePoint.WebPartPages.ContentEditorWebPart
Web Part Type	SharePoint
Group	Media and Content
Filename	MSContentEditor.dwp
Sealed	Yes
Feature	Basic Web Parts
Provider Connections	n/a
Consumer Connections	n/a

Data Form Web Part (DFWP)	
An XSLT-based Web Part that receives data from a DataSourceControl control	
Assembly	Microsoft.SharePoint
Class	Microsoft.SharePoint.WebPartPages.DataFormWebPart
Web Part Type	SharePoint
Group	n/a
Filename	n/a
Sealed	No
Feature	n/a
Provider Connections	IWebPartRow
Consumer Connections	IWebPartParameters

Data View Web Part (DVWP)	
Used by Microsoft Office FrontPage 2003 for data retrieval and presentation	
Assembly	Microsoft.SharePoint

Class	Microsoft.SharePoint.WebPartPages.DataViewWebPart
Web Part Type	SharePoint
Group	n/a
Filename	n/a
Sealed	Yes
Feature	n/a
Provider Connections	IRowProvider
Consumer Connections	IFilterConsumer

HTML Form Web Part

Can be used by authors to create simple forms

Assembly	Microsoft.SharePoint
Class	Microsoft.SharePoint.WebPartPages.SimpleFormWebPart
Web Part Type	SharePoint
Group	Forms
Filename	MSSimpleForm.dwp
Sealed	Yes
Feature	Basic Web Parts
Provider Connections	IRowProvider
Consumer Connections	n/a

Image Viewer

Allows the author to add an image to a page

Assembly	Microsoft.SharePoint
Class	Microsoft.SharePoint.WebPartPages.ImageWebPart
Web Part Type	SharePoint
Group	Media and Content
Filename	MSImage.dwp
Sealed	Yes
Feature	Basic Web Parts
Provider Connections	n/a
Consumer Connections	ICellConsumer

List View Web Part (LVWP)

Renders a SharePoint list in a Web Part—obsolete; use the new XSLT List View Web Part instead.

Assembly	`Microsoft.SharePoint`
Class	`Microsoft.SharePoint.WebPartPages.ListViewWebPart`
Web Part Type	SharePoint
Group	n/a
Filename	n/a
Sealed	Yes
Feature	n/a
Provider Connections	n/a
Consumer Connections	n/a

Page Viewer

Displays another web page on the page where this Web Part is added through an IFrame

Assembly	`Microsoft.SharePoint`
Class	`Microsoft.SharePoint.WebPartPages.PageViewerWebPart`
Web Part Type	SharePoint
Group	Media and Content
Filename	MSPageViewer.dwp
Sealed	Yes
Feature	Basic Web Parts
Provider Connections	n/a
Consumer Connections	n/a

Picture Library Slideshow Web Part

Shows a slide show of images from a Picture Gallery

Assembly	`Microsoft.SharePoint`
Class	`Microsoft.SharePoint.WebPartPages.PictureLibrarySlideshowWebPart`
Web Part Type	SharePoint
Group	Media and Content
Filename	MSPictureLibrarySlideshow.webpart
Sealed	Yes
Feature	Basic Web Parts

Provider Connections	n/a
Consumer Connections	n/a

Relevant Documents

Shows documents relevant to the current user

Assembly	`Microsoft.SharePoint`
Class	`Microsoft.SharePoint.WebPartPages.UserDocsWebPart`
Web Part Type	SharePoint
Group	Content Rollup
Filename	MSUserDocs.dwp
Sealed	Yes
Feature	Basic Web Parts
Provider Connections	n/a
Consumer Connections	n/a

Silverlight Web Part

Allows the author to add a Silverlight application to SharePoint

Assembly	`Microsoft.SharePoint`
Class	`Microsoft.SharePoint.WebPartPages.SilverlightWebPart`
Web Part Type	ASP.NET
Group	Media and Content
Filename	Silverlight.webpart
Sealed	Yes
Feature	Basic Web Parts
Provider Connections	n/a
Consumer Connections	n/a

Site Users

Shows a list of users and/or groups as well as online status

Assembly	`Microsoft.SharePoint`
Class	`Microsoft.SharePoint.WebPartPages.MembersWebPart`
Web Part Type	SharePoint
Group	Social Collaboration
Filename	MSMembers.dwp
Sealed	Yes

Feature	Basic Web Parts
Provider Connections	n/a
Consumer Connections	n/a

User Tasks

Shows tasks assigned to the user

Assembly	`Microsoft.SharePoint`
Class	`Microsoft.SharePoint.WebPartPages.UserTasksWebPart`
Web Part Type	SharePoint
Group	Social Collaboration
Filename	MSUserTasks.dwp
Sealed	Yes
Feature	Basic Web Parts
Provider Connections	n/a
Consumer Connections	n/a

XML Viewer

Transforms XML data using XSL and shows the results

Assembly	`Microsoft.SharePoint`
Class	`Microsoft.SharePoint.WebPartPages.XmlWebPart`
Web Part Type	SharePoint
Group	Content Rollup
Filename	MSXml.dwp
Sealed	Yes
Feature	Basic Web Parts
Provider Connections	n/a
Consumer Connections	n/a

XSLT List View Web Part (XLV)

XSLT-based Web Part that renders default lists such as document libraries; highly customizable

Assembly	`Microsoft.SharePoint`
Class	`Microsoft.SharePoint.WebPartPages.XsltListViewWebPart`
Web Part Type	SharePoint
Group	n/a
Filename	n/a

Sealed	Yes
Feature	n/a
Provider Connections	`IWebPartTable, IWebPartRow`
Consumer Connections	`IWebPartParameters`

A.2 *SharePoint 2010 Server Standard Web Parts*

These Web Parts are available in SharePoint 2010 Server Standard.

Advanced Search Box

The advanced search box that allows the user to parameterize their search options based on properties and word combinations

Assembly	`Microsoft.Office.Server.Search`
Class	`Microsoft.Office.Server.Search.WebControls.Advanced-SearchBox`
Web Part Type	SharePoint
Group	Search
Filename	AdvancedSearchBox.dwp
Sealed	Yes
Feature	SharePoint Server Standard Site Collection features, SharePoint Server Enterprise Site Collection Features, Search Server Web Parts
Provider Connections	n/a
Consumer Connections	n/a

Categories

Displays categories from Site Directory

Assembly	`Microsoft.SharePoint.Portal`
Class	`Microsoft.SharePoint.Portal.WebControls.CategoryWebPart`
Web Part Type	SharePoint
Group	Content Rollup
Filename	CategoryWebPart.dwp
Sealed	Yes
Feature	SharePoint Server Standard Site Collection features, SharePoint Server Enterprise Site Collection Features
Provider Connections	`IWebPartRow`
Consumer Connections	`IWebPartParameters`

Contact Details

Displays Visual Best Bet

Assembly	`Microsoft.SharePoint.Portal`
Class	`Microsoft.SharePoint.Portal.WebControls.ContactField-Control`
Web Part Type	SharePoint
Group	Social Collaboration
Filename	contactwp.dwp
Sealed	No
Feature	Portal Layouts Feature
Provider Connections	n/a
Consumer Connections	n/a

Content Query (CQWP)

Displays a dynamic view of content within a site collection

Assembly	`Microsoft.SharePoint.Publishing`
Class	`Microsoft.SharePoint.Publishing.WebControls.Content-ByQueryWebPart`
Web Part Type	SharePoint
Group	Content Rollup
Filename	ContentQuery.dwp
Sealed	No
Feature	SharePoint Server Publishing Infrastructure
Provider Connections	`IWebPartRow`
Consumer Connections	`IWebPartParameters`

Dual Chinese Search

Used to search Dual Chinese document and items at the same time

Assembly	`Microsoft.Office.Server.Search`
Class	`Microsoft.Office.Server.Search.WebControls.DualChinese-Webpart`
Web Part Type	SharePoint
Group	Search
Filename	DualChineseSearch.dwp
Sealed	No

Feature	SharePoint Server Standard Site Collection features, SharePoint Server Enterprise Site Collection Features, Search Server Web Parts
Provider Connections	n/a
Consumer Connections	n/a

Federated Results

Displays search results from a federated search

Assembly	`Microsoft.Office.Server.Search`
Class	`Microsoft.Office.Server.Search.WebControls.Federated-ResultsWebPart`
Web Part Type	SharePoint
Group	Search
Filename	SummaryResults.dwp
Sealed	No
Feature	Search Server Web Parts
Provider Connections	`IWebPartRow`
Consumer Connections	`IWebPartParameters`

Find By Document Id

Finds a document by specifying a document ID

Assembly	`Microsoft.Office.DocumentManagement`
Class	`Microsoft.Office.Server.WebControls.DocIDSearchWebPart`
Web Part Type	SharePoint
Group	Search
Filename	DocIDSearchWebPart.dwp
Sealed	No
Feature	Document ID Service
Provider Connections	n/a
Consumer Connections	n/a

Media Web Part

Used to embed media clips (video and audio) in a page

Assembly	`Microsoft.SharePoint.Publishing`
Class	`Microsoft.SharePoint.Publishing.WebControls.MediaWeb-Part`
Web Part Type	ASP.NET

Group	Media and Content
Filename	media.webpart
Sealed	Yes
Feature	SharePoint Server Publishing Infrastructure
Provider Connections	n/a
Consumer Connections	n/a

My Calendar

Displays your calendar using Outlook Web Access (Microsoft Exchange Server 2000 or later)

Assembly	`Microsoft.SharePoint.Portal`
Class	`Microsoft.SharePoint.Portal.WebControls.OWACalendar-Part`
Web Part Type	SharePoint
Group	Outlook Web App
Filename	Owacalendar.dwp
Sealed	No
Feature	SharePoint Server Standard Site Collection features, SharePoint Server Enterprise Site Collection Features, My Site Layouts Feature (hidden, stapled on My Site site definitions)
Provider Connections	n/a
Consumer Connections	n/a

My Contacts

Displays your contacts using Outlook Web Access (Microsoft Exchange Server 2000 or later)

Assembly	`Microsoft.SharePoint.Portal`
Class	`Microsoft.SharePoint.Portal.WebControls.OWAContacts-Part`
Web Part Type	SharePoint
Group	Outlook Web App
Filename	Owacontacts.dwp
Sealed	No
Feature	SharePoint Server Standard Site Collection features, SharePoint Server Enterprise Site Collection Features, My Site Layouts Feature (hidden, stapled on My Site site definitions)
Provider Connections	n/a
Consumer Connections	n/a

My Inbox

Displays your Inbox using Outlook Web Access (Microsoft Exchange Server 2000 or later)

Assembly	`Microsoft.SharePoint.Portal`
Class	`Microsoft.SharePoint.Portal.WebControls.OWAInboxPart`
Web Part Type	SharePoint
Group	Outlook Web App
Filename	owainbox.dwp
Sealed	No
Feature	SharePoint Server Standard Site Collection features, SharePoint Server Enterprise Site Collection Features, My Site Layouts Feature (hidden, stapled on My Site site definitions)
Provider Connections	n/a
Consumer Connections	n/a

My Mail Folder

Displays your mail folder using Outlook Web Access (Microsoft Exchange Server 2000 or later)

Assembly	`Microsoft.SharePoint.Portal`
Class	`Microsoft.SharePoint.Portal.WebControls.OWAPart`
Web Part Type	SharePoint
Group	Outlook Web App
Filename	Owa.dwp
Sealed	No
Feature	SharePoint Server Standard Site Collection features, SharePoint Server Enterprise Site Collection Features, My Site Layouts Feature (hidden, stapled on My Site site definitions)
Provider Connections	n/a
Consumer Connections	n/a

My Tasks

Displays your tasks using Outlook Web Access (Microsoft Exchange Server 2000 or later)

Assembly	`Microsoft.SharePoint.Portal`
Class	`Microsoft.SharePoint.Portal.WebControls.OWATasksPart`
Web Part Type	SharePoint
Group	Outlook Web App
Filename	owatasks.dwp

Sealed	No
Feature	SharePoint Server Standard Site Collection features, SharePoint Server Enterprise Site Collection Features, My Site Layouts Feature (hidden, stapled on My Site site definitions)
Provider Connections	n/a
Consumer Connections	n/a

Note Board

Enables users to comment publicly on a page

Assembly	`Microsoft.SharePoint.Portal`
Class	`Microsoft.SharePoint.Portal.WebControls.SocialComment WebPart`
Web Part Type	SharePoint
Group	Social Collaboration
Filename	SocialComment.dwp
Sealed	Yes
Feature	My Site Layouts Feature (hidden, stapled on My Site site definitions)
Provider Connections	n/a
Consumer Connections	n/a

Organization Browser

Shows an interactive view of each user in the reporting chain of the organization

Assembly	`Microsoft.SharePoint.Portal`
Class	`Microsoft.SharePoint.Portal.WebControls.ProfileBrowser`
Web Part Type	SharePoint
Group	Social Collaboration
Filename	ProfileBrowser.dwp
Sealed	No
Feature	SharePoint Server Standard Site Collection features, SharePoint Server Enterprise Site Collection Features, My Site Layouts Feature (hidden, stapled on My Site site definitions)
Provider Connections	n/a
Consumer Connections	n/a

People Refinement Panel

Used to help users refine the people search results

Assembly	`Microsoft.Office.Server.Search`

Class	Microsoft.Office.Server.Search.WebControls.People-RefinementWebPart
Web Part Type	SharePoint
Group	Search
Filename	PeopleRefinement.webpart
Sealed	No
Feature	SharePoint Server Standard Site Collection features, SharePoint Server Enterprise Site Collection Features, Search Server Web Parts
Provider Connections	IWebPartRow
Consumer Connections	IWebPartParameters

People Search Box

A search box that allows users to search for people

Assembly	Microsoft.SharePoint.Portal
Class	Microsoft.SharePoint.Portal.WebControls.PeopleSearch-BoxEx
Web Part Type	SharePoint
Group	Search
Filename	PeopleSearchBox.webpart
Sealed	No
Feature	SharePoint Server Standard Site Collection features, SharePoint Server Enterprise Site Collection Features, Search Server Web Parts
Provider Connections	n/a
Consumer Connections	n/a

People Search Core Results

Displays the results of a people search

Assembly	Microsoft.Office.Server.Search
Class	Microsoft.Office.Server.Search.WebControls.PeopleCore-ResultsWebPart
Web Part Type	SharePoint
Group	Search
Filename	PeopleSearchCoreResults.webpart
Sealed	Yes
Feature	SharePoint Server Standard Site Collection features, SharePoint Server Enterprise Site Collection Features, Search Server Web Parts

Provider Connections	IWebPartRow
Consumer Connections	IWebPartParameters

Query Suggestions

Displays related queries to a user query

Assembly	Microsoft.Office.Server.Search
Class	Microsoft.Office.Server.Search.WebControls.Query-SuggestionsWebPart
Web Part Type	SharePoint
Group	Search
Filename	QuerySuggestions.webpart
Sealed	No
Feature	SharePoint Server Standard Site Collection features, SharePoint Server Enterprise Site Collection Features, Search Server Web Parts
Provider Connections	IWebPartRow
Consumer Connections	IWebPartParameters

Refinement Panel

Allows users to refine their search result

Assembly	Microsoft.Office.Server.Search
Class	Microsoft.Office.Server.Search.WebControls.Refinement-WebPart
Web Part Type	SharePoint
Group	Search
Filename	Refinement.webpart
Sealed	No
Feature	SharePoint Server Standard Site Collection features, SharePoint Server Enterprise Site Collection Features, Search Server Web Parts
Provider Connections	IWebPartRow
Consumer Connections	IWebPartParameters

RSS Viewer

Displays an RSS feed

Assembly	Microsoft.SharePoint.Portal
Class	Microsoft.SharePoint.Portal.WebControls.RSSAggregator-WebPart
Web Part Type	SharePoint

Group	Content Rollup
Filename	RssViewer.dwp
Sealed	No
Feature	SharePoint Server Standard Site Collection features, SharePoint Server Enterprise Site Collection Features, My Site Layouts Feature (hidden, stapled on My Site site definitions)
Provider Connections	IWebPartRow
Consumer Connections	IWebPartParameters

Site Aggregator

Displays the contents (documents and tasks) of sites

Assembly	Microsoft.SharePoint.Portal
Class	Microsoft.SharePoint.Portal.WebControls.SiteDocuments
Web Part Type	SharePoint
Group	Content Rollup
Filename	siteFramer.dwp
Sealed	No
Feature	My Site Layouts Feature (hidden, stapled on My Site site definitions)
Provider Connections	n/a
Consumer Connections	n/a

Sites in Category

Displays sites from the Site Directory within a specific category

Assembly	Microsoft.SharePoint.Portal
Class	Microsoft.SharePoint.Portal.WebControls.Category-ResultsWebPart
Web Part Type	SharePoint
Group	Content Rollup
Filename	CategoryResultsWebPart.dwp
Sealed	Yes
Feature	SharePoint Server Standard Site Collection features, SharePoint Server Enterprise Site Collection Features
Provider Connections	IWebPartRow
Consumer Connections	IWebPartParameters

Search Action Links

Displays the search action links on the search results page

Assembly	`Microsoft.Office.Server.Search`
Class	`Microsoft.Office.Server.Search.WebControls.Core-ResultsWebPart`
Web Part Type	SharePoint
Group	Search
Filename	SearchActionLinks.webpart
Sealed	No
Feature	SharePoint Server Standard Site Collection features, SharePoint Server Enterprise Site Collection Features, Search Server Web Parts
Provider Connections	`IWebPartRow`
Consumer Connections	`IWebPartParameters`

Search Best Bets

Displays high-confidence results on a search results page

Assembly	`Microsoft.Office.Server.Search`
Class	`Microsoft.Office.Server.Search.WebControls.High-ConfidenceWebPart`
Web Part Type	SharePoint
Group	Search
Filename	SearchBestBets.webpart
Sealed	Yes
Feature	SharePoint Server Standard Site Collection features, SharePoint Server Enterprise Site Collection Features, Search Server Web Parts
Provider Connections	`IWebPartRow`
Consumer Connections	`IWebPartParameters`

Search Box

Displays a search box that allows users to search for information

Assembly	`Microsoft.Office.Server.Search`
Class	`Microsoft.Office.Server.Search.WebControls.SearchBoxEx`
Web Part Type	SharePoint
Group	Search
Filename	SearchBox.dwp

Sealed	No
Feature	SharePoint Server Standard Site Collection features, SharePoint Server Enterprise Site Collection Features, Search Server Web Parts
Provider Connections	n/a
Consumer Connections	n/a

Search Core Results

Displays the search result

Assembly	`Microsoft.Office.Server.Search`
Class	`Microsoft.Office.Server.Search.WebControls.Core-ResultsWebPart`
Web Part Type	SharePoint
Group	Search
Filename	SearchCoreResults.webpart
Sealed	No
Feature	SharePoint Server Standard Site Collection features, SharePoint Server Enterprise Site Collection Features, Search Server Web Parts
Provider Connections	`IWebPartRow`
Consumer Connections	`IWebPartParameters`

Search Paging

Displays links for navigating pages within the search results

Assembly	`Microsoft.Office.Server.Search`
Class	`Microsoft.Office.Server.Search.WebControls.Search-PagingWebPart`
Web Part Type	SharePoint
Group	Search
Filename	SearchPaging.dwp
Sealed	Yes
Feature	SharePoint Server Standard Site Collection features, SharePoint Server Enterprise Site Collection Features, Search Server Web Parts
Provider Connections	n/a
Consumer Connections	n/a

Search Statistics

Displays the search statistics for a search such as the time taken to perform the search

Assembly	`Microsoft.Office.Server.Search`

Class	Microsoft.Office.Server.Search.WebControls.Search-StatsWebPart
Web Part Type	SharePoint
Group	Search
Filename	SearchStats.dwp
Sealed	Yes
Feature	SharePoint Server Standard Site Collection features, SharePoint Server Enterprise Site Collection Features, Search Server Web Parts
Provider Connections	n/a
Consumer Connections	n/a

Search Summary

Displays suggestions for current search query

Assembly	Microsoft.Office.Server.Search
Class	Microsoft.Office.Server.Search.WebControls.Search-SummaryWebPart
Web Part Type	SharePoint
Group	Search
Filename	SearchSummary.dwp
Sealed	Yes
Feature	SharePoint Server Standard Site Collection features, SharePoint Server Enterprise Site Collection Features, Search Server Web Parts
Provider Connections	n/a
Consumer Connections	n/a

SQL Server Reporting Services Report Viewer

Shows reports from SQL Server Reporting Services

Assembly	Microsoft.ReportingServices.SharePoint.UI.WebParts
Class	Microsoft.ReportingServices.SharePoint.UI.WebParts-.ReportViewerWebPart
Web Part Type	SharePoint
Group	Miscellaneous
Filename	ReportViewer.dwp
Sealed	No
Feature	Report Server Integration Feature

Provider Connections	n/a
Consumer Connections	IFilterValues, IWebPartRow

Summary Links

Allows authors to create links that can be grouped and styled

Assembly	Microsoft.SharePoint.Publishing
Class	Microsoft.SharePoint.Publishing.WebControls.Summary-LinkWebPart
Web Part Type	SharePoint
Group	Content Rollup
Filename	SummaryLink.dwp
Sealed	Yes
Feature	SharePoint Server Publishing Infrastructure
Provider Connections	IWebPartRow
Consumer Connections	IWebPartParameters

Table of Contents

Displays the navigation hierarchy of a site

Assembly	Microsoft.SharePoint.Publishing
Class	Microsoft.SharePoint.Publishing.WebControls.TableOf-ContentsWebPart
Web Part Type	SharePoint
Group	Content Rollup
Filename	TableOfContents.dwp
Sealed	No
Feature	SharePoint Server Publishing Infrastructure
Provider Connections	IWebPartRow
Consumer Connections	IWebPartParameters

Tag Cloud

Displays the most popular subjects tagged inside your organization as a configurable tag cloud

Assembly	Microsoft.SharePoint.Portal
Class	Microsoft.SharePoint.Portal.WebControls.TagCloudWeb-Part
Web Part Type	SharePoint
Group	Social Collaboration

Filename	TagCloud.dwp
Sealed	No
Feature	SharePoint Server Standard Site Collection features, SharePoint Server Enterprise Site Collection Features, My Site Layouts Feature (hidden, stapled on My Site site definitions)
Provider Connections	n/a
Consumer Connections	n/a

Top Federated Results

Displays the top federated result from a federated search

Assembly	`Microsoft.Office.Server.Search`
Class	`Microsoft.Office.Server.Search.WebControls.Top-FederatedResultsWebPart`
Web Part Type	SharePoint
Group	Search
Filename	TopAnswer.webpart
Sealed	No
Feature	SharePoint Server Standard Site Collection features, SharePoint Server Enterprise Site Collection Features, Search Server Web Parts
Provider Connections	`IWebPartRow`
Consumer Connections	`IWebPartParameter`

Web Analytics Web Part

Displays the most viewed content, most frequent search queries from a site, or most frequent search queries from search center

Assembly	`Microsoft.Office.Server.WebAnalytics.UI`
Class	`Microsoft.Office.Server.WebAnalytics.Reporting.Whats-PopularWebPart`
Web Part Type	SharePoint
Group	Content Rollup
Filename	TableOfContents.dwp
Sealed	No
Feature	SharePoint Server Publishing Infrastructure
Provider Connections	n/a
Consumer Connections	n/a

A.3   *SharePoint Server 2010 Enterprise Web Parts*

These Web Parts are available in SharePoint Server 2010 Enterprise edition.

Business Data Actions	
Displays a list of actions from Business Connectivity Services	
Assembly	`Microsoft.SharePoint.Portal`
Class	`Microsoft.SharePoint.Portal.WebControls.BusinessData-` `ActionsWebPart`
Web Part Type	SharePoint
Group	Business Data
Filename	BusinessDataActionsWebPart.dwp
Sealed	Yes
Feature	SharePoint Server Enterprise Site Collection Features
Provider Connections	n/a
Consumer Connections	`IEntityInstanceProvider`

Business Data Related List	
Displays a list of items related to one or more parent items from a data source in the Business Connectivity Services	
Assembly	`Microsoft.SharePoint.Portal`
Class	`Microsoft.SharePoint.Portal.WebControls.BusinessData-` `AssociationWebPart`
Web Part Type	SharePoint
Group	Business Data
Filename	BusinessDataAssociationWebPart.dwp
Sealed	Yes
Feature	SharePoint Server Enterprise Site Collection Features
Provider Connections	`IWebPartRow, IEntityInstanceProvider`
Consumer Connections	`IWebPartParameters, IEntityInstanceProvider`

Business Data Item	
Displays one item from a data source in Business Connectivity Services	
Assembly	`Microsoft.SharePoint.Portal`
Class	`Microsoft.SharePoint.Portal.WebControls.BusinessData-` `DetailsWebPart`
Web Part Type	SharePoint

Group	Business Data
Filename	BusinessDataDetailsWebPart.dwp
Sealed	Yes
Feature	SharePoint Server Enterprise Site Collection Features
Provider Connections	`IWebPartRow, IEntityInstanceProvider`
Consumer Connections	`IWebPartParameters, IEntityInstanceProvider`

Business Data Connectivity Filter

Filters the contents of Web Parts using a list of values from Business Connectivity Services

Assembly	`Microsoft.SharePoint.Portal`
Class	`Microsoft.SharePoint.Portal.WebControls.BusinessData-FilterWebPart`
Web Part Type	SharePoint
Group	Business Data
Filename	BusinessDataFilter.dwp
Sealed	Yes
Feature	SharePoint Server Enterprise Site Collection Features
Provider Connections	`IDefaultFilterValue, ITransformableFilterValues`
Consumer Connections	`IDefaultFilterValue`

Business Data List

Displays a list of items from a data source in Business Connectivity Services

Assembly	`Microsoft.SharePoint.Portal`
Class	`Microsoft.SharePoint.Portal.WebControls.BusinessData-ListWebPart`
Web Part Type	SharePoint
Group	Business Data
Filename	BusinessDataListWebPart.dwp
Sealed	No
Feature	SharePoint Server Enterprise Site Collection Features
Provider Connections	`IEntityInstanceProvider, IWebPartRow`
Consumer Connections	`IWebPartParameters`

Chart Web Part

Shows a visualization of data as a chart

Assembly	`Microsoft.Office.Server.Chart`

Class	`Microsoft.Office.Server.WebControls.ChartWebPart`
Web Part Type	ASP.NET
Group	Business Data
Filename	MossChartWebPart.webpart
Sealed	No
Feature	SharePoint Server Enterprise Site Collection Features
Provider Connections	`IWebPartTable`
Consumer Connections	n/a

Choice Filter

Filters the contents of Web Parts by using values entered by the page author

Assembly	`Microsoft.Office.Server.FilterControls`
Class	`Microsoft.SharePoint.Portal.WebControls.SPSlicer-ChoicesWebPart`
Web Part Type	SharePoint
Group	Filters
Filename	AuthoredListFilter.webpart
Sealed	Yes
Feature	SharePoint Server Enterprise Site Collection Features
Provider Connections	`ITransformableFilterValues, IDefaultFilterValue`
Consumer Connections	`IDefaultFilterValue`

Current User Filter

Filters the contents of Web Parts by using properties of the current user

Assembly	`Microsoft.Office.Server.FilterControls`
Class	`Microsoft.SharePoint.Portal.WebControls.UserContext-FilterWebPart`
Web Part Type	SharePoint
Group	Filters
Filename	UserContextFilter.webpart
Sealed	Yes
Feature	SharePoint Server Enterprise Site Collection Features
Provider Connections	`ITransformableFilterValues, IDefaultFilterValue`
Consumer Connections	n/a

Date Filter

Filters the contents of Web Parts by using a date entered by the user

Assembly	`Microsoft.Office.Server.FilterControls`
Class	`Microsoft.SharePoint.Portal.WebControls.DateFilter-` `WebPart`
Web Part Type	SharePoint
Group	Filters
Filename	DateFilter.webpart
Sealed	Yes
Feature	SharePoint Server Enterprise Site Collection Features
Provider Connections	`ITransformableFilterValues, IDefaultFilterValue`
Consumer Connections	n/a

Excel Web Access

Shows an Excel Services Workbook

Assembly	`Microsoft.Office.Excel.WebUI`
Class	`Microsoft.Office.Excel.WebUI.ExcelWebRenderer`
Web Part Type	SharePoint
Group	Business Data
Filename	Microsoft.Office.Excel.WebUI.dwp
Sealed	Yes
Feature	SharePoint Server Enterprise Site Collection Features
Provider Connections	n/a
Consumer Connections	`IFilterValues, IWebPartParameters, IWebPartField`

Filter Actions

Used to synchronize the display of the filter results when there are two or more filter Web Parts on the same content page

Assembly	`Microsoft.Office.Server.FilterControls`
Class	`Microsoft.SharePoint.Portal.WebControls.ApplyFilters-` `WebPart`
Web Part Type	SharePoint
Group	Filters
Filename	FilterActions.webpart
Sealed	Yes

Feature	SharePoint Server Enterprise Site Collection Features
Provider Connections	n/a
Consumer Connections	n/a

Indicator Details

Displays the details of a single indicator

Assembly	`Microsoft.SharePoint.Portal`
Class	`Microsoft.SharePoint.Portal.WebControls.IndicatorWeb-Part`
Web Part Type	SharePoint
Group	Business Data
Filename	IndicatorWebPart.dwp
Sealed	No
Feature	SharePoint Server Enterprise Site Collection Features
Provider Connections	n/a
Consumer Connections	`IScorecardFilterValues`

InfoPath Form Web Part

Displays an InfoPath browser-enabled form

Assembly	`Microsoft.Office.InfoPath.Server`
Class	`Microsoft.Office.InfoPath.Server.Controls.WebUI.BrowserFormWebPart`
Web Part Type	SharePoint
Group	Forms
Filename	Microsoft.Office.InfoPath.Server.BrowserForm.webpart
Sealed	Yes
Feature	SharePoint Server Enterprise Site Collection Features
Provider Connections	`IWebPartRow`
Consumer Connections	`IWebPartParameters, IWebPartRow`

Status List

Shows a list of status indicators

Assembly	`Microsoft.SharePoint.Portal`
Class	`Microsoft.SharePoint.Portal.WebControls.KPIListWeb-Part`
Web Part Type	SharePoint

Group	Business Data
Filename	KpiListWebPart.dwp
Sealed	No
Feature	SharePoint Server Enterprise Site Collection Features
Provider Connections	n/a
Consumer Connections	`IScorecardFilterValues, IFilterValues`

Page Field Filter

Filters the contents of Web Parts using information about the current page

Assembly	`Microsoft.Office.Server.FilterControls`
Class	`Microsoft.SharePoint.Portal.WebControls.PageContext-` `FilterWebPart`
Web Part Type	SharePoint
Group	Filters
Filename	PageContextFilter.webpart
Sealed	Yes
Feature	SharePoint Server Enterprise Site Collection Features
Provider Connections	`ITransformableFilterValues, IDefaultFilterValue`
Consumer Connections	n/a

PerformancePoint Filter

Displays PerformancePoint filters

Assembly	`Microsoft.PerformancePoint.ScoreCards.WebControls`
Class	`Microsoft.PerformancePoint.ScoreCards.WebControls` `.FilterWebPart`
Web Part Type	ASP.NET
Group	PerformancePoint
Filename	FilterWebPart.webpart
Sealed	No
Feature	PerformancePoint Services Site Collection Features
Provider Connections	`ITransformableBIDataProvider`
Consumer Connections	`IBIDataProvider`

PerformancePoint Report

Displays PerformancePoint reports

Assembly	`Microsoft.PerformancePoint.ScoreCards.WebControls`

Class	Microsoft.PerformancePoint.ScoreCards.WebControls.ReportViewWebPart
Web Part Type	ASP.NET
Group	PerformancePoint
Filename	ReportViewWebPart.webpart
Sealed	Yes
Feature	PerformancePoint Services Site Collection Features
Provider Connections	n/a
Consumer Connections	IWebPartParameters, IBIDataProvider

PerformancePoint Scorecard

Displays a PerformancePoint scorecard

Assembly	Microsoft.PerformancePoint.ScoreCards.WebControls
Class	Microsoft.PerformancePoint.ScoreCards.WebControls.ScorecardWebPart
Web Part Type	ASP.NET
Group	PerformancePoint
Filename	ScorecardWebPart.webpart
Sealed	Yes
Feature	PerformancePoint Services Site Collection Features
Provider Connections	ITransformableBIDataProvider
Consumer Connections	IBIDataProvider, IFilterValues, IWebPartParameters

PerformancePoint Stack Selector

Displays a PerformancePoint Stack Selector

Assembly	Microsoft.PerformancePoint.ScoreCards.WebControls
Class	Microsoft.PerformancePoint.ScoreCards.WebControls.StackWebPart
Web Part Type	ASP.NET
Group	PerformancePoint
Filename	ScorecardWebPart.webpart
Sealed	No
Feature	PerformancePoint Services Site Collection Features
Provider Connections	n/a
Consumer Connections	n/a

Query String Filter

Filters the contents of Web Parts using values passed via the query string

Assembly	`Microsoft.Office.Server.FilterControls`
Class	`Microsoft.SharePoint.Portal.WebControls.QueryString-FilterWebPart`
Web Part Type	SharePoint
Group	Filters
Filename	QueryStringFilter.dwp
Sealed	Yes
Feature	SharePoint Server Enterprise Site Collection Features
Provider Connections	`ITransformableFilterValues, IDefaultFilterValue`
Consumer Connections	n/a

SharePoint List Filter

Filters the contents of Web Parts using a list of values

Assembly	`Microsoft.SharePoint.Portal`
Class	`Microsoft.SharePoint.Portal.WebControls.SpListFilter-WebPart`
Web Part Type	SharePoint
Group	Filters
Filename	SpListFilter.dwp
Sealed	Yes
Feature	SharePoint Server Enterprise Site Collection Features
Provider Connections	`ITransformableFilterValues, IDefaultFilterValue`
Consumer Connections	`IDefaultFilterValue`

SQL Server Analysis Services Filter

Filters the contents of Web Parts using a list of values from SQL Server Analysis Services cubes

Assembly	`Microsoft.SharePoint.Portal`
Class	`Microsoft.SharePoint.Portal.WebControls.Scorecard-FilterWebPart`
Web Part Type	SharePoint
Group	Filters
Filename	OlapFilter.dwp
Sealed	Yes

Feature	SharePoint Server Enterprise Site Collection Features
Provider Connections	`ITransformableFilterValues, IDefaultFilterValue, IScoreCardFilterValues`
Consumer Connections	`IDefaultFilterValues`

Text Filter

Filters the contents of Web Parts by allowing users to enter a text value

Assembly	`Microsoft.Office.Server.FilterControls`
Class	`Microsoft.SharePoint.Portal.WebControls.SPSlicerText-WebPart`
Web Part Type	SharePoint
Group	Filters
Filename	TextFilter.dwp
Sealed	Yes
Feature	SharePoint Server Enterprise Site Collection Features
Connections	`ITransformableFilterValues, IDefaultFilterValue`
Consumer Connections	`IDefaultFilterWebPart`

Visio Web Access

Enables viewing and refreshing of a Visio Web Drawing

Assembly	`Microsoft.Office.Visio.Server`
Class	`Microsoft.Office.Visio.Server.WebControls.VisioWeb-Access`
Web Part Type	SharePoint
Group	Business Data
Filename	VisioWebAccess.dwp
Sealed	Yes
Feature	SharePoint Server Enterprise Site Collection Features
Provider Connections	`IWebPartRow`
Consumer Connections	`IWebPartParameters, IWebPartTable, IWebPartParameters`

Search Visual Best Bet

Displays Visual Best Bet

Assembly	`Microsoft.Office.Server.Search`
Class	`Microsoft.Office.Server.Search.WebControls.Visual-BestBetWebPart`

Web Part Type	SharePoint
Group	Search
Filename	VisualBestBet.dwp
Sealed	No
Feature	SharePoint Server Enterprise Site Collection Features
Provider Connections	n/a
Consumer Connections	n/a

WSRP Viewer

Displays portlets from websites using WSRP 1.1

Assembly	`Microsoft.SharePoint.Portal`
Class	`Microsoft.SharePoint.Portal.WebControls.WSRPConsumer-WebPart`
Web Part Type	SharePoint
Group	Content Rollup
Filename	WSRPConsumerWebPart.dwp
Sealed	No
Feature	SharePoint Server Enterprise Site Collection Features
Provider Connections	n/a
Consumer Connections	n/a

index

RELATED MANNING TITLES

SharePoint 2010 Workflows in Action
by Phil Wicklund

    ISBN: 978-1-935182-71-9
    360 pages, $44.99
    February 2011

C# in Depth, Second Edition
by Jon Skeet

    ISBN: 978-1-935182-47-4
    584 pages, $49.99
    November 2010

Silverlight 4 in Action
Silverlight 4, ViewModel Pattern, and WCF RIA Services

by Pete Brown

    ISBN: 978-1-935182-37-5
    800 pages, $49.99
    September 2010

SQL Server 2008 Administration in Action
by Rod Colledge

    ISBN: 978-1-933988-72-6
    464 pages, $44.99
    August 2009

For ordering information go to www.manning.com